Pre-School Story Hour

Second Edition

by

VARDINE MOORE

The Scarecrow Press, Inc.
Metuchen, N. J.   1972

Library of Congress Cataloging in Publication Data

Moore, Vardine, 1906-
    Pre-school story hour.

    Includes bibliographies.
    1. Story-telling. 2. Education, Preschool--1945-
I. Title.
LB1042.M6 1972   027.62'51   78-188549
ISBN 0-8108-0474-3

Barter

Life has loveliness to sell,
All beautiful and splendid things,
Blue waves whitened on a cliff,
Soaring fire that sways and sings,
And children's faces looking up,
Holding wonder like a cup.

Sara Teasdale

Acknowledgments

My grateful acknowledgment goes to all who had a part in encouraging and aiding me in compiling this book.

To Bernice Bruner, Chief of Division of Work with Schools and Children in the Evansville Public Library and to all other staff members, for willing and helpful co-operation.

To Mildred Voelkel, staff member, who first asked me to conduct the pre-school story hour in the Children's Room.

To all the children who have attended the story hour through the years and to the grown-ups who brought them in with regularity and appreciation.

To Eugene Gula, art teacher, who illustrated "The Hanky Mouse."

Table of Contents

INTRODUCTION

"Books help you grow."
- Bruce

Bruce is four years old, attending his second year in the library pre-school story hour. His wise observation may have echoed the words of a beloved and respected adult. Or, just as likely, the discovery came from his own awareness of extended horizons reached by a year's experience with books and storytelling.

Young children need to feel at home in their ever-widening world. This desirable status can be achieved happily and effectively in a well organized and thoughtfully planned story hour for pre-schoolers. They learn what to expect of the world and what is expected of them through stories providing vicarious journeys into situations that could be their own. Vocabularies and the tools of communication develop readily in a vital word-learning environment. New levels of understanding are reached by contact with other personalities, both of their peers and of adults, in this tangible journey from home with its customary surroundings and familiar faces.

Most large communities offer nursery schools, day schools, museum classes, public recreation programs, and other forms of group participation for this eager age. In addition to these facilities, the library provides a unique means of enrichment with its wide array of beautifully illustrated picture books.

7

The pre-school hour differs from a nursery school program in that it is library-book-centered rather than nursery-education-centered. Also, I hasten to add, it is not a free baby-sitting service! Rather, it is part of the library's total story telling program and has the same basic goal: to lead children to literature. The pre-school hour should provide for the following:

1. First lesson in group experiences

2. The ability to sit quietly, to listen with open ears, to look at pictures with seeing eyes

3. An introduction to the best in children's literature (I would extend this to include the best in art for children)

4. First opportunities to select books for home reading[1]

Three to five year olds have come into their own as valued, loyal, library patrons with the introduction of the pre-school story hour in many libraries. A survey made in 1957 revealed that 121 (of 259) libraries in communities of 35,000 people or more and 70 (of 303) in smaller communities conduct pre-school story hours.

The survey supplied this further information:

Story hours for three-to-five-year-olds have flourished since World War II, when working mothers could not take full responsibility for the care, amusement, and education of their small children. Not all libraries today, however, agree that the library should provide story periods for very young children. Some children's librarians feel that the play activities usually included in programs for this age have no place in the library, where the prime concern is with books. Others feel that, all too often, mothers use such programs as a baby-sitting service in order to have freedom to shop or pursue their own interests. Many librarians, on the other hand, believe that the child's introduction to libraries and books cannot begin too early, and that story

> hours arouse his awareness of the importance of books at his most impressionable age.
>
> Some respondents also comment that younger children are welcome to their regular story hour if no special one is planned for them, and a few libraries provide book and film programs for mothers while the pre-school story hour is in progress.
>
> Most of the libraries which conduct these picture book or story periods have learned that the value for young children in a program of this kind is best achieved when the group is kept to a manageable number. Programs for groups of twenty or under seem to provide the most worthwhile experience for small children.[2]

In her later book, <u>Public Library Service to Children,</u>[3] 1967, Elizabeth H. Gross further emphasized the purpose of introducing young children to books, to the library, and to association with children of their own age group.

Since then programs geared to the pre-school level are more widely accepted and are in ever-increasing demand. Kindergarten and first grade teachers often require their beginners to know the familiar nursery rhymes and suggest that the parents send their young children to a pre-school story hour. One mother came into the library children's room asking for "one of those riddle books about Jack and Jill." Her six-year-old had never heard a Mother Goose rhyme!

Authorities agree that until the age of three, most children have a very short span of attention and are not ready for group activities. They are preoccupied with their own pursuits and primarily with themselves. The average three-year-old, however, has developed greater listening ability and a wider interest in other persons. This is the age when the seeds of imagination are beginning to stir and curiosity in the wonderful outside world is growing.

This is not to say that there is a definite line of de-
marcation on the dawn of a child's third birthday. There are
various rates of growth socially and mentally as well as
physically. However, the invitation to enroll children at the
age of three is generally best for all concerned. If a child
has reached this age and is found to lack readiness for the
experience, parents are almost always willing to see the ad-
visability of a waiting period. No child should be compelled
to attend or forced to join in any activity. (Some children
are content to sit quietly and listen attentively but balk at
even such a simple activity as standing up to stretch.)

In some cases an almost-three is very well adjusted
and ready for participation with already-three's. If there is
room, these children can often be admitted at the beginning
of a season, particularly when an older brother or sister is
a regular member of the group.

The ideal situation, however, would be to have all
three-year-olds in one group and all four-year-olds in another
since some books are better used with one age than the other.
Also, beginners need a period of orientation and should be in
a separate group from those who have attended before.

It should be remembered that a pre-school story hour
is not a nursery school, which is concerned with the overall
development of the young child in an environment offering the
basic experiences and training that a good home offers. Nor
should it be confused with a babysitting agency or parking
place with no co-operation shown by the parents in the carry-
over of interests and purposes from the library to the home.
Generally, a baby sitter is simply someone "there" with children to keep them out of mischief and from physical harm.
In saying, "This is not a baby sitting service," the library
is saying, "We have something constructive, something of val-

ue to offer.   This is not a passive 'minding the children' for half an hour or more."

A good story hour provides the occasion to bring together young children and books in a joyous, meaningful situation.   Here, they have the opportunity to browse through a larger collection than is available in most homes and to make their own selections for borrowing books to take home.

Many libraries discuss the purposes and structure of the program with parents and suggest methods of mutual helpfulness.   The role of the parent is given in a later chapter (See Chapter 6).

Books and stories are only a part of the story hour program although they are the motivation for presenting a wide choice of related material and should never be subordinated.   Along with stories and books, there is value and good reason for including art, music, poetry, fingerplays, nursery rhymes and jingles, rhythm and simple dramatization.   Not only is the program thereby enriched, but diversity of activity with a change of pace is a recognized need for children of pre-school age.

Since there are frequently unexpected diversions and interruptions, a story hour for pre-schoolers has a more informal atmosphere than one for older children.   The program should be flexible to allow for spontaneous participation and free self-expression.

No library is too small and none too large to include a pre-school story hour.   No special room is needed.   Even the smallest library usually has a few shelves of books for children in a location which lends itself to becoming the story hour "nook" or "corner."   In any situation, the background of books is always a pleasing and natural arrangement. Gathered together, away from the general flow of traffic, the group will not interfere with those coming into the library for other purposes.

It is not unusual to have older children, even an occasional grown-up, quietly join the edge of the group to observe with fascinated attention. Those coming in will not usually disturb the children. They seldom look around or become disturbed by other persons. Only a fire truck clanging by in the street will divert attention, and even this is only a brief interruption. The incident may even spark an interesting discussion!

In a large library, the logical place to hold the story hour is in the children's room or department containing the collection of children's books with a special section of shelves for picture books and story books for the youngest. There may even be a separate room for story telling, the showing of films, and other special programs where quiet and freedom from interruptions are assured.

The time set for the session is not arbitrary. Mornings are usually chosen because most young children take a nap in the afternoon. The time chosen should fit the best interests of the children. There might be situations where a late afternoon session is indicated. There is even an early evening story hour called "The Bedtime Story Hour," near a large shopping center. The time of day may vary to conform to a particular community so long as it is one that is convenient, appropriate, and right for the children.

The choice of day is also flexible. It can be any day of the week, or any day of the month if only one day a month is possible. It should, however, be a regular day at a regular time rather than a hit-and-miss schedule.

The length of the term is also selected at the discretion of each individual library. Some are held during the

regular school term from September through May, others
continue through the summer months, some only during the
summer.   There are library storytellers who go to summer
playgrounds or parks for pre-school storytelling.   In some
instances it has worked out best to hold a series of five-
week sessions, but there are many possible variations.

While this service is called an "Hour," the length of
the session is variable.   The occasions should be one of
joyful anticipation and happy participation in achieving worthwhile goals, not an endurance test for the storyteller or for
the children.   A half hour is considered long enough by
some; an hour is scarcely long enough for others.

Regardless of the duration of the term or of each
meeting, it should be a time of enrichment.   Children are
exposed to every sort of stimulation on radio and TV, from
singing commercials and adult entertainment to the sometimes garbled and often violent children's programs.   Lives
of young children are influenced by stories and books in the
impressionable years before they begin school.   The pre-
school story hour can lay the cornerstone for future reading
pleasure and should introduce the library's many facilities.
This is a challenge to be met by the storyteller's carefully
considered selection and presentation of material which can
satisfy the child's needs at the present level and can help
to establish a life-long attitude toward books and the library.

> Story hours have not been as universally adopted
> as one would think.   Answers to the questionnaires
> sent out indicate that there are many librarians
> who hesitate to attempt working with the pre-school
> child.   Others, challenged by the problems offered
> by this age child--the short attention span, the
> process of learning to listen without interruption,
> the exuberance or extreme shyness--find in this
> activity a most rewarding aspect of service to chil-

dren. Some libraries reported that staff members
who have been reluctant to conduct the more formal story hour for older children are willing to
take on a pre-school story hour, feeling that the
presentation of the picture book is easier and less
time-consuming in preparation, and that small
children are less critical than older children. [4]

Librarians now offering this service find it to be a
delightful and satisfying experience for themselves with enthusiastic response from parents and children.   There is a
wealth of material, both in the old standbys and in the excellent picture books being produced each year.   There is
no question of values, which have been formulated and clearly defined.

In many ways, the preschool program for the
three- and four-year-olds is both the hardest and
the easiest to execute.   It is the hardest because
it requires more careful planning and more understanding on the part of the librarian than any other
type.   It is the easiest because the pre-schoolers
nearly always make an enthusiastic audience and
are usually available in large numbers. [5]

Where there is enough imagination and enthusiasm to
bring children and books together, any library can extend its
services to include pre-school children.

Notes

1.   Peterson, Ellin F., "The Pre-School Hour," Top of
     the News, vol. 18, No. 2, December 1961, p. 47.

2.   Gross, Elizabeth Henry, and Namoviez, Gene Inyart.
     Children's Service in Public Libraries.   Chicago,
     American Library Association, 1963, p. 80.

3.   Gross, Elizabeth Henry, Public Library Service to
     Children.   Dobbs Ferry, N.Y., Oceana Publications,

Inc., 1967, p. 96.

4.   Hardendorff, Jeanne B., "Storytelling and the Story
     Hour," Library Trends, July 1963, p. 60.

5.   Broderick, Dorothy M., An Introduction to Children's
     Work in Public Libraries. New York, H. W. Wilson
     Company, 1965, p. 71.

Chapter 1

PRACTICES AND PROCEDURES

"I like to see how you do it."
-A Parent

Story telling is considered one of the oldest arts, and infant schools flourished more than a century ago, yet preschool story hours are not a standard practice. In most libraries where they have been introduced, parents and children have been enthusiastic, the programs have been successful even without any special training for the story tellers, and the children's librarians have found joy and satisfaction in working with young children in pre-school story hours. How did they begin, and how did they develop?

> The pre-school hour for the 3 to 5 year olds is relatively new in library work. It followed the growth of children's rooms, the new interest in child development, and early childhood education, which came to the fore in the 1930's and the tremendous production of picture books which followed World War II as the result of better and more varied technical processes. As far as I can ascertain, the first pre-school hour in a public library was held in the early 40's, though I suspect there were some in the late thirties. [1]

Many children's librarians have recognized the values inherent in such a program and of the need to launch special programs for the youngest patrons. Pre-schoolers often accompany older brothers and sisters to the regular story hour in the library. While much of the program is above their

16

level of comprehension, they sit quietly with absorbed attention and return time after time.   In many cases the parents
themselves have requested a story hour at the library for
the little ones, even in communities which offer other types
of pre-school programs.

There seems to be no prescribed routine, no widely
accepted definition of goals, functions, and purposes, and no
formulation of techniques.   In a pioneering spirit individual
libraries have introduced the pre-school story hour on an
experimental basis, and like Topsy, "they have just growed."
Some libraries have had picture book story hours for many
years, introducing the collection on their shelves to create
a desire for exploring them further.   Others have followed
the practice of traditional story telling with a simple and
direct approach suitable for the nursery age child, adding
suitable activities in the way of fingerplays, music and dramatization.

Some of these established programs have been recorded in pamphlets and periodicals.   Examination of practices and procedures reveals interesting similarities, although the approach varies in different localities.

According to Miss Bernice Bruner, chief of Division
of Work with Schools and Children, Evansville, Indiana, Public Library, a pre-school story hour began in the children's
room of Central Library in 1953.   Parents, who had been
taking their children to a group at the Y.W.C.A., saw the
possibilities of a pre-school story hour in the library when
they brought their youngsters into the children's room.   It
was at the request of a dozen or so of these parents that a
group was started on a regular schedule.   It was handled by
a young assistant who was interested in this age group and
was taking college courses in nursery school education.

The size of the group soon grew to such proportions that more sessions were added. A story teller with kindergarten and nursery school experience was hired to be in charge for a few hours each week, since it was necessary to have someone who would not be interrupted by other library duties, who could present the picture books and tell stories for this age level, who could think up games, rhythms and songs for any occasion, and who had time to hear the many tales of the talkative ones and patiently draw out the painfully shy child. Creative and spontaneous dramatization played a large part in the program as reported by Miss Bruner. [2]

Registrations are accepted at any time during the year that the child reaches the age of three. (This has some disadvantages since a new member may require some individual orientation.) Registrations on file cards contain the following information, supplied by the parent or other responsible adult: name of the child and name of parent or guardian, address, telephone number, age of the child, and birthday. Name tags are made for each child. Names are printed large enough for the story teller to read at a distance, on colorful construction paper, in shapes to suit the season or units of interest.

Upon arrival the children receive their name tags, which are spread on a low table in alphabetical order. There are some children who learn to identify their own. When the story hour is over, the tags are returned to the table to be used the next time. They are taken home at the end of the season and can be used as book marks.

After the children receive their name tags they spend some time with the parent or a librarian, browsing through the books, choosing some to take home or looking at exhibits or seasonal displays around the room. (This opportunity is repeated at the end of the session.) Others engage in conversation with the story teller or with each other until all have arrived and music signals time for stories.

Small chairs are arranged in a semicircle in the area of books for the youngest patrons. The story teller's low chair, facing the semicircle, is near a table holding the books she plans to use, a record player with appropriate recordings, pictures, and other related material.

The program generally follows this procedure: recorded music with appropriate activity for opening the period, a sharing time instigated by the children who bring a favorite toy or interesting object to show. Stories are told or read from a book while showing the pictures, with fingerplays, poems, rhythms, dramatization, games or rhythm band and with alternating quiet and active times. There is occasional use of film strips, movies, parties for special events such as birthdays, Hallowe'en, Christmas, or a visitor from outside with an interest or talent to share. Good-by's are said and the name tags are returned to the table. Each session lasts one hour.

The programs run from the first week in October through the last week in May. A summer program continues through June and July. Parents may follow their own inclinations. They may stay, or shop, or browse in the adult book collection, as their interests dictate.

One of the pioneers in this field was the pre-kindergarten story hour in the Montclair Public Library, which was operated with Junior Service League members.[3]

The stories were told at the library by the head of the childrens' division, who observed that the children developed rapidly under this program. The librarian, in addition to

telling stories, started the children on finger plays and on
acting out the tales. The youngsters came with their mothers a week or two before the course began, giving the librarian a chance to judge whether the three and four year
olds were mature enough or whether they should wait for a
later series. It also gave the children a chance to meet
their story teller and to see where they would meet. The
meeting was scheduled for five consecutive Tuesday mornings each fall and spring and it lasted thirty minutes. Emphasis was placed on acting out familiar tales such as
"Three Bears" and "Three Billy Goats Gruff" on a short
double flight of blue stairsteps which the Junior League of
Montclair had built and painted. (These steps were good for
dramatization, and would be good for sitting on with a small
group.)

As early as 1955, the Children's Department of the
Gary Public Library prepared a handbook[4] covering its well-
organized, well-planned, well-developed, well-directed pre-
school story hour called Story Time for Wee Wigglers. The
handbook included a bibliography of stories, records, and
picture books especially suited to the pre-school child. The
goals specified were: to introduce children to books, to por-
tray reading as a pleasant leisure-time activity, and to help
make known the varied services of the library.

These story hours were started in response to requests from parents, particularly where there were limited
nursery school and kindergarten facilities. Programs included stories, records, and games, and gave the child an
opportunity to associate with other children of his own age.
Held on weekday mornings, each session lasted for one-half
hour. The parent or other adult was required to accompany
the child and to remain during the program. Participation

of the parents in the games was encouraged but not required. Emphasis was placed on the varied collection of
picture books and stories to read to children that was available for the patron to take home.

> Because of space limitations, the parents are gen-
> erally passive although appreciative observers.
> This year we plan to encourage them to see their
> own responsibilities in this area. We intend to
> carry on a simultaneous program for mothers in
> as many branches as possible. We shall outline
> for them the purposes and structure of the pre-
> school program, and then suggest ways they can
> help--before, during and after. [5]

Ellin F. Peterson tells of her experiences in the pre-
school hour which operated as a series of six-to-eight week
programs. They were scheduled when the library was least
busy.

> Usually not much publicity is needed for the pre-
> school hour. If the program is brought to the at-
> tention of parents who came to the library with
> their pre-school children, news of it will spread
> quickly by word of mouth. Post a notice in both
> the children's and adult departments. If you still
> feel the program needs a little 'pushing,' ask to
> have it announced at the next meeting of the local
> P. T. A.

Miss Peterson goes on to say:

> The usual problem is to keep the program from
> snowballing. A small group, and the same group,
> is best for this age. The size of the group can
> be controlled, and I believe it is wise to do so.
> [Some story tellers disagree on this point!] One
> method of control is to keep a registration file on
> 3" x 5" index cards. The card should give the
> child's name, age, birthday, parent's name, ad-
> dress, phone number and date of registration.
> (The date of registration is important in the event
> of over-registration.) Fill the group by date of
> registration except when you know there is going

to be greater response than you can handle.   In
that event, fill the group with the four-to-five-
year olds before taking the three-year-olds.   Tell
the parent his three-year-old can come if there is
room in the group.   Keep a waiting list and let the
parent know when space is available.[6]

Another pioneer in the field is the Enoch Pratt Free
Library, Baltimore, Maryland, with a fine pamphlet, Story
Hour for the Three to Five Year Old, [7] prepared by Beth
Caples, Head of Children's Department, December, 1953.

The program was held the first Saturday morning in
October and continued every Saturday morning at 11 o'clock
until the last Saturday in May.   The children began arriving
at 10:30 for a conversation period.   They watched feeding of
the goldfish and got acquainted.   When the theme song was
played on a record player they took hands and walked softly
to the story room.   With the children seated on pillows there
followed half an hour of stories, games, finger plays and
music.   Stories were interspersed with activities in connection with the stories, then back to the pillows for finger
plays and singing, with the theme song serving as the signal
to put pillows away.

Miss Caples says a small group of children is preferable, and that while a group of 12-15 children is ideal,
20-30 can be managed with help.   For every ten children
there should be help from another children's librarian or
from one of the mothers.

She reports that the story hour is not publicized, but
that a registration file of children who are 3-5 years old is
made by the children's librarian with the help of mothers
who bring their children into the library.   About a week pri-
or to the first story hour the children's librarian consults
her file and sends each eligible child a personal invitation.

The story of the Jackson Pre-School Cooperative
Story Hour, reported in Top of the News, shows one of the
many possible ways to organize the story hour.[8]

At first the children's department offered a story
hour for a limited number of pre-school children. A mother
who enrolled her two young sons saw the need for expanding
this service. As a former kindergarten teacher she knew
how to tell stories and had access to what she called "trim-
mings," such as rhythm band instruments, picture scripts,
and even a live turtle. She organized a volunteer core of
mothers who, with the librarian, planned a program to handle
a larger number of children. These mothers, who were out-
standing in the community and well prepared with talents and
professional training, quickly volunteered to help as coordi-
nators. Mothers planning to give a presentation were asked
to observe one before taking on their duties. The children's
librarian acted as the general chairman and attended every
session. She was responsible for the materials used, for
planning the units, for occasional participation in the story
telling, and for providing continuing leadership to the enterprise.

The program grew into a "Little Children's Day" at
the library every Wednesday from 9:30 A.M. until 2:30 P.M.,
with a morning story hour from 10 to 10:45. The afternoon
program filled one hour, 1:30 to 2:30. These programs continued from September until May.

This co-operative pre-school story hour showed that
the children benefit, the community benefits and the library
benefits. The young mother who comes with her child often
stops for a book for herself or to inquire about other services the library offers, and new young families become regular library patrons.

In Baerrien Springs, Michigan a pretty, smiling woman devotes her talents and a good deal of time to making
children happy.   Primrose Glasgow holds story hours in
small libraries in surrounding towns.

She reports that the program is held on Saturday
mornings from 10 until 11 A.M. for children ranging in age
from 3-1/2 to 10, and consists of a straight story, a nature
story, and reviewing of several children's books found in
that particular library.   The small children sit on the floor,
the older ones in chairs.   Mothers often attend the programs
and there are always candy treats.   The program is very
informal, with participation from the children.

Mrs. Glasgow adds a seasonal touch to her costumes.
For Easter she wears a hat topped by an Easter bunny with
a nest of tiny rabbits and candy eggs.   She carries her own
collection of large and colorful pictures and a collection of
unusual stuffed, cuddly animals, each with its own name.
She also brings in real bird nests, hornet nests, fossils,
rocks, and various kinds of leaves to show.

Trips are made to each library for four seasonal programs and an extra summer program.   Her purpose is to
co-operate with the librarians by bringing more children into
the library and to develop a love of good books and interest
in using the books in their own local collections.

Libraries from coast to coast, in large cities and in
small communities, are now offering story hours for pre-
schoolers.   Successful programs often follow a simple, basic pattern consisting of stories and picture books, perhaps
ending with a finger play or stretching activity.   The children, then, have an opportunity to explore books on their
own and to choose those they wish to borrow.

There are many other active pre-school story hours

in public libraries; some are new, some have been operating smoothly and effectively for years. Each one has its own individual situation, each has its own strengths and weaknesses.

A concise handbook, <u>How to Conduct Effective Picture Book Programs</u>,[9] covering questions and brief answers pertaining to pre-school story hours, is an excellent resource for quick reference. This thorough handbook was prepared for the Westchester (N.Y.) Library System by Joanna Foster and complements the 16mm color film, "The Pleasure Is Mutual," which was made with the assistance of Anne Izard, Children's Services Consultant of the Westchester Library System.

Purchase of the film and the handbook may be made through The Children's Book Council, Inc., 175 Fifth Avenue, New York, N.Y. 10010. The film may also be borrowed from most state libraries and is available on a rental basis from a number of university film libraries.

Pre-school story hours in libraries need not be regimented. Indeed, it would be limiting to future growth, and stultifying to have every library doing the same program at the same time. But keeping the basic goals, purposes and functions as the cornerstone, each one can build with imagination and enthusiasm, using the particular resources at hand.

With all the variations, certain salient features occur in each situation. All are in accord with the basic goal which is to lead children to literature. Programs follow a similar pattern with some variations:

<u>Schedules followed are:</u>

> Each fall and spring for five consecutive Tuesday mornings.

Five times a year, four seasonal programs with an
extra summer program.
The same as the school year from September or October until June.
Twice a week if the group grows too large and must
be divided.
Some continue with a summer session.

The length of the meeting varies:

One half hour.
Three-quarters of an hour.
One hour, part of which time is spent in prelimi-
naries and farewells.

Publicity includes:

Word of mouth.
Notices in adult and childrens' departments.
Announcements at P. T. A. meetings.
Newspaper announcements, feature articles, and pic-
tures.
TV and radio programs.
Talks to interested groups.
Invitations sent out prior to the first meeting to par-
ents who have shown interest.
Demonstrations at Book Fairs.
A demonstration was once given in a corner display
window of Sears, Roebuck and Company during a
week of showing various library services.

Registration practices:

Any time the child reaches the age of three.
A week or two before the first session.
At the time of the first session.
Cards are dated and filed.   When the group is filled
according to the date of registration, others must
wait.

What to do with the parents:

Some frankly say, "Let them follow their own pur-
suits."
Encourage them to browse in the library.
Carry on a simultaneous program for the parents.
Some insist that they remain during the program.

Some insist that they leave.
Some allow parents to stay for the first meeting or until a fearful child becomes oriented.

Programs follow a pattern:

Greeting children as they enter.
Using a name tag for identification, pinned on or hung around the neck of the child.
Give each child a book to look at until all have arrived, or let the children browse at will among the children's books.
Observing points of interest in the room (special exhibits, permanent exhibits).
As a signal that stories are about to begin, some have the ceremony of lighting a candle which is extinguished when the story hour is ended.
Start program on time with a theme song, when children may take hands and march into the story telling room or corner.
Simply sit down and sing or clap to the music.
Follow theme song with other appropriate actions, a train, an airplane.
Spend a few minutes in conversation... what happened during the week, or sharing something brought from home--a favorite toy or interesting object.
Finger play to bring all to attention.
First story. (Many say use the longest one first.)
If a child has a birthday sing "Happy Birthday."
Some celebrate once a month for all who have had birthdays that month.
Lively action, rhythms, dramatization.
Another story, or poems, or nursery rhymes.
For longer periods, filmstrips, movies, flannelboards, special occasion parties with treats, a visit from some outside person with a special interest or talent.
Good-by's are said, with or without a puppet.
Name tags are returned.
Selection of books to take home.

Notes

1.   Peterson, Ellin F., "The Pre-School Hour," Top of the News, vol. 18, No. 2, December 1961, p. 47.

2. Bruner, Bernice, "Creative Activities in a Public Library Children's Room," Illinois Libraries, September, 1958, p. 649.

3. Waugh, Dorothy, Wilson Library Bulletin, Vol. 32, No. 2, October 1957, p. 139.

4. Story Time for Wee Wigglers. Gary, Indiana, Children's Department, Gary Public Library, 1955.

5. Horner, Margaret, Wilson Library Bulletin, December 1962, p. 337.

6. Peterson, Ellin F., Top of the News, vol. 18, No. 2, December 1961, p. 48.

7. Story Hour for the Three to Five Year Old, prepared by Beth Caples. Baltimore, Maryland, Enoch Pratt Free Library, 1953.

8. Burnside, Frances E., "Here's a Story," Top of the News, vol. 14, No. 3, March 1958, p. 20.

9. How to Conduct Effective Picture Book Programs, compiled by Joanna Foster. Westchester, N.Y., Westchester Library System, 1967.

Chapter 2

NEW INSIGHTS

"I can't 'cause I aint never done it before."
-Billy

This is the cry of a child lacking the experiences and background we have come to accept as normal and ordinary in the lives of pre-school children, whether they come from so-called "good" homes or from those of low socio-economic status. Recognition of this lack and the growing concern for children deprived of the opportunities to develop to their fullest extent have led to numerous avenues of providing help to all children.

Establishment of day nurseries, child-care centers, private nurseries, church-sponsored nurseries, parent-cooperative nursery schools, college development centers, parent education groups and high school homemaking nursery schools is making available facilities for large numbers of children. However, there are children in many areas of our country who have no opportunity for any sort of pre-school training.

Emphasis on the needs of this group, composed largely of children from the lower socio-economic class, led in the summer of 1965 to the educational program "Head Start." The Office of Economic Opportunity, which was responsible for the program, planned a $17 million summer program for 100,000 pre-school children in 300 communities. As soon

29

as the project was announced, more than 3,500 communities
deluged the OEO with requests for help in setting up such
programs.   With evidence that the early years of childhood
are the most critical point in the poverty cycle, the task acquired new urgency.   Dr. Julius Richmond, dean of New
York Medical School at Syracuse, pointed out that the failure
to tackle poverty problems at this early age results in con-
signing a vast number of children to failure in every phase
of their future lives.

Because many disadvantaged children have never
looked at a book or visited a library and have never even
heard hundreds of words that are well within the grasp of
young children, Francis Keppel, then U.S. Commissioner of
Education, recommended beginning the program for underprivileged children at the ages of three to five by getting
them started on the vital word-learning process.   In this
way, the talents and prospects of some of these youngsters
could be salvaged.

> Many of these children come from overcrowded
> homes that are barren of any kind of intellectual
> stimulation.   They are exposed to violence, not on-
> ly through the TV shows they watch, but also in
> their daily living.   Their vocabularies are small
> but they often include a number of unprintable
> words.   Their knowledge of the real world is con-
> fused and magical.   No one listens to them seri-
> ously and no one really straightens out their think-
> ing.   If grownups hear what they say, they are as
> likely as not either to laugh at them or tell them
> to 'shut up.'[1]

Other educators stressed the importance of recognizing the needs of young children.

> Foundations for vital attitudes, habits, and knowl-
> edge originate in the pre-school experience of chil-
> dren.   Ideally, the pre-school child would receive

> attention, affection, and guidance within his home
> environment, but for many children the ideal never
> becomes a reality. For these children, vital as-
> pects of growing and learning must be provided
> through some other medium. [2]

By 1969 the Head Start Program came under the direct administration of the Office of Child Development, a division of Health, Education and Welfare. Encouraged by the
OCD, plans continued to move forward to extend existing
programs with local and federal co-operation.

There were 249,000 children in federal day-care programs in 1970, and the programs were funded at $222.1
million--a significant increase from the $73.4 million which
the federal government spent for day-care only three years
earlier.

A survey of the growth of various day-care facilities,
presented in Saturday Review, February 20, 1971, offered
new insights:

> At the time the day-care movement gained adher-
> ents and momentum in America we wanted to pro-
> tect young children from such hazards as inade-
> quate supervision, insufficient food, lack of shelter,
> and physical abuse. As today's knowledge about
> the importance of early experience for child devel-
> opment was only faintly limned in our conscious-
> ness at that time, it is not surprising that the pre-
> vailing concept of quality day care failed to recog-
> nize education as an integral part of 'care and
> protection.'
>
> At the 1970 White House Conference on Children
> last December, delegates representing various
> women's groups were among the most vocal in
> their demands that child care be made available
> around the clock throughout the year for all who
> want it, not just for indigent or minority groups. [3]

The television program, "Sesame Street," designed
for children from three to five, was introduced in 1969.

Presented weekdays by the Children's Television Workshop
of National Education Television in New York City and broad-
cast to nearly two hundred television stations, "Sesame
Street" reached a large viewing audience of children from
all socio-economic levels.

Although many prominent children's librarians were
asked to help in book selections, the use of story books was
not entirely satisfying.

> Too frequent interruption, and the simple fact that
> a fast-paced program like Sesame Street really
> can't slow down for a book....

> The program is hardly a library tie-in per se...
> yet it suggests the vast coordinative function that
> libraries can play, and in fact were asked to play
> ...it may move libraries more in the direction of
> community work and keep them from repeating
> what was, for the most part, a largely unimagina-
> tive response which tended to turn this effort to
> reach the disadvantaged child into just one more
> promotion for the traditional, middle-class story
> hour. [4]

Testing of children's reactions led to further changes
designed to make TV more rewarding and constructive for
all pre-schoolers. Showing picture books on the program
and reading parts of the stories encourage children to explore the wider world of books.

Along with other media mentioned, the pre-school
story hour in the public library has much of value to contribute. Although it does not offer all the features of nursery school training, the public library can assume a vital
role by extending its services to include pre-school story
hours. New insights and research reveal the significance
verbal communication has in developing a potential for learning and for success both in school and beyond. This sig-

nificance is in direct line with the basic goals, purposes, and functions of a well-planned pre-school story hour.

Since one of the principal goals is an introduction to the best in children's literature and inclusion of the best in art for children, it is interesting to note that Miss Brunner mentions "development of communication skills, of the ability to think quantitatively, and of esthetic values through experiences in art, literature, and music."[5]

She also stresses the importance of creating an interest in books as sources of pleasure and information.

> Books are not always readily accessible to children in depressed areas, and it is hoped that these children can be provided with experiences that will lead them to use the library regularly. [6]

The importance of the pre-school story hour is further revealed in this statement by Dr. James L. Hymes, Jr.: "It is good to see some children beginning to get the break that all young children deserve. These children are frequently called 'culturally deprived'--a terrible term! ....all Threes and Fours and Fives are 'culturally deprived' ....even children from more privileged homes. Youngsters this age are reaching out for more ideas, more sights, more friends, more new experiences than even the best homes can usually provide."[7]

Group experience is not only valuable as a way to find new friends and of getting along better with other children; there is added enrichment when adults provide a climate of warm love and deep respect for children as human beings.

> For being loved and loving, in return, facilitates identification with parents, relatives, teachers and peers by which the culture is internalized more

readily and organizing attitudes and values are es-
tablished easily. When one feels loved and loves
in return it is easy to believe that which one's objects of love believe, and it is easy to aspire in
the directions encouraged by one's objects of identification. The unloved child feels so much inse-
curity that he scarcely dares to try his wings in
learning. Or he is so full of hostility that he
tends to reject what he is told and to refuse to
meet the expectancies that face him, as a way of
demonstrating his power to himself. Obviously
the readiness of loving persons to provide meaningful experiences and to aid him in the learning
process are further facilitations that give great advantages to loved children. [8]

Great love and great patience is required of the story
teller as it is of the teacher of young children.

Teacher attitude is extremely important in helping
disadvantaged children. The teacher needs to
realize that vocabulary and language concepts develop slowly. He must learn to accept each child
as he is and to respect him as an individual. [9]

Thus it can be seen that there is a real challenge to
libraries, whose goals for all children and the methods in
achieving these goals are much the same. It is not to be
supposed that children from disadvantaged homes are lacking
in potential or in eagerness to learn; they simply lack opportunities. J. McVicker Hunt states:

The intellectual inferiority apparent among so
many children of low educational and socio-economic status, regardless of race, is already evi-
dent by the time they begin kindergarten or first
grade at age 5 or 6. Such children are apt to
have articulation, and syntactical deficiencies that
are revealed in the tendency to rely on unusually
short sentences with faulty grammar. They also
show perceptual deficiencies in the sense that they
recognize fewer objects and situations than do most
middle class children. And perhaps more important, they usually have fewer interests than do the

> middle class children who are the pace setters in
> the schools. Moreover, the objects recognized
> by and the interests of children typical of the low-
> er class differ from those of children of the mid-
> dle class. These deficiencies give such children
> the poor start which so commonly handicaps them
> ever after in scholastic competition. [10]

According to Jean Piaget, a Swiss psychologist, the
child first develops a store of sensorimotor meanings largely through trial and error responses to things he can manip-
ulate and see in the beginning years. Having acquired some
degree of perceptual-motor control and enlarged his sphere
of activity, he begins, by the age of two to four, to acquire
notions about objects in his environment; their size, feel and
consequences. Seeing the new in the light of the old helps
to develop the goal of mature thinking.

If there is any doubt concerning the value and importance of the role that can be played by the pre-school
story hour in the library, with its emphasis on books, pictures, verbal communication, and exploration into new experiences, Mr. Hunt's counteracting measures are illumi-
nating:

> Children aged 3 and 4 should have the opportunity
> to hear people speak who provide syntactical mod-
> els of standard grammar. The behavioral models
> would lead gradually to interest in pictures, writ-
> ten words, and books. The objects provided and
> appropriate answers to the 'why' questions would
> lead to interest in understanding the workings of
> things and the consequences of social conduct.
> Thus, the child might gradually overcome most of
> the typical handicaps of his lower-class rearing by
> the time he enters grade school. [11]

Based on the fundamental goals and purposes of the
pre-school story hour in the library, using the same basic
programs, it would be appropriate to consider the deter-

mined needs of particular groups; in this case, the so-
called "culturally deprived," "educationally deprived," "underprivileged," "lower class," or "lower socio-economic
class."

> These terms are generally used as synonyms in
> describing the people affected. In less elegant
> terms, we mean poor people. They include Ne-
> groes, Puerto Ricans, Mexican Americans, Euro-
> pean immigrants, and white people from rural
> southern communities in large numbers. There
> are others as well. [12]

Warren G. Cutts suggested that the language approach
to these children might well be the same as if one were
teaching a foreign language.

> If these children are to master the basic language
> skills of listening and speaking, they must have a
> wider range of experiences--both real and vicari-
> ous--than their more fortunate counterparts.
>
> Such experiences should include listening to stories
> told or read by the teacher; taking field trips to
> parks, farms, zoos, airports, fire stations, and
> other points of interest; using and listening to tape
> recorders, hearing records; and seeing movies and
> filmstrips. In all these activities, the main ob-
> jective is to provide pupils with opportunities for
> language experience. They must, therefore, have
> plenty of time to react to and talk about the things
> they have seen and heard. [13]

Obviously, the field trips mentioned by Mr. Cutts are
not part of a library-centered program, but the many lovely
picture-story books of farms, zoos, fire stations, and other
points of interest can be presented as part of the vicarious
experiences children need. Most of the other activities are
part of any well-planned pre-school story hour.

His suggested approach to presentation of selected
material in dealing with children who speak or understand

little of the English language, whether foreign-born or underprivileged, is further developed by Alice Dalgliesh in her
delightful book, First Experiences with Literature. [14]

Miss Dalgliesh says, "Apart from the language difficulty there is the fact that the children may come from
homes where books are practically unknown and where wholesome childlike experiences are sadly lacking."

In such situations many pictures should be used for,
as she says, the language of pictures is universal--a dog is
a dog, a river is a river, a bridge is a bridge, and "a
rose is a rose."

There are many charming picture books to be used,
so many well illustrated story books, and books of information on the pre-school level to add to the traditional stories
and nursery rhymes with which every child should be familiar. There could well be collections of pictures from magazines and other sources for children to examine and talk
about.

It has been noted that the goals and purposes, the
basic programs, and the needs of pre-school children are
the same in every group of the social structure. It should
be said that the role of the parent is also much the same.

> Before moving to implications for the schools, and
> proposed action programs, it would be well to
> point out some of the positive aspects of condi-
> tions among low income families. Frank Reiss-
> man (1955) cites responses from underprivileged
> groups which may seem surprising. He asked low
> socio-economic class interviewees, 'What do you
> miss most in life that you would like your chil-
> dren to have?" Over 50 per cent of the white re-
> spondents and 70 per cent of the Negro respond-
> ents said 'education.'
>
> Reissman also reports a study (1962) in which
> some 55 per cent of children who had learned to

read before coming to school came from lower
socio-economic homes--probably learning from the
older brother or sister--and other studies which
show that education enjoys high status among many
adults and youth of the lower socio-economic
group. [15]

Considering this report, it would seem logical to
publicize the program of pre-school story hours in the library, to gain the interest, confidence, and cooperation of
parents with much the same methods used in any group or
any community.

There will be some parents in all groups who do not
care what happens to their children and who would make no
effort to step inside a public library nor see that their children attend a story hour. However, programs for those
parents who are willing to come should follow the same pattern as given in the chapter on the role of the parent.

Parents of underprivileged children, themselves underprivileged, may need to be encouraged to borrow books
from the library to take home. They may need help in understanding the purposes and goals. They should be given
periods to stay and observe. Some of the parent programs
might include suggestions for helping their children.

(a) Help children to notice the changes in the
seasons; observe trees, bushes, flowers, leaves,
clouds, sun and moon; (b) Call attention to
trucks, buses, cars, street signs, lamp posts,
fire hydrants, manholes, mailboxes, telephone
posts...

Parents are encouraged to read stories and nursery rhymes to their children and to play 'sound
games' such as playing games with words starting
with the sound of 's' during mealtime.

In addition, the parents are encouraged to converse
with their children. They are urged to ask their

> children such questions as 'What did you play out-
> side?' 'What happened at kindergarten today?'
> 'Tell me about the children you played with today.'
> Further, parents are encouraged to stimulate self-
> expression in their children by asking them a se-
> ries of questions as they look at pictures in popu-
> lar magazines together. Parents are also urged
> to count objects with their children, help them to
> know and write their names, develop motor con-
> trol, and teach them to discriminate colors. [16]

These suggestions will, of course, be adapted to the library pre-school story hour situation. Instead of "What happened at kindergarten today?" it would be something like "What did you do or hear at story hour today?"

Again stressing the importance of verbal stimuli to the intellectual development of pre-school children, it is interesting to note the following from J. McVicker Hunt's article on "How Children Develop Intellectually:"

> 1. Hopi infants reared on cradleboards, where
>   the movements of arms and legs are inhibited
>   during waking hours, learn to walk at the same
>   age as Hopi infants reared with arms and legs
>   free.
>
> 2. Eighty-five per cent of the 4-year olds in a
>   Teheran orphanage, where variations in audi-
>   tory and visual input were extremely limited,
>   did not walk alone. [17]

The conclusion drawn should be significant to any library with a children's department, which offers a collection of books to enrich the auditory and visual experiences of pre-school children, the physical facilities for a story hour, however small and inadequate or however grand and complete, and even more compelling--the ideal and desire to extend the library's services to all children.

To quote Warren G. Cutts again:

> More and more educators are recognizing the im-
> portance of working with culturally disadvantaged
> children during the early formative years...pre-
> school enrichment programs may never be able to
> compensate fully for deficiencies in the experience
> and training provided by the home.   Nevertheless,
> such programs can go a long way toward overcom-
> ing the handicap of a poor start, and without such
> enrichment, culturally disadvantaged children are
> certain to show irreparable gaps in their learning
> and to fall hopelessly behind the rest of society. [18]

Since that statement in 1963, the gap is rapidly closing through the growth of private and public nursery schools,
day-care centers and other programs of pre-school training
including the government project "Head Start."   Even with
the phenomenal growth of interest and concern, there are
areas where no facilities for the development of young children are available.   It is a challenge to libraries to keep
pace with this growth, and they are doing so with more and
more new libraries being built, the introduction of the bookmobile to outlying districts, and the enlargement of services
to children.

Where there are no pre-school programs available,
and even where they are plentiful, the library pre-school
story hour can offer a unique contribution to existing programs with its free access to books and to library-centered
activities.

Augusta Baker, coordinator of children's services at
the New York Public Library says, "We do not see these
as new opportunities for service; they are rather extensions
of a program that is over half a century old..."   Ernestine
Rose, branch librarian at 135th Street, recognized in 1925
that dedicated staff, as well as carefully chosen books, must
be provided for these boys and girls.

> Nursery schools brought pre-schoolers to the
> children's room; for some, this was a first intro-
> duction to fine picture books and story telling. [19]

A pamphlet illustrated with photographs from the

Queens Borough Public Library tells this story:

> Eager children and parents arrive for an OPERA-
> TION HEAD START program. Now, the picture
> book hour is on: all eyes are on the pictures and
> all ears are tuned to the story. When the candle
> goes out, the children know the picture book tell-
> ing is over for the day and it is time for them to
> do some of their own picture book exploring.
> Meantime, parents of newcomers have been regis-
> tering their children for a regular weekly picture
> book program... and hearing about adult programs
> being especially planned for themselves by the li-
> brary. Like all good things, 'Library Time' must
> come to an end. Children and parents head for
> home... but they will be back next week to hear
> more picture book stories and get acquainted with
> new books. [20]

There is not always a responsible adult interested

enough to bring children to the library, and pre-schoolers

seldom wander into the children's room alone. It may be

possible for the story-teller to go to the children where they

live or gather. A bookmobile might stop in their neighbor-

hood for a story hour. (For many years story tellers have

gone into the parks every summer for a weekly story hour.)

Once the children are attracted, perhaps out of curi-

osity, they become interested in stories and books. They

may persuade their parents to bring them to the story hour

at the library, where they discover that books are meant to

be held and looked at and may be borrowed to take home.

In an article on "The Deprived Child," Mrs. Sara H.

Wheeler concluded with this statement: "Although we have

a clear sense of the difficulties of a successful program, we

anticipate a brighter future, in which all Americans can participate impartially in the American dream.   Children's librarians can indeed play an important part in making such
participation possible."[21]

Notes

1. Holsley, Eleanor, "Culturally Deprived Children in
    Day-Care Programs," Children, September-October
    1963, p. 176.

2. Brunner, Catherine, "Project Help," The Education
    Digest, vol. 29, No. 7, March 1964, p. 25.

3. Caldwell, Bettye M., "The Timid Giant Grows Bolder,"
    Saturday Review, February 30, 1971, p. 47.

4. "Sesame Street - What Next?" Library Journal,
    November 15, 1970, p. 3958.

5. Brunner, op. cit., p. 23.

6. Ibid., p. 24.

7. Hymes, James L., Jr., "Schools for the Culturally
    Deprived," Grade Teacher, May 1964, p. 107.

8. Prescott, Daniel A., "The Role of Love in Pre-School
    Education," Childhood Education, February 1962,
    p. 273.

9. Cutts, Warren G., "Reading Unreadiness in the Under-
    privileged," NEA Journal, April 1963, p. 24.

10. Hunt, J. McVicker, "How Children Develop Intellectu-
    ally," Children, May-June 1964, p. 87.

11. Ibid., p. 89.

12. Della-Dora, Delmo, "The Culturally Disadvantaged:
    Further Observations," Exceptional Children, Janu-
    ary 1963, p. 226.

13. Cutts, op. cit., p. 23.

14. Dalgliesh, Alice, First Experiences with Literature. New York, Charles Scribner's Sons, 1932, pp. 111-114.

15. Della-Dora, op. cit., p. 229.

16. U.S. Department of Health, Education and Welfare. Office of Education, School-Home Partnership in Depressed, Urban Neighborhoods, p. 25.

17. Hunt, op. cit., p. 87.

18. Cutts, op. cit., p. 24.

19. Baker, Augusta, "Pioneer in the War on Poverty: NYPL," Library Journal, vol. 89, No. 16, September 15, 1964, pp. 24-27.

20. On the Way to Their Head Start at the Queens Borough Public Library, Queens Borough, N.Y. (Pamphlet), 1965.

21. Wheeler, Sara H., "Children's Libraries," Wilson Library Bulletin, December 1964, p. 342.

Additional Reading

Hechinger, Fred M., ed. Pre-School Education Today. New York, Doubleday & Company, Inc., 1966.
    (New approaches to learning and development of the city pre-school child.)

"Providing School Library Services for the Culturally Disadvantaged," ALA Bulletin, February 1965.
    (A reprint for The American Association of School Librarians of articles which appeared in ALA Bulletin June 1964-January 1965.)

Chapter 3

CHARACTERISTICS OF THE PRE-SCHOOL CHILD

"Here Comes Julie all dressed up!"
-Julie

As she enters the door for pre-school story hour, Julie announces herself. Dressed in her best ruffles and bows, she is full of exuberance, knowing that life is packed with exciting possibilities. Her shining eyes express Walt Whitman's line of poetry, "I celebrate myself."[1]

There will be many children like Julie, confident and outgoing, ready for any new adventure. There will be others, quiet and composed, who enter with great dignity and solemn demeanor, nevertheless filled with expectancy of something special in this visit to the library for a story hour of their own.

There may be a few who are openly tearful, clutching mother's hand, but with all the potentials of the personal spirit trying to understand everything in their world, particularly other personal spirits.

Pre-schoolers are definitely individual and cannot be lumped together like a bowl of bland mashed potatoes. They are more like a shower of snowflakes, each with his own pattern. In the first few meetings there should be a gradual smoothing of the boisterous ones and soothing of the shy and fearful without trying to make all conform to a single pattern. The sparklers will always be ready to sparkle and the less confident will always need reassurance and encouragement.

Fortunately, similarities are to be expected as well as differences. While no two children are exactly alike at any age level, there are certain characteristics and needs, certain aspects of behavior, common to all normal children.

It is necessary to understand the characteristics of pre-school children in order to help this group experience a happy time of adjustment and growth. According to Ilg and Ames, at three years old:

> Greater maturity has led him to feel much more secure--secure within himself and secure in his relations to others ... But above all, his increased ability with and interest in language help him to be a delightful companion, an interesting group member. His own vocabulary and ability to use language have increased tremendously in most cases. His own application of the language of others has increased similarly. Now he can not only be controlled by language, but he can be entertained and himself can entertain. He loves new words, and they can often act like magic in influencing him to behave as we would wish. Such words as 'new,' 'different,' 'big,' 'surprise,' 'secret,' all suggest his increased awareness in the excitement of new horizons. Such words as 'help,' 'might,' 'could,' 'guess,' are active motivators to get him to perform necessary tasks... Three goes forward positively to meet each new adventure. [2]

Part of the joy of working with pre-schoolers is their charming responsiveness. They are a most eager and receptive audience, radiantly ready to smile or even to laugh uproariously. Anticipation and interest are evidenced by "children's faces looking up, holding wonder like a cup." [3]

To engage this interest, the story teller should be keenly interested in the proceedings herself, for children are quick to reflect moods, emotions, and the slightest nuances of feeling.

A strong characteristic of these children is their

readiness to imitate not only the attitudes and feelings, but
also the actions of those around them. If one wants a drink
of water, they are all likely to want a drink of water; if one
cries, others may start. Loud laughter sometimes develops
into boisterous hilarity. One trip to the toilet may start a
whole chain of reaction. If one says "I have a dog," everybody wants to tell about his dog or other pet. All these imi-
tative responses can be handled tactfully, as explained in other chapters.

This pleasure in imitation helps to guide activities and
ideas in group participation: the rhythm band, simple body
rhythms, and the more involved activity of "acting out" stories and nursery rhymes after they are repeated several
times. Vocabulary and language skills develop largely through
imitation, particularly at the pre-school level.

> The young child acquires his linguistic and thinking
> habits only through communication with other human
> beings. It is only this association that makes a
> human being out of him, that is, a speaking and
> thinking being. But, if this communication with
> other human beings did not evoke in him, for even
> a short period of time, a special, heightened sensi-
> tivity to the materials of speech which adults share
> with him, he would remain, to the end of his days,
> a foreigner to the realm of his own language--as
> though repeating lifelessly the dull rules of text-
> books. [4]

Repetition is part of the general plan of the program
since children enjoy and expect repetition. It is a universal
characteristic of young children to find satisfaction in following a familiar routine.

While they enjoy repetition, they also reach out for
the unknown. They are not ashamed to ask questions for
they are as full of "'satiable curiosity" as Kipling's ele-
phant child. [5]

It is said that children and wise men ask questions.

The child learns many things quickly and permanently. Throughout his childhood years he is learning to communicate, to listen, to know and understand, and to speak more effectively. He is learning to be at home in his world, learning to read
its signs and portents, learning to read people,
learning to act less on impulse and more with purpose. [6]

If possible, children's questions should be answered
immediately. When the right answer is unknown to the story
teller, it is good to say, "I don't know, but we can find out.
Let's look it up." Locate a book on the subject and find out
together. This will be a demonstration to the children that
books contain answers to questions, even those that some
adults do not know.

To help the child think independently, now and then
there are questions which could be answered by a challenge,
"What do you think?" Try not to put off satisfying curiosity,
and never give a thoughtless, flippant answer.

Children need answers. The story hour situation can
also make valuable contributions to other basic needs of
young children:

Need for security;

Need for belonging;

Need to feel accepted;

Need to feel adequate;

Need for recognition;

Need for play;

Need for inner resources.

The need for security can be met partly by routine
and repetition, along with a loving, dependable relationship
with leaders of the story hour. "Children feel secure when

the adults who work with them value them to the point of
empathy with them.   They develop rapidly, and learning takes
place at an optimum rate."[7]

The child needs to feel safe and to be as comfortable
as possible.   Emotional security is equally important.   This
can be found in stories of family affection and other happy
relationships, showing love, courage and gaiety, not only in
the human realm but also in animals stories.

The need for belonging finds fulfillment in group participation with the companionship of his peers.   "The teacher
who is aware of this does not leave to chance the relationships of the children.   Daily she builds a 'we-feeling' as she
works with the children in group situations.   'Aren't we having fun?' she may ask."[8]

Sooner or later, this need to belong to a group includes the need to feel a part of the world in which one lives.
It extends beyond MY family, MY neighbors, MY friends,
MY library.   Books can bring a feeling of belonging to people
outside their immediate environment.   In many libraries,
children also have contact with children from other neighborhoods than their own, other races, and other family back-
grounds.

The need for self-realization is found as the child is
given simple choices, such as choosing books to take home.
He learns to appreciate himself as an individual, a unique
person of importance when:

> he comes to understand that what he wants is given
> due consideration by those around him... He asks,
> and he receives either what he asks for or a sim-
> ple explanation supplemented, perhaps, by a rea-
> sonable substitute for what he wants.   As he devel-
> ops an awareness of his self-importance, he begins
> to develop an appreciation of the importance of
> others... [9]

A child who was told in the story hour, "We are proud of you for sitting still today," replied, "I'm proud of you too," which indicates a need for feeling accepted. This is often accomplished by conforming to rules and regulations, with approval of his actions by other children as well as by adults in charge.

This ties in with the need for feeling adequate. Praise is not only an excellent means for cultivating desirable behavior, it is also a means for meeting the need of children to feel adequate. Appreciation should be shown at every opportunity. Given any small task such as moving a chair or picking up a piece of paper from the floor, the child should be thanked.

Children learn independence and begin to feel adequate when they come into the group alone and are willing to stay without a parent nearby. Learning to be responsible for taking care of books and returning them safely helps build a feeling of adequacy.

The need for recognition is met in the story hour by having someone who is reading to him on his own level and listening to his confidences and experiences. As children identify themselves with characters in stories, they find many ways of looking at the world through new eyes. Having something to talk about to parents, neighbors, brothers and sisters, he is helped to gain recognition outside the story hour, giving him some status in society.

Play has been defined as part of the desire for change and relief from pressure, a basic need of the human organism. Humorous tales offer relief from the restriction of being "little." There is need for the emotional release provided by laughter.

Children also need books which will help and comfort

them in times of distress, just like Pooh Bear in his distress.   Pooh Bear began to sigh, and then found he couldn't
because he was so tightly stuck; and a tear rolled down his
eye, as he said: "Then would you read a Sustaining Book,
such as would help and comfort a Wedged Bear in a Great
Tightness?"[10]

Along with sustaining books, children need books to
help build inner resources.   A mind stored with happy
thoughts, gleaned from stories and poetry to be recalled when
the way looks dark, helps to combat loneliness, to overcome
fear, and to understand a world that is often strange and difficult.

It is not to be hoped nor expected that a library pre-
school story hour will fill all needs of the young child, but
there are particular needs which seem pertinent.   Not only
can social needs be satisfied through association with others,
but the child finds new interests awakened by the stories he
hears and the books he takes home.   His solitude is no longer empty and fretful.   He is learning to direct his own activities.

Notes

1.   Whitman, Walt, Leaves of Grass.

2.   Ilg, Frances L. and Louise Bates Ames, Child Be-
     havior.   New York, Harper & Brothers, 1955, p. 27.

3.   Teasdale, Sara, Barter.

4.   Chukovsky, Kornei, From Two to Five.   Berkeley and
     Los Angeles, University of California Press, 1963,
     p. 9.

5.   Kipling, Rudyard, Just So Stories.

6.   Jennings, Frank, "Most Dangerous Profession," Satur-

day Review of Literature, March 8, 1958, p. 22.

7. Todd, Vivian Edmiston, and Heffernan, Helen. The Years Before School: Guiding Pre-School Children. New York, The MacMillan Company, 1964, p. 63.

8. Ibid., p. 63.

9. Op. cit., p. 64.

10. Milne, A. A., Winnie the Pooh.

Additional Reading

Bereiter, Carl, Teaching Disadvantaged Children in the Pre-School. Englewood Cliffs, N. J., Prentice-Hall, Inc., 1966.

Chukovsky, Kornei, From Two to Five, trans. by Miraim Morton. Berkeley and Los Angeles, University of California Press, 1963.
    ("This is a book of immediate and large importance
    for parents, teachers, and writers of books for chil-
    dren--for everyone concerned with children and the
    pattern of the future. Moreover, it is a delight to
    read this skillful and perceptive translation which in-
    cludes the rendering into English of one of Chukov-
    sky's small, rhymed 'epics' of nonsense. It offers,
    besides its knowledge and insight, the companionship
    of a wise and loving spirit."--Frances Clarke Sayers.)

Hymes, James L., Jr., The Child Under Six. Englewood Cliffs, N. J., Prentice-Hall, Inc., 1963.
    (A highly perceptive look at a child's first exciting
    years of discovery, adventure, and exploration.)

Ilg, Frances L., and Ames, Louise Bates, Child Behavior. New York, Harper & Brothers, 1955.

Ilg, Frances L., and Ames, Louise Bates, School Readi-ness. New York, Harper & Row, 1964.
    (Behavior tests used at the Gesel Institute.)

Leeper, Dales, Skipper, Witherspoon, Good Schools for Young Children. New York, The Macmillan Company, 1968.
    (A guide for understanding three, four and five-year-
    old children.) Second edition.

Lewis, Claudia, Writing for Young Children. New York,
Simon and Schuster, 1954.
> ("A book to enjoy and to learn from. It is a book
> about children and how their language reveals what
> is going on inside them..." --Lucy Sprague Mitchell)

Logan, Lillian M. Teaching the Young Child. Boston,
Houghton Mifflin Company; Cambridge, The Riverside Press,
1960.
> (Written primarily for students preparing to teach, it
> is helpful to those concerned with the significance and
> development of children of nursery school age.)

Read, Katherine H., The Nursery School. Philadelphia,
W. B. Saunders Company, 1966.
> (Child behavior in early years.) Fourth edition.

Todd, Vivian Edmiston, and Heffernan, Helen, The Years
Before School: Guiding Pre-School Children. New York,
The Macmillan Company, 1964.
> (A comprehensive, detailed study of pre-school
> groups in America.)

Chapter 4

THE STORY TELLER

"She wore orange shoes today."
-David

Young children notice everything and are affected by
all that they see and all that they hear. While it takes more
than orange shoes to win and hold their attention, the appearance of the story teller is an important factor. What she is
wearing and the expression on her face often speak more effectively than what she says.

Children love bright colors, not necessarily gaudy but
certainly not somber. If it is necessary for the story teller
to wear a dark dress for attending some function afterward,
or if her wardrobe is predominately subdued, a colorful, becoming smock would not only protect her dress but would be
more cheerful and attractive to the children. A bit of jewelry is pleasing, but dangling, jingly jewelry is distracting and
should be avoided.

In the long run, neatness and good taste do as much
for the story teller's attitude as they do for the children who
must look at her for this hour. For they do care, and her
appearance tells them that she cares. Do the best to make
it appealing and then forget about it.

A cheerful disposition and good manners add charm
to appearance. Children respond to friendliness and courtesy,
to enthusiasm, and to sympathy. Consider, also, good pos-

ture and carriage. A slumping, dejected figure is depressing to look at. So, whether standing or sitting, keep the
head poised, the back straight, and the knees together, for
children are mimics. They will quickly pick up undesirable
habits. This is particularly true of facial expressions such
as deliberate distortions and nervous mannerisms. However,
a "dead-pan" face with no change of expression is not recommended. An animated, interested face showing the story
teller's own interest will quickly engage the interest of the
children.

A good voice is a great asset to the story teller and
certain qualities should be cultivated. Try for a well-modu-
lated tone and clear enunciation, using an intimate, personal
approach--gentle and easy, as if in conversation, never
stagey nor overly dramatic. Speak slowly and softly. When
the children get too loud, talk under rather than over the
noise. This has a calming, quieting effect. In fact, if you
whisper to a child, you will usually get a whisper in return.

Avoid baby-talk and "talking down" and never put on
an artificial, saccharin-sweet story voice.

The pre-school story hour differs from the story hour
for older children in presentation as well as in content.
There are many fine books on the art of story telling, and
it is good to be familiar with many techniques in order to
be fully aware of this difference.

The story hour for older children is more formal
and more dramatic. The story teller stands before the audience as if on a stage. The story is memorized, either
word for word or told in her own words. It is usually told
independently of a book.

In the pre-school story hour, however, the picture
book is of paramount interest and importance. The book is

held open at the pictures, the pages turned leisurely as the story unfolds to give every child time to drink in the details. It may be necessary to turn the book slowly from side to side for all to see, particularly if the group is large.

It is best to know the contents of the book well enough to turn the pages so that the picture won't be shown before the sequence or action of the story. Also, being familiar with the story, the story teller's eyes will not be glued to each page; it will take only a glance at the picture for continuity, condensing the story if it is too long.

The classics used with the pre-schoolers, however, should be told (or read) as nearly as possible in the language of the original. Even so, some child may correct the telling if he has heard different wording at home: In the story of "The Three Bears," someone may say, "It's not who's been eating my porridge? It's who's been tasting my soup?" Try to find the best version, then quietly answer, "Yes, sometimes people say it that way." Never argue that only one way is right.

Nursery rhymes, poems, and jingles that accompany finger plays must be memorized and should be repeated accurately since they are usually picked up word for word by the children and recited for members of the family, from grandparents to baby sister--even for the neighbors. When asked by a neighbor who listened with admiration, "Where did you learn that?" one little boy is reported to have replied, "From the library. The story lady was on today."

Whether the story is memorized or told as the book is shown, the story teller should look in turn at all members of the group, not just those directly in front of her. She must also be sure that they are all facing her! Frequently, in the beginning, when everything is new and customs are unknown, a child will sit with his back to the story teller, facing the children. No doubt he is more interested in them, at least until the stories capture his attention.

Others will want to stand close beside the story teller, some even climb upon her lap. Demonstrations of affection can be handled tactfully with a quick hug or a gentle pat on the head followed by the suggestion, "Now we are all going to sit in our own places so we can have a story and see the pictures." Even Hans Christian Andersen, the great story teller and beloved friend of children, never allowed them to climb over him. Story telling, in his words, was "a ceremony and too delicate a process to have children climbing on his back or sitting on his lap." Children will understand and be happier when they understand the rules of conduct and abide by them.

Of course, they will not be expected to sit rigidly at attention. If they are obviously bored with one story, be ready to switch to another one or to some lively activity. Do not be afraid to stop when attention is wandering. Save that story for another time if it seems worth trying again later.

On the other hand, do not hesitate to repeat a story the children particularly enjoy. They want to hear favorites over and over. Often a child will ask, "Tell it again." If it is not convenient to do so just then, it is generally satisfactory to say, "We will have that one again some time."

There are certain techniques which little children enjoy and which are valuable for gaining and for holding their attention. Finger plays just before a story, such as "Open, shut them...," or "Here are Grandma's glasses...," help to quiet wigglers and squirmers.

Wandering attention can often be brought back by lowering the voice or by inserting the child's name: "And the little rabbit went hopping down the road, Tony, looking for a home."

Variety in tempo is also good for holding attention. A monotonous, one-level tone can put everybody near sleep. So make use of pauses and stressing important words. Slow the pace at appropriate parts of the story, then increase the speed when the action is swift.

Some books, such as <u>Benny's Four Hats</u> (page 140), invite participation by the children, and offer a lively change from concentrated listening. Allow them to express themselves freely for they will be eager, responsive and vocal.

Mimicry is another means of effective participation. Children love to imitate sounds. There will often be a chorus of mooing, baaing, neighing, cock-a-doodle-dooing, squealing like pigs and squeaking like mice, and all sorts of other animal voices. Some stories inspire the imitation of mechanical sound, such as the tooting of whistles, the chugging of trains, and the ticking of clocks.

Spontaneous participation is natural and includes many enthusiastic sound effects, even stomping of feet and hilarious laughter on occasion, but should not bring the story to a complete halt. If it should go on too long, some other sound or movement can be used by the story teller to break the chain reaction. Or it could be a combination of sound and movement such as clapping the hands over the head, then rolling the fists over and over, bringing them folded into the lap. And, lo, everybody is ready to listen. If this happens not to work, tap a triangle or employ some other arresting sound.

Interruptions are to be expected, and the story teller

must know how to handle them tactfully but firmly.   Someone
will surely ask to have a shoestring tied during the course
of a story.   Rather than distract the entire group by stopping
the story for interruptions of this kind, such requests may
be answered by a smiling nod of the head and the assuring
word, "Later."

Emergency interruptions demand immediate attention,
of course.   It is good to have an assistant for a quick trip
to the toilet, or to have a tissue ready for a sudden, drippy
sneeze.   Requests for a drink of water are not usually considered emergencies, and can be postponed graciously by a
quiet, "After a while.   You don't want to miss any of the
fun."

Some children will interrupt by bouncing up to find
another seat or even to climb on a chair or table, particularly during the orientation period when they have not
learned the ways of the story hour.   Avoid a negative response by using a suggestion such as, "We all stay in our
places during the story, Betsy," or "We will all stand up
and stretch after the story."

Occasionally a discipline problem may arise and
should be handled in a positive and loving manner.   More
harm than good results from using a negative approach.   It
is much more effective to say, "We are all going to sit
quietly and listen to a story" rather than, "Don't wiggle
around and don't talk until the story is over."

Tensions are increased by demanding too much too
strenuously.   Many children will fight back, answer argument with argument, yell in response to a raised voice, get
bossy when bossed.   Encourage acceptable behavior by ac-
cepting the child's feelings with a sympathetic remark such
as, "I know how you feel, but now we're all going to have

a good time." A pat on the shoulder and the reminder,
"We're big people now; we all help at story hour," usually
proves that the all-important "we" works wonders.

A crying spell can be met with the suggestion, "If
you could tell me why you are crying, maybe we could do
something about it." Usually the tears are explained by, "I
want my mother," and can be stopped by the cheerful assur-
ance, "Your mother will be back soon. We'll have a story
and a game, then all the mothers will come back."

Sometimes the child needs to go to the toilet and is
afraid to ask. Sometimes he does not know why he is crying. In any case, try to find the reason. If none is apparent, offer comfort and consolation by a show of affection and
by sympathetic identification.

If a full-blown tantrum should develop, calm can often
be restored by diverting the child's attention without becoming too upset oneself. It may be necessary for an assistant
to take the child aside temporarily for a quiet talk in order
not to disturb the entire group.

Some interruptions are merely attention-getters, but
the disturber should not be ignored or his tactics may become more demanding. Children often get up and walk to
the story teller's side to show a new dress or a skinned
knee, or to tell what the family had for breakfast. After a
brief word of recognition, admiration or sympathy, the story
can be resumed smoothly. If there is no move to go back
and sit down again, it is best for the story teller to put her
arm around the child and go on with the story. Never reject a child, but always be ready for questions and confidences with a sympathetic attitude and a friendly response.

Little children often interrupt a story with comments
about the subject: "I have a doggy," or "I have a turtle."

It is good to stop briefly to listen, or to say, "You may tell us all about it at the end of the story."

At that time there will be many more who have dog stories and turtle stories, which can develop into a whole array of family pets from goldfish to parakeets. It may be necessary to change the program that has been planned. However, it does not usually take much of the prepared time since most children will be satisfied just to announce that they have a pet. If there is time, further discussion can be encouraged by "What is his name?" or "Where does he sleep?" Generally, three-year-olds will have to be drawn out a little when they actually have the spotlight, although there will be an occasional child who outshines the story teller's best efforts in holding attention and dramatizing an event or experience.

The story teller should not interrupt the story herself to ask questions such as, "What do you suppose he did next?" or "What do you think he saw?" The response may be over-whelming, for everybody will have an answer. Neither should the story teller interrupt the story for explanations which insult the intelligence of the children and check the flow of the narrative.

For best results with pre-school children the story teller must know her story well, whether she tells it with or without a book. She tells it simply and naturally with the amount of dramatic feeling and humor that the story de-mands. She does not talk down to the children. She knows how to handle their interruptions with patience and tact, and does not interrupt herself unnecessarily.

In addition, a good story teller should be a good lis-tener, a good admirer of skinned knees, and good at tying shoe strings.

Recommended Reading

Allstrom, Elizabeth, You Can Teach Creatively. Nashville,
Tennessee, Abingdon Press, 1970.
(For workers with children in libraries, day schools,
church school, Head Start, and all groups where
children are growing and learning.)

Bereiter, Carl, Teaching Disadvantaged Children in the Pre-
School. Englewood Cliffs, N.J., Prentice-Hall, Inc., 1966.

Cundiff, Ruby Ethel and Webb, Barbara, Storytelling for
You. Yellow Springs, Ohio, The Antioch Press, 1957.
(Pre-school helps scattered throughout.)

Dalgliesh, Alice, First Experiences with Literature. New
York, Charles Scribner's Sons, 1931.
("The future usefulness of this little volume may be
predicted without risk."--Patty Smith Hill)

Emerson, Laura S., Storytelling, The Art and the Purpose.
Grand Rapids, Michigan, Zondervan Publishing House, 1959.
(Pre-school, p. 35.)

Hymes, James L., Jr., Teaching the Child Under Six.
Columbus, Ohio, Charles E. Merrill Publishing Company,
1968.

Lewis, Claudia, Writing for Young Children. New York,
Simon and Schuster, 1954.
(Invaluable to all who use language in their relation-
ships with children.)

Mitchell, Lucy Sprague, Here and Now Story Book. New
York, E. P. Dutton and Company, Inc., 1948.
(Stories and technique for two through seven-year-
olds.)

Sawyer, Ruth, The Way of the Storyteller. New York, The
Viking Press, 1949. Revised edition, 1962.
(Not how to tell nor what to tell, but a call to go
questing for the spiritual experience which makes
good stories.)

Shedlock, Marie L. , <u>Art of the Storyteller</u>. New York,
Dover, 1951.
    (A standard approach to story telling.)

Tooze, Ruth, <u>Storytelling</u>.   Englewood Cliffs, N. J. , Prentice-
Hall, 1959.
    (A storehouse of useful information.)

Chapter 5

PHYSICAL ARRANGEMENTS

"Our library is too small--not enough
time and not enough staff!"
--Many librarians.

Objections of this kind are most often heard from librarians who are reluctant to introduce a library pre-school
story hour.

These laments are understandable. However, any library which has the tiniest corner, nook or cubicle with
shelves of books for the pre-school age has a place to gather
a group, albeit a small one, for a story hour. A mother's
lap is not too small an area for a story. Dewey on one end
of a log with a child on the other end has been cited as con-
ducive to learning. Hans Christian Andersen on a street corner with children clustered before him held their spellbound
attention. The size of the place and the location are not
nearly so important as the story teller, her material, and
her listeners.

The amount of space and facilities available will be,
of course, deciding factors in the necessary arrangements
for a pre-school story hour. The story teller and the children should be comfortably seated during the stories. There
are many possibilities for seating; some are selected from
necessity and some by choice. Small chairs or benches,
perhaps both, can be found in most children's rooms. Wob-

bly stools and seats without backs are not recommended because of the danger of having a child fall off (although they sometimes tumble off a chair with a good, sturdy back). Reasonable precautions should be taken to avoid such incidents.

If there are not enough low seats to go around, even with spillover to a convenient window seat, small individual rugs or pillows may be supplied for the overflow, and placed on the floor in the open section of the semi-circle. Some children prefer the rugs. It would be satisfactory to use only the individual rugs or pillows or one big story rug. One large rug, which can be rolled up and put away, is a good choice. Or the children may sit on the bare floor as they do in most kindergartens and nursery schools. Sitting on the floor, whether it is bare or covered, has some features that make it preferable to sitting on chairs. There are some little legs that are too short to reach the floor when the child is sitting on a chair. Dangling legs become uncomfortable after a short time. Short legs can be curled under or folded tailor fashion on a rug or bare floor.

A story rug, also, has a sort of magic carpet atmosphere and gives the children a cozy feeling. It should be large enough to accommodate all the children without crowding. There should be sufficient space between children whether they are seated on chairs, pillows or rugs. The seating should be informal, close together, but not touching. It is sometimes good to say, "If you are touching anybody, you're sitting too close."

The story rug is brought out only for story hour; first of all, to give a feeling of special occasion, and for the more practical reason that it would soon become dirty from being walked upon constantly. Individual rugs or pillows should also be stored when not in use. The children enjoy making their selections from a large box gaily painted in childlike designs or from a large cardboard carton which has been covered with bright-colored book jackets and given a coat of shellac.

In some communities, Girl Scout Troops make "Sit-Upons" as a service project for the library pre-schoolers. These are individual squares made from plastic or oilcloth of double thickness sewed together with a buttonhole stitch or bound with bias tape. Single thicknesses could simply be finished by cutting with pinking shears.

One library uses a double flight of stairs for acting out stories they have heard. If there is enough seating capacity, stairs make a good seating arrangement for listening to stories, too. A sort of amphitheatre effect can be achieved in a library with a short flight of stairs as part of the natural setting, where there is no danger of children falling. For outdoor story telling, a grassy spot in the shade of a tree, steps, or a low coping provide convenient seating arrangements. Ingenuity and imagination are helpful in determining which situation offers the best advantages.

Whatever arrangement is chosen, the children should be facing away from the windows to avoid glare from outside. There should be good ventilation and a comfortable temperature. To encourage good listening, the children should be seated in a semi-circle so that all can see and hear.

The story teller should be seated on the children's level or slightly elevated (never standing to tell a story) and as close to the children as possible. A low table or stand of some kind near at hand is convenient for holding the books and all material to be used at a particular session, plus the record player and records. (A box of cleansing tissues is also handy as a substitute for a forgotten hanky!)

There must be some arrangement for hanging outdoor clothing. Children should not keep coats on during the story hour; they should not throw them over a chair nor pile them on a table to be unscrambled later. The ideal arrangement would be to have low racks in a hallway where the children could learn responsibility in taking care of their own belongings.

However, there might be low hooks in a hallway, or a pipe with small coat hangers. Where there is no hallway, provisions have been made right in the room by installing a pipe under high book shelves. Older children are able to reach the books, and the little folks can reach the low hangers. Not every room can make this adaptation, so perhaps a commercial rolling coat rack could be used and rolled into a storage space when not in use.

Some libraries consist of only one room offering services to both children and adults. In many libraries, all work with children is conducted in one room; some have a separate room for story telling and other activities. What is needed ideally is not a children's room, but a children's suite according to Lionel McColvin:

> One could think of such a suite comprising, for example, a room for the younger children, a lending library for the older ones with a separate reference library and study room, and a story hour or lecture room (films, television) room. Most of us, however, will be grateful for one trained children's librarian with a little, probably one-roomed kingdom over which she can reign. [1]

In these one-roomed kingdoms, there is usually a distinct area with its own shelves, tables and chairs for children, for, as Mr. McColvin says, "They deserve their due share of attention."

Part of this attention should be devoted to making the children's corner, room, or "suite" as attractive and child-like as possible.   Naturally, there will be books lying about on the table for browsing.   Shadow boxes and collections such as dolls and shells add pleasing centers of interest.   Flowers and seasonal objects are always appealing.   One children's room has a "seasonal tree," which was made from an inter-esting branch about two feet high, stuck into a flower pot of sand.   The limbs are convenient for decorating and can be left natural or painted to harmonize with the trimming.   It has been decorated in turn with little ghosts (made of white Kleenex) at Hallowe'en, candy canes and sugar plums (made of frosted prunes) during the Christmas season, decorated eggs for Easter, and bright paper butterflies for later spring.

Colorful cardboard posters or advertising pieces do-nated by places of business have been used effectively-- Easter rabbits, Santas and reindeer, trains, planes and even a castle.

Children's books with their bright-colored jackets are an attractive decoration in themselves, and should be dis-played in a way to encourage children to enjoy handling the books.   The colorful jackets often help the youngest patrons decide which book to check out for home use.   Choices are made for various reasons: because they are tiny like the Beatrix Potter books and some of Joan Walsh Anglund's, be-cause they are large like many of the Golden Books, but mainly because the child "reads" the pictures long before he is able to read the words.

Besides encouraging children to use and enjoy books, another purpose of the story hour is to help children learn to respect books whether their own or those from the library collection, and to keep them clean and attractive. It will be necessary to make these points clear very early in the story hour program. Some of the youngest will look at a book briefly, but find it as much fun to sit upon, stand upon, or carry around by the cover. There is no doubt that most children instinctively love books but it might be cautioned that a few "love" them too much or in the wrong way, even to the extent of trying to eat them by chewing at the corners or nibbling the pages.

Children need to be shown how to take care of books at the earliest opportunity. The demonstration should include these points:

 a. We must have clean hands before we touch the books.

 b. We must open the book carefully, and turn the pages from the upper right hand corner. (He may not know his right hand from his left, but he can see what you are doing.)

 c. When we are finished with the book, we must return it carefully to the shelf or to the table, where we found it.

 d. When we choose a book to take home, we must have it checked out at the desk, and we must return it to the same place.

Children are interested in the check-out procedure, and it is a good idea to show them exactly how it is done and to explain why. At the same time, they should be shown where books are returned so they will not be dropped on a table, stuck back on a shelf, or left where they hang their coats. In this way, the children will soon learn the meaning of borrowing books, how to check them out and return them properly, which is one of the goals of the pre-school story hour: "First opportunities to select books for home reading."

There will no doubt have to be reminders, but generally speaking, children with respect for books will not deliberately harm them or lose them. So the invitation to borrow books can safely be given: "Now you may choose a book to take home."

Then the question arises, "How can all this be accomplished with shortage of staff?" This is a problem in big libraries as well as in one-room libraries with only one trained librarian. In any library there are many time-consuming demands to be met.

> For years many public library children's rooms have been carrying work that should have been done by school libraries. The trends in the development of elementary-school libraries should bring some definite changes of emphasis and focus in the public children's library. ...The public librarian will still be meeting school classes; but she will be able to talk more about books, since the lessons on how to use the library will be taught in the school. She will have more time for story hours in the library, for speaking and story telling outside the library. ...The children's librarian will do more with parents, using this collection (outstanding children's books) as a background for talks, perhaps even for series of lectures on children's books. [2]

It is recognized that assistance is necessary to cope with a large group of pre-schoolers, and it is considered best to have one adult present for each ten or twelve children. For this reason alone, many libraries hesitate to adopt a program solely for young children. However, the problem has been solved satisfactorily where the need has been felt and the challenge accepted.

These are some of the ways that have been found practical in providing valuable assistance to understaffed libraries:

a. Volunteers from civic groups and service groups such as Junior Service League, Child Study Association, A.A.U.W., Girl Scouts, 4-H Club members.

b. Cooperative mothers.

c. Library trainees or clerks interested in children's work.

d. Practice teachers from local colleges.

e. Ex-teachers with nursery school or kindergarten experience.

f. Story telling specialists hired for this specific program.

Some assistants give aid simply by being present to help with wraps, with registrations, name tags, with sudden emergencies, and by giving attention to an individual child who is disturbing the group. Others have particular talents to offer such as music and drama, or ability and training in working with young children.

Assistants should, of course, be sympathetic and sensitive to young children and can be given pointers in procedures and techniques of the story hour by observing actual presentations. A series of workshops could be conducted by a qualified person for those who are interested in active participation. In-service training of library personnel has also been used in some libraries.

A trained, experienced story teller might be added to the payroll just to conduct story hours at the central library and branches and to give training to members of the staff and volunteers.

For such is the popularity of this service to the pre-school age that even the smallest groups often grow beyond capacity. The best possible physical arrangements must be

made in each situation, always trying to create an atmosphere that plainly says, "This is a pleasant place with friendly people having a happy time."

Notes

1. McColvin, Lionel R., <u>Libraries for Children.</u>   London,
    Phoenix House Ltd. , 1961, p. 60.

2. Viguers, Ruth Hill, <u>Margin for Surprise; About Books,
    Children, and Libraries.</u>   Boston, Little, Brown &
    Company, 1964, p. 96.

Additional Reading

Goldhor, Herbert and Joseph L. Wheeler, <u>Practical Administration of Public Libraries.</u>   New York and Evanston, Harper
& Row, 1962.
        (Children's Services, p. 373, Chapter 21.)

Chapter 6

THE ROLE OF THE PARENT

"Story Hour is the highlight of our week."
-A Parent

Parents are usually the instigators of a pre-school story hour. It is unlikely that a pre-schooler would ever make the request, "Why don't you start a story hour for us here in the library?" Once it is begun, they are eager to attend every session and frequently provide the momentum to take on more duties with shortage of staff, time and space. Although they may be willing, they are reluctant to begin a story hour for young children without knowledge of specific techniques for the pre-school hour. In most cases, there-fore, the service begins at the request of parents, who are responsible for bringing the children in and picking them up week after week. They are always appreciative and are in-terested in the program, and yet the problem of what to do with the parents is one of the most difficult to solve.

Policies vary in regard to the role of the parent in es-tablished story hour programs. Some libraries quite frankly ignore the problem, allowing the parents to follow their own pursuits and inclinations. Some mothers send their children with a neighbor and never appear; some visit with other moth-ers in a nearby coffee shop after leaving their children at the library. Other libraries near a shopping center or in the downtown area report that the mothers are grateful for a

72

chance to shop or keep a dental appointment while their children are having a meaningful experience of their own. They do not consider the story hour a free babysitting service, but they do realize that there is not space for everybody.

Most parents prefer to remain in the room to observe the story hour program. Where there is space, some sit unobtrusively knitting or catching up on their mending. They often volunteer to help with the children when needed. Some choose to read or browse in the adult department of the library.

The ideal situation would be to have a program for the parents at the time of the children's hour. This has been done where there is room available and a staff member can be in charge. In some cases the mothers can take turns as leader of the group and an outside speaker can be brought in occasionally.

When this service is offered it is appreciated by most parents but none should be required to attend. It would be impossible in cases where the mother has an outside job, or when she sends her child with someone else and must stay at home with younger children.

Programs could consist of talks about books and recordings for young children, building a home library, family reading aloud, and subjects of that nature. Talks on child care and nutrition, first aid and home nursing, arts and crafts for children or adults, also make interesting and worthwhile programs. Parents appreciate reviews and discussions of adult books, and there may be other suggestions from the parents themselves.

It is a sound policy to have a member of the professional staff meet with the parents at the beginning of the series to explain the goals, purposes and procedures of the

pre-school story hour. This encourages parents to feel that
they are part of the program and helps them to understand
their responsibilities in making the program a success.

It is also advisable to have another meeting with the
parents at the end of the series to discuss with the librarians
ways of continuing the objectives of the story hour in home
activities. These ways might include suggestions for them:

To schedule a reading-aloud period for each day.

To encourage children to ask questions about what
is read.

To show enthusiasm for beautiful pictures and rhythmical language.

To convince the children that people in stories are
friends.

To encourage curiosity about the meaning of words.

To allow the pre-schooler some voice in selecting
books to take home from the library.

There are always a few parents who would like to observe every story hour to see how their children behave in
a similar age group and to learn the finger plays and techniques so that they can use them at home. It has been
found, however, that some children are distracted by the
presence of their parents. They will jump up from time to
time and run to the mother's lap. Some will not leave her
side as long as she is present.

There are other obvious disadvantages to having parents in attendance. For one, there is not usually room
enough to accommodate all who want to stay. It is reported
that in one situation, thirty-six mothers stayed to watch the
program. This practice is not only impossible in most
cases, but would cause overcrowding in any case and might

easily turn the story hour into a show. The continued presence of parents also thwarts any possibility of teaching the
child to be independent, which is one of the recognized needs
of young children.

It is understandable that parents want to observe their
children and the problem has been solved in some instances
by allowing the parents to stand outside the story hour room
to watch the activities through a glass door. Also, where
parents are eager to observe, small groups could be permitted to take turns observing on specified occasions, even par-
ticipating in some of the activities.

This is particularly recommended for parents who volunteer to help carry out the program. Some of the help may
be simply assisting with the physical needs of the children.
Others often help with stories or dramatization when they are
familiar with methods and techniques, whether from observation or from their previous experience and training as teachers in kindergarten and nursery school.

Any child who is excessively shy or fearful in any
way needs to have a parent or familiar adult remain in sight
and easily accessible. After the first few times, he will
gradually adjust to the group and be proud of his new-found
independence. This gradual process of withdrawal can be
accomplished by having the parent leave for only a short
time, perhaps to put money in the parking meter, saying,
"I'll be right back." The time can be lengthened to a visit
to another part of the library, and finally to her absence for
the entire period.

After this procedure, these reluctant children have
been known to rush the parents away with a cheerful fare-
well; "Good-by, you'd better go now." One such child even
confided to the story teller, "I wouldn't be afraid if my

mother went away on a long trip."

Parents should never leave without telling the child
good-by and saying that they will be back soon. It is disastrous for a parent to wait until the child is absorbed in the
group activities and slip away unnoticed without telling the
child where she is going and that she will be back. This
ruse is a breach of faith and will tend to destroy the child's
confidence and trust, making him cling to the parent more
tenaciously from them on.

When the child discovers the disappearance of the
parent, the ensuing storm will be much greater than the little
shower of tears that might occur if the child had been told in
the first place. It has been found that a child will stop crying soon after the parent leaves if he has been prepared for
the departure. If he does not, he is either ill or too imma-
ture for the story hour experience, and should not be in the
group at that time.

Parents are very willing to cooperate when the understand the point of view of the librarians in charge of the
story hour. Taking into consideration what has been done
and what can be done, these suggestions are offered:

> Permit the parents to do whatever they choose during
> the story hour insofar as it does not disrupt the
> program.
>
> Sanction observation--
> a) in small groups at specified times.
> b) at some location where they will not distract
>   the children.
> c) for a parent whose child has difficulty adjusting.
> d) to train volunteer assistants.
>
> Encourage parents to remain in the library building--
> a) for browsing, reading or study.
> b) for listening to music if there is a special
>   music room.

c) for programs of their own, conducted by a member of the staff or by the mothers themselves. (One mother, who brought her knitting each time, offered to teach the others during story hour since they showed interest in learning to knit.)

Suggestions for Parent Programs

Talks about books and recordings for young children.

Building a home library and family reading aloud.

Talks on child care and nutrition.

Talks on first aid and home nursing.

Talks on arts and crafts.

Book reviews and discussions of adult books.

Outside speakers on subjects chosen by the group.

Music.

Films.

The following statements by parents are worth considering:

"I like to observe and see how you manage to keep children of this age quiet and interested."

"Johnny is quieter at home now. He is not so rambunctious and will sit still and look at books or listen to his records."

"I notice you speak in a low, soft voice. I used to shout at Kevin and it didn't do any good. Now he listens when I talk softly."

"Attending story hour has overcome my son's excessive shyness. He is more communicative and outgoing."

"The routine of story hour and hearing her favorite stories gives my child a feeling of security."

"Coming to story hour gives my child something to talk about at home."

"My child plays 'story hour' all week and reads to

her dolls."

"I like to observe so we can carry out the same activities at home."

"It is my only free time all week, but I would like a
book review once in a while."

"It's a good chance to get out of the house and do
something different for a change."

One parent wrote a letter to the story teller giving
her reactions to this service. Her remarks illustrate the
aims and purposes of the story hour:

> It is almost fantastic the enthusiasm that 'Story
> Hour' creates. It is truly the highlight of our
> week's activites.
>
> The weekly excursion in the library has opened
> up the world outside the family and neighborhood.
> It is the first association with any large number
> of children. And my child particularly enjoys
> meeting children from other sections of the city.
>
> While many of the activities have been introduced
> at home, the setting is conducive to good behavior
> and full attention--no ringing telephones, younger
> children, or household activities to distract.
>
> My child has learned to sit quietly for a length of
> time, to listen attentively, and to participate ac-
> tively before and with a group. She has achieved
> a certain amount of independence by going along
> to 'The Children's Room' (when I couldn't find a
> nearby parking place), taking care of her coat, re-
> turning her books, and recognizing her name on
> the name tags.
>
> These are traits that would be developed in a nurs-
> ery school. So the important difference is the in-
> terest in books that is created.
>
> We have many children's books at home, but to
> borrow books from the library has become SO im-
> portant. She helps choose her books and carries
> them home to proudly display to Daddy and Grand-

parents. Borrowing from the library means she can have so many more books--fun ones, information ones, and those with fine illustrations-- than we or any family could afford to give for home use. She and the others at home have learned special care of library books because they are borrowed. This in turn has taught respect for the property of others.

I feel this first introduction to the library program will prove more valuable in years to come. My child loves to visit the library, knows she has friends among the librarians and in the books too! This way, she will feel at home when the time comes to use the library for research and study as well as for pleasure.

OUR 'Story Lady' and 'Story Hour' are the first conscious recognition of something GREAT outside the family circle. No wonder it is such a highlight for both child and mother!

Thus it can be concluded that a successful pre-school story hour program is the result of combined efforts.

Books for Parents

Arbuthnot, May Hill, Children's Reading in the Home. Glenview, Illinois, Foresman and Company, 1969.

Arnold, Arnold, Teaching Your Child to Learn from birth to school. Englewood Cliffs, N. J., Prentice-Hall, Inc., 1971.

Baruch, Dorothy Walter, New Ways in Discipline. New York, McGraw-Hill Book Co., Inc., 1949.

Bernhardt, Karl, Discipline and Child Guidance. New York, McGraw-Hill Book Co., Inc., 1964.

Dodson, Fitzhugh, How to Parent, Los Angeles, Nash Publishing, 1970.

Duvall, Evelyn M., Family Development, 4th edition, Philadelphia, J. B. Lippincott Co., 1971.

Engelmann, Siegfried, Give Your Child a Superior Mind.
    New York, Simon and Schuster, 1966.

Ginott, Dr. Haim, Between Parent and Child, new solutions
    for old problems. New York, Macmillan Co., 1965.

Goodman, Dr. David, A Parent's Guide to the Emotional
    Needs of Children. New York, Hawthorne Books,
    Revised edition, 1969.

Hymes, James L., Jr., The Child Under Six, Englewood
    Cliffs, N. J., Prentice-Hall, Inc., 1963.

Ilg, Frances L., and Louise Bates Ames, Child Behavior.
    New York, Harper & Brothers, 1955; (Paperback vol-
    ume, New York, Dell Publishing Co., 1960.)

Jones, Molly Mason, Guiding Your Child from 2 to 5. New
    York, Harcourt, Brace & World, Inc., 1967.

Larrick, Nancy, A Parent's Guide to Children's Reading,
    3rd Edition, Garden City, N. Y., Doubleday, 1969.

Schwartz, Berthold Eric, You Can Raise Decent Children.
    New Rochelle, N. Y., Arlington House, 1971.

Spock, Benjamin, Baby and Child Care. New York, Pocket
    Books, Inc., 1968.

Chapter 7

PLANNING THE PROGRAM

"This is a story hour just for us!"
-Alice

A well-planned program, on the young child's level,
is an aid to the success of a pre-school story hour.   Children enjoy a familiar routine and repetition gives them a
sense of security.   It is wise to plan programs ahead to
avoid last-minute frantic preparations since the story teller
needs to have the content for each session and the continuity
firmly in mind for her own feeling of security and confidence.

The best guide to planning is to keep everything informal and flexible enough to meet unexpected interruptions
and unforeseen interests of the children with calmness and
consideration rather than being dominated by the program.
There is loss of spontaneity and joy in a rigid program demanding that it must start with a set greeting, then a story,
then a finger play, then a story, then a lively activity, and
must all come out even in the end.

A pre-school program can seldom be timed accurately; time may be over or there may not be time to finish
everything that was anticipated.   In the first instance, it is
wise to have a few extras at hand; in the second, left-over
material can be saved for another time.   There should be no
feeling of panic or such thoughts as "What will I do if I finish too soon?" or "What if there isn't enough time to include

81

everything I had planned?"

The greatest satisfaction for all concerned is to
choose a certain theme or unit of interest for each session
with enough books, pictures, nursery rhymes, finger plays,
and other related material to avoid the possibility of running
short.

Programs are built on subjects suggested in many instances by the children themselves.   Their interests include
everything from dinosaurs to turtles, from toy trains to
space ships, from sea shells to snakes.   A child once
brought in a huge black snake his father had killed and stored
in the deep freeze until he could bring it for "Show and
Tell." There was an interesting session on snakes! Another
child brought in a bleeding-tooth shell, which the story teller
and the children learned about together from The Book of
Sea Shells, by Michael H. Bevans.

Since recognizing the seasons of the year is a joyful
part of the pre-school child's development, programs should
be designed for spring, summer, fall and winter.   "As children experience the succession of birthdays and holidays
throughout the year, and as they enjoy activities appropriate
to each season, they build up an understanding of the year
as a series of recurring events."[1]

There can be programs planned to celebrate holidays,
birthdays, and other special occasions.   Several sessions
may be needed leading up to Hallowe'en, Christmas, and
Easter because of the sustained interest of the children and
the wealth of material available.

It is advisable to have books laid aside for future
programs so that they will be on hand at the time when they
are needed.   Material for a rainy-day program or a snowy-
day program will then be ready on the appropriate occasion.

Weather is not always predictable! Holiday materials and seasonal materials are best anticipated in plenty of time to be sure of having the book you plan to use. Of course, many programs can be used any time during the year, and no one should feel obligated to make every program seasonal or fill a stated need or a stated interest.

To quote Ruth Hill Viguers, there should be a "margin for surprise."

> Today we have many fine books for children, some of them works of art; but we still expect children to use that art rather than to receive it. Much book criticism is concerned with analyzing books in terms of social values as well as curriculum values. Some of us make a great point of emphasizing that a book teaches brotherhood, or kindness to animals, or a dozen other specific things. We forget that the child who has fine books available to him will receive all this naturally. Every book a child reads becomes a part of him. He does not have to have books angled at his specific problems or needs. [2]

It is hoped that the more general acceptance of the pre-school story hour as part of library services to children, and the understanding of its particular techniques will not lead to conformity and to stereotyped programs.

These suggested programs are not meant to be followed exactly step by step, but are given to help you create your own programs. There are many themes to build on that are not mentioned here. Use your imagination and enjoy each session.

SUGGESTED PROGRAMS

General Framework

1) Preliminaries:

   Greetings, helping with wraps, putting on name tags,

conversation, book browsing, listening to music.

2) Signal for story hour to begin:

A musical signal to gather children together: theme song on record player or piano, lighting a candle, or simply a chord on a piano or tap on a triangle from the rhythm band.

3) Opening period:

Conversation, period of sharing experiences or objects brought in by the children or story teller.

4) Story:

Told as the picture book is shown, after a quieting finger play.

5) Active period:

Stretching or rhythmic activity;

Pantomime or dramatization of the story.

6) Another listening time:

Story told with or without a book, or nursery rhymes, or poetry.

7) Active time:

Simple games;   Birthday celebration;

Rhythm band;   Holiday party.

8) Good-by time:

Repetition of theme song;

Lightly touching each one with a hand puppet;

Blowing out the candle.

9) After the program:

Returning name tags;

Choosing books to take home;

Looking at books or listening to music while waiting for a delayed parent.

Choices can be made according to the available time allowed for each program and according to the intentions of each individual story teller.

The First Day

The children may not be familiar with the library; may not be acquainted with the story teller nor with the other children; may not understand how to behave during a library story hour. This is a time of introductions, (which may have to be repeated for several sessions).

1) Preliminaries:

Be sure there is plenty of time allowed to make friends with the children and parents by talking with each one. The mothers are sometimes invited to stay in the room or in some part of the library, at least for a while.

Put on name tags, explaining "Now, we'll know who you are." The story teller might wear a name tag herself or simply tell each child her name and the names of other librarians and helpers present. This shows courtesy and respect for the child and will encourage him to show respect by calling the right name instead of "Hey, Teacher" or just "Hey." Names will be learned gradually.

2) Signal for going to their places:

Explain that when we have this signal, we will all gather in a particular place for stories.

3) Opening period:

Explain further what the story hour is and what to expect. Listen and comment on remarks from the children.

If some child has brought a toy, he might be asked to show it and tell about it in front of the group.

This encourages verbal communication, but can run
into problems. There may be a constant stream of
little trucks and cars, of guns and cowboy pistols, of
little girls' purses with monotonous contents to be revealed. However, valuable time can be saved and nobody's feelings will be hurt if everyone with the same
category is invited to come up at the same time and
show them all at once. If there is time, individual
children should have opportunity for telling about a
trip, a new baby, a pet, a personal experience; for
showing and telling about a toy, clothing, a possession; for sharing original stories or songs.

4) Story:

Since security is found in recognizing the familiar,
begin with one the children may have heard at home,
"The Three Bears," or "The Three Billy Goats Gruff,"
or "Thumbelina" ... (particularly good for a first time
since Thumbelina makes a happy journey away from
home).
Follow with a familiar nursery rhyme with the children joining in.

5) Active period:

Finger plays of nursery rhymes, "Little Miss Muffet,"
"Jack and Jill," "Hickory, Dickory Dock."
Stand up and stretch or flopping like a rag doll.

6) Another listening time:

Try a new story, a short one from one of the current
books with beautiful illustrations, turning the pages
slowly as you show the pictures.

7) Active time:

Take a walk around the room showing points of interest, showing location of the books they may borrow

to take home.   Give demonstration of checking out
books.

8) Good-by time:

Return to seats and tell where to put their name tags
if they are to be used again; if not, tell them they
may be taken home and used for book marks.

Use any signal chosen for departure, saying, "Good-
by. We'll see you next week, I hope."

9) After the program:

Be sure each child has someone to go home with.   It
is advisable to have an adult stationed at the door to
see that no one leaves alone, even if some child with
a great deal of imagination explains, as one little boy
did, "But I have on my safety belt!"

Comfort any fearful ones by giving them a book to
look at "until Mother comes. "   Others may choose
books to take home, either with a librarian, assistant,
or parent.

Program on Bears

The "Bear Unit" can be used after somebody brings
in a favorite teddy bear to show, or tells about seeing a
bear at the zoo or on a trip.   The conversation period about
bears is followed by the first story.

"Here is a story about a boy and his toy bear.   It
isn't a teddy bear, but another kind of toy bear--a wind-up
bear."

Hold the book up so that everyone can see the front
cover.   "The name of the book is 'Beady Bear'."   (See
Book List)

Tell or read the story, turning the pages and showing

each picture as the story unfolds. Comments are not to be encouraged during this story, which follows a well-developed plot.

After the story, welcome comments and discussion of different kinds of bears, from polar bears to bears in the zoo. Show pictures of bears.

For an active period, have the children stand up and imitate the shambling gait of a bear to slow music. Or ask, "How does the bear walk?" and let them show you. Some may decide to crawl on all fours. "Walk like a bear," "Roll your head like a bear," "Dance like a bear," are a few suggestions for rhythmic activity.

Next choose the familiar story of "The Three Bears," told with or without a book. Follow a dramatization of the story. "Let's play 'The Three Bears' and choose somebody to be Goldilocks and others for the three bears. The rest of us can be the audience."

Mouse Program

It has been discovered that some children express alarm at the introduction of stories about mice, relating them to rats, particularly children who have encountered live rats. A mouse theme helps to overcome this aversion or fear.

All of the Mousekin books by Edna Miller are excellent, both for the interesting stories and for the beautiful illustrations in color.

Other good mouse stories are Leo Lionni's Alexander and the Wind-up Mouse and his fantasy of Frederick.

Include such poems as "I Think Mice are Rather Nice" by Elizabeth Coatsworth and "Has Anybody Seen My Mouse" by A. A. Milne.

Children enjoy singing the nursery rhyme, "Three Blind Mice." Some adults have considered this verse objectionable, along with other traditional nursery rhymes, but children do not seem to find it gruesome. They even like to dramatize the action, used as an activity pantomime with children scampering around like mice. (See Booklist, Chapter 9, and Hanky Mouse directions in Chapter 10, Page 162.)

Program on Hats

Children enjoy wearing different kinds of hats which identify different occupations or activities. Sometimes a child comes to the story hour wearing a princess crown, a sailor cap, an Indian head dress, or the hat of a cowboy, policeman, or fireman. Others will want to wear a favorite hat or make up one, suggesting a program on hats.

There are many good books for this theme. Jennie's Hat is a delightful story with imaginative ideas for an impromptu hat. Jenny tries on a straw basket, a lampshade, even a shiny pan.

A lively discussion can be generated by using Benny's Four Hats, a participation book, to "let off steam."

This theme might be used any time of the year. It is especially appropriate at the Easter season with The Horse in the Easter Bonnet for a starter. The story lends itself to spontaneous dramatization.

For stretching muscles and moving about, an Easter parade is fun. The children walk gaily and lightly to a recording of Irving Berlin's "The Easter Parade," found on individual record or record of Easter music. (See Book List, Chapter 9, and List of Recordings, Chapter 10.)

Circus Program

A circus is coming to town or has appeared, and the children are talking about it. This is a good time for a circus theme.

Effective books for this program include Circus by Beatrice de Regniers and Brian Wildsmith's Circus.

Children can make up their own story by looking at the pictures without words in The Chimp and the Clown by Ruth Carroll.

Book of Clowns (Grosset & Dunlap) has pictures showing the transformation of everyday people to various clown characters. It might be possible to invite a person in to give a "live" demonstration. This has been done by members of the Shrine Funsters, a group of men who perform as clowns at Shrine amusements. Other sources to contact are local little theater groups and school drama departments.

The choice of activities between stories is abundant: a circus parade with high-stepping ponies, dancing bears, roaring lions, the antics of the clowns, using circus music.

"Walking the tightrope" becomes very realistic when a string is placed on the floor and each child takes a turn balancing with outstretched arms to walk along the string without falling off. The feat becomes more challenging when the walking is done while looking at the string through the long distance end of a pair of binoculars. (See Book List, Chapter 9, and List of Recordings, Chapter 10.)

Program on Gardens

Start the conversation period with some comment like, "It's springtime and many people are planting seeds to make a garden."

Stop for comments from the children, with a discussion of gardens.

Begin the story with, "This is a book about a little boy who planted a seed." Hold up the closed book. "It is called, The Carrot Seed." (See Book List)

Open the book and begin turning the pages so that everyone can see as you tell the story, which can be told word for word as you glance at each page. Take plenty of time to show each picture.

Be ready for comments at the end. If a record is available, say, "Let's listen to a record about the little boy who planted a carrot seed." The book is short enough for quiet listening without stopping for a moving-about activity.

After the record is over, stand up and say, "We could pretend that we are that little boy." Play the record again, following the action of the story. The children go through the actions with you--of spading the ground, dropping the seed into the hole, pulling the weeds, filling the watering can, and sprinkling the ground. They even shake their heads when the little boy says, "But it didn't come up."

Follow with the familiar Little Red Hen. This can be dramatized with the animals played almost word for word by the children.

If there is time, cut off the top of a carrot and place it in a container of water. The children enjoy watching the progress of the green shoots week after week.

Hallowe'en

Children will be seeing and hearing about "ghosts," "witches," "scary black cats," and all sorts of frightening

creatures outside the library long before the Hallowe'en date
arrives. It is good to prepare young children to the fact
that people do dress up funny and wear masks for Hallowe'en.

Programs in the pre-school story hour with picture
books, finger plays, and plans for a party will help dispel
fears and make the celebration a happy time.

There is good material for a sharing period with contributions from the story teller as well as from the children.
The story teller might show a mask and talk about it: "See,
it's just a painted face. I'll try it on. Don't I look funny!"
Then let a child try it on; "Look at Julie! She looks scary,
but it's really your friend behind the mask."

One year a little girl brought a live black kitten in an
orange basket for everyone to see. She had named it "Hallowe'en."

After the preliminaries, use a story such as A Tiger
Called Thomas by Charlotte Zolotow, showing the pictures of
children dressed up for Hallowe'en. Another excellent book
for this time is Tell Me, Mr. Owl by Doris Van Liew Foster.

For activity, the children might go for a walk like the
Weenky Days in Tell Me, Mr. Owl.

Another good book to use is Mousekin's Golden House,
by Edna Miller.

Activity following this story could be a pretend hunt
for a pumpkin. If there is time enough and the story teller
is willing to take the trouble, a real pumpkin might be found,
hidden in some part of the room, to use for making a jack-
o-lantern. The children watch in fascination as the top is
cut off, and enjoy giving directions as the eyes, nose, and
mouth are cut out. A few seeds could be planted in a container to keep in the library. The children will watch the

growth of their pumpkin vine with great interest.

A good finger play to use at this time would be "Here's a pumpkin big and yellow;" also "Five little jack-o-lanterns."

Farm Program

Just before Thanksgiving or in the springtime, farm stories are appropriate and very appealing to the children.

The theme song of "Old MacDonald Had a Farm" brings enthusiastic singing from the children.

The first story might be The Animals of Farmer Jones or Wake Up Farm.

Activity of imitating farm animals joyfully follows either story. Or the choice may be to dramatize the story of Farmer Jones and his variety of animals waiting for supper.

In the fall, Autumn Harvest is a good choice. After this story, the children enjoy a pantomime of gathering the autumn harvest.

For springtime on the farm, Who Took the Farmer's Hat? lends itself to spontaneous dramatization.

Christmas

Christmastime is enriched by the telling of the legendary stories and hearing the traditional carols. Current books and familiar songs such as "Rudolph, the Red-Nosed Reindeer" are also part of the Christmas programs. The children begin talking about Christmas early in December, so plans can be made for several sessions leading up to the holiday.

As the children arrive, traditional Christmas carols

played softly make a pleasant and appropriate background.

The story hour can begin with a recording of "Jingle Bells" with the children singing and pretending to hold the reins as they ride in the sleigh.

Opening with The Night Before Christmas enchants all children.   There will be an enthusiastic discussion of what Santa may bring.

This could be followed by playing the game of "Here We Go Round the Christmas Tree."

The Little Fir Tree, is excellent for dramatization.

Children also enjoy the pantomime of decorating a pretend Christmas tree, following the suggestions, "Now we'll hang this shining red ornament, now a silver one away up high."   Many ideas will come from the children; stars, candy canes, angels and "Now a star on the high tip-top."

Suggested stories for the season are listed in Chapter 9.

Christmas music played again at the end of the sessions makes a happy goodbye time.

Easter

The Easter season is a delightful time for presenting stories of Easter customs on the pre-school level, and for discovering the fascination of springtime.

The Bunny Who Found Easter is a good choice for the first story.

For a finger play, Here's a Bunny is good to use here and is quickly memorized by the children.

A second story might be Happy Easter.

The children enjoy following this story with a pantomime of Mother Rabbit sending her children out to get eggs.

Other suggestions for Easter stories are listed in

Chapter 10.

The traditional activity of hunting for Easter eggs
could be pantomimed following an Easter story. The children enjoy the imaginative experience as they walk softly
around the room peering here and there. "I see a pink one!"
"I see a red one!" can be heard as imaginary baskets are
found with imaginary eggs. Someone may even call out, "I
see the Easter Bunny!"

Program for a Rainy Day

A rainy day offers an opportunity for stories, discussions, and activities leading to awareness of changes in
weather. The children come in their rainy day boots, gal-
oshes, rain coats, slickers, and some with small umbrellas.
There is generally an air of high spirits, restlessness, and
a tendency to be talkative.

The talk can be about preparing for the weather and
observations of the differences in the day. "Everyone came
prepared for the wet weather." "Rain is good for the grass
and the trees; it helps the flowers to grow." "It washes
everything clean."

The children make many of these observations themselves, along with happy comments: "I caught some rain-
drops on my tongue." "I like to walk in the rain."

After the discussion, the story Umbrella by Taro
Yashima presents an interesting experience of a little girl
hoping for a rainy day so that she may use her new red rub-
ber boots and big umbrella. The beautiful illustrations extend the story with interesting detail.

The finger play, "The busy windshield wiper goes
a-dash, a-dash, a-dash," offers appropriate participation.

For the second story, Wet World by Norma Simon is a good choice.

For active play suggest, "Let's go walking in the rain and splash through the puddles."

Scatter irregular shaped "puddles," previously cut from old wall paper samples, newspaper or brown wrapping paper, at random on the floor.

"We'll put on our boots, a raincoat and rain hat." Pantomime the action saying the words slowly with time between for each act.

"Now we are ready." Walk with splashy steps through the puddles. This may be done to music or to the chant, "Splish, splash - splish, splash."

The paper may also represent stepping stones lined up so the children can step from one to another. "Now the water is getting deeper. We'll try to step from stone to stone without stepping off."

After the first time around, move the stones farther apart for greater challenge in balancing.

The record, "Rainy Day," gives many excellent rainy day acitivites with music and directions.

Program for a Snowy Day

A program on the pleasant experiences of a winter season might be given on a snowy day, or might be used for a vicarious experience in a locality where snow never falls.

The Snowy Day, by Ezra Keats, tells about a little boy who enjoys snow activities and then goes out again to enjoy them with a friend.

After the action rhythm "My zipper suit is bunny brown," the children will be ready to pantomime the activities of Peter's snowy day.

Choices for a second story include <u>White Snow, Bright Snow</u> by Alvin Tresselt and <u>The Happy Day</u>.

Children enjoy the activity of snowflakes falling. This can be done either with the rhythm of whirling and twirling to music and then all falling softly down, or by sitting quietly in their places with arms raised high as fingers dance lightly to their laps.   A good action story is <u>Playing in the Snow</u> (p. 157).

A Summer Program

There are many delightful books to choose for planning summer sessions, although they may be used any time of the year.   Some libraries may not have summer story hours, others may have "summer" weather most of the year.

Warm evenings when the moon is full may suggest the lovely mood book, <u>Moon Jumpers.</u>   The sense of mystery in story and pictures holds the children quietly entranced as they become absorbed in the details--the dancing of the children and the appearance of the cat who seems to be enjoying the moonlight as much as the children, in his own way.

After the story, suggest, "Maybe we can be moon jumpers.   Let's pretend that we are dancing in the moonlight."   Someone may volunteer to be the silent cat, watching quietly.   Others may be chosen to be the adults who call the children indoors.

Another good story for dramatizing a summer activity is <u>The Little Fish That Got Away</u>.   Going fishing is an interesting pantomime for activity after this story.   For a pretend fishing trip suggest, "Let's get out our fishing pole (or a rod and reel).   Now we can dig for some worms."   When

the can is full, "We'll walk over here and find a good place
to fish." Baiting the hook, casting and reeling in, then
putting the fish in a bucket are all part of the fun. Someone will say, "My fish got away!" But everyone is sure to
come back with a bucket full of fish.

Notes

1. Todd, Vivian Edmiston and Heffernan, Helen, The Years
    Before School: Guiding Pre-School Children. New
    York, The Macmillan Company, 1964, p. 350.

2. Viguers, Ruth Hill, Margin for Surprise; About Books,
    Children, and Libraries. Boston, Little, Brown &
    Company, 1964, p. 21.

Chapter 8

EXTENDED PROGRAM (AND EXTRAS)

"When do we have the story?"
-Jerry

Even the youngest children know what they have come for--a story.

However, extras need not overshadow the real purpose of the pre-school story hour. A program consisting of story, finger play, story, goodby, could be tiring to young children and become wooden, monotonous or formal. A group of children, much like a group of adults, sometimes needs gathering together, warming up or quieting down, bringing to attention, and so it is good to have a few extras in reserve. If not too far afield, they add appeal like parsley on the potatoes with plus value of their own.

Actually the term "story hour" does not always indicate the length of time the program is in session. There are those who say that a half hour of concentrated listening is enough for the young child. This is true. It would be difficult for anybody, old or young, to listen attentively for more than half an hour. In some cases the period lasts for three-quarters of an hour; in others for an entire hour.

This does not mean that stories are read or told for a solid hour of listening. Even in half-hour sessions the time is broken with finger plays and conversation, or other activities. Part of the time is taken up with assembling;

wraps to be removed, greetings to be exchanged, and name
tags put on.   Then at the end, with name tags removed,
books chosen to take home, good-by's said, and wraps put on
again, an hour is scarcely long enough.   Little children cannot be rushed successfully, and the atmosphere of their story
hour should be leisurely.   Also, for those who bring the
children, it would hardly seem worthwhile to dress up and
drive some distance for one-half hour.

However, when a half hour or three-quarters is all
the time possible to give to the program, it should consist
of the basic activities of a pre-school story hour; stories,
finger plays, nursery rhymes, and perhaps some rthythmic
or lively activity.

For those libraries which can reasonably give more
time, there are many related activities.   In her chapter on
the heritage of story telling, Ruth Tooze, Director of Children's Book Caravan, reminds us that, "Over and over one
sees the arts of music, poetry, dance and story telling in-
terwoven."[1]   There is value in music, rhythms, informal
dramatization, and games.   Along with the stories and books,
finger plays, rhymes and jingles, children of pre-school age
need a change of pace and diversity of activity.   Music adds
joy to the experience and is recommended where facilities
are available.   This may be supplied by a record player,
with records selected for different purposes; in some cases
by a piano; in others the music may be provided by singing.
A piano would be ideal for these activities, and where there
is one available and someone can play it, by all means use
it for the activities mentioned above.   The piano with an on-
the-scene musician gives closer rapport.

The record collection could include music for listening, singing nursery rhymes, lullabies for quiet times, simple

classics, and marches. It is not advisable to use a story
record to replace the live story for several reasons. Children have difficulty understanding the delivery in most recordings, there is no personal contact between the listener
and story teller, no face to smile, no warmth of the human
voice, no breaking off for a child's spontaneous comment.
A recorded story is handy to use, however, in an emergency
when the story teller without an assistant must halt opera-
tions briefly. She can then use a record to fill the gap.

The record player can also be used with records to
accompany simple rhythms for stretching and swaying, bending or bouncing when little bodies get restless or tense from
sitting. There are many good ones, some with directions.

Simple percussion instruments and bells can be used
for a rhythm band to the accompaniment of lively records
with a strong beat. Keeping time to the music under the direction of a child as leader of the band is always a favorite
participation activity for "letting off steam" and having a
session of group co-operation. The rhythm can be introduced
by first clapping to music, imitating cymbals, guessing instruments such as violin, drum, flute, guitar, slide trom-
bone, harp. (This usually fools them.)

Then they are ready for the simple percussion instruments and bells. Playing instruments familiar to a rhythm
band should be a very simple procedure for pre-schoolers.
Later, in kindergarten and the primary grades, they will
learn to use the instruments for different effects, in sections
and singly. When used in the story hour, the purpose is to
allow the children the pleasure of rhythm, the release from
concentrated listening. Instruments to be used satisfactorily
would include jingle bells, cymbals, rhythm sticks, clappers,
tom-toms, drums, triangles, and small tambourines. The

rhythm sticks are a little too unwieldy for beginners and
might lead to accidental poking.   Children like to take turns
being the leader, with a baton small enough for little hands
to handle.

The accompanying music should be a march or selection with a definite beat.   In the beginning hold up each instrument in turn and tell its name.   "This is called a triangle because of its shape."   (We've had concept books.)
"We tap it gently like this."   (Demonstrate.)   "Johnny, would
you like to play the triangle?"   It is also good to say, "We
will hold our instruments quietly until everybody is ready
and the music tells us to start."

There is often a child who will hold the instrument
quietly as he watches the other children.   He may sway to
the music without making a sound.   There should be no pressure to make him join in, for each child moves at his own
rate of speed; when he is ready, he will start playing.
There will be those who keep accurate time, and others seem
not to hear the beat at all; but there is no emphasis on perfection.

Children may come up and choose an instrument from
the box in which they are kept, but it is better to hand out
the instruments; otherwise the children will often stand for
a long, long time trying to make a choice, picking up each
one in turn and experimenting with it.

When all the instruments are passed out and a leader
is chosen, say, "Now we will let the music talk to us before
we start.   The leader will tell us when to start so that we
can all begin at the same time, and when the music is ended
we will all stop at the same time."   This will not happen
the first time, but praise for trying to follow the leader
goes a long way in bringing it about.

After the first number the children may want to exchange instruments.   This is a good way to demonstrate sharing as they hear, "Now you may trade instruments with your neighbor." Most children know the meaning of the word "trade," particularly if they have heard the book Was It a Good Trade?

When the rhythm band activity is over the children should return each instrument to the box, one at a time. This may be accomplished smoothly by touching each child in turn with a hand puppet after saying, "Now we will put the instruments back into the box so softly that no one can hear a sound."

Singing is a natural part of the child's experience with music. There are times for song in the story hour, with or without accompaniment: singing games, singing nursery rhymes, singing "Happy Birthday," singing "Jingle Bells" and other familiar Christmas songs. They all love to sing "Old MacDonald Had a Farm" during a farm unit. Many of these songs are available on children's records which can be used as accompaniment.

Children begin to move rhythmically long before they come into contact with adult leaders. They move freely and spontaneously to music and enjoy beating out their own rhythm with toy drums or even a battered kitchen pan or other percussion instruments. In the pre-school story hour they can be encouraged to respond to music with more purpose and direction, although no effort should be made toward perfection of specific actions. Body rhythms, pantomimic movement (including the finger plays), the rhythm band and simple games encourage expressive movements. It is not necessary to stress that everybody do exactly the same thing in a certain way, but it is fun for the children to learn doing the same thing at the same time.

After a period of sitting still, little bodies need to stretch and move about to get out the kinks. Types of loco-motor movements to a musical accompaniment include walk-ing, hopping, stretching, bending, swaying and shaking.

Directions given for walking rhythms might be: "Now we are going to walk around the room, one behind the other, following the leader." They enjoy following the leader (who, at first, should be an adult--later, children taking turns.) They will not all stay in line at first. This can be accom-plished by playing train. Each child puts his hand on the shoulder of the child in front of him. The first one is the engine, the last one is the caboose. The ones in between are the various parts of the train. This activity might well follow a train story.

Later the children can march individually, with or without the rhythm band instruments. There could be a tip-toe march, or a walk out hunting for bears after a bear story, or looking for a pumpkin after a Hallowe'en story.

A variation of walking with hands on the shoulders of the person in front could be a "snake march," weaving in and out around tables and chairs. The walk could follow the leader into an open space, go around and around until a cir-cle is formed. Then all take hands. Give directions such as, "Now we have a circle. Let's keep our circle round like a ring or round like a hoop, or round like a kiss." These directions are easier to follow after hearing a con-cept book of roundness such as A Kiss is Round.[2]

When the children have discovered the circle forma-tion, keeping the circle round, they are ready for simple, traditional games.

Hopping can be suggested after a rabbit story. "Let's

hop like a rabbit, very softly on velvet feet so that nobody hears us." (This discourages stomping and overzealous hops.)

Stretching can be done to music, showing the action as directions are given: "Stretch your arms forward, now back, now forward and up above your head. Now stretch one arm high, now the other. Now bring your arms slowly down to your sides."

Variations of stretching can be done without music. "Let's stand very tall and reach for the stars (or the moon, or the ceiling.) Both arms stretch, then one after the other." Another is "Let's stretch very high, now stoop very low, now stand on tip-toes, let your fingers wiggle. Now let's give our shoulders a shake, shake, shake, and all sit down."

Swaying movements can be followed with everybody standing, arms up: "Let's bend and sway like a tall tree, at first very gently in a soft, little breeze. Now the branches are bending in a strong wind. Now the tree stands tall and still."

Children delight in pantomime play. This may be imitating animals in the zoo after a zoo story. They enjoy being elephants with hands placed together to form a long trunk. Bending forward, they take slow and heavy steps with trunk swinging from side to side. They may stop to take a drink of water with their long trunks, then splash water over their backs by swinging the trunk over their shoulders. They may even catch an imaginary peanut in that long trunk when the story teller or one of the children tosses them a pretend treat.

It is great fun and good release from tension to be a stalking lion or a bear walking on his hind legs with a slow lumbering gait, wagging his head and shaking his hands. The

children may want to imitate bears dancing clumsily about;
then dropping to all fours, they scamper back to their seats.

There are many good suggestions for walking like
other animals in the books, This Is the Way the Animals
Walk, by Louise Woodcock, and Just Me, by Marie Hall Etz.
(See book list.)

Imitation of animated toys often comes at the Christmas season while singing "What do You Want Old Santa to
Bring?" to the tune of "Here We Go Round the Mulberry
Bush." There may be jumping jacks, airplaines, trains,
walking, talking dolls who take stiff, hesitant steps.

Pantomime may be used with nursery rhymes; "Jack
be Nimble." A real candlestick on the floor gives everybody
a turn to be nimble and quick as "Jack jumps over the candlestick." "Sing a Song of Sixpence" gives everyone a chance
to participate with any number of blackbirds flapping their
wings "When the pie was opened." "Humpty Dumpty" uses
a large group of "king's horses" and "king's men" trying to
put Humpty together again.

"The Three Bears," "The Three Billy Goats Gruff,"
"The Three Little Pigs," and other classic tales can be
acted out as the story teller repeats the story.

In addition to pantomiming traditional nursery rhymes
and traditional tales, many contemporary stories lend themselves to spontaneous dramatization without any attempt to
perfect the roles. There are no "lines" to be learned and
no formal presentation of the action.

The stage is merely a chosen area of the room.
Props are unnecessary since imagination supplies all, and
"The play is the thing."

In dramatizations when only a few characters are
used, the other children make an enthusiastic audience.

Some of the shy ones will not participate at first, but after being in the audience for a while, they can be drawn into the play itself. Some even volunteer after they see how it is done by watching.

The child must never feel that his interpretation and response might not be accepted. Rhythms and dramatic expressions are not "taught" activities, but are an outlet for creativity.

A flannelboard with a collection of pictures is sometimes used in presenting ideas, although nothing equals the value of the original book illustrations. The flannelboard can be made from a large but lightweight piece of wall board covered with a piece of flannel at least four inches larger than the board. The extra material is turned over the edges of the board and sewed into place or fastened with upholstery staples.

Complete directions for making and using the flannelboard are given in the book, Story Telling With the Flannel Board.[3]

A collection of pictures is also valuable for presenting ideas. Sets of pictures such as Mother Goose Rhymes[4] and Peter Rabbit[5] may be obtained commercially or may be gathered by the story teller from magazines and advertising pieces.

Hand puppets such as plush bears, dogs, kittens, clowns, etc. are an interesting and useful addition. They can be used for conversation and often help to draw out the shy or self-conscious child. A puppet is also good for choosing a child to do something since the puppet's nod or touch seems to eliminate any favoritism on the part of the story teller. In saying goodby at the end of a session, to avoid having everyone jump at the same time, the puppet can be

used to touch one after the other with "Goodby, Janis, Good-
by, Harold." Then each child leaves quietly, although some
will stop briefly to give the puppet an affectionate squeeze or
a light kiss.

Other extras which prove helpful in getting attention
and in changing pace from concentrated listening are paper
folding, handkerchief folding and string manipulation. Children will watch in rapt attention when the story teller folds
a handkerchief into a white mouse after hearing <u>Has Anybody</u>
<u>Seen My Mouse?</u>[6] (Directions for folding the Hanky Mouse
are given in Chapter 10.)

Films may also be used such as those produced by Weston Woods, Weston, Conn. When using a film based on a story
book, (or when a recording such as "The Carrot Seed" is used)
the book should be shown first. The children will then know
where the story came from. Seeing the story on a screen or
hearing a recording after presentation of the book will give the
heightened pleasure of recognition. Presenting an unfamiliar
story in book form is, also, a more intimate situation and gives
the story teller time to stop for questions and comments.

Although parties are taboo in some libraries, particularly when food is served, others welcome the opportunity
for a celebration. The occasion may be a seasonal one such
as Hallowe'en, Christmas, or Easter. A child's birthday is
sometimes celebrated at the story hour with the mother bringing in treats. If the group is large and too many birthdays
pop up, it would be better to celebrate once a month. The
mothers of those children could get together and share the
planning.

If treats are permissible, it is wiser to serve indi-
vidually-wrapped candies or cookies than cake, which crumble
in warm little hands, like the cake Epaminondas carried home

from his auntie's house. Icing can be disastrous! Too
much time is needed for the mop-up afterward.

While these extras lend variety and attraction, they
must be kept subordinate to the main purpose of the program which is to introduce children to the best literature on
the pre-school level. Too many extras may lead to confusion and over-stimulation; they should be kept within the
bounds of good judgment.

If each library strives to retain its own individuality
with emphasis on the distinctive characteristics of each locality and on the strengths and interests of the personnel in
charge, then programs will be presented with enthusiasm and
vitality. Each one can be a truly creative experience for
the story teller as well as for the children. The service
will have the opportunity and freedom to grow in substance
and in meaning as a worthwhile contribution.

Notes

1. Tooze, Ruth, Story Telling. Englewood Cliffs, N. J.,
   Prentice-Hall, Inc., p. 12.

2. Budney, Blossom, A Kiss is Round. New York, Lothrop, Lee & Shepard, Inc., 1954.

3. Anderson, Paul S., Story Telling With the Flannel Board.
   Minneapolis, T. S. Denison & Company, Inc., 1963.

4. Rojankovsky, Feodor, Simon and Schuster, Inc., Artists
   and Writers Guild, 1945.

5. Beatrix Potter Prints, Frederick Warne & Co., Ltd.,
   Great Britain.

6. Milne, A. A., When We Were Very Young. New York,
   E. P. Dutton & Co., Inc.

Chapter 9

BOOK SELECTION

"I want to look at the book."
-Charles

It is important to choose books and stories which have
appeal and significance to the three and four year old. If
they also hold appeal for the story teller herself, the children will sense the adult's enjoyment and respond in propor-
tion to her enthusiasm. It is unnecessary to be bored by
books that lack true worth or appear dull.

There is an ample supply of nursery classics, stories
of contemporary life, stories with an element of fancy, stories that spark laughter, books that invite participation, books
that answer questions, and poetry for all occasions.

There are said to be two inherent joys in life: the
joy of recognition and the joy of creation. Hearing the nursery rhymes and nursery tales, which most children have
heard at home, is like meeting an old friend. There will be
enthusiastic responses to this joy of recognition: "I know
Goldilocks and the three bears," "My mother knows 'Hickory,
Dickory Dock' and 'Jack and Jill'." (Glory be to those children who may never have heard these heritages of literature
and who first hear them at story hour!)

There is wonder and excitement in familiar things:
first haircuts, birthday parties, picnics, circuses and zoos,
staying all night away from home, new babies in the family,

household pets, the change of seasons and familiar holidays. Children enjoy hearing stories about experiences of others who speak and act as they do.

Along with these and with the old favorites, children find pleasure and need stories of experiences they have never had, of situations beyond the boundaries of everyday life, of stories that stretch the imagination. Security is found in recognizing things they know about, understand and love, while venturing forth to explore the strange and the new.

Some children have never been to a farm. Horses and cows, chickens and pigs may be as unfamiliar to them as dinosaurs. Life on a farm may be as remote and exciting as life on another planet. Others may never have been to a city with its subways and elevators, its skyscrapers, steam shovels, and tug boats. The sight of an ocean, the height of a mountain, the view of a river are like an unknown fairy tale world to many children.

Stories about animals are always popular, both those which are realistic and those of friendly animals and their young having experiences that children might have themselves. There is fascination in books about the zoo with lions, tigers, monkeys, elephants and all of its inhabitants.

Most children of pre-school age are intrigued by books about buses, trucks, steam shovels, boats, trains, fire trucks, planes and space ships. These can be realistic picture books of information or fanciful tales with dramatic plots.

The pre-schooler is ready for stories with plot; something happening in exciting sequences, with suspense, climax, and a satisfying ending. Presentation of these stories can begin with events that have happened in his own contacts with life and go on to adventures he wishes might happen any bright, unexpected day. He stretches his imagination to see himself zooming to the moon or swimming under the sea.

There should be books with new ideas to ponder, books that arouse curiosity and create a desire to know more.

Books without plot have a definite place in the program: A B C books with their lovely illustrations, offered for pleasure and for the knowledge that letters exist--not for instruction, number books for the same reasons, concept books, mood books, and books for audience participation.

Aesthetic appreciation of language is an important consideration. Children are involved from birth with words and the task of learning their meanings and appreciating the beauty of their sounds. Children in a pre-school story hour have an opportunity to continue this growth by learning new words and by expressing themselves freely. They enjoy simple rhythmic style, repetition, nonsense words and sound effects.

Poetry delights the ear and increases awareness. Perhaps that is why it is called the first literature of childhood. Upon hearing "This little pig went to market," a baby has no idea of pigs nor markets nor roast beef. It is the rhythm of the language and the strangeness of the words that catch his attention and hold enchantment. There is an ever-widening stream of poetry to continue this enchantment and awareness in programs for pre-schoolers.

In selecting books to use in their story hour, it is necessary to be guided by illustrations and format. Books for this age are meant to be looked at. The artist, Lynd Ward, once made this statement at a meeting of children's librarians: "Pictures extend the story." The artist often puts in details that are not mentioned in the text, and the children delight in these extensions of the story. The process of putting names to things he sees begins with a baby's first picture book wherein a cup is a cup, a shoe is a shoe, and a bed is a bed, with pictures accompanying the words. Being visual-minded, children want to see the pictures and pore over details, for it is difficult for them to conjure up images.

The format of the book should be attractive with many pictures and few words, although it is possible to condense some stories as the story teller follows the pictures. The book should be large enough and the pictures clear enough for all the children to see from the distance they are sitting. (Books chosen to borrow for home use can be big, little, tall, short, thin or fat, with more story and smaller pictures since they will be used in a different situation.)

Illustrations in books used for the story hour should be colorful, crisp, and have interesting details. Strong, vibrant colors appeal to children more than those which are pale, fuzzy or over-stylized. Children are likely to be confused by distortions and by pictures that do not present true colors.

The purpose of seeking the excellent and of selecting the right book for the right time and the right age is to help children live more fully and more enjoyably. It is to help them act, feel, and think with greater satisfaction.

> In the pursuit of excellence in books for boys and girls there are certain qualities we look for: those of making a child respect books; persuading him that, no matter how hard it may seem to learn, reading is worth the effort; giving him an experience that is worth having and that he might not be able to have for himself; broadening his acquaintance with people by giving him friends he would never know except through books; setting his imagination free; and leading him into the great world of books. All these qualities make for excellence;

yet excellence itself cannot be defined.   It can only be experienced. [1]

While not persuading pre-schoolers to read, except in-
directly, these qualities of excellence are applicable to the
pre-school story hour.

There are so many beautiful and worthwhile books for
children that it is difficult to choose among them.   There
are also many attractive and excellent books which must be
put aside for one reason or another.

Among the fine books which are beyond this age level
and should be saved until later are picture books with longer
stories.   These are best used with children in the primary
grades.   It is also a mistake to include beginning readers,
however charming, or books for the child to read for himself.   They will be "old hat" when he is ready for them.

Illustrations which are distorted or terrifying to the
pre-school age will defeat the purpose of presenting literature as enjoyable.   The large, ferocious face of a cat in an
otherwise beautiful book of nursery rhymes was so frightening to a little boy in one pre-school group that he screamed
in terror and never came back.   The prize-winning book,
Where the Wild Things Are, by Maurice Sendak, is delightful and amusing to older children, but pre-schoolers find
such stories good material for nightmares.   Save the "scary"
stories until a later age when children are thrilled by spine-
tingling pictures and love to be "scared" by hair-raising stories.

Most fairy tales and folk tales are too complicated
and involved for very young children.   Underlying meanings
and symbolism are beyond their comprehension.   Of course,
there are exceptions such as Hans Andersen's "Thumbelina"
and the classic nursery folk tales such as "The Little Red
Hen."

Fairy tales about elves, gnomes, giants, disagreeable witches, stepmothers, and godmothers are not appropriate for pre-schoolers (although the troll in "The Three Billy Goats Gruff" is generally acceptable).

Learning about the here-and-now world is sufficiently filled with magic, wonder, and surprise, and should be recognized and understood before taking off for fairy land.

There is wisdom in the words of Alice Dalgliesh written in 1932: "We need to keep the best of the old, and add to it the best of the new, for literature must reflect life and to reflect it truly it must keep pace with our ever-changing world."[2]

This good advice holds true today and, no doubt, always will.

The following books, listed in various categories, have been tried and found successful with story hour groups. No list could be complete with so many beautiful and excellent ones to choose from. These may be a yardstick for further choices. Make your own selections to fit the occasion from those which appeal to you.

BOOK LIST

A B C Books

    Traditionally a child's first book was an ABC book
and there are many beautifully designed present-day ABC
books for use with pre-school groups. Although these books
are not presented as a lesson in learning the alphabet con-
secutively, they will give the child a feeling for letters and
a consciousness of their shapes.

Alexander, Anne, ABC of Cars and Trucks.
    (ABC's using all sorts of cars and trucks.)
Anglund, Joan, A Mother Goose ABC in a Pumpkin Shell.
    (A combination of the alphabet and nursery rhymes,
    charming illustrations.)
Batherman, Muriel, The Alphabet Tale.
    (A participation book along with the alphabet.)
Falls, C. B., ABC Book.
    (Big and beautiful, a letter and picture on each page;
    wood cuts large and distinct.)
Gag, Wanda, The ABC Bunny.
    (Lovely to look at, funny to read; large, soft litho-
    graphs.)
Heide, Florence Parry, Alphabet Zoop.
    (A modern ABC book using different examples of let-
    ters.)
Munari, Bruno, Bruno Munari's ABC.
    (An imaginative alphabet book from an ant to a fly
    going "Zzzz.")
Seuss, Dr., Dr. Seuss's ABC.

(From A to Z in the Seuss inimitable style.)

Shuttlesworth, Dorothy, ABC of Buses.

(Definite appeal to boys.)

Tudor, Tasha, A Is for Annabelle.

(Delicate pictures; quaint figures.)

Wildsmith, Brian, Brian Wildsmith's ABC.

(An animal ABC book in stunning colors.)

Animal Stories

Children enjoy stories about animals in their natural habitats as well as stories of animals having experiences that they might have and behaving as they might behave. There are so many to choose from that it is not difficult to find the right one to suit needs and themes.

Bennett, Rainey, The Secret Hiding Place.

(Little children appreciate Little Hippo's efforts to find a secret hiding place of his own where he can be alone.)

Brown, Margaret Wise, Home For a Bunny.

(Large, beautiful illustrations for a simple "suspense" story told in rhythmic language.)

Brown, Margaret Wise, Three Little Animals.

(A humorous story of three little animals who dress up like human beings and have some interesting experiences.)

Brown, Margaret Wise, The Country Noisy Book.

(Sounds made by country animals, many of which are left for the children to supply.)

Cook, Bernadine, The Curious Little Kitten.

(A kitten's curiosity leads him into a suspenseful adventure with a turtle.)

Crawford, Mel, Old MacDonald Had a Farm.
    (Large, realistic pictures in color bring visual
    pleasure to the familiar song about Old MacDonald
    and his animals.)
Davis, Alice Vaught, Timothy Turtle.
    (An exciting story of a turtle whose friends help him
    out of trouble.)
Ets, Marie Hall, In the Forest.
    (A small boy's adventures with his forest friends.)
Ets, Marie Hall, Just Me.
    (This is the way the animals walk--and the children
    will enjoy imitating them.)
Ets, Marie Hall, Play With Me.
    (A little girl makes friends with the animals by sit-
    ting still.)
Fischer, Ellen, Tell Me, Cat.
    (Cats and kittens tell about themselves in verse.
    Colored photographs of enchanting cats against a
    background of interesting stitchery by Virginia Tif-
    fany.)
Freeman, Don, Beady Bear.
    (A wind-up toy bear's adventures on a snowy night.)
Gale, Leah, The Animals of Farmer Jones.
    (Excellent pictures by Richard Scarry accompany the
    rhythmic story of the farm animals waiting for their
    supper and being fed by Farmer Jones.)
Gay, Zhenya, What's Your Name?
    (Guess the name of the animal from the description
    and a rhyme.)
Great Big Golden Books,   Great Big Animal Book.
                                   Baby Animals.
                                   Baby Farm Animals.

(All are delightful to use with a group of children.)

Hazen, Barbara Shook, Where Do Bears Sleep?

(Where all the animals sleep, including moles, snakes, dragonflies, even a mite. But lucky you! You sleep on a bed with a teddy bear beside you.)

Hoban, Russell, Bedtime for Frances.

(A little badger delays going to bed just as a child does.)

Johnson, Crockett, Terrible, Terrifying Toby.

(Toby, the little dog, terrifies everyone including himself.)

Kessler, Ethel and Leonard, Do Baby Bears Sit in Chairs?

(No, but they do other things that children do.)

Lionni, Leo, Alexander and the Wind-up Mouse.

(Alexander, a real mouse, envies the pampered life of Willy, the toy mouse who lives in the same household. Bold, brightly colored collage illustrations by the author.)

Lionni, Leo, Fish is Fish.

(The life of a small fish in a small pond told with wit and wisdom.)

Lionni, Leo, Frederick.

(Outdoor mice get ready for winter collecting supplies. Frederick's surprise collection turns out better than expected.)

Lionni, Leo. Swimmy.

(A remarkable little fish discovers the beauty of his world and finds a way to enjoy it.)

McCloskey, Robert, Make Way for the Ducklings.

(The Mallard family and the commotion they create in Boston as they search for a home.)

Miller, Edna, Mousekin's Family.

(Mouskin's difficulties as a woodland teacher.)

Miller, Edna, Mousekin Finds a Friend.

   (As Mousekin searches for another creature like himself, dark things in the forest can fool a mouse.)

Rojankowsky, Feodor, Animals on the Farm.

   (All the ordinary animals become extraordinary in vibrant, four-color drawings full of imagination.)

Slobodkin, Louis, Dinny and Danny.

   (Pre-schoolers are interested even in dinosaurs and
   enjoy this story of long ago when Danny and his friend,
   the dinosaur, help each other.)

Stobbs, William, Henny-Penny.

   (A picture book with bright colors, showing details
   that add to the ever-popular Joseph Jacob's tale.)

Tresselt, Alvin, Wake Up Farm.

   (After the rooster crows, the farm creatures wake up,
   and, at last, the little boy hears his mother call
   "Breakfast." Another day has begun.)

Williams, Gweneira, Timid Timothy.

   (The little kitten was afraid of everything until his
   mother taught him how to be brave.)

Woodcock, Louise, This is the Way the Animals Walk.

   (An act-it-out story.)

Zion, Gene, Harry, the Dirty Dog.

   (Harry gets into trouble when he tries to avoid having
   a bath.)

Circus Books

Carroll, Ruth, The Chimp and the Clown.

   (Pictures of lively humor without words. The children
   make up the story by following the pictures.)

de Regniers, Beatrice Schenk, Circus.

(Delightful circus photographs by Al Griese with rhythmical text in a circus beat.)

Johnson, Crockett, Harold's Circus.

(Harold and his purple crayon create an astounding and imaginative circus.)

Maley, Anne, Have You Seen My Mother?

(The bright ball Barnabus goes to all the circus animals looking for his mother. Children enjoy the illustrations by Yutaka Sugita in bold, bright colors, and the unexpected ending.)

Sutton, Felix, Book of Clowns.

(Shows various types of clowns, even dog clowns. A step-by-step demonstration of putting on make-up.)

Wildsmith, Brian, Brian Wildsmith's Circus.

(Double-page spreads of circus parading and performing.)

Books of Concepts

Almost every book helps a child develop some sort of concept about life as he learns to understand the social order as well as the physical and natural world around him. He will understand some of the fundamental science concepts from these well-illustrated picture books.

Adelson, Leone, Please Pass the Grass.

(A meadow full of interests close to the ground.)

Blair, Mary, The Up and Down Book.

("Ups" and "downs"--from grass and clouds to a child standing on his head.)

Brenner, Barbara, Faces.

(A joyous appreciation of the senses in simple, lyric

prose with photographs by George Ancona.)

Budney, Blossom, A Kiss is Round.

   (What is round?)

Carle, Eric, The Tiny Seed.

   (An ideal introduction to the cycle of the seasons.)

de Regniers, Beatrice Schenk, The Shadow Book.

   (A child enjoys shadows throughout the day.)

Emberley, Ed, The Wing on a Flea.

   (Rhymes about shapes of everyday objects.)

Jackson, Kathryn, Wheels.

   (Children are interested in wheels on wheelbarrows,
   roller skates, buses, and all everyday things.)

Kessler, Ethel and Leonard, Plink, Plink.

   (Goldfish, ducks, ships, flowers and trees--all need
   water; and so do we.)

Lionni, Lee, Inch by Inch.

   (The measuring worm inches through the grass and
   out of sight.)

Oppenheim, Joanne, Have You Seen Roads?

   (Designed by Gerard Nook, photographs, pictures and
   verse explore the variety of roads and pathways from
   bumpy country roads to super-highways.)

Schlein, Miriam, Fast Is Not a Ladybug.

   (About fast and slow things, from ladybugs to jet
   planes.)

Schlein, Miriam, Heavy Is a Hippopotamus.

   (What is heavy; what is light?)

Schlein, Miriam, Shapes.

   (Shows fundamental shapes in simple language with
   pictures children will try to imitate.)

Schwartz, Julius, I Know a Magic House.

   (Wonders in the home--the faucet, telephone, toaster

and other familiar articles.)

Schwartz, Julius, Now I Know.

   (Experiences with wind, lightning, shadows and other
   phenomena.)

Shaw, Charles G., It Looked Like Spilt Milk.

   (The different shapes a cloud may take encourages
   children to make discoveries of their own.)

Slobodkin, Louis, Millions, Millions, Millions.

   (Millions and millions of other things, but only one
   you and one me.)

Steiner, Charlotte, Listen to My Seashell.

   (A good book of sounds.)

Steiner, Charlotte, My Bunny Feels Soft.

   (Definition of soft along with twelve other words.)

Steiner, Charlotte, My Slippers Are Red.

   (Brightly colored pictures of familiar objects help
   children identify colors.)

Zion, Gene and M. Graham, All Falling Down.

   (Petals of flowers and water of fountains, all fall
   down.)

Counting Books

   During the pre-school years, children become very
interested in numbers and in learning to count. "I am three
years old," they will say, holding up three fingers. (Or
four or five years old.) They enjoy helping to count the
number of children present each day. Many finger plays use
digits from one to ten, which have value in learning to count.
Here are some of the beautiful picture books in which the
child can see the numeral as he listens to the counting
games or stories.

Cooke, Barbara, My Daddy and I.
    (Gay couplets and imaginative pictures of all sorts of city sights and country sights.)

Eichenberg, Fritz, Dancing in the Moon.
    (Counting rhymes up to twenty with delightfully funny pictures.)

Friskey, Margaret, Chicken Little, Count-to-Ten.
    (Bright pictures illustrate the story of a little chick that went out to see the world.)

Gretz, Susanna, Teddy Bears 1 to 10.
    (Teddy bears, drawn in vividly warm colors illustrate the appropriate numbers opposite the bold, black print.)

Kuskin, Karla, James and the Rain.
    (Gay and funny counting book with birds and animals James meets on a rainy day.)

Langstaff, John, Over in the Meadow.
    (A picture book based on an old animal counting song.)

McLeod, Mary, One Snail for Me.
    (A funny and fanciful book about numbers of animals crowding into a bathtub with a surprised child.)

Moore, Lillian, My Big Golden Counting Book.
    (A charming, large picture book with interesting text and all sorts of things to be counted, from acorns and cabbages to lambs and ducklings.)

Tudor, Tasha, 1 is One.
    (Original verses and delicate pastel illustrations; animals, children, and flowers to count.)

Werner, Jane, The Fuzzy Duckling.
    (A Big Golden Book--counting farm animals.)

Wildsmith, Brian, Brian Wildsmith's 1, 2, 3's.

(Unique and colorful counting book.)

Experiences - Familiar and Otherwise

Books that reflect the child's every-day world and those which create awareness of wider horizons are received with equal enthusiasm. Although the pre-school child's interests are mainly with his own family and his own limited experiences, he is beginning to have curiosity about other people, places and times.

Brown, Margaret Wise, The Dead Bird.
    (Children face death realistically as they bury the dead bird they find.)
Brown, Myra Berry, First Night Away From Home.
    (Stevie packs his suitcase to spend his first night away from home--a new and exciting experience.)
Burton, Virginia, The Little House.
    (Story of a little house in the country that becomes part of the city through years of change and progress.)
Emberley, Ed and Barbara, Drummer Hoff.
    (Lively folk verse about building a cannon, with each character bringing a part of the remarkable machine.)
Felt, Sue, Rosa-Too-Little.
    (Appealing picture book about a little girl who wanted to have her own library card.)
Fenton, Edward, Fierce John.
    (John pretends to be many different characters, but finds it best to be himself.)
Freeman, Don, Corduroy.
    (Nobody seemed to want the toy bear with a button missing on his green overalls as he waits to be pur-

chased in a large department store. After a series
of amusing adventures searching through the store for
his button, wishes come true for Corduroy and the
little girl who buys him.)

Freeman, Don, Mop Top.
> (An amusing story about a boy who tries to avoid get-
> ting a haircut.)

Freeman, Don, The Night the Lights Went Out.
> (What happens in a family when the electricity goes
> off.)

Freeman, Don, Quiet: There's a Canary in the Library.
> (The day that animals visit the library in a little
> girl's imagination is full of quiet comedy that children
> will appreciate and understand.)

Johnson, Crockett, Harold and the Purple Crayon.
> (Harold uses his magic crayon to draw a moon and
> starts off on a moonlight walk, creating his own ad-
> ventures along the way.)

Keats, Ezra Jack, Goggles.
> (A motorcycle is involved in a story of high adventure
> in another of Peter's experiences.)

Keats, Ezra Jack, Hi, Cat!
> (Another story of the little black boy named Peter,
> who makes a mistake at the beginning of a neighbor-
> hood adventure.)

Keats, Ezra Jack, Jennie's Hat.
> (Illustrations by the author with full-color collage
> pictures in rich and fanciful detail, show how Jennie's
> disappointment in her new hat turns into a wonderful
> surprise.)

Keats, Ezra Jack, Peter's Chair.
> (When the new baby comes, Peter finds that he is

growing up and finally accepts the difficulties with
good grace.)

Krasilovsky, Phyllis, The Very Little Girl.

(Although she was small, the little girl became big
enough to help with the baby.)

Krauss, Ruth, The Carrot Seed.

(A little boy faces discouragement valiantly and gains
recognition. Also available in record form.)

Leaf, Munro, The Story of Ferdinand.

(Dramatic story of a bull fight and the bull who
wanted only to sit and smell flowers.)

Mahy, Margaret, A Lion in the Meadow.

(Children follow the dreamy pictures with wide-eyed
understanding of the imaginative fantasy.)

Matsui, Tadashi, Puka the Traffic Light.

(Text and pictures of the familiar traffic light holds
fascination in the setting of Tokyo, Japan.)

Mayer, Mercer, The Nightmare in My Closet.

(A small boy makes friends with his nightmares, with
a humorous twist to a frightening situation.)

Merrill, Jean, Emily Emerson's Moon.

(Emily finally gets a moon with the help of her father.)

Parks, Gale T., Here Comes Daddy.

(As Peter and Ann watch for Daddy to come home
from work, they see many other workers.)

Sauer, Julia L., Mike's House.

(Robert visits the library after an adventure on the
way, and finds his favorite book about Mike Mulligan's
steamshovel.)

Sharmat, Marjorie Weinman, Gladys Told Me to Meet Her
Here. (A delightfully funny story of friendship with
a zoo background.)

Steig, William, <u>Sylvester and the Magic Pebble.</u>
    (A young donkey finds a magic pebble that grants
    wishes. He gets into trouble, but all ends well in
    this unusual fantasy.)

Thayer, Jane, <u>The Pussy that Went to the Moon.</u>
    (A pussy that likes to wander is rescued from the top
    of a tree, and even from the moon, by his owners.)

Tresselt, Alvin, <u>Wake Up, City.</u>
    (The gradual awakening of the city from the earliest
    hour of dawn.)

Udry, Janice May, <u>The Moon Jumpers.</u>
    (Maurice Sendak's pictures capture the magic of moon-
    light as children respond to the loveliness of a sum-
    mer night.)

Wells, Rosemary, <u>Martha's Birthday.</u>
    (Disappointed at first, Martha finally gets what she
    wanted for a birthday--a baby skunk! Simple, uncom-
    plicated pictures with short text.)

Zemach, Harve and Margot, <u>Mommy, Buy Me a China Doll.</u>
    (This delightfully funny cumulative tale adapted from
    an Ozark children's song is enchanting.)

Zion, Gene, <u>Dear Garbage Man.</u>
    (An amusing story about the garbage collector that
    helps children understand how he feels about his work.)

Zolotow, Charlotte, <u>Mr. Rabbit and the Lovely Present.</u>
    (A little girl meets Mr. Rabbit, and together they find
    the perfect gift for her mother.)

Zolotow, Charlotte, <u>The Night When Mother Was Away.</u>
    (Daddy takes care of his little girl in a most under-
    standing and heart-warming response to her loneliness
    until Mother comes back the next day.)

Mother Goose Books

     Nursery rhymes and Mother Goose rhymes are part
of every child's literary heritage.   Some of these are listed
as reference books and some can be used to show as picture
books.

Anglund, Joan Walsh, In a Pumpkin Shell.
     (Mother Goose ABC book.)
Brooks, Leslie, Ring O'Roses.
     (Amusing drawings make this a perennial favorite.)
de Angeli, Marguerite, Book of Nursery and Mother Goose
     Rhymes.   (A big and beautifully illustrated collection
     of 376 rhymes.)
Fish, Helen D., Four and Twenty Blackbirds.
     (Nursery rhymes of yesterday, illustrated by Robert
     Lawson.)
Fisher, Blanche, The Real Mother Goose.
     (Old and traditional.)
Fujikawa, Gyo, Mother Goose.
     (A large book with an extensive collection, beautifully
     illustrated.)
Greenaway, Kate, Mother Goose; or The Old Nursery Rhymes.
     (Characteristic drawings in color by a famous illus-
     trator.)
Reed, Philip, Mother Goose and Nursery Rhymes.
     (Old favorites and lesser known verses, highlighted by
     woodcuts in six colors.)
Rojankovsky, Feodor, The Tall Book of Mother Goose.
     (One hundred old favorites with fresh illustrations.)
Scarry, Richard, Richard Scarry's Best Mother Goose Ever.
     (Rollicking illustrations of favorite Mother Goose
     rhymes with animal characters.)

Tenggren, Gustav, The Tenggren Mother Goose.
> (Charming pictures in color illustrate many of the
> rhymes.   Twelve rhymes set to music with special
> arrangements by Inez Bertail.)

Tudor, Tasha, Mother Goose.
> (Tasha Tudor's characteristic pictures illustrate
> seventy-seven nursery rhymes.)

Wildsmith, Brian, Brian Wildsmith's Mother Goose.
> (Brightly colored illustrations.)

Poetry

Poetry has an important place in the pre-school
group.   Little children enjoy its rhythmic patterns, colorful
expressions, and its word pictures, stories and ideas.   Wonderful adventures in poetry may be had from these books:

Aldis, Dorothy, All Together.

Barrows, Marjorie, Read-Aloud Poems.

Brown, Margaret Wise, Nibble Nibble.

Doane, Pelagie, A Small Child's Book of Verse.

Fisher, Aileen, We Went Looking.

Frank, Josette, Poems to Read to the Very Young.

Hillert, Margaret, Farther Than Far.

Hopkins, Lee Burnett, compiler, Me!

McGovern, Ann, Black Is Beautiful.

Milne, A. A., When We Were Very Young.

Moore, Clement, The Night Before Christmas.   New York,
> Grosset and Dunlap, 1949.   (Large, beautiful illus-
> trations by Leonard Weisgard make this edition ex-
> cellent for showing.)

Moore, John Travers, There's Motion Everywhere.

Prelutsky, Jack, Lazy Blackbird.

Rosen, Ellsworth, To Be a Bee.

Roy, Cal, A Friend Can Be.

Sicotte, Virginia, A Riot of Quiet.

Smith, William Jay, Laughing Time.

Suter, Antoinette, and Barbara Geismer, Very Young Verses.

Thompson, Jean McKee, Poems to Grow On.

Withers, Carl, A Rocket in My Pocket.

Seasons and Holidays

     Books help children to become aware of the oustand-
ing characteristics of the seasons and of the succession of
holidays.   Through pictures and stories, the child develops
an appreciation of the world about him.

Ets, Marie Hall, Gilberto and the Wind.
     (A small Mexican boy finds the wind a fascinating
     playmate.)

Foster, Doris Van Liew, A Pocketful of Seasons.
     (Each season Andy picks up something for his pocket.)

McCloskey, Robert, Time of Wonder.
     (The change of seasons on an island in Penobscot Bay.)

Piatti, Celestino, The Happy Owls.
     (Two wise owls try to explain their joy in the chang-
     ing seasons to the barnyard fowl.)

Udrey, Janice May, A Tree Is Nice.
     (The many delights offered by trees; picking apples,
     raking leaves, swinging, or just sitting in the shade.)

Zolotow, Charlotte, Over and Over.
     (Each year has the same succession of holidays.)

Zolotow, Charlotte, The Storm Book.
     (A little boy and his mother watch the beauty of a
     storm.)

RAIN

Bright, Robert, My Red Umbrella.
> (A very little girl and all the animals that take shelter under her umbrella.)

Simon, Norma, Wet World.
> (The feeling of snugness indoors and adventures into the wet world outside suggest the pleasures of a rainy day.)

Tresselt, Alvin, Rain Drop Splash.
> (Striking pictures and simple, poetic text describe the journey of a raindrop in terms a small child can understand.)

Yashima, Taro, Umbrella.
> (A three year old Japanese girl, born in New York, longs for a rainy day so she may use her new umbrella and her red rubber boots.)

FALL

Bancroft, Henrietta, Down Come the Leaves.
> (Autumn is a gay time of busy activity. Many leaves and trees are identified in story and pictures.)

Lenski, Lois, Now It's Fall.
> (Joys of the fall season in pictures and verses.)

Tresselt, Alvin, Autumn Harvest.
> (From the first autumn chill until Thanksgiving Day celebrations, children help with the autumn harvest.)

Tresselt, Alvin, Johnny Maple Leaf.
> (Story and pictures of a maple leaf's cycle of seasons until his descent to the ground.)

WINTER

Adelson, Leone, All Ready for Winter.
    (Each creature has its own way of preparing for win-
    ter, from squirrels to caterpillars. Even children
    have to be prepared for snow and cold.)
de Regniers, Beatrice, The Snow Party.
    (A snowstorm maroons an interesting group of char-
    acters in a farmhouse, which makes a delightful oc-
    casion for all.)
Hader, Berta and Elmer, The Big Snow.
    (A beautiful picture book of how the animals and birds
    prepare for the long winter. The winter of the big
    snow was an especially difficult one and they all need-
    ed help.)
Hoban, Lillian and Russell, Some Snow Said Hello.
    (A family of children find fun in the snow after a
    quarrelsome time indoors.)
Kay, Helen, One Mitten Lewis.
    (Lewis keeps losing one mitten, but his trouble is
    solved in a most interesting way.)
Keats, Ezra Jack, The Snowy Day.
    (A boy's quiet pleasure on a day of deep, new-fallen
    snow.)
Kessler, Ethel and Leonard, The Day Daddy Stayed Home.
    (A special winter day when the snow covered every-
    thing and Daddy stayed home with his family.)
Krauss, Ruth, The Happy Day.
    (Animals of the forest come out of their winter homes
    to find a surprise in the snow.)
Lenski, Lois, I Like Winter.
    (Gay pictures and verses depicting the delights of winter.)

Tresselt, Alvin, White Snow, Bright Snow.

    (Puts into words and distinguished pictures the excitement that snow brings to children and how it affects different people.)

SPRING

Hausman, Leon Augustus, A Book of Song Birds.

    (Well-known song birds with a record of authentic songs captured in their natural habitat.)

Henry, Marguerite, Birds at Home.

    (A large book with brilliant pictures by Jacob Bates Abbott for showing. Text as reference for the story teller.)

Johnson, Crockett, Time for Spring.

    (Imaginative story about Irene's snowman who wanted to stay until the 4th of July, though Irene thought it was time for spring.)

Kruss, Ruth, The Carrot Seed.

    (The little boy planted a carrot seed and nobody thought his carrot would come up. Faithfully, he watered it and pulled the weeds--and finally it did!)

Lenski, Lois, Spring Is Here.

    (About children's activities in the spring.)

Nodset, Joan L., Who Took the Farmer's Hat?

    (With the help of his animal friends, a farmer finds his old brown hat which had been stolen by the wind.)

Parker, Bertha Morris, Birds in Your Backyard.

    (Pictures in clear, true color of familiar birds with short, simple descriptive text.)

Schlein, Miriam, Little Red Nose.

    (The little boy discovers spring as he helped his

father plant a garden, looked at the birds coming
back, and felt the sun on his nose. He also discovered that spring had discovered him when his nose
turns as red as a rose.)

SUMMER

Bevans, Michael H., The Book of Sea Shells.
(The large, colored pictures are accurate and de-
tailed. The text furnishes information for the story
teller to tell in her own words.)
Cook, Bernadine, The Little Fish That Got Away.
(An amusing story with delightful repetition.)
Lenski, Lois, On a Summer Day.
(The joys of a summer day in pictures and verses.)
Paull, Grace, Come to the Country.
(What you can see, feel, and smell on a summer day
in the country.)
Udry, Janice May, Moon Jumpers.
(Children enjoy the mystery of moonlight as they play
outdoors on a summer night.)

HALLOWE'EN

Balian, Lorna, Humbug Witch.
(Suspense grows as the little witch fails at witchcraft.
A delightful surprise ending. Wonderful pictures.)
Bright, Robert, Georgie.
Georgie's Hallowe'en.
Georgie and the Magician.
Georgie to the Rescue.
(About a friendly little ghost and the family he haunts.)
Calhoun, Mary, Wobbly, the Witch Cat.

(An amusing story about a motherly witch and her
black cat that kept falling off the magic broom until
a safer ride was found.)

Foster, Doris Van Liew, Tell Me, Mr. Owl.

(Mr. Owl explains some spooky sounds and masquer-
ades to a little boy on Hallowe'en night.)

Freeman, Don, Space Witch.

(A modern-minded witch designs a "Zoom Broom" and
switches around the planets. She thinks she is stuck
on Mars when she lands among a strange-looking
group, but it turns out to be a group of trick-or-
treaters on earth.)

Miller, Edna, Mousekin's Golden House.

(A little mouse made his home in a Jack-o-lantern
after Hallowe'en was over.)

Zolotow, Charlotte, A Tiger Called Thomas.

(Dressed in his tiger suit, Thomas made many friends
on Hallowe'en night.)

CHRISTMAS

Brown, Margaret Wise, The Little Fir Tree.

(Excellent for dramatization and enriches the child's
feeling for the Christmas tree.)

Chalmers, Mary, A Christmas Story.

(A little girl, a dog, a cat, and a rabbit search for
a star for the top of their Christmas tree.)

Françoise, Noel for Jeanne-Marie.

(A picture-story about a little pet sheep and a pair of
wooden shoes.)

Hoff, Syd, Where's Prancer?

(An after-Christmas story tells how Santa loses one

of his reindeer and returns for a lively search.)

Hurd, Edith and Clement, Christmas Eve.

(Picture-story of the traditional animals' Christmas Eve.)

Keats, Ezra Jack, The Little Drummer Boy.

(A favorite Christmas song with pictures children enjoy.)

Miller, Edna, Mousekin's Christmas Eve.

(When Mousekin ventures into a happy house, he finds all the warmth and peaceful beauty of Christmas Eve.)

Moore, Clement, The Night Before Christmas.

(The classic poem of a visit from St. Nick. The edition illustrated by Leonard Weisgard is good for showing with a large group. New York, Grosset and Dunlap, 1949.)

Partch, Virgil, The Christmas Cookie Sprinkle Snitcher.

(A humorous story in verse about a horrible creature who learns a good lesson from Little Nat, the boy hero.)

Politi, Leo, Rosa.

(A little Mexican girl longs for a new doll for Christmas, but finds that a new baby sister is even more wonderful.)

Whitcomb, Joh, Pom-Pom's Christmas.

(Colorful pictures accompany the story of a delightful poodle that became a Christmas gift for a little girl.)

EASTER

Duvoisin, Roger, Easter Treat.

(Santa decides to visit a city in the Springtime and has an exciting adventure that turns out happily.)

Friedrich, Priscilla and Otto, The Easter Bunny That Overslept. (An imaginative tale of the adventures that befell the Easter Bunny the year he slept through Easter.)

Heyward, DuBose, The Country Bunny and the Little Gold
    Shoes. (Cottontail, the mother of 21 bunnies, finally
    realizes her ambition to be an Easter Bunny, too.)

Thayer, Jane, The Horse in the Easter Bonnet.
    (Nobody wants to pay for a ride through the park in
    a carriage drawn by a slow, dismal horse. The un-
    expected gift of a beautiful hat lifts the spirits of the
    droopy horse and helps earn a living for him and his
    master.)

Wiese, Kurt, Happy Easter.
    (A mother rabbit sends her children out to get eggs
    to color for the holiday with results that are unex-
    pected and delightful.)

Zolotow, Charlotte, The Bunny Who Found Easter.
    (Easter time is a delightful season for discovering all
    the fascinations of Springtime.)

Wheels and Wings and Moving Things

    There is fascination for the pre-school age in books
about wheels and machinery. In most of the books listed below, there is a story; in others, the text is subordinate to
the informative illustrations.

The Big Book of Boats and Ships.
    (The Big Book series includes books about fire en-
    gines, trains, trucks, and building and wrecking ma-
    chines.)

Brown, Margaret Wise, Two Little Trains.
    (The journey of two little trains is a picture story told
    in rhythmic prose.)

Burton, Virginia, Mike Mulligan and His Steam Shovel.
    (Mike and his faithful steam shovel dig their way to

a happy ending in an exciting race against time.)

Ets, Marie Hall, Little Old Automobile.

(The little old automobile whose favorite saying was
"I won't" finds what happened when he said it once
too often.)

Gramatky, Hardie, Creeper's Jeep.

(The story of a jeep that became a hero and was
saved from the junk shop.)

Gramatky, Hardie, Great Big Car and Truck Book.

(Everything from a cattle truck to the big, stream-
lined double-decker bus, in absorbing text and large
pictures by Richard Scarry.)

Gramatky, Hardie, Little Toot.

(A fun-loving little tugboat, in disgrace because of
his frivolous ways, proves himself a hero in a crisis.)

Gramatky, Hardie, Loopy.

(Loopy, the little airplane who wishes he could go up
without a pilot, gets a chance and makes a good landing.)

Jackson, Kathryn, Wheels.

(Wheels on wheelbarrows, roller skates, buses, and
all sorts of everyday things.)

Lenski, Lois, Little Aute, Little Sailboat, Little Train, and
Little Fire Engine. (Adventures of the famous Mr.
Small.)

Piper, Watty, The Little Engine That Could.

(The little engine saves the day after all the other
engines refuse to pull a trainful of toys over the
mountain.)

Potter, Marian, Little Red Caboose.

(Life becomes exciting for the little red caboose on
the day he gets a chance to be a hero.)

Wright, Ethel A., Saturday Walk.

> (Large, vivid pictures of cars, ships, and trains.)

Young, Miriam, If I Flew a Plane.

> (Off we go into the sky by passenger plane, sports
> plane, sky writer, spaceship, helicopter, and a
> glider. The text may be a little too much for pre-
> schoolers, but the interest is high, and the pictures
> by Robert Quackenbush are exciting.)

Zaffo, George, J., The Giant Nursery Book of Things That
Go.

PARTICIPATION BOOKS

Brown, Margaret Wise, The Noisy Book.

> (One of a series of "noisy" books, which give chil-
> dren greater awareness of sound in the city, the
> country, in summer and in winter.)

de Regniers, Beatrice, Was It a Good Trade?

de Regniers, Beatrice, What Can You do With a Shoe?

Ets, Marie Hall, Just Me.

Gay, Zhenya, What's Your Name?

Jaynes, Ruth, Benny's Four Hats.

> (Colorful photographs of a boy wearing different hats.
> Children enjoy guessing why Benny wears each hat
> and seeing what he does.)

Kessler, Esther and Leonard, Do Baby Bears Sit in Chairs?

Mace, Katherine, Let's Dance a Story.

Wolff, Janet and Bernard Owett, Imagination Books.

> Let's Imagine Being Places.
> Let's Imagine Colors.
> Let's Imagine Numbers.
> Let's Imagine Sounds.

Let's Imagine Thinking Up Things.

Woodcock, Louise, This Is the Way the Animals Walk.

Notes

1. Viguers, Ruth Hill, Margin for Surprise; About Books Children, and Librarians. Boston, Little, Brown & Company, 1964, p. 15.

2. Dalgliesh, Alice, First Experiences With Literature. New York, Charles Scribner's Sons, 1932, p. 10.

Additional Reading

Arbuthnot, May Hill, Children and Books. Chicago, Scott Foresman, 1964. 3rd edition.

Dodson, Fitzhugh, How to Parent. Los Angeles, Nash Publishing, 1970. (Annotated books for the pre-school years, pp. 329-381.)

Duff, Annis, Bequest of Wings. New York, Viking, 1944.

Fenner, Phyllis, Proof of the Pudding. New York, John Day, 1957.

The Horn Book, Magazine of books and reading for children and young people. 585 Boylston Street, Boston, Mass., Horn Book, Inc.

Larrick, Nancy, Children's Reading. Garden City, N.Y., Doubleday & Co., Inc., 1958.

The Lively Art of Picture Books. Weston, Conn., Weston Woods Studies, 1964. (A full-color film introducing the work of Robert McCloskey, Barbara Cooney, and Maurice Sendak.)

Smith, Lillian, Unreluctant Years. Chicago, American Library Association, 1953.

Todd, Vivian Edmiston and Heffernan, Helen, The Years Before School: Guiding Pre-School Children. New York, The Macmillan Company, 1964. (Stories for pre-school children, p. 409.)

White, Dorothy, <u>Books Before Five</u>. New York, Oxford
    University Press, 1954.

Winn, Marie and Mary Ann Porcher, <u>The Playgroup Book.</u>
    New York, The Macmillan Company, 1967. (Titles
    listed under subject matter, pp. 138-146.)

Chapter 10

RELATED ACTIVITIES

"Grandpa and I get stiff if we sit too long."
                                                -Stanley

Finger plays, group games, and rhythmic play give the story hour variety and provide an opportunity to relax after a period of sitting still and help to develop motor skills and alertness.

Finger plays are valuable for focusing wandering attention, for use in following a particular theme, or just for fun. When introducing a new one, say the words slowly, showing the action. After the children have caught the meaning, go through it again one line at a time, inviting the children to repeat it with you. Then try the entire finger play together without a break. Most children are able to follow straight through by this third time around.

Simple games teach the fundamentals of group activity and co-operation by following directions, by taking turns, and by moving in formation. Freedom of action is encouraged; however, some conformity is not only desirable but even necessary, particularly in an emergency when directions must be followed quickly and in an orderly manner.

Children usually respond enthusiastically to music, with movement ranging from the simple action of clapping hands to exercising large muscles in running, jumping, hopping, stretching, and acting out dramatic play.

143

Records listed at the end of this chapter include music with directions for rhythms, games, songs, finger plays, and rhythm band. When using records, prepare the children for what the record is about. "Let's listen for the sounds the animals make." "Let's listen to the directions for this game." "Let's listen for the sounds of the different instruments." "Let's listen to see how the music makes you feel."

These related activities contribute to growth in self-expression and foster friendly feeling within the group. Some children show reluctance to make the slightest move at first. Again it should be emphasized that coaxing or demanding participation defeat the purpose of these activities. Offer the invitation and allow response to come naturally in its own good time.

FINGER PLAYS FOR QUIETING

1. Here are Grandma's glasses.

    (Make circles with forefingers and thumb.   Hold them over your eyes to resemble glasses.)

    Here is Grandma's cap.

    (Put both hands on your head to make a pointed cap.)

    This is the way she folds her hands

    And puts them in her lap.

    (Fold hands and place them in your lap.)

    Here are Grandpa's glasses.

    (Make circles with fingers.)

    And here is Grandpa's hat.

    (Make larger pointed hat, or put hand over the forehead.)

    This is the way he folds his arms

    (Fold your arms across your chest.)

    And sits like that.

2. Open, shut them - open, shut them,
    (Follow the words with action of the hands.)
    Give a little clap.
    Open, shut them - open, shut them,
    Put them in your lap.

3. Touch your head and shoulders, knees and toes.
    Head and shoulders, knees and toes.
    (Suit action to the words.)
    Head and shoulders, knees and toes.
    And we'll all sit down together.
    I'll touch my hair, my lips, my eyes.
    I'll sit up straight and then I'll rise.
    I'll touch my ears, my nose, my chin.
    Then quietly sit down again.

4. Two little eyes that open and close,
    (Suit action to words.)
    Two little ears, and one little nose,
    (Point to ears and nose.)
    Two little cheeks and one little chin,
    (Point to cheeks and chin.)
    Two little lips with teeth closed in.
    (Point to lips and smile.)

5. A little mouse went creeping, creeping, creeping into
    the house.
    (Start with right hand at right foot, fingers creep up
    right leg and around to the back.)
    The big black cat went creeping, creeping, creeping
    into the house.
    (Fingers of left hand creep up the left leg and around

to the back.)

The big black cat went creeping, creeping, creeping
    into the house.

(Fingers of left hand creep up the left leg and around
to the back.   Pause.)

Away ran the mouse - out of the house!

(Right hand scampers off.)

6.   Here is an airplane flying about.

(Right hand moving high.)

Here is the landing field down on the ground.

(Left hand held low, palm up and open.)

The man in the tower tells the plane when to land.

(Raise thumb of left hand.)

Zoom - the plane lands right in my hand.

(Right hand into left hand.)

7.   Big clocks make a sound like Tick-Tock, Tick-Tock.

(While standing, swing the right arm from side to
side in front of the body with wide sweeps.)

Small clocks make a sound like Ticktock, ticktock,
    ticktock.)

(Bend the arm at the elbow, swinging the hand from
side to side.)

And the little tiny clocks say Tick, tick, tick, tick,
    tick, tick.

(Cup the right hand over the right ear.)

LIMBERING RHYMES

1.   Flop your arms, flop your feet,

(Suit action to words.)

Let your hands go free.

Be the raggiest doll you ever did see.

2. Fee, Fi, Fo, Fum,
    Measure my arm, measure my nose.
    (Fingers of right hand creep along to measure.)
    Measure myself way down to my toes.

3. Hands on shoulders, hands on knees.
    Hands behind you, if you please.
    (Suit action to words.)
    Touch your shoulders, now your nose,
    Now your hair and now your toes.
    Hands high up in the air,
    Down at your sides; now touch your hair.
    Hands up high as before,
    Now clap your hands - one, two, three, four.

4. This is my right hand.
    (Suit action to words.)
    I'll raise it up high.
    This is my left hand.
    I'll touch the sky.
    Right hand, left hand.
    Roll them around.
    Left hand, right hand,
    Pound, pound, pound!
    (Pound one fist on the other.)

5. I'm a floppy rag doll,
    Drooping in my chair.
    My rag head rolls from, side to side;
    It shakes my wooly hair.
    My floppy arms are loose and limp
    My body's floppy too.

But I'll stand up and shake and shake,

And flop back when I'm through.

(Suit action to words.)

6. Little leaves fall gently down, red and yellow, orange, brown.

(Raise and lower arms, fluttering fingers like falling leaves.)

Whirling, whirling round and round.

(Repeat arm motion, turning body slowly on tiptoe.)

Quietly without a sound.

Falling softly to the ground,

(Lower body gradually to the floor.)

Down - and down - and down - and down.

7. I can make myself get smaller, smaller, smaller.

(Gradually stoop to the floor.)

I can make myself get taller, taller, taller.

(Gradually rise to tiptoes.)

I can make myself go faster, faster, faster.

(Run in place.)

I can make myself go slower, slower, slower.

(Come to a gradual stop.)

Clapping to music: Clap loud, clap soft, Clap with hands brushing, Clap with fingertips touching.

WEATHER

1. My zipper suit is bunny brown.

The top zips up and the legs zip down.

(Suit action to words.)

My daddy brought it out from town.

Zip it up and zip it down.

And then go out to play.

2. The busy windshield wiper goes

A-dash, a-dash, a-dash.

(With elbow bent, right hand up, facing out, let your hand move back and forth.)

It pushes all the drops away,

Splash, splash, splash.

(Same action, only faster.)

3. The eensie, teensie spider climbed up the water spout.

(Left arm extended forward and downward, right fingers creep up.)

Down came the rain and washed the spider out.

(Right hand sweeps down left arm.)

Out came the sun and dried up all the rain.

(Both hands circle head.)

And the eensie, teensie spider climbed up the spout again.

(Repeat first action.)

EASTER

1. Here's a bunny

(Hold up first and second fingers of right hand.)

With ears so funny.

(Bend the two fingers forward.)

And here's his hole in the ground.

(Close thumb and first finger of left hand, making a circle.)

At the least, little sound,

He pricks up his ears

(Straighten the two fingers of right hand.)

And Pop! he goes into the ground.

(Pop right fingers through the circle.)

2.   Once I saw a bunny

(Make ears with two fingers of right hand.)

And a green cabbage head,

(Make a fist with left hand.)

"I think I'll have some cabbage,"

(Make bunny hop to the cabbage.)

The little bunny said.

So he nibbled and he nibbled,

(Make nibbling motions with right hand.)

Then he pricked up his ears to say,

(Straighten the two right fingers.)

Now I think it's time for me to hop away."

(Let bunny hop away.)

3.   Here comes a rabbit; hippity, hop, hop.

(Hands on hips; 3 short hops.)

See how his long ears - flippity, flop, flop.

(Hands above head; flip 3 times.)

See how his nose goes - twink, twink, twink.

(Twitch nose 3 times.)

See how his eyes go - wink, wink, wink.

(Wink 3 times.)

Stroke his warm coat, soft and furry.

(Stroking motion.)

Hippity, hop, hop - he's off in a hurry.

(3 short hops to seat.)

4.   A little boy went walking, walking, walking,

(While sitting, "walk" first two fingers down
thighs to knees.)

On a lovely day.

He saw a little rabbit,

(Hold up first two fingers above ears.)

Who quickly hopped away.

(First two fingers held together hop down thoughts to knees.)

HALLOWE'EN

1. Five little jack-o-lanterns sitting on a gate,

    (Hold up fingers of right hand and point to each one with the left.)

    Said the first little jack-o-lantern, "It's growing very late."

    Said the second little jack-o-lantern, "I see a witch in the air."

    Said the third little jack-o-lantern, "Who goes there?"

    Said the fourth little jack-o-lantern, "Let's run, let's run."

    Said the fifth little jack-o-lantern, "Oh, it's just Hallowe'en fun."

    The "Poof" went the wind and out went the light,

    And away ran all their little jack-o-lanterns on Hallowe'en night.

    (With fingers wiggling, let them run behind your back.)

2. Here's a pumpkin big and yellow

    Let's make a jolly, smiling fellow.

    (Arms rounded, fingers touching.)

    Cut two eyes, a nose, and smile

    (Pantomime action.)

    Put a candle inside to glow for a while.

MOTHER GOOSE FINGERPLAYS

1. Hickory, dickory, dock,

    (Left arm bent up, palm out.   Right hand under left
    elbow.   Move left hand sideways, back and forth.)

    The mouse ran up the clock.

    (Right hand fingers run from elbow up to left hand.)

    The clock struck one,

    (Clap hands together one time.)

    The mouse ran down.

    (Right hand fingers run down to left elbow.)

    Hickory, dickory, dock.

    (Repeat first movement.)

2. Jack and Jill went up the hill

    (Both hands, palms down in lap; lift one after the
    other in steps.)

    To fetch a pail of water.

    Jack fell down and broke his crown,

    (Right hand falls to lap.)

    And Jill came tumbling after.

    (Left hand circles to lap.)

3. Little Miss Muffet sat on a tuffet

    (Make fist of right hand, thumb up.)

    Eating her curds and whey.

    (Wiggle thumb.)

    Along came a spider

    (Left arm high, fingers make crawling motion toward
    right hand.)

    And sat down beside her

    And frightened Miss Muffet away.

    (Right hand rushes behind back.)

STORY FINGER PLAYS AND ACTION STORIES

1. This is the house with the sloping roof
        (Place finger tips together.)
    Where I live.
        (Point to self.)
    This is the tree so straight and tall
        (Hands high over head.)
    That shades the house with the sloping roof
        (Make roof.)
    Where I live.
        (Point to self.)
    This is the dog with ears so long
        (Hands pointing up at ears.)
    That plays under the tree so straight and tall
        (Hands over head.)
    That shades the house with the sloping roof
        (Make roof.)
    Where I live.
        (Point to self.)
    This is the cat so furry and soft
        (Cradle cat in left arm and stroke with right hand.)
    That worries the dog with ears so long
        (Repeat action for dog.)
    That plays under the tree so straight and tall
        (Repeat action for tree.)
    That shades the house with the sloping roof
        (Repeat action for roof.)
    Where I live.
        (Point to self.)
    And last comes me as you can see
        (Point to self.)

Who loves the cat so furry and soft
  (Repeat action of stroking cat.)
That worries the dog with ears so long
  (Repeat dog action.)
That plays under the tree so straight and tall
  (Repeat tree action.)
That shades the house with the sloping roof
  (Repeat roof action.)
Where I live.
  (Point to self.)

2. I looked up in an apple tree.
      (Look up.)
    And a great big apple looked down at me.
      (Form circle with hands.)
    I shook that tree as hard as I could.
      (Shaking motion with hands together.)
    Down fell the apple.
      (Take a bite.)
    Ummm - good.
      (Rub tummy.)
    I looked up in an orange tree.
      (Look up.)
    And a great big orange looked down at me.
      (Form circle with hands.)
    I shook that tree as hard as I could.
      (Shaking motion with hands together.)
    Down fell the orange.
      (Take a bite.)
    Ummm - good.
      (Rub tummy.)
    I looked up in a lemon tree.

(Look up.)

And a great big lemon looked down at me.

(Form circle with hands.)

I shook that tree as hard as I could.

(Shaking motion with hands together.)

Down fell the lemon.

(Take a bite.)

Oh!

(Make a wry face.)

The Dance of the Shaggy Bear

3. (Children follow the action as the story is told.)

The bear crawls out of his cave.

He yawns and stretches.

He looks around, then turns around one time.

He shambles off through the forest.

The bear stops to catch some fish with his paws.

Smack!

(Smack with your hands.)

He shambles off again.

He looks around and turns around two times.

Next he rolls over and shambles off again.

He looks around and turns around three times.

He yawns and stretches.

Then he crawls back into his cave for a snooze.

The Ten Little Farmers

4. Ten little farmers got up one day.

(Outstretch fingers of both hands, palms outward.)

Five wanted to work - five wanted to play.

(Hold up left hand first and then right hand.)

Five started to work on the run.

(Fingers of the right hand "run" to and fro.)

For the day was good and chores had to be done.

The first little farmer said, "I'll feed the hens,"

(Hold up left hand, fingers outstretched. Point to successive fingers with finger of right hand for all five.)

The second little farmer said, "I'll clean the pens."

The third little farmer said, "I'll milk the cow."

The fourth little farmer said, "I'll work the plow."

The fifth little farmer said, "I'm off to town.
    to sell all the produce we grew in the ground."

But the five little farmers who stayed home all day

(Hold up fingers of right hand.)

Had trouble deciding just what they would play.

The first little farmer said, "Hide and go seek?"

(Hold up right hand, fingers outstretched. Point to successive fingers with finger of left hand for all five.)

The second little farmer said, "No, you peek."

The third little farmer said, "Blind Man's Buff?"

The fourth little farmer said, "You play too rough."

The fifth little farmer said, "Let's have a fight."

And that's what they did right into the night.

When the little farmers who worked all day

Came home, they had supper, then started to play.

(Cup left hand. Go through the motions of eating with right hand.)

But the little farmers who fought the whole day through

Had nothing to eat and nothing to do.

(Outstretch both hands, palms up denoting "nothing.")

This finger play is also adaptable for use as a dramatic activity. Children are chosen for all the characters, including the cow and the pigs in the pen. Nobody needs to be left out, since there can be as many "pigs" as there are children who wish to participate but are too shy to take an active part.

Playing in the Snow

Pantomime the actions of getting ready to go out into the cold.

"Let's put on a warm coat and zip it up to the chin.

"Put on your cap and pull it over your ears.

"Now, pull on your boots and stamp your feet in.

"Are we ready to go? What have we forgotten?"
There may be shouts of "Mittens!" or "A scarf!"

"Oh yes. Let's draw on our mittens and tie on a scarf. Now we're ready to go."

"Take big giant steps in the deep, fluffy snow.

"First we'll roll a big, big ball to make a snowman's body.

"Now we'll make a smaller ball and put it on top for his head.

"Put in two eyes, a nose, and a mouth.

"Now let's roll a snowball and throw it straight and true.

"Throw it at the snowman. He won't get mad at you.

"And another! And another! And another!"

"Now we'll go inside to get warm.

"Lets hang up our wet outdoor clothes to dry.

"Let's all sit down and have a nice cup of hot cocoa."

This pantomime may also be used to go ice skating by sliding in long sweeps to a waltz record.

Or try going for a sleigh ride by taking little jogging steps to the tune of "Jingle Bells."

The Crooked Mouth Family

There are many versions of this action story. This one, however, appeals to young children and never fails to bring laughter and requests to have it repeated. Before beginning the story, quietly light a candle--preferably a dripless one.

Once there was a family called The Crooked Mouth Family.

The father had a mouth like this.

(Twist mouth to the right.)

The mother had a mouth like this.

(Twist mouth to the left.)

The Big Brother had a mouth like this.

(Bring lower lip over upper lip.)

The Big Sister had a mouth like this

(Bring upper lip over lower lip.)

But the Baby Sister had a pretty mouth just like yours.

(Smile naturally.)

(Repeat mouth positions as each character speaks.)

One night they forgot to blow the candle out when they went upstairs to bed.

The father said, "I'd better go downstairs and blow that candle out."

(With mouth still twisted to the right, blow at the flame being careful not to blow it out.)

"What's the matter with this candle? It won't go out."

(Repeat blowing several times.)

"I guess I'd better call Mother. Mother! Please come down and blow the candle out."

Mother said, "Why can't you blow the candle out? Anybody can blow a candle out. You just go like this."

(She blows at the flame, mouth still twisted to the left.)

"I can't blow it out either. We'd better call Big Brother."

(Change to father's mouth.)

"Brother! Please come down and blow the candle out."

Big Brother said, "That's easy. All you have to do is blow hard."

(With lower lip over upper, hold the candle low and blow.)

Father said, "See. You can't blow it out either. We'll have to call Big Sister. Sister! Please come down and blow the candle out!

Big Sister said, "I can blow it out. Watch me."

(With upper lip over lower, candle held high, blow several times.)

Father said, "That's a funny candle. I told you I couldn't blow it out."

Mother said, "I couldn't blow it out, either."

Big Brother said, "Neither could I."

Big Sister said, "I tried and tried, and I couldn't blow it out."

Father said, "I guess we'll have to call Baby Sister. Baby! Please come down and blow the candle out."

Baby Sister came downstairs, rubbing her eyes because she had been asleep. She asked, "What's the matter?"

Father said, "I can't blow the candle out."

Mother said, "I can't blow it out either."

Big Brother said, "Neither can I."

Big Sister said, "I can't either."

Baby Sister said, "Anybody can blow a candle out. That's easy." And she did.

(Gently blow out the candle.)

The Hanky Mouse

This simple folding trick is fascinating to children
and fits in well with a mouse program or to gain wandering
attention and relieve restlessness.

During the folding process questions and answers
might run like this:

Story teller: "Do you know what this is?"
      (Holding up the handkerchief.)

Children: "It's a hanky."

Story teller: "It could be a tablecloth."

Children: "That's too small for a tablecloth."

Story teller: "It might be a doll's tablecloth or a tablecloth
      for a fairy."

When the triangle is folded, the storyteller might ask:

"What does this look like?"

Some children say, "A dolly's scarf," "A baby's diaper,"
"A half a cheese sandwich," or very realistically, "A triangle."

To make the mouse use a medium-sized handkerchief
with a plain edge. Lay it in your lap or on a flat surface
with one corner toward you (Fig. 1). Now fold the hanky in
half, bringing point A to point C, so that a triangle is
formed (Fig. 2). Fold corner D into the center of the bottom edge and do the same with corner B so that corners B
and D touch (Fig. 3). Keeping the hanky in the same position, make a one-inch fold up from the bottom and smooth.
Make a second fold and smooth. Now make a third fold
(Fig. 4). Now turn the handkerchief over, keeping the point
CA at the top (Fig. 5). Bring the two little rolls E and F
into the center so that they touch (Fig. 6). Holding the little

rolls firmly, turn them up one fold from the bottom toward point CA. Now turn point CA down and tuck it into the space between the fold and the two rolls (Fig. 7). The rolls are now completely covered (Fig. 8). This completes the folds.

Now pick up the hanky roll, keeping it in the same position as it was on the flat surface. Slip your thumbs into the slot (Fig. 9). Holding the hanky firmly, begin rolling the hanky away from you as you would roll up a pair of socks. On the third roll, two little tails will pop out (Fig. 10). Take one of these ends and, holding the "tail" so that the point is up, roll gently between the fingers until you have two tiny little rolls which you can tie in a knot to make the head and ears. Now the mouse is completed (Fig. 11).

Lay the hanky mouse in the palm of your left hand with the head pointing up the arm. Curve your fingers so that they are touching the roll. The tail hangs out over the fingers (Fig. 12). Cover the mouse lightly with the right hand, making a stroking motion. As your hand moves from your wrist down toward your fingertips, make a quick motion with the fingers of the left hand. The mouse will be propelled up your arm. The mouse will appear to be alive. If you occasionally use enough force to let the mouse jump off your arm, the children shout with glee.

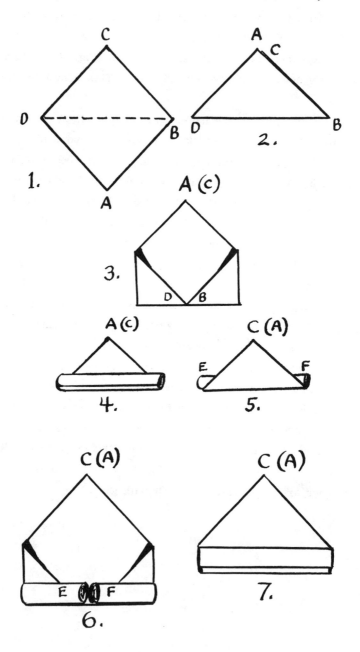

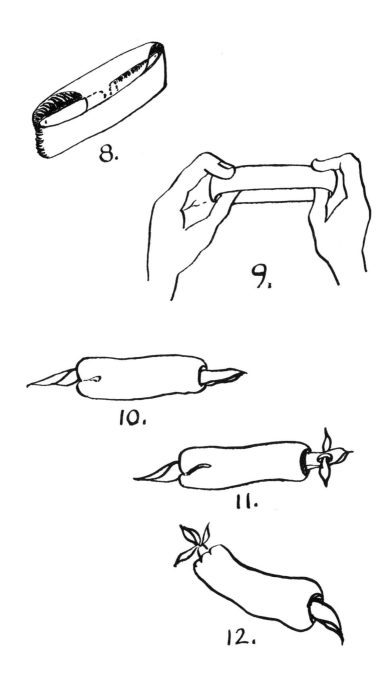

8.

9.

10.

11.

12.

GAMES

Ring Around the Rosie

Ring around the rosie,

Pocket full of posie.

One, two, three,

And we all stoop down.

(One child may stand in the of the circle to represent the rosie. The others circle around, hands joined. All stoop down at the last line.)

Did You Ever See a Lassie (or Laddie) Go This Way?

Did you ever see a lassie,

A lassie, a lassie

Did you ever see a lassie

Go this way and that?

(One child stands in the middle of the circle. The others circle around, hands joined.)

Go this way and that way,

Go this way and that way,

Did you ever see a lassie

Go this way and that?

(The child in the middle shows some action. The others drop hands and follow the action, which may be clapping hands, tapping one foot, nodding the head, swinging the arms, or other movement the child makes. He chooses another child and the game is repeated.)

Looby Loo

Here we go looby loo,

> (Hands joined, circle around, walking, gliding, or skipping.)

Here we go looby light.

Here we go looby loo,

All on a Saturday night.

1. I put my left hand in.

> (Actions to suit the words.)

I take my left hand out.

I give my hand a shake, shake, shake,

And turn myself about.

2. Repeat with right hand.
3. Repeat with left foot.
4. Repeat with right foot.
5. Repeat with little head.
6. Repeat with little self.

Here We Go Round the Mulberry Bush

This is a singing game which the children pantomime, with each child giving his own interpretation of the words. The children circle between each verse, repeating the first.

In addition to the traditional words, this music may be used for "Here we go round the Christmas tree, etc." "What do you want Old Santa to bring, etc.?" followed by pantomime of rocking a doll, skating, riding a rocking horse, chugging like a toy train, and other activities suggested by the children, ending with "So early Christmas morning."

1. Here we go round the mulberry bush

> (Hands joined, circle around, walking, gliding, or skipping.)

The mulberry bush, the mulberry bush.

Here we go round the mulberry bush

So early in the morning.

2. This is the way we wash our clothes,

Wash our clothes, wash our clothes,

> (Circle facing in, make motions of washing clothes on a wash board.)

This is the way we wash our clothes
So early Monday morning.

3. This is the way we iron our clothes,
Iron our clothes, iron our clothes.
(Motion of ironing.)
This is the way we iron our clothes
So early Tuesday morning.

4. This is the way we scrub our floors,
Scrub our floors, scrub our floors.
(Mopping motions.)
This is the way we scrub our floors
So early Wednesday morning.

5. This is the way we mend our clothes,
Mend our clothes, mend our clothes.
(Motions of sewing with needle and thread.)
This is the way we mend our clothes
So early Thursday morning.

6. This is the way we sweep the house,
Sweep the house, sweep the house.
(Wide sweeping motions.)
This is the way we sweep the house
So early Friday morning.

7. We play when all our work is done,
Our work is done, our work is done.
(Dance around the circle.)
We play when all our work is done
So early Saturday morning.

8. This is the way we go to church,
Go to church, go to church,
(Join hands and walk slowly around the circle.)

This is the way we go to church

So early Sunday morning.

London Bridge

London Bridge is falling down,

Falling down, falling down.

London Bridge is falling down,

My fair lady.

(Repeat until all the children
are caught.)

(Two children form a bridge by joining hands and holding them high. The others march in line under the bridge until one is caught on the last word.)

Froggie in the Middle

Froggie in the middle

Can't get out.

Froggie in the middle

Can't get out.

Poor little froggie

Can't get out.

(Choose one child to be the frog. The rest join hands and circle around.)

He hops to a friend

To let him out.

He hops to another

To let him out.

Out he jumps!

(Frog hops to two children who keep hands joined. On the last line, two hands are dropped and the frog jumps out. He chooses another frog to repeat the game.)

Books of Finger Plays, Games and Rhythms

Bevan, Edna, Christian Finger Plays and Games. Grand
     Rapids, Mich., Zondervan.

Ellis, Mary J., Finger Play Approach to Dramatization.
     Minneapolis, Minn.

Ellis, Mary J. and Lyons, Frances, Finger Playtime.
     Minneapolis, Minn.

Grayson, Marion F., Let's Do Fingerplays. Washington,
     D.C., Robert B. Luce, Inc., 1962.

Jacobs, Frances E., Finger Plays and Action Rhymes.
     New York, Lothrop.

Lewis, Shari and Jacquelyn Reinbach, Be Nimble and Be
     Quick. New York, McGraw-Hill.

Miller, Mary and Paul Zajan, Finger Plays. New York,
     G. Schirmer.

Montgomerie, Norah, This Little Pig Went to Market.
     New York, Franklin Watts, Inc. (Toe and Finger
     Counting, Foot Patting, Leg Wagging, Finger Plays,
     Hand Clapping, Jig Jogging, Singing Games.)

Pierce, June, (ed.), Wonder Book of Finger Plays and Ac-
     tion Rhymes. New York, Grosset. (Wonder Books)

Poulsson, Emilie, Finger Plays. New York, Lothrop.

Raebeck, Lois, Who Am I? Chicago, Follett. (Finger Plays
     and Activities.)

Romper Room Book of Finger Plays and Action Rhythms.
     New York, Grosset. (Wonder Books)

Scott, Louise B. and Thompson, J. J. Rhymes for Fingers
     and Flannelboards. New York, McGraw.

Yamaguchi, Marianne, Finger Plays. New York, Holt.
     (Full-color paintings illustrate sprightly rhymes.)

Recordings

A Child's Introduction to Rhythm. Gold LP99 (Rhythm.)

Activity Songs for Kids. Marcia Berman, Folk FC7023 (Rhythm.)

Adventures in Resting. Dec4204 (For quiet time - listening.)

American Game & Activity Songs for Children. Folk FC7002 (Games.)

Animal Rhythms. Ed. rec. R. R. 2 (Rhythm.)

Children Sing Around the Year. Dec DL4406 (Singing.)

Circus Time. Decca Records, DL 8451 (Circus marches and fanfare.)

Counting Games & Rhythms for the Little Ones. Folk FC7056 (Rhythm.)

Dance a Story About Little Duck. Vic LE101 (Rhythm.)

Dance a Story About Noah's Ark. Vic LE102 (Rhythm.)

Dance a Story - Balloons. Vic LE104 (Rhythm.)

Dance a Story - The Magic Mountain. Vic LE103 (Rhythm.)

Eensie, Beensie Spider. CRG1002 (Game; includes Skip to My Lou.)

Favorite Marches for Children. (The Children's Marching Chorus and the Toyland Band.) MGM CH109 (Rhythm Band.)

First Easter Record for Children. Columbia, HL 9555 (Peter Cottontail, Easter Parade and other favorite Easter music.)

Golden Treasury of Mother Goose & Nursery Songs. GRC12 (Singing.)

Golden Treasury of Train Songs. GR GLP33 (Rhythm.)

Happy Instruments. Col CL1026 (Rhythm Band.)

Hop, Skip and Sing. Pacific Cascade Records, LPL 7015
     (Activities.)

Jingle Bells and Other Songs for Winter Fun. Young People's
     Records, YPR 718 (Directed dramatic play.)

Lead a Little Orchestra. Col MJV115 (Rhythm Band.)

Let's Play a Musical Game. Harmony, HL 9522 (Directed
     activities.)

Let's Play Zoo. Sung by Tom Glazer, YPR802 (Rhythm.)

Little White Duck & Other Children's Favorites. Col HL
     9507 (Rhythm.)

Majorettes on Parade. Sta 1011 (Rhythm Band.)

Me, Myself and I. Young People's Records, YPR 10012.

Merry-Go-Sounds at the Zoo. BR101 (Rhythm.)

More Music Time and Stories. Folkways Records, FC 7528
     (Songs, dances and improvised expressive movements.)

Mother Goose. Read by Cyril Ritchard, Celeste Holm, and
     Boris Karloff, Coed TC1091 (Listening.)

My Playful Scarf. Children's Record Guild, 1019. (Dra-
     matic rhythmic movements.)

Party Time. Des DLP32 (Birthdays.)

Play Your Instruments and Make a Pretty Sound. Folkways
     Records, FC7665 (Rhythm band and song.)

Rainy Day. YPR712 (Rhythm.)

Singing Games. Educational Recordings of America, Inc.,
     SG1. (Group games and creative rhythmic activities.)

Sleep-Time. Folkways Records, FC7525. (Rhythmic ac-
     tivities, songs and stories.)

Strike Up the Band. (Creative and musical use of rhythm
     band instruments,) CRG5027.

This is Rhythm. Folk FC 7652.

Children's Small Records

Old MacDonald Had a Farm.

Down by the Station.

Parade of the Wooden Soldiers.

Here We Go, Looby Loo.

Happy Birthday.

Jingle Bells.

Rudolph, the Red-Nosed Reindeer.

Frosty, the Snowman.

I Wish You a Merry Christmas.

Silent Night.

There are many other small records for children suitable for the rhythm band, for marching, playing train, airplane and other rhythmic activities. There are also small records of Christmas music.

INDEX

THE COMPLETE NOVELS
OF
MARK TWAIN

THE PRINCE
AND THE PAUPER
*A Tale for Young People
of all Ages*

❀

THOSE
EXTRAORDINARY
TWINS

❀

BY

MARK TWAIN

NELSON DOUBLEDAY, Inc.
GARDEN CITY, NEW YORK

Published by arrangement with
HARPER & ROW, PUBLISHERS, INCORPORATED

TRADE (BY
S. L. CLEMENS.
MARK TWAIN.) MARK.

[TRADE MARK.]

To those good-mannered and agreeable
children, Susy and Clara Clemens, this book
is affectionately inscribed by their father

The quality of mercy . . .
                is twice bless'd;
It blesseth him that gives, and him that takes;
'Tis mightiest in the mightiest: it becomes
The thronèd monarch better than his crown.

Merchant of Venice.

CONTENTS

PREFACE

I WILL set down a tale as it was told to me by one who had it of his father, which latter had it of *his* father, this last having in like manner had it of *his* father—and so on, back and still back, three hundred years and more, the fathers transmitting it to the sons and so preserving it. It may be history, it may be only legend, a tradition. It may have happened, it may not have happened: but it *could* have happened. It may be that the wise and the learned believed it in the old days; it may be that only the unlearned and the simple loved it and credited it.

Hugh Latimer, *Bishop of Worcester,* to Lord Cromwell, *on the birth of the* Prince of Wales *(afterward* Edward VI.)

FROM THE NATIONAL MANUSCRIPTS
PRESERVED BY THE BRITISH GOVERNMENT

HUGH LATIMER, *Bishop of Worcester, to* LORD CROMWELL, *on the
birth of the* PRINCE OF WALES (*afterward* EDWARD VI.)

FROM THE NATIONAL MANUSCRIPT
PRESERVED BY THE BRITISH GOVERNMENT

Ryght honorable, *Salutem in Christo Jesu,* and Syr here ys no lesse
joynge and rejossynge in thes partees for the byrth of our prynce,
hoom we hungurde for so longe, then ther was (I trow), *inter vicinos*
att the byrth of S. I. Baptyste, as thys berer, Master Erance, can telle
you. Gode gyffe us alle grace, to yelde dew thankes to our Lorde
Gode, Gode of Inglonde, for verely He hathe shoyd Hym selff Gode
of Inglonde, or rather an Inglyssh Gode, yf we consydyr and pondyr
welle alle Hys procedynges with us from tyme to tyme. He hath over-
cumme alle our yllnesse with Hys excedynge goodnesse, so that we
ar now moor then compellyd to serve Hym, seke Hys glory, promott
Hys wurde, yf the Devylle of alle Devylles be natt in us. We have
now the stooppe of vayne trustes ande the stey of vayne expectations;
lett us alle pray for hys preservatione. And I for my partt wylle wyssh
that hys Grace allways have, and evyn now from the begynynge,
Governares, Instructores and offyceres of ryght jugmente, *ne optimum
ingenium non optimâ educatione depravetur.*

Butt whatt a grett fowlle am I! So, whatt devotione shoyth many
tymys butt lytelle dyscretione! Ande thus the Gode of Inglonde be
ever with you in alle your procedynges.

The 19 of October.

Youres, H. L. B. of Wurcestere, now att Hartlebury.

Yf you wolde excytt thys berere to be moore hartye ayen the abuse
of ymagry or mor forwarde to promotte the veryte, ytt myght doo
goode. Natt that ytt came of me, butt of your selffe, &c.

(*Addressed*) To the Ryght Honorable Loorde P. Sealle hys
synguler gode Lorde.

THE COMPLETE NOVELS
OF
MARK TWAIN

THE PRINCE
AND THE PAUPER

1

The Birth of the Prince and the Pauper

IN THE ANCIENT CITY of London, on a certain autumn day in the second quarter of the sixteenth century, a boy was born to a poor family of the name of Canty, who did not want him. On the same day another English child was born to a rich family of the name of Tudor, who did want him. All England wanted him too. England had so longed for him, and hoped for him, and prayed God for him, that, now that he was really come, the people went nearly mad for joy. Mere acquaintances hugged and kissed each other and cried. Everybody took a holiday, and high and low, rich and poor, feasted and danced and sang, and got very mellow; and they kept this up for days and nights together. By day, London was a sight to see, with gay banners waving from every balcony and housetop, and splendid pageants marching along. By night, it was again a sight to see, with its great bonfires at every corner, and its troops of revelers making merry around them. There was no talk in all England but of the new baby, Edward Tudor, Prince of Wales, who lay lapped in silks and satins, unconscious of all this fuss, and not knowing that great lords and ladies were tending him and watching over him—and not caring, either. But there was no talk about the other baby, Tom Canty, lapped in his poor rags, except among the family of paupers whom he had just come to trouble with his presence.

2

Tom's Early Life

LET US SKIP a number of years.

London was fifteen hundred years old, and was a great town—for that day. It had a hundred thousand inhabitants—some think double as many. The streets were very narrow, and crooked, and dirty, especially in the part where Tom Canty lived, which was not far from London Bridge. The houses were of wood, with the second story projecting over the first, and the third sticking its elbows out beyond the second. The higher the houses grew, the broader they grew. They were skeletons of strong crisscross beams, with solid material between, coated with plaster. The beams were painted red or blue or black, according to the owner's taste, and this gave the houses a very picturesque look. The windows were small, glazed with little diamond-shaped panes, and they opened outward, on hinges, like doors.

The house which Tom's father lived in was up a foul little pocket called Offal Court, out of Pudding Lane. It was small, decayed, and rickety, but it was packed full of wretchedly poor families. Canty's tribe occupied a room on the third floor. The mother and father had a sort of bedstead in the corner; but Tom, his grandmother, and his two sisters, Bet and Nan, were not restricted—they had all the floor to themselves, and might sleep where they chose. There were the remains of a blanket or two, and some bundles of ancient and dirty straw, but these could not rightly be called beds, for they were not organized; they were kicked into a general pile mornings, and selections made from the mass at night, for service.

Bet and Nan were fifteen years old—twins. They were good-hearted girls, unclean, clothed in rags, and profoundly ignorant. Their mother was like them. But the father and the grandmother were a couple of fiends. They got drunk whenever they could; then they fought each other or anybody else who came in the way; they cursed and swore always, drunk or sober; John Canty was a thief, and his mother a beggar. They made beggars of the children, but failed to make thieves of them. Among, but not of, the dreadful rabble that inhabited the house, was a good old priest whom the king had turned out of house and home with a pension of a few farthings, and he used to get the children aside and teach them right ways secretly. Father Andrew also taught Tom a little Latin, and how to read and write; and would have done the same with the girls, but they were afraid of the jeers of their friends, who could not have endured such a queer accomplishment in them.

All Offal Court was just such another hive as Canty's house. Drunkenness, riot, and brawling were the order there, every night and nearly all night long. Broken heads were as common as hunger in that place. Yet little Tom was not unhappy. He had a hard time of it, but did not know it. It was the sort of time that all the Offal Court boys had, therefore he supposed it was the correct and comfortable thing. When he came home empty-handed at night, he knew his father would curse him and thrash him first, and that when he was done the awful grandmother would do it all over again and improve on it; and that away in the night his starving mother would slip to him stealthily with any miserable scrap or crust she had been able to save for him by going hungry herself, notwithstanding she was often caught in that sort of treason and soundly beaten for it by her husband.

No, Tom's life went along well enough, especially in summer. He only begged just enough to save himself, for the laws against mendicancy were stringent, and the penalties heavy; so he put in a good deal of his time listening to good Father Andrew's charming old tales and legends about giants and fairies, dwarfs and genii, and enchanted castles, and gorgeous kings and princes. His head grew to be full of these wonderful things, and many a night as he lay in the dark on his scant and offensive straw, tired, hungry, and smarting from a thrashing, he unleashed his imagination and soon forgot his aches and pains in delicious picturings to himself of the charmed life of a petted prince in a regal palace. One desire came in time to haunt him day and night; it was to see a real prince, with his own eyes. He spoke of it once to some of his Offal Court comrades; but they jeered him and scoffed him so unmercifully that he was glad to keep his dream to himself after that.

He often read the priest's old books and got him to explain and enlarge upon them. His dreamings and readings worked certain changes in him by and by. His dream-people were so fine that he grew to lament his shabby clothing and his dirt, and to wish to be clean and better clad. He went on playing in the mud just the same, and enjoying it, too; but instead of splashing around in the Thames solely for the fun of it, he began to find an added value in it because of the washings and cleansings it afforded.

Tom could always find something going on around the Maypole in Cheapside, and at the fairs; and now and then he and the rest of London had a chance to see a military parade when some famous unfortunate was carried prisoner to the Tower, by land or boat. One summer's day he saw poor Anne Askew and three men burned at the stake in Smithfield, and heard an ex-bishop preach a sermon to them which did not interest him. Yes, Tom's life was varied and pleasant enough, on the whole.

By and by Tom's reading and dreaming about princely life wrought such a strong effect upon him that he began to *act* the prince, unconsciously. His speech and manners became curiously ceremonious and courtly, to the vast admiration and amusement of his intimates. But Tom's influence among these young people began to grow now, day by day; and in time he came to be looked up to by them with a sort of wondering awe, as a superior being. He seemed to know so much! and he could do and say such marvelous things! and withal, he was so deep and wise! Tom's remarks and Tom's performances were reported by the boys to their elders; and these, also, presently began to discuss Tom Canty, and to regard him as a most gifted and extraordinary creature. Full-grown people brought their perplexities to Tom for solution, and were often astonished at the wit and wisdom of his decisions. In fact, he was become a hero to all who knew him except his own family—these only saw nothing in him.

Privately, after a while, Tom organized a royal court! He was the prince; his special comrades were guards, chamberlains, equerries, lords and ladies in waiting, and the royal family. Daily the mock prince was received with elaborate ceremonials borrowed by Tom from his romantic readings; daily the great affairs of the mimic kingdom were discussed in the royal council, and daily his mimic highness issued decrees to his imaginary armies, navies, and viceroyalties.

After which he would go forth in his rags and beg a few farthings, eat his poor crust, take his customary cuffs and abuse, and then stretch himself upon his handful of foul straw, and resume his empty grandeurs in his dreams.

And still his desire to look just once upon a real prince, in the flesh, grew upon him, day by day, and week by week, until at last it absorbed all other desires, and became the one passion of his life.

One January day, on his usual begging tour, he tramped despondently up and down the region round about Mincing Lane and Little East Cheap, hour after hour, barefooted and cold, looking in at cook-shop windows and longing for the dreadful pork-pies and other deadly inventions displayed there—for to him these were dainties fit for the angels; that is, judging by the smell, they were—for it had never been his good luck to own and eat one. There was a cold drizzle of rain; the atmosphere was murky; it was a melancholy day. At night Tom reached home so wet and tired and hungry that it was not possible for his father and grandmother to observe his forlorn condition and not be moved—after their fashion; wherefore they gave him a brisk cuffing at once and sent him to bed. For a long time his pain and hunger, and the swearing and fighting going on in the building, kept him awake; but at last his thoughts drifted away to far, romantic lands, and he fell asleep in the company of jeweled and gilded princelings who lived in vast palaces, and had servants salaaming before them or flying to execute their orders. And then, as usual, he dreamed that *he* was a princeling himself.

All night long the glories of his royal estate shone upon him; he moved among great lords and ladies, in a blaze of light, breathing perfumes, drinking in delicious music, and answering the reverent obeisances of the glittering throng as it parted to make way for him, with here a smile, and there a nod of his princely head.

And when he awoke in the morning and looked upon the wretchedness about him, his dream had had its usual effect—it had intensified the sordidness of his surroundings a thousandfold. Then came bitterness, and heartbreak, and tears.

3

Tom's Meeting with the Prince

TOM GOT UP hungry, and sauntered hungry away, but with his thoughts busy with the shadowy splendors of his night's dreams. He wandered here and there in the city, hardly noticing where he was going, or what was happening around him. People jostled him and some gave him rough speech; but it was all lost on the musing boy. By and by he found himself at Temple Bar, the farthest from home he had ever traveled in that direction. He stopped and considered a moment, then fell into his imaginings again, and passed on outside the walls of London. The Strand had ceased to be a country-road then, and regarded itself as a street, but by a strained construction; for, though there was a tolerably compact row of houses on one side of it, there were only some scattering great buildings on the other, these being palaces of rich nobles, with ample and beautiful grounds stretching to the river—grounds that are now closely packed with grim acres of brick and stone.

Tom discovered Charing Village presently, and rested himself at the beautiful cross built there by a bereaved king of earlier days; then idled down a quiet, lovely road, past the great cardinal's stately palace, toward a far more mighty and majestic palace beyond—Westminster. Tom stared in glad wonder at the vast pile of masonry, the wide-spreading wings, the frowning bastions and turrets, the huge stone gateway, with its gilded bars and its magnificent array of colossal granite lions, and the other signs and symbols of English royalty. Was the desire of his soul to be satisfied at last? Here, indeed, was a king's palace. Might he not hope to see a prince now—a prince of flesh and blood, if Heaven were willing?

At each side of the gilded gate stood a living statue, that is to say, an erect and stately and motionless man-at-arms, clad from head to heel in shining steel armor. At a respectful distance were many country-folk, and people from the city, waiting for any chance glimpse of royalty that might offer. Splendid carriages, with splendid people in them and splendid servants outside, were arriving and departing by several other noble gateways that pierced the royal inclosure.

Poor little Tom, in his rags, approached, and was moving slowly and timidly past the sentinels, with a beating heart and a rising hope, when all at once he caught sight through the golden bars of a spectacle that almost made him shout for joy. Within was a comely boy, tanned and brown with sturdy outdoor sports and exercises, whose clothing was all of lovely silks and satins, shining with jewels; at his hip a little jeweled sword and dagger; dainty buskins on his feet, with red heels; and on his head a jaunty crimson cap, with drooping plumes fastened with a great sparkling gem. Several gorgeous gentlemen stood near—his servants, without a doubt. Oh! he was a prince—a prince, a living prince, a real prince—without the shadow of a question; and the prayer of the pauper boy's heart was answered at last.

Tom's breath came quick and short with excitement, and his eyes grew big with wonder and delight. Everything gave way in his mind instantly to one desire: that was to get close to the prince, and have a good, devouring look at him. Before he knew what he was about, he had his face against the gate-bars. The next instant one of the soldiers snatched him rudely away, and sent him spinning among the gaping crowd of country gawks and London idlers. The soldier said:

"Mind thy manners, thou young beggar!"

The crowd jeered and laughed; but the young prince sprang to the gate with his face flushed, and his eyes flashing with indignation, and cried out:

"How dar'st thou use a poor lad like that! How dar'st thou use the king my father's meanest subject so! Open the gates, and let him in!"

You should have seen that fickle crowd snatch off their hats then. You should have heard them cheer, and shout, "Long live the Prince of Wales!"

The soldiers presented arms with their halberds, opened the gates, and presented again as the little Prince of Poverty passed in, in his fluttering rags, to join hands with the Prince of Limitless Plenty.

Edward Tudor said:

"Thou lookest tired and hungry; thou'st been treated ill. Come with me."

Half a dozen attendants sprang forward to—I don't know what; interfere, no doubt. But they were waved aside with a right royal gesture, and they stopped stock still where they were, like so many statues. Edward took Tom to a rich apartment in the palace, which he called his cabinet. By his command a repast was brought such as Tom had never encountered before except in books. The prince, with princely delicacy and breeding, sent away the servants, so that his humble guest might not be embarrassed by their critical presence; then he sat near by, and asked questions while Tom ate.

"What is thy name, lad?"

"Tom Canty, an it please thee, sir."

"'Tis an odd one. Where dost live?"

"In the city, please thee, sir. Offal Court, out of Pudding Lane."

"Offal Court! Truly, 'tis another odd one. Hast parents?"

"Parents have I, sir, and a grandam likewise that is but indifferently precious to me, God forgive me if it be offense to say it—also twin sisters, Nan and Bet."

"Then is thy grandam not overkind to thee, I take it."

"Neither to any other is she, so please your worship. She hath a wicked heart, and worketh evil all her days."

"Doth she mistreat thee?"

"There be times that she stayeth her hand, being asleep or overcome with drink; but when she hath her judgment clear again, she maketh it up to me with goodly beatings."

A fierce look came into the little prince's eyes, and he cried out: "What! Beatings?"

"Oh, indeed, yes, please you, sir."

"*Beatings!*—and thou so frail and little. Hark ye: before the night come, she shall hie her to the Tower. The king my father—"

"In sooth, you forget, sir, her low degree. The Tower is for the great alone."

"True, indeed. I had not thought of that. I will consider of her punishment. Is thy father kind to thee?"

"Not more than Gammer Canty, sir."

"Fathers be alike, mayhap. Mine hath not a doll's temper. He smiteth with a heavy hand, yet spareth me: he spareth me not always with his tongue, though, sooth to say. How doth thy mother use thee?"

"She is good, sir, and giveth me neither sorrow nor pain of any sort. And Nan and Bet are like to her in this."

"How old be these?"

"Fifteen, an it please you, sir."

"The Lady Elizabeth, my sister, is fourteen, and the Lady Jane Grey, my cousin, is of mine own age, and comely and gracious withal; but my sister the Lady Mary, with her gloomy mien and— Look you: do thy sisters forbid their servants to smile, lest the sin destroy their souls?"

"They? Oh, dost think, sir, that *they* have servants?"

The little prince contemplated the little pauper gravely a moment, then said:

"And prithee, why not? Who helpeth them undress at night? who attireth them when they rise?"

"None, sir. Wouldst have them take off their garment, and sleep without—like the beasts?"

"Their garment! Have they but one?"

"Ah, good your worship, what would they do with more? Truly, they have not two bodies each."

"It is a quaint and marvelous thought! Thy pardon, I had not meant to laugh. But thy good Nan and thy Bet shall have raiment and lackeys enow, and that soon, too: my cofferer shall look to it. No, thank me not; 'tis nothing. Thou speakest well; thou hast an easy grace in it. Art learned?"

"I know not if I am or not, sir. The good priest that is called Father Andrew taught me, of his kindness, from his books."

"Know'st thou the Latin?"

"But scantily, sir, I doubt."

"Learn it, lad: 'tis hard only at first. The Greek is harder; but neither these nor any tongues else, I think, are hard to the Lady Elizabeth and my cousin. Thou shouldst hear those damsels at it! But tell me of thy Offal Court. Hast thou a pleasant life there?"

"In truth, yes, so please you, sir, save when one is hungry. There be Punch-and-Judy shows, and monkeys—oh, such antic creatures! and so bravely dressed!—and there be plays wherein they that play do shout and fight till all are slain, and 'tis so fine to see, and costeth but a farthing—albeit 'tis main hard to get the farthing, please your worship."

"Tell me more."

"We lads of Offal Court do strive against each other with the cudgel, like to the fashion of the 'prentices, sometimes."

The prince's eyes flashed. Said he:

"Marry, that would I not mislike. Tell me more."

"We strive in races, sir, to see who of us shall be fleetest."

"That would I like also. Speak on."

"In summer, sir, we wade and swim in the canals and in the river, and each doth duck his neighbor, and spatter him with water, and dive and shout and tumble and—"

" 'Twould be worth my father's kingdom but to enjoy it once! Prithee go on."

"We dance and sing about the Maypole in Cheapside; we play in the sand, each covering his neighbor up; and times we make mud pastry—oh, the lovely mud, it hath not its like for delightfulness in all the world!—we do fairly wallow in the mud, sir, saving your worship's presence."

"Oh, prithee, say no more, 'tis glorious! If that I could but clothe me in raiment like to thine, and strip my feet, and revel in the mud once, just once, with none to rebuke me or forbid, meseemeth I could forego the crown!"

"And if that I could clothe me once, sweet sir, as thou art clad —just once—"

"Oho, wouldst like it? Then so shall it be. Doff thy rags, and don these splendors, lad! It is a brief happiness, but will be not less keen for that. We will have it while we may, and change again before any come to molest."

A few minutes later the little Prince of Wales was garlanded with Tom's fluttering odds and ends, and the little Prince of Pauperdom was tricked out in the gaudy plumage of royalty. The two went and stood side by side before a great mirror, and lo, a miracle: there did not seem to have been any change made! They stared at each other, then at the glass, then at each other again. At last the puzzled princeling said:

"What dost thou make of this?"

"Ah, good your worship, require me not to answer. It is not meet that one of my degree should utter the thing."

"Then will I utter it. Thou hast the same hair, the same eyes, the same voice and manner, the same form and stature, the same face and countenance, that I bear. Fared we forth naked, there is none could say which was you, and which the Prince of Wales. And, now that I am clothed as thou wert clothed, it seemeth I should be able the more nearly to feel as thou didst when the brute soldier— Hark ye, is not this a bruise upon your hand?"

"Yes; but it is a slight thing, and your worship knoweth that the poor man-at-arms—"

"Peace! It was a shameful thing and a cruel!" cried the little prince, stamping his bare foot. "If the king— Stir not a step till I come again! It is a command!"

In a moment he had snatched up and put away an article of national importance that lay upon a table, and was out at the door and flying through the palace grounds in his bannered rags, with a hot face and glowing eyes. As soon as he reached the great gate, he seized the bars, and tried to shake them, shouting:

"Open! Unbar the gates!"

The soldier that had maltreated Tom obeyed promptly; and as the prince burst through the portal, half smothered with royal wrath, the soldier fetched him a sounding box on the ear that sent him whirling to the roadway, and said:

"Take that, thou beggar's spawn for what thou got'st me from his Highness!"

The crowd roared with laughter. The prince picked himself out of the mud, and made fiercely at the sentry, shouting:

"I am the Prince of Wales, my person is sacred; and thou shalt hang for laying thy hand upon me!"

The soldier brought his halberd to a present-arms and said mockingly:

"I salute your gracious Highness." Then angrily, "Be off, thou crazy rubbish!"

Here the jeering crowd closed around the poor little prince, and hustled him far down the road, hooting him, and shouting, "Way for his royal Highness! way for the Prince of Wales!"

4

The Prince's Troubles Begin

AFTER HOURS of persistent pursuit and persecution, the little prince was at last deserted by the rabble and left to himself. As long as he had been able to rage against the mob, and threaten it royally, and royally utter commands that were good stuff to laugh at, he was very entertaining; but when weariness finally forced him to be silent, he was no longer of use to his tormentors, and they sought amusement elsewhere. He looked about him now, but could not recognize the locality. He was within the city of London—that was all he knew. He moved on, aimlessly, and in a little while the houses thinned, and the passers-by were infrequent. He bathed his bleeding feet in the brook which flowed then where Farringdon Street now is; rested a few moments, then passed on, and presently came upon a great space with only a few scattered houses in it, and a prodigious church. He recognized this church. Scaffoldings were about, everywhere, and swarms of workmen; for it was undergoing elaborate repairs. The prince took heart at once—he felt that his troubles were at an end now. He said to himself, "It is the ancient Grey Friars' church, which the king my father hath taken from the monks and given for a home forever for poor and forsaken children, and new-named it Christ's church. Right gladly will they serve the son of him who hath done so generously by them—and the more that that son is himself as poor and as forlorn as any that be sheltered here this day, or ever shall be."

He was soon in the midst of a crowd of boys who were running, jumping, playing at ball and leap-frog and otherwise disporting themselves, and right noisily, too. They were all dressed alike, and in the fashion which in that day prevailed among serving-men and 'prentices—that is to say, each had on the crown of his head a flat black cap about the size of a saucer, which was not useful as a covering, it being of such scanty dimensions, neither was it ornamental; from beneath it the hair fell, unparted, to the middle of the forehead, and was cropped straight around; a clerical band at the neck; a blue gown that fitted closely and hung as low as the knees or lower; full sleeves; a broad red belt; bright yellow stockings, gartered above the knees; low shoes with large metal buckles. It was a sufficiently ugly costume.

The boys stopped their play and flocked about the prince, who said with native dignity:

"Good lads, say to your master that Edward Prince of Wales desireth speech with him."

A great shout went up at this, and one rude fellow said:

"Marry, art thou his grace's messenger, beggar?"

The prince's face flushed with anger, and his ready hand flew to his hip, but there was nothing there. There was a storm of laughter, and one boy said:

"Didst mark that? He fancied he had a sword—belike he is the prince himself."

This sally brought more laughter. Poor Edward drew himself up proudly and said:

"I am the prince; and it ill beseemeth you that feed upon the king my father's bounty to use me so."

This was vastly enjoyed, as the laughter testified. The youth who had first spoken shouted to his comrades:

"Ho, swine, slaves, pensioners of his grace's princely father, where be your manners? Down on your marrow bones, all of ye, and do reverence to his kingly port and royal rags!"

With boisterous mirth they dropped upon their knees in a body and did mock homage to their prey. The prince spurned the near-est boy with his foot, and said fiercely:

"Take thou that, till the morrow come and I build thee a gibbet!"

Ah, but this was not a joke—this was going beyond fun. The

laughter ceased on the instant, and fury took its place. A dozen shouted:

"Hale him forth! To the horse-pond, to the horse-pond! Where be the dogs? Ho, there, Lion! ho, Fangs!"

Then followed such a thing as England had never seen before —the sacred person of the heir to the throne rudely buffeted by plebeian hands, and set upon and torn by dogs.

As night drew to a close that day, the prince found himself far down in the close-built portion of the city. His body was bruised, his hands were bleeding, and his rags were all besmirched with mud. He wandered on and on, and grew more and more bewildered, and so tired and faint he could hardly drag one foot after the other. He had ceased to ask questions of any one, since they brought him only insult instead of information. He kept muttering to himself, "Offal Court—that is the name; if I can but find it before my strength is wholly spent and I drop, then am I saved—for his people will take me to the palace and prove that I am none of theirs, but the true prince, and I shall have mine own again." And now and then his mind reverted to his treatment by those rude Christ's Hospital boys, and he said, "When I am king, they shall not have bread and shelter only, but also teachings out of books; for a full belly is little worth where the mind is starved, and the heart. I will keep this diligently in my remembrance, that this day's lesson be not lost upon me, and my people suffer thereby; for learning softeneth the heart and breedeth gentleness and charity."

The lights began to twinkle, it came on to rain, the wind rose, and a raw and gusty night set in. The houseless prince, the homeless heir to the throne of England, still moved on, drifting deeper into the maze of squalid alleys where the swarming hives of poverty and misery were massed together.

Suddenly a great drunken ruffian collared him and said:

"Out to this time of night again, and hast not brought a farthing home, I warrant me! If it be so, an I do not break all the bones in thy lean body, then am I not John Canty, but some other."

The prince twisted himself loose, unconsciously brushed his profaned shoulder, and eagerly said:

"Oh, art *his* father, truly? Sweet heaven grant it be so—then wilt thou fetch him away and restore me!"

"*His* father? I know not what thou mean'st; I but know I am *thy* father, as thou shalt soon have cause to—"

"Oh, jest not, palter not, delay not!—I am worn, I am wounded, I can bear no more. Take me to the king my father, and he will make thee rich beyond thy wildest dreams. Believe me, man, believe me!—I speak no lie, but only the truth!—put forth thy hand and save me! I am indeed the Prince of Wales!"

The man stared down, stupefied, upon the lad, then shook his head and muttered:

"Gone stark mad as any Tom o' Bedlam!"—then collared him once more, and said with a coarse laugh and an oath, "but mad or no mad, I and thy Gammer Canty will soon find where the soft places in thy bones lie, or I'm no true man!"

With this he dragged the frantic and struggling prince away, and disappeared up a front court followed by a delighted and noisy swarm of human vermin.

5

Tom as a Patrician

Tom Canty, left alone in the prince's cabinet, made good use of his opportunity. He turned himself this way and that before the great mirror, admiring his finery; then walked away, imitating the prince's high-bred carriage, and still observing results in the glass. Next he drew the beautiful sword, and bowed, kissing the blade, and laying it across his breast, as he had seen a noble knight do, by way of salute to the lieutenant of the Tower, five or six weeks before, when delivering the great lords of Norfolk and Surrey into his hands for captivity. Tom played with the jeweled dagger that hung upon his thigh; he examined the costly and exquisite ornaments of the room; he tried each of the sumptuous chairs, and thought how proud he would be if the Offal Court herd could only peep in and see him in his grandeur. He wondered if they would believe the marvelous tale he should tell when he got home, or if they would shake their heads, and say his overtaxed imagination had at last upset his reason.

At the end of half an hour it suddenly occurred to him that the prince was gone a long time; then right away he began to feel lonely; very soon he fell to listening and longing, and ceased to toy with the pretty things about him; he grew uneasy, then restless, then distressed. Suppose some one should come, and catch him in the prince's clothes, and the prince not there to explain. Might they not hang him at once, and inquire into his case afterward? He had heard that the great were prompt about small matters. His fears rose higher and higher; and trembling he softly opened the door to the antechamber, resolved to fly and seek the prince, and through him, protection and release. Six gorgeous gentlemen-servants and two young pages of high degree, clothed like butterflies, sprung to their feet, and bowed low before him. He stepped quickly back, and shut the door. He said:

"Oh, they mock at me! They will go and tell. Oh! why came I here to cast away my life?"

He walked up and down the floor, filled with nameless fears, listening, starting at every trifling sound. Presently the door swung open, and a silken page said:

"The Lady Jane Grey."

The door closed, and a sweet young girl, richly clad, bounded toward him. But she stopped suddenly, and said in a distressed voice:

"Oh, what aileth thee, my lord?"

Tom's breath was nearly failing him; but he made shift to stammer out:

"Ah, be merciful, thou! In sooth I am no lord, but only poor Tom Canty of Offal Court in the city. Prithee let me see the prince, and he will of his grace restore to me my rags, and let me hence unhurt. Oh, be thou merciful, and save me!"

By this time the boy was on his knees, and supplicating with his eyes and uplifted hands as well as with his tongue. The young girl seemed horror-stricken. She cried out:

"Oh, my lord, on thy knees?—and to *me!*"

Then she fled away in fright; and Tom, smitten with despair, sank down, murmuring:

"There is no help, there is no hope. Now will they come and take me."

Whilst he lay there benumbed with terror, dreadful tidings were speeding through the palace. The whisper, for it was whispered always, flew from menial to menial, from lord to lady, down all the long corridors, from story to story, from saloon to saloon, "The prince hath gone mad, the prince hath gone mad!" Soon every saloon, every marble hall, had its groups of glittering lords and ladies, and other groups of dazzling lesser folk, talking earnestly together in whispers, and every face had in it dismay. Presently a splendid official came marching by these groups, making solemn proclamation:

"IN THE NAME OF THE KING.

Let none list to this false and foolish matter, upon pain of death, nor discuss the same, nor carry it abroad. In the name of the king!"

The whisperings ceased as suddenly as if the whisperers had been stricken dumb.

Soon there was a general buzz along the corridors, of "The prince! See, the prince comes!"

Poor Tom came slowly walking past the low-bowing groups, trying to bow in return, and meekly gazing upon his strange surroundings with bewildered and pathetic eyes. Great nobles walked upon each side of him, making him lean upon them, and so steady his steps. Behind him followed the court physicians and some servants.

Presently Tom found himself in a noble apartment of the palace, and heard the door close behind him. Around him stood those who had come with him.

Before him, at a little distance, reclined a very large and very fat man, with a wide, pulpy face, and a stern expression. His large head was very gray; and his whiskers, which he wore only around his face, like a frame, were gray also. His clothing was of rich stuff, but old, and slightly frayed in places. One of his swollen legs had a pillow under it, and was wrapped in bandages. There was silence now; and there was no head there but was bent in reverence, except this man's. This stern-countenanced invalid was the dread Henry VIII. He said—and his face grew gentle as he began to speak:

"How now, my lord Edward, my prince? Hast been minded to cozen me, the good king thy father, who loveth thee, and kindly useth thee, with a sorry jest?"

Poor Tom was listening, as well as his dazed faculties would let him, to the beginning of this speech; but when the words "me the good king" fell upon his ear, his face blanched, and he dropped as instantly upon his knees as if a shot had brought him there. Lifting up his hands, he exclaimed:

"Thou the *king*? Then am I undone indeed!"

This speech seemed to stun the king. His eyes wandered from face to face aimlessly, then rested, bewildered, upon the boy before him. Then he said in a tone of deep disappointment:

"Alack, I had believed the rumor disproportioned to the truth; but I fear me 'tis not so." He breathed a heavy sigh, and said in a gentle voice, "Come to thy father, child; thou art not well."

Tom was assisted to his feet, and approached the Majesty of England, humble and trembling. The king took the frightened face between his hands, and gazed earnestly and lovingly into it awhile, as if seeking some grateful sign of returning reason there, then pressed the curly head against his breast, and patted it tenderly. Presently he said:

"Dost thou know thy father, child? Break not mine old heart; say thou know'st me. Thou *dost* know me, dost thou not?"

"Yea; thou art my dread lord the king, whom God preserve!"

"True, true—that is well—be comforted, tremble not so; there is none here who would hurt thee; there is none here but loves thee. Thou art better now; thy ill dream passeth—is't not so? And thou knowest thyself now also—is't not so? Thou wilt not miscall thyself again, as they say thou didst a little while agone?"

"I pray thee of thy grace believe me, I did but speak the truth, most dread lord; for I am the meanest among thy subjects, being a pauper born, and 'tis by a sore mischance and accident I am here, albeit I was therein nothing blameful. I am but young to die, and thou canst save me with one little word. Oh, speak it, sir!"

"Die? Talk not so, sweet prince—peace, peace, to thy troubled heart—thou shalt not die!"

Tom dropped upon his knees with a glad cry:

"God requite thy mercy, oh my king, and save thee long to bless thy land!" Then springing up, he turned a joyful face toward the two lords in waiting, and exclaimed, "Thou heard'st it! I am not to die: the king hath said it!" There was no movement, save that all bowed with grave respect; but no one spoke. He hesitated, a little confused, then turned timidly toward the king, saying, "I may go now?"

"Go? Surely, if thou desirest. But why not tarry yet a little? Whither wouldst go?"

Tom dropped his eyes, and answered humbly:

"Peradventure I mistook; but I did think me free, and so was I moved to seek again the kennel where I was born and bred to misery, yet which harboreth my mother and my sisters, and so is home to me; whereas these pomps and splendors whereunto I am not used—oh, please you, sir, to let me go!"

The king was silent and thoughtful awhile, and his face betrayed a growing distress and uneasiness. Presently he said, with something of hope in his voice:

"Perchance he is but mad upon this one strain, and hath his wits unmarred as toucheth other matter. God send it may be so! We will make trial."

Then he asked Tom a question in Latin, and Tom answered him lamely in the same tongue. The king was delighted, and showed it. The lords and doctors manifested their gratification also. The king said:

" 'Twas not according to his schooling and ability, but sheweth that his mind is but diseased, not stricken fatally. How say you, sir?"

The physician addressed bowed low, and replied:

"It jumpeth with mine own conviction, sire, that thou hast divined aright."

The king looked pleased with this encouragement, coming as it did from so excellent authority, and continued with good heart:

"Now mark ye all: we will try him further."

He put a question to Tom in French. Tom stood silent a moment, embarrassed by having so many eyes centered upon him, then said diffidently:

"I have no knowledge of this tongue, so please your majesty."

The king fell back upon his couch. The attendants flew to his assistance; but he put them aside, and said:

"Trouble me not—it is nothing but a scurvy faintness. Raise me! there, 'tis sufficient. Come hither, child; there, rest thy poor troubled head upon thy father's heart, and be at peace. Thou'lt soon be well; 'tis but a passing fantasy. Fear thou not; thou'lt soon be well." Then he turned toward the company; his gentle manner changed, and baleful lightnings began to play from his eyes. He said:

"List ye all! This my son is mad; but it is not permanent. Over-study hath done this, and somewhat too much of confinement. Away with his books and teachers! see ye to it. Pleasure him with sports, beguile him in wholesome ways, so that his health come again." He raised himself higher still, and went on with energy. "He is mad; but he is my son, and England's heir; and, mad or sane, still shall he reign! And hear ye further, and proclaim it: whoso speaketh of this his distemper worketh against the peace and order of these realms, and shall to the gallows! . . . Give me to drink—I burn: This sorrow sappeth my strength. . . . There, take away the cup. . . . Support me. There, that is well. Mad, is he? Were he a thousand times mad, yet is he

Prince of Wales, and I the king will confirm it. This very morrow shall he be installed in his princely dignity in due and ancient form. Take instant order for it, my Lord Hertford."

One of the nobles knelt at the royal couch, and said:

"The king's majesty knoweth that the Hereditary Great Marshal of England lieth attainted in the Tower. It were not meet that one attainted—"

"Peace! Insult not mine ears with his hated name. Is this man to live forever? Am I to be balked of my will? Is the prince to tarry uninstalled, because, forsooth, the realm lacketh an earl marshal free of treasonable taint to invest him with his honors? No, by the splendor of God! Warn my parliament to bring me Norfolk's doom before the sun rise again, else shall they answer for it grievously!"

Lord Hertford said:

"The king's will is law"; and, rising, returned to his former place.

Gradually the wrath faded out of the old king's face, and he said:

"Kiss me, my prince. There . . . what fearest thou? Am I not thy loving father?"

"Thou art good to me that am unworthy, O mighty and gracious lord; that in truth I know. But—but—it grieveth me to think of him that is to die, and—"

"Ah, 'tis like thee, 'tis like thee! I know thy heart is still the same, even though thy mind hath suffered hurt, for thou wert ever of a gentle spirit. But this duke standeth between thee and thine honors: I will have another in his stead that shall bring no taint to his great office. Comfort thee, my prince: trouble not thy poor head with this matter."

"But is it not I that speed him hence, my liege? How long might he not live, but for me?"

"Take no thought of him, my prince: he is not worthy. Kiss me once again, and go to thy trifles and amusements; for my malady distresseth me. I am aweary, and would rest. Go with thine uncle Hertford and thy people, and come again when my body is refreshed."

Tom, heavy-hearted, was conducted from the presence, for this last sentence was a death-blow to the hope he had cherished that now he would be set free. Once more he heard the buzz of low voices exclaiming, "The prince, the prince comes!"

His spirits sank lower and lower as he moved between the glittering files of bowing courtiers; for he recognized that he was indeed a captive now, and might remain forever shut up in this gilded cage, a forlorn and friendless prince, except God in his mercy take pity on him and set him free.

And, turn where he would, he seemed to see floating in the air the severed head and the remembered face of the great Duke of Norfolk, the eyes fixed on him reproachfully.

His old dreams had been so pleasant; but this reality was so dreary!

6

Tom Receives Instructions

Tom was conducted to the principal apartment of a noble suite, and made to sit down—a thing which he was loath to do, since there were elderly men and men of high degree about him. He begged them to be seated, also, but they only bowed their thanks or murmured them, and remained standing. He would have insisted, but his "uncle," the Earl of Hertford, whispered in his ear:

"Prithee, insist not, my lord; it is not meet that they sit in thy presence."

The Lord St. John was announced, and, after making obeisance to Tom, he said:

"I come upon the king's errand, concerning a matter which

requireth privacy. Will it please your royal highness to dismiss all that attend you here, save my lord the Earl of Hertford?"

Observing that Tom did not seem to know how to proceed, Hertford whispered him to make a sign with his hand and not trouble himself to speak unless he chose. When the waiting gentlemen had retired, Lord St. John said:

"His majesty commandeth, that for due and weighty reasons of state, the prince's grace shall hide his infirmity in all ways that be within his power, till it be passed and he be as he was before. To wit, that he shall deny to none that he is the true prince, and heir to England's greatness; that he shall uphold his princely dignity, and shall receive, without word or sign of protest, that reverence and observance which unto it do appertain of right and ancient usage; that he shall cease to speak to any of that lowly birth and life his malady hath conjured out of the unwholesome imaginings of o'erwrought fancy; that he shall strive with diligence to bring unto his memory again those faces which he was wont to know—and where he faileth he shall hold his peace, neither betraying by semblance of surprise, or other sign, that he hath forgot; that upon occasions of state, whensoever any matter shall perplex him as to the thing he should do or the utterance he should make, he shall show naught of unrest to the curious that look on, but take advice in that matter of the Lord Hertford, or my humble self, which are commanded of the king to be upon this service and close at call, till this commandment be dissolved. Thus saith the king's majesty, who sendeth greeting to your royal highness and prayeth that God will of His mercy quickly heal you and have you now and ever in His holy keeping."

The Lord St. John made reverence and stood aside. Tom replied, resignedly:

"The king hath said it. None may palter with the king's command, or fit it to his ease, where it doth chafe, with deft evasions. The king shall be obeyed."

Lord Hertford said:

"Touching the king's majesty's ordainment concerning books and such like serious matters, it may peradventure please your highness to ease your time with lightsome entertainment, lest you go wearied to the banquet and suffer harm thereby."

Tom's face showed inquiring surprise; and a blush followed when he saw Lord St. John's eyes bent sorrowfully upon him. His lordship said:

"Thy memory still wrongeth thee, and thou hast shown surprise—but suffer it not to trouble thee, for 'tis a matter that will not bide, but depart with thy mending malady. My Lord of Hertford speaketh of the city's banquet which the king's majesty did promise two months flown, your highness should attend. Thou recallest it now?"

"It grieves me to confess it had indeed escaped me," said Tom, in a hesitating voice; and blushed again.

At that moment the Lady Elizabeth and the Lady Jane Grey were announced. The two lords exchanged significant glances, and Hertford stepped quickly toward the door. As the young girls passed him, he said in a low voice:

"I pray ye, ladies, seem not to observe his humors, nor show surprise when his memory doth lapse—it will grieve you to note how it doth stick at every trifle."

Meanwhile Lord St. John was saying in Tom's ear:

"Please you, sir, keep diligently in mind his majesty's desire. Remember all thou canst—*seem* to remember all else. Let them not perceive that thou art much changed from thy wont, for thou knowest how tenderly thy old playfellows bear thee in their hearts and how 'twould grieve them. Art willing, sir, that I remain?—and thine uncle?"

Tom signified assent with a gesture and a murmured word, for he was already learning, and in his simple heart was resolved to acquit himself as best he might, according to the king's command.

In spite of every precaution, the conversation among the young people became a little embarrassing at times. More than once, in truth, Tom was near to breaking down and confessing himself unequal to his tremendous part; but the tact of the Princess Elizabeth saved him, or a word from one or the other of the vigilant lords, thrown in apparently by chance, had the same happy effect. Once the little Lady Jane turned to Tom and dismayed him with this question:

"Hast paid thy duty to the queen's majesty to-day, my lord?"

Tom hesitated, looked distressed, and was about to stammer out something at hazard, when Lord St. John took the word and answered for him with the easy grace of a courtier accustomed to encounter delicate difficulties and to be ready for them:

"He hath indeed, madam, and she did greatly hearten him, as touching his majesty's condition; is it not so, your highness?"

Tom mumbled something that stood for assent, but felt that he was getting upon dangerous ground. Somewhat later it was mentioned that Tom was to study no more at present, whereupon her little ladyship exclaimed:

"'Tis a pity, 'tis such a pity! Thou were proceeding bravely. But bide thy time in patience; it will not be for long. Thou'lt yet be graced with learning like thy father, and make thy tongue master of as many languages as his, good my prince."

"My father!" cried Tom, off his guard for the moment. "I trow he cannot speak his own so that any but the swine that wallow in the sties may tell his meaning; and as for learning of any sort soever—"

He looked up and encountered a solemn warning in my Lord St. John's eyes.

He stopped, blushed, then continued low and sadly: "Ah, my malady persecuteth me again, and my mind wandereth. I meant the king's grace no irreverence."

"We know it, sir," said the Princess Elizabeth, taking her "brother's" hand between her two palms, respectfully but caressingly; "trouble not thyself as to that. The fault is none of thine, but thy distemper's."

"Thou'rt a gentle comforter, sweet lady," said Tom, gratefully, "and my heart moveth me to thank thee for't, an I may be so bold."

Once the giddy little Lady Jane fired a simple Greek phrase at Tom. The Princess Elizabeth's quick eye saw by the serene blankness of the target's front that the shaft was overshot; so she tranquilly delivered a return volley of sounding Greek on

Tom's behalf, and then straightway changed the talk to other matters.

Time wore on pleasantly, and likewise smoothly, on the whole. Snags and sand-bars grew less and less frequent, and Tom grew more and more at his ease, seeing that all were so lovingly bent upon helping him and overlooking his mistakes. When it came out that the little ladies were to accompany him to the Lord Mayor's banquet in the evening, his heart gave a bound of relief and delight, for he felt that he should not be friendless now, among that multitude of strangers, whereas, an hour earlier, the idea of their going with him would have been an insupportable terror to him.

Tom's guardian angels, the two lords, had had less comfort in the interview than the other parties to it. They felt much as if they were piloting a great ship through a dangerous channel; they were on the alert constantly, and found their office no child's play. Wherefore, at last, when the ladies' visit was drawing to a close and the Lord Guilford Dudley was announced, they not only felt that their charge had been sufficiently taxed for the present, but also that they themselves were not in the best condition to take their ship back and make their anxious voyage all over again. So they respectfully advised Tom to excuse himself, which he was very glad to do, although a slight shade of disappointment might have been observed upon my Lady Jane's face when she heard the splendid stripling denied admittance.

There was a pause now, a sort of waiting silence which Tom could not understand. He glanced at Lord Hertford, who gave him a sign—but he failed to understand that also. The ready Elizabeth came to the rescue with her usual easy grace. She made reverence and said:

"Have we leave of the prince's grace my brother to go?"

Tom said:

"Indeed, your ladyships can have whatsoever of me they will, for the asking; yet would I rather give them any other thing that in my poor power lieth, than leave to take the light and blessing of their presence hence. Give ye good den, and God be with ye!" Then he smiled inwardly at the thought, "'tis not for naught I have dwelt but among princes in my reading, and taught my tongue some slight trick of their broidered and gracious speech withal!"

When the illustrious maidens were gone, Tom turned wearily to his keepers and said:

"May it please your lordships to grant me leave to go into some corner and rest me!"

Lord Hertford said:

"So please your highness, it is for you to command, it is for us to obey. That thou shouldst rest, is indeed a needful thing, since thou must journey to the city presently."

He touched a bell, and a page appeared, who was ordered to desire the presence of Sir William Herbert. This gentleman came straightway, and conducted Tom to an inner apartment. Tom's first movement there was to reach for a cup of water; but a silk-and-velvet servitor seized it, dropped upon one knee, and offered it to him on a golden salver.

Next, the tired captive sat down and was going to take off his buskins, timidly asking leave with his eye, but another silk-and-velvet discomforter went down upon his knees and took the office from him. He made two or three further efforts to help himself, but being promptly forestalled each time, he finally gave up, with a sigh of resignation and a murmured "Beshrew me, but I marvel they do not require to breathe for me also!" Slippered, and wrapped in a sumptuous robe, he laid himself down at last to rest, but not to sleep, for his head was too full of thoughts and the room too full of people. He could not dismiss the former, so they stayed; he did not know enough to dismiss the latter, so they stayed also, to his vast regret—and theirs.

Tom's departure had left his two noble guardians alone. They mused awhile, with much headshaking and walking the floor, then Lord St. John said:

"Plainly, what dost thou think?"

"Plainly, then, this. The king is near his end, my nephew is mad, mad will mount the throne, and mad remain. God protect England, since she will need it!"

"Verily it promiseth so, indeed. But . . . have you no misgivings as to . . . as to . . ."

The speaker hesitated, and finally stopped. He evidently felt that he was upon delicate ground. Lord Hertford stopped before him, looked into his face with a clear, frank eye, and said:

"Speak on—there is none to hear but me. Misgivings as to what?"

"I am loath to word the thing that is in my mind, and thou so near to him in blood, my lord. But craving pardon if I do offend, seemeth it not strange that madness could so change his port and manner!—not but that his port and speech are princely still, but that they *differ* in one unweighty trifle or another, from what his custom was aforetime. Seemeth it not strange that madness should filch from his memory his father's very lineaments; the customs and observances that are his due from such as be about him; and, leaving him his Latin, strip him of his Greek and French? My lord, be not offended, but ease my mind of its disquiet and receive my grateful thanks. It haunteth me, his saying he was not the prince, and so—"

"Peace, my lord, thou utterest treason! Hast forgot the king's command? Remember I am party to thy crime, if I but listen."

St. John paled, and hastened to say:

"I was in fault, I do confess it. Betray me not, grant me this grace out of thy courtesy, and I will neither think nor speak of this thing more. Deal not hardly with me, sir, else am I ruined."

"I am content, my lord. So thou offend not again, here or in the ears of others, it shall be as though thou hadst not spoken. But thou needst not have misgivings. He is my sister's son; are not his voice, his face, his form, familiar to me from his cradle? Madness can do all the odd conflicting things thou seest in him, and more. Dost not recall how that the old Baron Marley, being mad, forgot the favor of his own countenance that he had known for sixty years, and held it was another's; nay, even claimed he was the son of Mary Magdalene, and that his head was made of Spanish glass; and sooth to say, he suffered none to touch it, lest by mischance some heedless hand might shiver it. Give thy misgivings easement, good my lord. This is the very prince, I know him well—and soon will be thy king; it may advantage thee to bear this in mind and more dwell upon it than the other."

After some further talk, in which the Lord St. John covered up his mistake as well as he could by repeated protests that his faith was thoroughly grounded now, and could not be assailed by doubts again, the Lord Hertford relieved his fellow-keeper, and sat down to keep watch and ward alone. He was soon deep in meditation. And evidently the longer he thought, the more he was bothered. By and by he began to pace the floor and mutter.

"Tush, he *must* be the prince! Will any he in all the land maintain there can be two, not of one blood and birth, so marvelously twinned? And even were it so, 'twere yet a stranger miracle that chance should cast the one into the other's place. Nay, 'tis folly, folly, folly!"

Presently he said:

"Now were he impostor and called himself prince, look you *that* would be natural; that would be reasonable. But lived ever an impostor yet, who, being called prince by the king, prince by the court, prince by all, *denied* his dignity and pleaded against his exaltation? *No!* By the soul of St. Swithin, no! This is the true prince, gone mad!"

7

Tom's First Royal Dinner

Somewhat after one in the afternoon, Tom resignedly underwent the ordeal of being dressed for dinner. He found himself as finely clothed as before, but everything different, everything changed, from his ruff to his stockings. He was presently conducted with much state to a spacious and ornate apartment, where a table was already set for one. Its furniture was all of massy gold, and beautified with designs which well-nigh made it priceless, since they were the work of Benvenuto. The room was half filled with noble servitors. A chaplain said grace, and Tom was about to fall to, for hunger had long been constitutional with him, but was interrupted by my lord the Earl of Berkeley, who fastened a napkin about his neck; for the great post of Diaperers to the Princes of Wales was hereditary in this nobleman's family. Tom's cupbearer was present, and forestalled all his attempts to help himself to wine. The Taster to his Highness the Prince of Wales was there also, prepared to taste any suspicious dish upon requirement, and run the risk of being poisoned. He was only an ornamental appendage at this time, and was seldom called to exercise his function; but there had been times, not many generations past, when the office of taster had its perils, and was not a grandeur to be desired. Why they did not use a dog or a plumber seems strange; but all the ways of royalty are strange. My Lord d'Arcy, First Groom of the Chamber, was there, to do goodness knows what; but there he was—let that suffice. The Lord Chief Butler was there, and stood behind Tom's chair, overseeing the solemnities, under command of the Lord Great Steward and the Lord Head Cook, who stood near. Tom had three hundred and eighty-four servants besides these; but they were not all in that room, of course, nor the quarter of them; neither was Tom aware yet that they existed.

All those that were present had been well drilled within the hour to remember that the prince was temporarily out of his head, and to be careful to show no surprise at his vagaries. These "vagaries" were soon on exhibition before them; but they only moved their compassion and their sorrow, not their mirth. It was a heavy affliction to them to see the beloved prince so stricken.

Poor Tom ate with his fingers mainly; but no one smiled at it, or even seemed to observe it. He inspected his napkin curiously and with deep interest, for it was of a very dainty and beautiful fabric, then said with simplicity:

"Prithee, take it away, lest in mine unheedfulness it be soiled."

The Hereditary Diaperer took it away with reverent manner, and without word or protest of any sort.

Tom examined the turnips and the lettuce with interest, and asked what they were, and if they were to be eaten; for it was only recently that men had begun to raise these things in England in place of importing them as luxuries from Holland. His question was answered with grave respect, and no surprise manifested. When he had finished his dessert, he filled his pockets with nuts; but nobody appeared to be aware of it, or disturbed by it. But the next moment he was himself disturbed by it, and showed discomposure; for this was the only service he had been permitted to do with his own hands during the meal, and he did not doubt that he had done a most improper and unprincely thing. At that moment the muscles of his nose began to twitch, and the end of that organ to lift and wrinkle. This continued, and Tom began to evince a growing distress. He looked appealingly, first at one and then another of the lords about him, and tears came into his eyes. They sprang forward with dismay in their faces, and begged to know his trouble. Tom said with genuine anguish:

"I crave your indulgence; my nose itcheth cruelly. What is the custom and usage in this emergence? Prithee speed, for 'tis but a little time that I can bear it."

None smiled; but all were sore perplexed, and looked one to the other in deep tribulation for counsel. But, behold, here was a dead wall, and nothing in English history to tell how to get over it. The Master of Ceremonies was not present; there was no one who felt safe to venture upon this uncharted sea, or risk the attempt to solve this solemn problem. Alas! there was no Hereditary Scratcher. Meantime the tears had overflowed their banks, and begun to trickle down Tom's cheeks. His twitching nose was pleading more urgently than ever for relief. At last nature broke down the barriers of etiquette; Tom lifted up an inward prayer for pardon if he was doing wrong, and brought relief to the burdened hearts of his court by scratching his nose himself.

His meal being ended, a lord came and held before him a broad, shallow, golden dish with fragrant rose-water in it, to cleanse his mouth and fingers with; and my lord the Hereditary Diaperer stood by with a napkin for his use. Tom gazed at the dish a puzzled moment or two, then raised it to his lips, and gravely took a draught. Then he returned it to the waiting lord, and said:

"Nay, it likes me not, my lord; it hath a pretty flavor, but it wanteth strength."

This new eccentricity of the prince's ruined mind made all the hearts about him ache; but the sad sight moved none to merriment.

Tom's next unconscious blunder was to get up and leave the table just when the chaplain had taken his stand behind his chair and with uplifted hands and closed uplifted eyes, was in the act of beginning the blessing. Still nobody seemed to perceive that the prince had done a thing unusual.

By his own request, our small friend was now conducted to his private cabinet, and left there alone to his own devices. Hanging upon hooks in the oaken wainscoting were the several pieces of a suit of shining steel armor, covered all over with beautiful designs exquisitely inlaid in gold. This martial panoply belonged to the true prince—a recent present from Madam Parr, the queen. Tom put on the greaves, the gauntlets, the plumed helmet, and such other pieces as he could don without assistance, and for a while was minded to call for help and complete the matter, but bethought him of the nuts he had brought away from dinner, and the joy it would be to eat them with no crowd to eye him, and no Grand Hereditaries to pester him with undesired services; so he restored the pretty things to their several places, and soon was cracking nuts, and feeling almost naturally happy for the first time since God for his sins had made him a prince. When the nuts were all gone, he stumbled upon some inviting books in a closet, among them one about the etiquette of the English court. This was a prize. He lay down upon a sumptuous divan, and proceeded to instruct himself with honest zeal. Let us leave him there for the present.

8

The Question of the Seal

ABOUT five o'clock Henry VIII. awoke out of an unrefreshing nap, and muttered to himself, "Troublous dreams, troublous dreams! Mine end is now at hand; so say these warnings, and my failing pulses do confirm it." Presently a wicked light flamed up in his eye, and he muttered, "Yet will not I die till *he* go before."

His attendants perceiving that he was awake, one of them asked his pleasure concerning the Lord Chancellor, who was waiting without.

"Admit him, admit him!" exclaimed the king eagerly.

The Lord Chancellor entered, and knelt by the king's couch, saying:

"I have given order, and, according to the king's command, the peers of the realm, in their robes, do now stand at the bar of the House, where, having confirmed the Duke of Norfolk's doom, they humbly wait his majesty's further pleasure in the matter."

The king's face lit up with a fierce joy. Said he:

"Lift me up! In mine own person will I go before my Parliament, and with mine own hand will I seal the warrant that rids me of—"

His voice failed; an ashen pallor swept the flush from his cheeks; and the attendants eased him back upon his pillows, and hurriedly assisted him with restoratives. Presently he said sorrowfully:

"Alack, how have I longed for this sweet hour! and lo, too late it cometh, and I am robbed of this so coveted chance. But speed ye, speed ye! let others do this happy office sith 'tis denied to me.

I put my great seal in commission: choose thou the lords that shall compose it, and get ye to your work. Speed ye, man! Before the sun shall rise and set again, bring me his head that I may see it."

"According to the king's command, so shall it be. Will't please your majesty to order that the Seal be now restored to me, so that I may forth upon the business?"

"The Seal! Who keepeth the Seal but thou?"

"Please your majesty, you did take it from me two days since, saying it should no more do its office till your own royal hand should use it upon the Duke of Norfolk's warrant."

"Why, so in sooth I did; I do remember it. . . . What did I with it! . . . I am very feeble. . . . So oft these days doth my memory play the traitor with me. . . . 'Tis strange, strange—"

The king dropped into inarticulate mumblings, shaking his gray head weakly from time to time, and gropingly trying to recollect what he had done with the Seal. At last my Lord Hertford ventured to kneel and offer information—

"Sire, if that I may be so bold, here be several that do remember with me how that you gave the Great Seal into the hands of his Highness the Prince of Wales to keep against the day that—"

"True, most true!" interrupted the king. "Fetch it! Go: time flieth!"

Lord Hertford flew to Tom, but returned to the king before very long, troubled and empty-handed. He delivered himself to this effect:

"It grieveth me, my lord the king, to bear so heavy and unwelcome tidings; but it is the will of God that the prince's affliction abideth still, and he cannot recall to mind that he received the Seal. So came I quickly to report, thinking it were waste of precious time, and little worth withal, that any should attempt to search the long array of chambers and saloons that belong unto his royal high—"

A groan from the king interrupted my lord at this point. After a little while his majesty said, with a deep sadness in his tone:

"Trouble him no more, poor child. The hand of God lieth heavy upon him, and my heart goeth out in loving compassion for him, and sorrow that I may not bear his burden on mine own old trouble-weighted shoulders, and so bring him peace."

He closed his eyes, fell to mumbling, and presently was silent. After a time he opened his eyes again, and gazed vacantly around until his glance rested upon the kneeling Lord Chancellor. Instantly his face flushed with wrath:

"What, thou here yet! By the glory of God, an thou gettest not about that traitor's business, thy miter shall have holiday the morrow for lack of a head to grace withal!"

The trembling Chancellor answered:

"Good your majesty, I cry you mercy! I but waited for the Seal."

"Man, hast lost thy wits? The small Seal which aforetime I was wont to take with me abroad lieth in my treasury. And, since the Great Seal hath flown away, shall not it suffice? Hast lost thy wits? Begone! And hark ye—come no more till thou do bring his head."

The poor Chancellor was not long in removing himself from this dangerous vicinity; nor did the commission waste time in giving the royal assent to the work of the slavish Parliament, and appointing the morrow for the beheading of the premier peer of England, the luckless Duke of Norfolk.

9

The River Pageant

AT NINE in the evening the whole vast river-front of the palace was blazing with light. The river itself, as far as the eye could reach cityward, was so thickly covered with watermen's boats and with pleasure barges, all fringed with colored lanterns, and gently agitated by the waves, that it resembled a glowing and limitless garden of flowers stirred to soft motion by summer winds. The grand terrace of stone steps leading down to the water, spacious enough to mass the army of a German principality upon, was a picture to see, with its ranks of royal halberdiers in polished armor, and its troops of brilliantly costumed servitors flitting up and down, and to and fro, in the hurry of preparation.

Presently a command was given, and immediately all living creatures vanished from the steps. Now the air was heavy with the hush of suspense and expectancy. As far as one's vision could carry, he might see the myriads of people in the boats rise up, and shade their eyes from the glare of lanterns and torches, and gaze toward the palace.

A file of forty or fifty state barges drew up to the steps. They were richly gilt, and their lofty prows and sterns were elaborately carved. Some of them were decorated with banners and streamers; some with cloth-of-gold and arras embroidered with coats of arms; others with silken flags that had numberless little silver bells fastened to them, which shook out tiny showers of joyous music whenever the breezes fluttered them; others of yet higher pretensions, since they belonged to nobles in the prince's immediate service, had their sides picturesquely fenced with shields gorgeously emblazoned with armorial bearings. Each state barge was towed by a tender. Besides the rowers, these tenders carried each a number of men-at-arms in glossy helmet and breastplate, and a company of musicians.

The advance-guard of the expected procession now appeared in the great gateway, a troop of halberdiers. "They were dressed in striped hose of black and tawny, velvet caps graced at the sides with silver roses, and doublets of murrey and blue cloth, embroidered on the front and back with the three feathers, the prince's blazon, woven in gold. Their halbered staves were covered with crimson velvet, fastened with gilt nails, and ornamented with gold tassels. Filing off on the right and left, they formed two long lines, extending from the gateway of the palace to the water's edge. A thick, rayed cloth or carpet was then unfolded, and laid down between them by attendants in the gold-and-crimson liveries of the prince. This done, a flourish of trumpets resounded from within. A lively prelude arose from the musicians on the water; and two ushers with white wands marched with a slow and stately pace from the portal. They were followed by an officer bearing the civic mace, after whom came another carrying the city's sword; then several sergeants of the city guard, in their full accoutrements, and with badges on their sleeves; then the Garter king-at-arms, in his tabard; then several knights of the Bath, each with a white lace on his sleeve; then their esquires; then the judges, in their robes of scarlet and coifs; then the Lord High Chancellor of England, in a robe of scarlet, open before, and purfled with minever; then a deputation of aldermen, in their scarlet cloaks; and then the heads of the different civic companies, in their robes of state. Now came twelve French gentlemen, in splendid habiliments, consisting of pour-points of white damask barred with gold, short mantles of crimson velvet lined with violet taffeta, and carnation-colored *hauts-de-chausses,* and took their way down the steps. They were of the suite of the French ambassador, and were followed by twelve cavaliers of the suite of the Spanish ambassador, clothed in black velvet, unrelieved by any ornament. Following these came several great English nobles with their attendants."

There was a flourish of trumpets within; and the prince's uncle, the future great Duke of Somerset, emerged from the gateway, arrayed in a "doublet of black cloth-of-gold, and a cloak of crimson satin flowered with gold, and ribanded with nets of silver." He turned, doffed his plumed cap, bent his body in a low reverence, and began to step backward, bowing at each step. A prolonged trumpet-blast followed, and a proclamation, "Way for the high and mighty, the Lord Edward, Prince of Wales!" High aloft on the palace walls a long line of red tongues of flame leaped forth with a thunder-crash; the massed world on the river burst into a mighty roar of welcome; and Tom Canty, the cause and hero of it all, stepped into view, and slightly bowed his princely head.

He was "magnificently habited in a doublet of white satin, with a front-piece of purple cloth-of-tissue, powdered with diamonds, and edged with ermine. Over this he wore a mantle of white cloth-of-gold, pounced with the triple-feather crest, lined with blue satin, set with pearls and precious stones, and fastened with a clasp of brilliants. About his neck hung the order of the Garter, and several princely foreign orders"; and wherever light fell upon him jewels responded with a blinding flash. O, Tom Canty, born in a hovel, bred in the gutters of London, familiar with rags and dirt and misery, what a spectacle is this!

10

The Prince in the Toils

WE LEFT John Canty dragging the rightful prince into Offal Court, with a noisy and delighted mob at his heels. There was but one person in it who offered a pleading word for the captive, and he was not heeded; he was hardly even heard, so great was the turmoil. The prince continued to struggle for freedom, and to rage against the treatment he was suffering, until John Canty lost what little patience was left in him, and raised his oaken cudgel in a sudden fury over the prince's head. The single pleader for the lad sprang to stop the man's arm, and the blow descended upon his own wrist. Canty roared out:

"Thou'lt meddle, wilt thou? Then have thy reward."

His cudgel crashed down upon the meddler's head; there was a groan, a dim form sank to the ground among the feet of the crowd, and the next moment it lay there in the dark alone. The mob pressed on, their enjoyment nothing disturbed by this episode.

Presently the prince found himself in John Canty's abode, with the door closed against the outsiders. By the vague light of a tallow candle which was thrust into a bottle, he made out the main features of the loathsome den, and also of the occupants of it. Two frowsy girls and a middle-aged woman cowered against the wall in one corner, with the aspect of animals habituated to harsh usage, and expecting and dreading it now. From another corner stole a withered hag with streaming gray hair and malignant eyes. John Canty said to this one:

"Tarry! There's fine mummeries here. Mar them not till thou'st enjoyed them; then let thy hand be heavy as thou wilt. Stand forth, lad. Now say thy foolery again, an thou'st not forgot it. Name thy name. Who art thou?"

The insulted blood mounted to the little prince's cheek once more, and he lifted a steady and indignant gaze to the man's face, and said:

"'Tis but ill-breeding in such as thou to command me to speak. I tell thee now, as I told thee before, I am Edward, Prince of Wales, and none other."

The stunning surprise of this reply nailed the hag's feet to the floor where she stood, and almost took her breath. She stared at the prince in stupid amazement, which so amused her ruffianly son that he burst into a roar of laughter. But the effect upon Tom Canty's mother and sisters was different. Their dread of bodily injury gave way at once to distress of a different sort. They ran forward with woe and dismay in their faces, exclaiming:

"Oh, poor Tom, poor lad!"

The mother fell on her knees before the prince, put her hands upon his shoulders, and gazed yearningly into his face through her rising tears. Then she said:

"Oh, my poor boy! thy foolish reading hath wrought its woeful work at last, and ta'en thy wit away. Ah! why didst thou cleave to it when I so warned thee 'gainst it? Thou'st broke thy mother's heart."

The prince looked into her face, and said gently:

"Thy son is well and hath not lost his wits, good dame. Comfort thee; let me to the palace where he is, and straightway will the king my father restore him to thee."

"The king thy father! Oh, my child! unsay these words that be freighted with death for thee, and ruin for all that be near to thee. Shake off this gruesome dream. Call back thy poor wandering memory. Look upon me. Am not I thy mother that bore thee, and loveth thee?"

The prince shook his head, and reluctantly said:

"God knoweth I am loath to grieve thy heart; but truly have I never looked upon thy face before."

The woman sank back to a sitting posture on the floor, and, covering her eyes with her hands, gave way to heartbroken sobs and wailings.

"Let the show go on!" shouted Canty. "What, Nan! what, Bet! Mannerless wenches! will ye stand in the prince's presence? Upon your knees, ye pauper scum, and do him reverence!"

He followed this with another horse-laugh. The girls began to plead timidly for their brother; and Nan said:

"An thou wilt but let him to bed, father, rest and sleep will heal his madness; prithee, do."

"Do, father," said Bet; "he is more worn than is his wont. To-morrow will he be himself again, and will beg with diligence, and come not empty home again."

This remark sobered the father's joviality, and brought his mind to business. He turned angrily upon the prince, and said:

"The morrow must we pay two pennies to him that owns this hole; two pennies mark ye—all this money for a half-year's rent, else out of this we go. Show what thou'st gathered with thy lazy begging."

The prince said:

"Offend me not with thy sordid matters. I tell thee again I am the king's son."

A sounding blow upon the prince's shoulder from Canty's broad palm sent him staggering into good-wife Canty's arms, who clasped him to her breast, and sheltered him from a pelting rain of cuffs and slaps by interposing her own person.

The frightened girls retreated to their corner; but the grand-mother stepped eagerly forward to assist her son. The prince sprang away from Mrs. Canty, exclaiming:

"Thou shalt not suffer for me, madam. Let these swine do their will upon me alone."

This speech infuriated the swine to such a degree that they set

about their work without waste of time. Between them they be-
labored the boy right soundly, and then gave the girls and their
mother a beating for showing sympathy for the victim.

"Now," said Canty, "to bed, all of ye. The entertainment has
tired me."

The light was put out, and the family retired. As soon as the
snorings of the head of the house and his mother showed that
they were asleep, the young girls crept to where the prince lay,
and covered him tenderly from the cold with straw and rags;
and their mother crept to him also, and stroked his hair, and
cried over him, whispering broken words of comfort and compassion in his ear the while. She had saved a morsel for him to eat
also; but the boy's pains had swept away all appetite—at least
for black and tasteless crusts. He was touched by her brave and
costly defense of him, and by her commiseration; and he thanked
her in very noble and princely words, and begged her to go to
her sleep and try to forget her sorrows. And he added that the
king his father would not let her loyal kindness and devotion go
unrewarded. This return to his "madness" broke her heart anew,
and she strained him to her breast again and again and then went
back, drowned in tears, to her bed.

As she lay thinking and mourning, the suggestion began to
creep into her mind that there was an undefinable something
about this boy that was lacking in Tom Canty, mad or sane. She
could not describe it, she could not tell just what it was, and yet
her sharp mother-instinct seemed to detect it and perceive it.
What if the boy were really not her son, after all? Oh, absurd! She
almost smiled at the idea, spite of her griefs and troubles. No
matter, she found that it was an idea that would not "down," but
persisted in haunting her. It pursued her, it harassed her, it clung
to her, and refused to be put away or ignored. At last she perceived that there was not going to be any peace for her until she
should devise a test that should prove, clearly and without question, whether this lad was her son or not, and so banish these
wearing and worrying doubts. Ah, yes, this was plainly the right
way out of the difficulty; therefore she set her wits to work at
once to contrive that test. But it was an easier thing to propose

than to accomplish. She turned over in her mind one promising test after another, but was obliged to relinquish them all—none of them were absolutely sure, absolutely perfect; and an imperfect one could not satisfy her. Evidently she was racking her head in vain—it seemed manifest that she must give the matter up. While this depressing thought was passing through her mind, her ear caught the regular breathing of the boy, and she knew he had fallen asleep. And while she listened, the measured breathing was broken by a soft, startled cry, such as one utters in a troubled dream. This chance occurrence furnished her instantly with a plan worth all her labored tests combined. She at once set herself feverishly, but noiselessly, to work to relight her candle, muttering to herself, "Had I but seen him *then,* I should have known! Since that day, when he was little, that the powder burst in his face, he hath never been startled of a sudden out of his dreams or out of his thinkings, but he hath cast his hand before his eyes, even as he did that day, and not as others would do it, with the palm inward, but always with the palm turned outward—I have seen it a hundred times, and it hath never varied nor ever failed. Yes, I shall soon know now!"

By this time she had crept to the slumbering boy's side, with the candle shaded in her hand. She bent heedfully and warily over him, scarcely breathing, in her suppressed excitement, and suddenly flashed the light in his face and struck the floor by his ear with her knuckles. The sleeper's eyes sprung wide open, and he cast a startled stare about him—but he made no special movement with his hands.

The poor woman was smitten almost helpless with surprise and grief; but she contrived to hide her emotions, and to soothe the boy to sleep again; then she crept apart and communed miserably with herself upon the disastrous result of her experiment. She tried to believe that her Tom's madness had banished this habitual gesture of his; but she could not do it. "No," she said, "his *hands* are not mad, they could not unlearn so old a habit in so brief a time. Oh, this is a heavy day for me!"

Still, hope was as stubborn now as doubt had been before; she could not bring herself to accept the verdict of the test; she must try the thing again—the failure must have been only an accident; so she startled the boy out of his sleep a second and a third time, at intervals—with the same result which had marked the first test—then she dragged herself to bed, and fell sorrowfully asleep, saying, "But I cannot give him up—oh, no, I cannot, I cannot—he *must* be my boy!"

The poor mother's interruptions having ceased, and the prince's pains having gradually lost their power to disturb him, utter weariness at last sealed his eyes in a profound and restful sleep. Hour after hour slipped away, and still he slept like the dead. Thus four or five hours passed. Then his stupor began to lighten. Presently, while half asleep and half awake, he murmured:

"Sir William!"

After a moment:

"Ho, Sir William Herbert! Hie thee hither, and list to the strangest dream that ever. . . . Sir William! Dost hear? Man, I did think me changed to a pauper, and . . . Ho there! Guards! Sir William! What! is there no groom of the chamber in waiting? Alack it shall go hard with—"

"What aileth thee?" asked a whisper near him. "Who art thou calling?"

"Sir William Herbert. Who art thou?"

"I? Who should I be, but thy sister Nan? Oh, Tom, I had forgot! Thou'rt mad yet—poor lad thou'rt mad yet, would I had never woke to know it again! But, prithee, master thy tongue, lest we be all beaten till we die!"

The startled prince sprang partly up, but a sharp reminder from his stiffened bruises brought him to himself, and he sunk back among his foul straw with a moan and the ejaculation:

"Alas, it was no dream, then!"

In a moment all the heavy sorrow and misery which sleep had banished were upon him again, and he realized that he was no longer a petted prince in a palace, with the adoring eyes of a nation upon him, but a pauper, an outcast, clothed in rags, prisoner in a den fit only for beasts, and consorting with beggars and thieves.

In the midst of his grief he began to be conscious of hilarious noises and shoutings, apparently but a block or two away. The next moment there were several sharp raps at the door; John Canty ceased from snoring and said:

"Who knocketh? What wilt thou?"

A voice answered:

"Know'st thou who it was thou laid thy cudgel on?"

"No. Neither know I, nor care."

"Belike thou'lt change thy note eftsoons. An thou would save thy neck, nothing but flight may stead thee. The man is this moment delivering up the ghost. 'Tis the priest, Father Andrew!"

"God-a-mercy!" exclaimed Canty. He roused his family, and hoarsely commanded, "Up with ye all and fly—or bide where ye are and perish!"

Scarcely five minutes later the Canty household were in the street and flying for their lives. John Canty held the prince by the wrist, and hurried him along the dark way, giving him this caution in a low voice:

"Mind thy tongue, thou mad fool, and speak not our name. I will choose me a new name, speedily, to throw the law's dogs off the scent. Mind thy tongue, I tell thee!"

He growled these words to the rest of the family:

"If it so chance that we be separated, let each make for London Bridge; whoso findeth himself as far as the last linen-draper's shop on the bridge, let him tarry there till the others be come, then will we flee into Southwark together."

At this moment the party burst suddenly out of darkness into light; and not only into light, but into the midst of a multitude of singing, dancing, and shouting people, massed together on the river-frontage. There was a line of bonfires stretching as far as one could see, up and down the Thames; London Bridge was illuminated; Southwark Bridge likewise; the entire river was aglow with the flash and sheen of colored lights, and constant explosions of fireworks filled the skies with an intricate commingling of shooting splendors and a thick rain of dazzling sparks that almost turned night into day; everywhere were crowds of revelers; all London seemed to be at large.

John Canty delivered himself of a furious curse and com-

manded a retreat; but it was too late. He and his tribe were
swallowed up in that swarming hive of humanity, and hopelessly
separated from each other in an instant. We are not considering
that the prince was one of his tribe; Canty still kept his grip
upon him. The prince's heart was beating high with hopes of
escape now. A burly waterman, considerably exalted with liquor,
found himself rudely shoved by Canty in his efforts to plow
through the crowd; he laid his great hand on Canty's shoulder
and said:

"Nay, whither so fast, friend? Dost canker thy soul with sordid
business when all that be leal men and true make holiday?"

"Mine affairs are mine own, they concern thee not," answered
Canty, roughly; "take away thy hand and let me pass."

"Sith that is thy humor, thou'lt *not* pass till thou'st drunk to the
Prince of Wales, I tell thee that," said the waterman, barring the
way resolutely.

"Give me the cup, then, and make speed, make speed."

Other revelers were interested by this time. They cried out:

"The loving-cup, the loving-cup! make the sour knave drink
the loving-cup, else will we feed him to the fishes."

So a huge loving-cup was brought; the waterman, grasping it
by one of its handles, and with his other hand bearing up the end
of an imaginary napkin, presented it in due and ancient form to
Canty, who had to grasp the opposite handle with one of his
hands and take off the lid with the other, according to ancient
custom. This left the prince handfree for a second, of course. He
wasted no time, but dived among the forest of legs about him and
disappeared. In another moment he could not have been harder
to find, under that tossing sea of life, if its billows had been the
Atlantic's and he a lost sixpence.

He very soon realized this fact, and straightway busied himself
about his own affairs without further thought of John Canty. He
quickly realized another thing, too. To wit, that a spurious Prince
of Wales was being feasted by the city in his stead. He easily
concluded that the pauper lad, Tom Canty, had deliberately
taken advantage of his stupendous opportunity and become a
usurper.

Therefore there was but one course to pursue—find his way to the Guildhall, make himself known, and denounce the impostor. He also made up his mind that Tom should be allowed a reasonable time for spiritual preparation, and then be hanged, drawn, and quartered, according to the law and usage of the day, in cases of high treason.

11

At Guildhall

THE ROYAL BARGE, attended by its gorgeous fleet, took its stately way down the Thames through the wilderness of illuminated boats. The air was laden with music; the river-banks were be-ruffled with joy-flames; the distant city lay in a soft luminous glow from its countless invisible bonfires; above it rose many a slender spire into the sky, incrusted with sparkling lights, wherefore in their remoteness they seemed like jeweled lances thrust aloft; as the fleet swept along, it was greeted from the banks with a continuous hoarse roar of cheers and the ceaseless flash and boom of artillery.

To Tom Canty, half buried in his silken cushions, these sounds and this spectacle were a wonder unspeakably sublime and astonishing. To his little friends at his side, the Princess Elizabeth and the Lady Jane Grey, they were nothing.

Arrived at the Dowgate, the fleet was towed up the limpid Walbrook (whose channel has now been for two centuries buried out of sight under acres of buildings) to Bucklersbury, past houses and under bridges populous with merry-makers and brilliantly lighted, and at last came to a halt in a basin where now is Barge Yard, in the center of the ancient city of London. Tom disembarked, and he and his gallant procession crossed Cheapside and made a short march through the Old Jewry and Basinghall Street to the Guildhall.

Tom and his little ladies were received with due ceremony by the Lord Mayor and the Fathers of the City, in their gold chains and scarlet robes of state, and conducted to a rich canopy of state at the head of the great hall, preceded by heralds making proclamation, and by the Mace and the City Sword. The lords and ladies who were to attend upon Tom and his two small friends took their places behind their chairs.

At a lower table the court grandees and other guests of noble degree were seated, with the magnates of the city; the commoners took places at a multitude of tables on the main floor of the hall. From their lofty vantage ground, the giants Gog and Magog, the ancient guardians of the city, contemplated the spectacle below them with eyes grown familiar to it in forgotten generations. There was a bugle-blast and a proclamation, and a fat butler appeared in a high perch in the leftward wall, followed by his servitors bearing with impressive solemnity a royal Baron of Beef, smoking hot and ready for the knife.

After grace, Tom (being instructed) rose—and the whole house with him—and drank from a portly golden loving-cup with the Princess Elizabeth; from her it passed to the Lady Jane, and then traversed the general assemblage. So the banquet began.

By midnight the revelry was at its height. Now came one of those picturesque spectacles so admired in that old day. A description of it is still extant in the quaint wording of a chronicler who witnessed it:

"Space being made, presently entered a baron and an earl appareled after the Turkish fashion in long robes of bawdkin powdered with gold; hats on their heads of crimson velvet, with great rolls of gold, girded with two swords, called simitars, hanging by great bawdricks of gold. Next came yet another baron and another earl, in two long gowns of yellow satin, traversed with white satin, and in every bend of white was a bend of crimson satin, after the fashion of Russia, with furred hats of gray on their heads; either of them having an hatchet in their hands, and boots with *pykes*" (points a foot long), "turned up. And after them came a knight, then the Lord High Admiral, and with him five nobles, in doublets of crimson velvet, voyded low on the back and before to the cannel-bone, laced on the breasts with chains of silver; and, over that, short cloaks of crimson satin, and on their heads hats after the dancers' fashion, with pheasants' feather in them. These were appareled after the fashion of Prussia. The torch-bearers, which were about an hundred, were appareled in crimson satin and green, like Moors, their faces black. Next came in a *mommarye*. Then the minstrels, which were disguised, danced; and the lords and ladies did wildly dance also, that it was a pleasure to behold."

And while Tom, in his high seat, was gazing upon this "wild" dancing, lost in admiration of the dazzling commingling of kaleidoscopic colors which the whirling turmoil of gaudy figures below him presented, the ragged but real little Prince of Wales was proclaiming his rights and his wrongs, denouncing the impostor, and clamoring for admission at the gates of Guildhall! The crowd enjoyed this episode prodigiously, and pressed forward and craned their necks to see the small rioter. Presently they began to taunt him and mock at him, purposely to goad him into a higher and still more entertaining fury. Tears of mortification sprung to his eyes, but he stood his ground and defied the mob right royally. Other taunts followed, added mockings stung him, and he exclaimed:

"I tell ye again, you pack of unmannerly curs, I am the Prince of Wales! And all forlorn and friendless as I be, with none to give me word of grace or help me in my need, yet will not I be driven from my ground, but will maintain it!"

"Though thou be prince or no prince, 'tis all one, thou be'st a gallant lad, and not friendless neither! Here stand I by thy side to prove it; and mind I tell thee thou might'st have a worser friend than Miles Hendon and yet not tire thy legs with seeking. Rest thy small jaw, my child, I talk the language of these base kennel-rats like to a very native."

The speaker was a sort of Don Cæsar de Bazan in dress, aspect, and bearing. He was tall, trim-built, muscular. His doublet and trunks were of rich material, but faded and threadbare, and their gold-lace adornments were sadly tarnished; his ruff was rumpled and damaged; the plume in his slouched hat was broken and had a bedraggled and disreputable look; at his side he wore a long rapier in a rusty iron sheath; his swaggering carriage marked him at once as a ruffler of the camp. The speech of this fantastic figure was received with an explosion of jeers and laughter. Some cried, "'Tis another prince in disguise!" "'Ware thy tongue, friend, belike he is dangerous!" "Marry, he looketh it—mark his eye!" "Pluck the lad from him—to the horse-pond wi' the cub!"

Instantly a hand was laid upon the prince, under the impulse of this happy thought; as instantly the stranger's long sword was out and the meddler went to the earth under a sounding thump with the flat of it. The next moment a score of voices shouted "Kill the dog! kill him! kill him!" and the mob closed in on the warrior, who backed himself against a wall and began to lay about him with his long weapon like a madman. His victims sprawled this way and that, but the mob-tide poured over their prostrate forms and dashed itself against the champion with undiminished fury. His moments seemed numbered, his destruction certain, when suddenly a trumpet-blast sounded, a voice shouted, "Way for the king's messenger!" and a troop of horsemen came charging down upon the mob, who fled out of harm's reach as fast as their legs could carry them. The bold stranger caught up the prince in his arms, and was soon far away from danger and the multitude.

Return we within the Guildhall. Suddenly, high above the jubilant roar and thunder of the revel, broke the clear peal of a bugle-note. There was instant silence—a deep hush; then a single voice rose—that of the messenger from the palace—and began to pipe forth a proclamation, the whole multitude standing, listening. The closing words, solemnly pronounced, were:

"The king is dead!"

The great assemblage bent their heads upon their breasts with one accord; remained so, in profound silence, a few moments; then all sunk upon their knees in a body, stretched out their hands toward Tom, and a mighty shout burst forth that seemed to shake the building:

"Long live the king!"

Poor Tom's dazed eyes wandered abroad over this stupefying spectacle, and finally rested dreamily upon the kneeling princesses beside him a moment, then upon the Earl of Hertford. A sudden purpose dawned in his face. He said, in a low tone, at Lord Hertford's ear:

"Answer me truly, on thy faith and honor! Uttered I here a command, the which none but a king might hold privilege and prerogative to utter, would such commandment be obeyed, and none rise up to say me nay?"

"None, my liege, in all these realms. In thy person bides the majesty of England. Thou art the king—thy word is law."

Tom responded, in a strong, earnest voice, and with great animation:

"Then shall the king's law be law of mercy, from this day, and never more be law of blood! Up from thy knees and away! To the Tower and say the king decrees the Duke of Norfolk shall not die!"

The words were caught up and carried eagerly from lip to lip far and wide over the hall, and as Hertford hurried from the presence, another prodigious shout burst forth:

"The reign of blood is ended! Long live Edward, king of England!"

12

The Prince and His Deliverer

As SOON as Miles Hendon and the little prince were clear of the mob, they struck down through back lanes and alleys toward the river. Their way was unobstructed until they approached London Bridge; then they plowed into the multitude again, Hendon keeping a fast grip upon the prince's—no, the king's—wrist. The tremendous news was already abroad, and the boy learned it from a thousand voices at once—"The king is dead!" The tidings struck a chill to the heart of the poor little waif, and sent a shudder through his frame. He realized the greatness of his loss, and was filled with a bitter grief; for the grim tyrant who had been such a terror to others had always been gentle with him. The tears sprung to his eyes and blurred all objects. For an instant he felt himself the most forlorn, outcast, and forsaken of God's creatures—then another cry shook the night with its far-reaching thunders: "Long live King Edward the Sixth!" and this made his eyes kindle, and thrilled him with pride to his fingers' ends. "Ah," he thought, "how grand and strange it seems—I AM KING!"

Our friends threaded their way slowly through the throngs upon the Bridge. This structure, which had stood for six hundred years, and had been a noisy and populous thoroughfare all that time, was a curious affair, for a closely packed rank of stores and shops, with family quarters overhead, stretched along both sides of it, from one bank of the river to the other. The Bridge was a sort of town to itself; it had its inn, its beerhouses, its bakeries, its haberdasheries, its food markets, its manufacturing industries, and even its church. It looked upon the two neighbors which it linked together—London and Southwark—as being well enough, as suburbs, but not otherwise particularly important. It was a close corporation, so to speak; it was a narrow town, of a single street a fifth of a mile long, its population was but a village population, and everybody in it knew all his fellow-townsmen intimately, and had known their fathers and mothers before them—and all their little family affairs into the bargain. It had its aristocracy, of course—its fine old families of butchers, and bakers, and what not, who had occupied the same old premises for five or six hundred years, and knew the great history of the Bridge from beginning to end, and all its strange legends; and who always talked bridgy talk, and thought bridgy thoughts, and lied in a long, level, direct, substantial bridgy way. It was just the sort of population to be narrow and ignorant and self-conceited. Children were born on the Bridge, were reared there, grew to old age and finally died without ever having set a foot upon any part of the world but London Bridge alone. Such people would naturally imagine that the mighty and interminable procession which moved through its street night and day, with its confused roar of shouts and cries, its neighings and bellowings and bleatings and its muffled thunder-tramp, was the one great thing in this world, and themselves somehow the proprietors of it. And so they were in effect—at least they could exhibit it from their windows, and did—for a consideration—whenever a returning king or hero gave it a fleeting splendor, for there was no place like it for affording a long, straight, uninterrupted view of marching columns.

Men born and reared upon the Bridge found life unendurably dull and inane elsewhere. History tells of one of these who left the Bridge at the age of seventy-one and retired to the country. But he could only fret and toss in his bed; he could not go to sleep, the deep stillness was so painful, so awful, so oppressive. When he was worn out with it, at last, he fled back to his old home, a lean and haggard specter, and fell peacefully to rest and pleasant dreams under the lulling music of the lashing waters and the boom and crash and thunder of London Bridge.

In the times of which we are writing, the Bridge furnished
"object lessons" in English history, for its children—namely, the
livid and decaying heads of renowned men impaled upon iron
spikes atop of its gateways. But we digress.

Hendon's lodgings were in the little inn on the Bridge. As he
neared the door with his small friend, a rough voice said:

"So, thou'rt come at last! Thou'lt not escape again, I warrant
thee; and if pounding thy bones to a pudding can teach thee
somewhat, thou'lt not keep us waiting another time, mayhap"—
and John Canty put out his hand to seize the boy.

Miles Hendon stepped in the way, and said:

"Not too fast, friend. Thou art needlessly rough, methinks.
What is the lad to thee?"

"If it be any business of thine to make and meddle in others'
affairs, he is my son."

" 'Tis a lie!" cried the little king, hotly.

"Boldly said, and I believe thee, whether thy small head-piece
be sound or cracked, my boy. But whether this scurvy ruffian be
thy father or no, 'tis all one, he shall not have thee to beat thee
and abuse, according to his threat, so thou prefer to abide with
me."

"I do, I do—I know him not, I loathe him, and will die before
I will go with him."

"Then 'tis settled, and there is naught more to say."

"We will see, as to that!" exclaimed John Canty, striding past
Hendon to get at the boy; "by force shall he—"

"If thou do but touch him, thou animated offal, I will spit thee
like a goose!" said Hendon, barring the way and laying his hand
upon his sword-hilt. Canty drew back. "Now mark ye," continued Hendon, "I took this lad under my protection when a mob
of such as thou would have mishandled him, mayhap killed him;
dost imagine I will desert him now to a worser fate?—for whether
thou art his father or no—and sooth to say, I think it is a lie—a
decent swift death were better for such a lad than life in such
brute hands as thine. So go thy ways, and set quick about it,
for I like not much bandying of words, being not overpatient in
my nature."

John Canty moved off, muttering threats and curses, and was swallowed from sight in the crowd. Hendon ascended three flights of stairs to his room, with his charge, after ordering a meal to be sent thither. It was a poor apartment, with a shabby bed and some odds and ends of old furniture in it, and was vaguely lighted by a couple of sickly candles. The little king dragged himself to the bed and lay down upon it, almost exhausted with hunger and fatigue. He had been on his feet a good part of a day and a night, for it was now two or three o'clock in the morning, and had eaten nothing meantime. He murmured drowsily:

"Prithee, call me when the table is spread," and sunk into a deep sleep immediately.

A smile twinkled in Hendon's eye, and he said to himself:

"By the mass, the little beggar takes to one's quarters and usurps one's bed with as natural and easy a grace as if he owned them—with never a by-your-leave or so-please-it-you, or anything of the sort. In his diseased ravings he called himself the Prince of Wales, and bravely doth he keep up the character. Poor little friendless rat, doubtless his mind has been disordered with ill usage. Well, I will be his friend; I have saved him, and it draweth me strongly to him; already I love the bold-tongued little rascal. How soldierlike he faced the smutty rabble and flung back his high defiance! And what a comely, sweet and gentle face he hath, now that sleep hath conjured away its troubles and its griefs. I will teach him, I will cure his malady; yea, I will be his elder brother, and care for him and watch over him; and whoso would shame him or do him hurt, may order his shroud, for though I be burnt for it he shall need it!"

He bent over the boy and contemplated him with kind and pitying interest, tapping the young cheek tenderly and smoothing back the tangled curls with his great brown hand. A slight shiver passed over the boy's form. Hendon muttered:

"See, now, how like a man it was to let him lie here uncovered and fill his body with deadly rheums. Now what shall I do? 'Twill wake him to take him up and put him within the bed, and he sorely needeth sleep."

He looked about for extra covering, but finding none, doffed his doublet and wrapped the lad in it, saying, "I am used to nipping air and scant apparel, 'tis little I shall mind the cold"— then walked up and down the room to keep his blood in motion, soliloquizing as before.

"His injured mind persuades him he is Prince of Wales; 'twill be odd to have a Prince of Wales still with us, now that he that *was* the prince is prince no more, but king—for this poor mind is set upon the one fantasy, and will not reason out that now it should cast by the prince and call itself the king. . . . If my father liveth still, after these seven years that I have heard naught from home in my foreign dungeon, he will welcome the poor lad and give him generous shelter for my sake; so will my good elder brother, Arthur; my other brother, Hugh—but I will crack his crown, and *he* interfere, the fox-hearted, ill-conditioned animal! Yes, thither will we fare—and straightway, too."

A servant entered with a smoking meal, disposed it upon a small deal table, placed the chairs, and took his departure, leaving such cheap lodgers as these to wait upon themselves. The door slammed after him, and the noise woke the boy, who sprung to a sitting posture, and shot a glad glance about him; then a grieved look came into his face and he murmured to himself, with a deep sigh, "Alack, it was but a dream. Woe is me." Next he noticed Miles Hendon's doublet—glanced from that to Hendon, comprehended the sacrifice that had been made for him, and said, gently:

"Thou art good to me, yes, thou art very good to me. Take it and put it on—I shall not need it more."

Then he got up and walked to the washstand in the corner, and stood there waiting. Hendon said in a cheery voice:

"We'll have a right hearty sup and bite now, for everything is savory and smoking hot, and that and thy nap together will make thee a little man again, never fear!"

The boy made no answer, but bent a steady look, that was filled with grave surprise, and also somewhat touched with impatience, upon the tall knight of the sword. Hendon was puzzled, and said:

"What's amiss?"

"Good sir, I would wash me."

"Oh, is that all! Ask no permission of Miles Hendon for aught thou cravest. Make thyself perfectly free here and welcome, with all that are his belongings."

Still the boy stood, and moved not; more, he tapped the floor once or twice with his small impatient foot. Hendon was wholly perplexed. Said he:

"Bless us, what is it?"

"Prithee, pour the water, and make not so many words!"

Hendon, suppressing a horse-laugh, and saying to himself, "By all the saints, but this is admirable!" stepped briskly forward and did the small insolent's bidding; then stood by, in a sort of stupefaction, until the command, "Come—the towel!" woke him sharply up. He took up a towel from under the boy's nose and handed it to him, without comment. He now proceeded to comfort his own face with a wash, and while he was at it his adopted child seated himself at the table and prepared to fall to. Hendon despatched his ablutions with alacrity, then drew back the other chair and was about to place himself at table, when the boy said, indignantly:

"Forbear! Wouldst sit in the presence of the king?"

This blow staggered Hendon to his foundations. He muttered to himself, "Lo, the poor thing's madness is up with the time! it hath changed with the great change that is come to the realm, and now in fancy is he *king!* Good lack, I must humor the conceit, too—there is no other way—faith, he would order me to the Tower, else!"

And pleased with this jest, he removed the chair from the table, took his stand behind the king, and proceeded to wait upon him in the courtliest way he was capable of.

When the king ate, the rigor of his royal dignity relaxed a little, and with his growing contentment came a desire to talk. He said:

"I think thou callest thyself Miles Hendon, if I heard thee aright?"

"Yes, sire," Miles replied; then observed to himself, "If I *must* humor the poor lad's madness, I must sire him, I must majesty

him, I must not go by halves, I must stick at nothing that be-
longeth to the part I play, else shall I play it ill and work evil to
this charitable and kindly cause."

The king warmed his heart with a second glass of wine, and
said: "I would know thee—tell me thy story. Thou hast a gallant
way with thee, and a noble—art nobly born?"

"We are of the tail of the nobility, good your majesty. My
father is a baronet—one of the smaller lords, by knight service[1]
—Sir Richard Hendon, of Hendon Hall, by Monk's Holm in
Kent."

"The name has escaped my memory. Go on—tell me thy story."

"'Tis not much, your majesty, yet perchance it may beguile a
short half-hour for want of a better. My father, Sir Richard, is very
rich, and of a most generous nature. My mother died whilst I was
yet a boy. I have two brothers: Arthur, my elder, with a soul like
to his father's; and Hugh, younger than I, a mean spirit, covetous,
treacherous, vicious, underhanded—a reptile. Such was he from
the cradle; such was he ten years past, when I last saw him—a
ripe rascal at nineteen, I being twenty then, and Arthur twenty-
two. There is none other of us but the Lady Edith, my cousin—
she was sixteen, then—beautiful, gentle, good, the daughter of an
earl, the last of her race, heiress of a great fortune and a lapsed
title. My father was her guardian. I loved her and she loved me;
but she was betrothed to Arthur from the cradle, and Sir Richard
would not suffer the contract to be broken. Arthur loved another
maid, and bade us be of good cheer and hold fast to the hope
that delay and luck together would some day give success to our
several causes. Hugh loved the Lady Edith's fortune, though in
truth he said it was herself he loved—but then 'twas his way,
alway, to say one thing and mean the other. But he lost his arts
upon the girl; he could deceive my father, but none else. My
father loved him best of us all, and trusted and believed him; for
he was the youngest child and others hated him—these qualities
being in all ages sufficient to win a parent's dearest love; and he

[1] He refers to the order of baronets, or baronettes—the *barones minores,* as
distinct from the parliamentary barons;—not, it need hardly be said, the
baronets of later creation.

had a smooth persuasive tongue, with an admirable gift of lying
—and these be qualities which do mightily assist a blind affection
to cozen itself. I was wild—in troth I might go yet farther and
say *very* wild, though 'twas a wildness of an innocent sort, since
it hurt none but me, brought shame to none, nor loss, nor had in
it any taint of crime or baseness, or what might not beseem mine
honorable degree.

"Yet did my brother Hugh turn these faults to good account
—he seeing that our brother Arthur's health was but indifferent,
and hoping the worst might work him profit were I swept out of
the path—so—but 'twere a long tale, good my liege, and little
worth the telling. Briefly, then, this brother did deftly magnify
my faults and make them crimes; ending his base work with
finding a silken ladder in mine apartments—conveyed thither by
his own means—and did convince my father by this, and suborned
evidence of servants and other lying knaves, that I was minded
to carry off my Edith and marry with her, in rank defiance of his
will.

"Three years of banishment from home and England might
make a soldier and a man of me, my father said, and teach me
some degree of wisdom. I fought out my long probation in the
continental wars, tasting sumptuously of hard knocks, privation,
and adventure; but in my last battle I was taken captive, and
during the seven years that have waxed and waned since then, a
foreign dungeon hath harbored me. Through wit and courage I
won to the free air at last, and fled hither straight; and am but
just arrived, right poor in purse and raiment, and poorer still in
knowledge of what these dull seven years have wrought at Hendon Hall, its people and belongings. So please you, sir, my
meager tale is told."

"Thou hast been shamefully abused!" said the little king, with
a flashing eye. "But I will right thee—by the cross will I! The
king hath said it."

Then, fired by the story of Miles's wrongs, he loosed his tongue
and poured the history of his own recent misfortunes into the
ears of his astonished listener. When he had finished, Miles said
to himself:

"Lo, what an imagination he hath! Verily this is no common mind; else, crazed or sane, it could not weave so straight and gaudy a tale as this out of the airy nothings wherewith it hath wrought this curious romaunt. Poor ruined little head, it shall not lack friend or shelter whilst I bide with the living. He shall never leave my side; he shall be my pet, my little comrade. And he shall be cured!—aye, made whole and sound—then will he make himself a name—and proud shall I be to say, 'Yes, he is mine—I took him, a homeless little ragamuffin, but I saw what was in him, and I said his name would be heard some day—behold him, observe him—was I right?'"

The king spoke—in a thoughtful, measured voice:

"Thou didst save me injury and shame, perchance my life, and so my crown. Such service demandeth rich reward. Name thy desire, and so it be within the compass of my royal power, it is thine."

This fantastic suggestion startled Hendon out of his reverie. He was about to thank the king and put the matter aside with saying he had only done his duty and desired no reward, but a wiser thought came into his head, and he asked leave to be silent a few moments and consider the gracious offer—an idea which the king gravely approved, remarking that it was best to be not too hasty with a thing of such great import.

Miles reflected during some moments, then said to himself, "Yes, that is the thing to do—by any other means it were impossible to get at it—and certes, this hour's experience has taught me 'twould be most wearing and inconvenient to continue it as it is. Yes, I will propose it; 'twas a happy accident that I did not throw the chance away." Then he dropped upon one knee and said:

"My poor service went not beyond the limit of a subject's simple duty, and therefore hath no merit; but since your majesty is pleased to hold it worthy some reward, I take heart of grace to make petition to this effect. Near four hundred years ago, as your grace knoweth, there being ill blood betwixt John, king of England, and the king of France, it was decreed that two champions should fight together in the lists, and so settle the dispute by what is called the arbitrament of God. These two kings, and the Spanish king, being assembled to witness and judge the conflict, the French champion appeared; but so redoubtable was he that our English knights refused to measure weapons with him. So the matter, which was a weighty one, was like to go against the English monarch by default. Now in the Tower lay the Lord de Courcy, the mightiest arm in England, stripped of his honors and possessions, and wasting with long captivity. Appeal was made to him; he gave assent, and came forth arrayed for battle; but no sooner did the Frenchman glimpse his huge frame and hear his famous name but he fled away, and the French king's cause was lost. King John restored De Courcy's titles and possessions, and said, 'Name thy wish and thou shalt have it, though it cost me half my kingdom'; whereat De Courcy, kneeling, as I do now, made answer, 'This, then, I ask, my liege; that I and my successors may have and hold the privilege of remaining covered in the presence of the kings of England, henceforth while the throne shall last.' The boon was granted, as your majesty knoweth; and there hath been no time, these four hundred years, that that line has failed of an heir; and so, even unto this day, the head of that ancient house still weareth his hat or helm before the king's majesty, without let or hindrance, and this none other may do.[1] Invoking this precedent in aid of my prayer, I beseech the king to grant to me but this one grace and privilege —to my more than sufficient reward—and none other, to wit: that I and my heirs, forever, may *sit* in the presence of the majesty of Engand!"

"Rise, Sir Miles Hendon, knight," said the king, gravely—giving the accolade with Hendon's sword—"rise, and seat thyself. Thy petition is granted. While England remains, and the crown continues, the privilege shall not lapse."

His majesty walked apart, musing, and Hendon dropped into a chair at table, observing to himself, "'Twas a brave thought, and hath wrought me a mighty deliverance; my legs are griev-

[1] The lords of Kingsale, descendants of De Courcy, still enjoy this curious privilege.

ously wearied. An I had not thought of that, I must have had to stand for weeks, till my poor lad's wits are cured." After a little he went on, "And so I am become a knight of the Kingdom of Dreams and Shadows! A most odd and strange position, truly, for one so matter-of-fact as I. I will not laugh—no, God forbid, for this thing which is so substanceless to me is *real* to him. And to me, also, in one way, it is not a falsity, for it reflects with truth the sweet and generous spirit that is in him." After a pause: "Ah, what if he should call me by my fine title before folk!—there'd be a merry contrast betwixt my glory and my raiment! But no matter; let him call me what he will, so it please him; I shall be content."

13

The Disappearance of the Prince

A HEAVY DROWSINESS presently fell upon the two comrades. The king said:

"Remove these rags"—meaning his clothing.

Hendon disappareled the boy without dissent or remark, tucked him up in bed, then glanced about the room, saying to himself, ruefully, "He hath taken my bed again, as before—marry, what shall *I* do?" The little king observed his perplexity, and dissipated it with a word. He said, sleepily:

"Thou wilt sleep athwart the door, and guard it." In a moment more he was out of his troubles, in a deep slumber.

"Dear heart, he should have been born a king!" muttered Hendon, admiringly; "he playeth the part to a marvel."

Then he stretched himself across the door, on the floor, saying contentedly:

"I have lodged worse for seven years; 'twould be but ill gratitude to Him above to find fault with this."

He dropped asleep as the dawn appeared. Toward noon he rose, uncovered his unconscious ward—a section at a time—and took his measure with a string. The king awoke, just as he had completed his work, complained of the cold, and asked what he was doing.

"'Tis done now, my liege," said Hendon; "I have a bit of business outside, but will presently return; sleep thou again—thou needest it. There—let me cover thy head also—thou'lt be warm the sooner."

The king was back in dreamland before this speech was ended. Miles slipped softly out, and slipped as softly in again, in the course of thirty or forty minutes, with a complete second-hand suit of boy's clothing, of cheap material, and showing signs of wear; but tidy, and suited to the season of the year. He seated himself, and began to overhaul his purchase, mumbling to himself:

"A longer purse would have got a better sort, but when one has not the long purse one must be content with what a short one may do—

"'There was a woman in our town,
In our town did dwell'—

"He stirred, methinks—I must sing in a less thunderous key; 'tis not good to mar his sleep, with this journey before him and he so wearied out, poor chap. . . . This garment—'tis well enough—a stitch here and another one there will set it aright. This other is better, albeit a stitch or two will not come amiss in it, likewise. . . . These be very good and sound, and will keep his small feet warm and dry—an odd new thing to him, belike, since he has doubtless been used to foot it bare, winters and summers the same. . . . Would thread were bread, seeing one getteth a year's sufficiency for a farthing, and such a brave big needle without cost, for mere love. Now shall I have the demon's own time to thread it!"

And so he had. He did as men have always done, and probably always will do, to the end of time—held the needle still, and tried to thrust the thread through the eye, which is the opposite of a woman's way. Time and time again the thread missed the mark, going sometimes on one side of the needle, sometimes on the other, sometimes doubling up against the shaft; but he was patient, having been through these experiences before, when he was soldiering. He succeeded at last, and took up the garment that had lain waiting, meantime, across his lap, and began his work. "The inn is paid—the breakfast that is to come, included—and there is wherewithal left to buy a couple of donkeys and meet our little costs for the two or three days betwixt this and the plenty that awaits us at Hendon Hall—

"'She loved her hus'—

"Body o' me! I have driven the needle under my nail! . . . It matters little—'tis not a novelty—yet 'tis not a convenience, neither. . . . We shall be merry there, little one, never doubt it! Thy troubles will vanish there, and likewise thy sad distemper—

"'She loved her husband dearilee,
But another man'—

"These be noble large stitches!"—holding the garment up and viewing it admiringly—"they have a grandeur and a majesty that do cause these small stingy ones of the tailor-man to look mighty paltry and plebeian—

"'She loved her husband dearilee,
But another man he loved she,'—

"Marry, 'tis done—a goodly piece of work, too, and wrought with expedition. Now will I wake him, apparel him, pour for him, feed him, and then will we hie us to the mart by the Tabard inn in Southwark and—be pleased to rise, my liege!—he answereth not—what ho, my liege!—of a truth must I profane his sacred person with a touch, sith his slumber is deaf to speech. What!"

He threw back the covers—the boy was gone!

He stared about him in speechless astonishment for a moment; noticed for the first time that his ward's ragged raiment was also missing, then he began to rage and storm, and shout for the innkeeper. At that moment a servant entered with the breakfast.

"Explain, thou limb of Satan, or thy time is come!" roared the man of war, and made so savage a spring toward the waiter that this latter could not find his tongue, for the instant, for fright and surprise. "Where is the boy?"

In disjointed and trembling syllables the man gave the information desired.

"You were hardly gone from the place, your worship, when a youth came running and said it was your worship's will that the boy come to you straight, at the bridge-end on the Southwark side. I brought him thither; and when he woke the lad and gave his message, the lad did grumble some little for being disturbed 'so early,' as he called it, but straightway trussed on his rags and went with the youth, only saying it had been better manners that your worship came yourself, not sent a stranger—and so—"

"And so thou'rt a fool!—a fool, and easily cozened—hang all thy breed! Yet mayhap no hurt is done. Possibly no harm is meant the boy. I will go fetch him. Make the table ready. Stay! the coverings of the bed were disposed as if one lay beneath them—happened that by accident?"

"I know not, good your worship. I saw the youth meddle with them—he that came for the boy."

"Thousand deaths! 'twas done to deceive me—'tis plain 'twas done to gain time. Hark ye! Was that youth alone?"

"All alone, your worship."

"Art sure?"

"Sure, your worship."

"Collect thy scattered wits—bethink thee—take time, man."

After a moment's thought, the servant said:

"When he came, none came with him; but now I remember me that as the two stepped into the throng of the Bridge, a ruffian-looking man plunged out from some near place; and just as he was joining them—"

"What *then?*—out with it!" thundered the impatient Hendon, interrupting.

"Just then the crowd lapped them up and closed them in, and I saw no more, being called by my master, who was in a rage because a joint that the scrivener had ordered was forgot, though I take all the saints to witness that to blame *me* for that miscarriage were like holding the unborn babe to judgment for sins com—"

"Out of my sight, idiot! Thy prating drives me mad! Hold! whither art flying? Canst not bide still an instant? Went they toward Southwark?"

"Even so, your worship—for, as I said before, as to that detestable joint, the babe unborn is no whit more blameless than—"

"Art here *yet!* And prating still? Vanish, lest I throttle thee!" The servitor vanished. Hendon followed after him, passed him, and plunged down the stairs two steps at a stride, muttering, "'Tis that scurvy villain that claimed he was his son. I have lost thee, my poor little mad master—it is a bitter thought—and I had come to love thee so! No! by book and bell, *not* lost! Not lost, for I will ransack the land till I find thee again. Poor child, yonder is his breakfast—and mine, but I have no hunger now—so, let the rats have it—speed, speed! that is the word!" As he wormed his swift way through the noisy multitudes upon the Bridge, he several times said to himself—clinging to the thought as if it were a particularly pleasing one: "He grumbled, but he *went*—he went, yes, because he thought Miles Hendon asked it, sweet lad—he would ne'er have done it for another, I know it well!"

14

TOWARD DAYLIGHT of the same morning, Tom Canty stirred out of a heavy sleep and opened his eyes in the dark. He lay silent a few moments, trying to analyze his confused thoughts and impressions, and get some sort of meaning out of them, then suddenly he burst out in a rapturous but guarded voice:

"I see it all, I see it all! Now God be thanked, I am, indeed, awake at last! Come, joy! vanish, sorrow! Ho, Nan! Bet! kick off your straw and hie ye hither to my side, till I do pour into your unbelieving ears the wildest madcap dream that ever the spirits of night did conjure up to astonish the soul of man withal! . . . Ho, Nan, I say! Bet!" . . .

A dim form appeared at his side, and a voice said:

"Wilt deign to deliver thy commands?"

"Commands? . . . Oh, woe is me, I know thy voice! Speak, thou—who am I?"

"Thou? In sooth, yesternight wert thou the Prince of Wales, to-day art thou my most gracious liege, Edward, king of England."

Tom buried his head among his pillows, murmuring plaintively:

"Alack, it was no dream! Go to thy rest, sweet sir—leave me to my sorrows."

Tom slept again, and after a time he had this pleasant dream. He thought it was summer and he was playing, all alone, in the fair meadow called Goodman's Fields, when a dwarf only a foot high, with long red whiskers and a humped back, appeared to him suddenly and said, "Dig, by that stump." He did so, and found twelve bright new pennies—wonderful riches! Yet this was not the best of it; for the dwarf said:

"I know thee. Thou art a good lad and deserving; thy distresses shall end, for the day of thy reward is come. Dig here every seventh day, and thou shalt find always the same treasure, twelve bright new pennies. Tell none—keep the secret."

Then the dwarf vanished, and Tom flew to Offal Court with his prize, saying to himself, "Every night will I give my father a penny; he will think I begged it, it will glad his heart, and I shall no more be beaten. One penny every week the good priest that teacheth me shall have; mother, Nan, and Bet the other four. We be done with hunger and rags now, done with fears and frets and savage usage."

In his dream he reached his sordid home all out of breath, but with eyes dancing with grateful enthusiasm; cast four of his pennies into his mother's lap and cried out:

"They are for thee!—all of them, every one!—for thee and Nan and Bet—and honestly come by, not begged nor stolen!"

The happy and astonished mother strained him to her breast and exclaimed:

"It waxeth late—may it please your majesty to rise?"

Ah, that was not the answer he was expecting. The dream had snapped asunder—he was awake.

He opened his eyes—the richly clad First Lord of the Bed-chamber was kneeling by his couch. The gladness of the lying dream faded away—the poor boy recognized that he was still a captive and a king. The room was filled with courtiers clothed in purple mantles—the mourning color—and with noble servants of the monarch. Tom sat up in bed and gazed out from the heavy silken curtains upon this fine company.

The weighty business of dressing began, and one courtier after another knelt and paid his court and offered to the little king his condolences upon his heavy loss, while the dressing proceeded. In the beginning, a shirt was taken up by the Chief Equerry in Waiting, who passed it to the First Lord of the Buckhounds, who passed it to the Second Gentleman of the Bedchamber, who passed it to the Head Ranger of Windsor Forest, who passed it to the Third Groom of the Stole, who passed it to the Chancellor Royal of the Duchy of Lancaster, who passed it to the Master of the Wardrobe, who passed it to Norroy King-at-Arms, who passed it to the Constable of the Tower, who passed it to the Chief Steward of the Household, who passed it to the Hereditary Grand Diaperer, who passed it to the Lord High Admiral of England, who passed it to the Archbishop of Canterbury, who passed it to the First Lord of the Bedchamber, who took what was left of it and put it on Tom. Poor little wondering chap, it reminded him of passing buckets at a fire.

Each garment in its turn had to go through this slow and solemn process; consequently Tom grew very weary of the ceremony; so weary that he felt an almost gushing gratefulness when he at last saw his long silken hose begin the journey down the line and knew that the end of the matter was drawing near. But he exulted too soon. The First Lord of the Bedchamber received the hose and was about to incase Tom's legs in them, when a sudden flush invaded his face and he hurriedly hustled the things back into the hands of the Archbishop of Canterbury with an astounded look and a whispered, "See, my lord!"—pointing to a something connected with the hose. The Archbishop paled, then flushed, and passed the hose to the Lord High Admiral, whispering, "See, my lord!" The Admiral passed the hose to the Hereditary Grand Diaperer, and had hardly breath enough in his body to ejaculate, "See, my lord!" The hose drifted backward along the line, to the Chief Steward of the Household, the Constable of the Tower, Norroy King-at-Arms, the Master of the Wardrobe, the Chancellor Royal of the Duchy of Lancaster, the Third Groom of the Stole, the Head Ranger of Windsor Forest, the Second Gentleman of the Bedchamber, the First Lord of the Buckhounds—accompanied always with that amazed and frightened "See! see!"—till they finally reached the hands of the Chief Equerry in Waiting, who gazed a moment, with a pallid face, upon what had caused all this dismay, then hoarsely whispered, "Body of my life, a tag gone from a truss point!—to the Tower with the Head Keeper of the King's Hose!"—after which he leaned upon the shoulder of the First Lord of the Buckhounds to regather his vanished strength while fresh hose, without any damaged strings to them, were brought.

But all things must have an end, and so in time Tom Canty was in a condition to get out of bed. The proper official poured water, the proper official engineered the washing, the proper official stood by with a towel, and by and by Tom got safely through the purifying stage and was ready for the services of the Hairdresser-royal. When he at length emerged from his master's hands, he was a gracious figure and as pretty as a girl, in his mantle and trunks of purple satin, and purple-plumed cap. He now moved in state toward his breakfast-room, through the midst of the courtly assemblage; and as he passed, these fell back, leaving his way free, and dropped upon their knees.

After breakfast he was conducted, with regal ceremony, attended by his great officers and his guard of fifty Gentlemen Pensioners bearing gilt battle-axes, to the throne-room, where he proceeded to transact business of state. His "uncle," Lord Hertford, took his stand by the throne, to assist the royal mind with wise counsel.

The body of illustrious men named by the late king as his executors, appeared, to ask Tom's approval of certain acts of theirs —rather a form, and yet not wholly a form, since there was no Protector as yet. The Archbishop of Canterbury made report of the decree of the Council of Executors concerning the obsequies of his late most illustrious majesty, and finished by reading the signatures of the executors, to wit: the Archbishop of Canterbury; the Lord Chancellor of England; William Lord St. John; John Lord Russell; Edward Earl of Hertford; John Viscount Lisle; Cuthbert Bishop of Durham—

Tom was not listening—an earlier clause of the document was puzzling him. At this point he turned and whispered to Lord Hertford:

"What day did he say the burial hath been appointed for?"

"The 16th of the coming month, my liege."

" 'Tis a strange folly. Will he keep?"

Poor chap, he was still new to the customs of royalty; he was used to seeing the forlorn dead of Offal Court hustled out of the way with a very different sort of expedition. However, the Lord Hertford set his mind at rest with a word or two.

A secretary of state presented an order of the council appointing the morrow at eleven for the reception of the foreign ambassadors, and desired the king's assent.

Tom turned an inquiring look toward Hertford, who whispered:

"Your majesty will signify consent. They come to testify their royal masters' sense of the heavy calamity which hath visited your grace and the realm of England."

Tom did as he was bidden. Another secretary began to read a preamble concerning the expenses of the late king's household, which had amounted to £28,000 during the preceding six months—a sum so vast that it made Tom Canty gasp; he gasped again when the fact appeared that £20,000 of this money were still owing and unpaid;[1] and once more when it appeared that the king's coffers were about empty, and his twelve hundred servants much embarrassed for lack of the wages due them. Tom spoke out, with lively apprehension.

"We be going to the dogs, 'tis plain. 'Tis meet and necessary that we take a smaller house and set the servants at large, sith they be of no value but to make delay, and trouble one with offices that harass the spirit and shame the soul, they misbecoming any but a doll, that hath nor brains nor hands to help itself withal. I remember me of a small house that standeth over against the fish-market, by Billingsgate—"

A sharp pressure upon Tom's arm stopped his foolish tongue and sent a blush to his face; but no countenance there betrayed any sign that this strange speech had been remarked or given concern.

A secretary made report that forasmuch as the late king had provided in his will for conferring the ducal degree upon the Earl of Hertford and raising his brother, Sir Thomas Seymour, to the peerage, and likewise Hertford's son to an earldom, to-

---

[1] Hume.

gether with similar aggrandizements to other great servants of the crown, the council had resolved to hold a sitting on the 16th of February for the delivering and confirming of these honors; and that meantime the late king not having granted, in writing, estates suitable to the support of these dignities, the council, knowing his private wishes in that regard, had thought proper to grant to Seymour "500 pound lands," and to Hertford's son "800 pound lands, and 300 pound of the next bishop's lands which should fall vacant,"—his present majesty being willing.[1]

Tom was about to blurt out something about the propriety of paying the late king's debts first before squandering all his money; but a timely touch upon his arm, from the thoughtful Hertford, saved him this indiscretion; wherefore he gave the royal assent, without spoken comment, but with much inward discomfort. While he sat reflecting a moment over the ease with which he was doing strange and glittering miracles, a happy thought shot into his mind: why not make his mother Duchess of Offal Court and give her an estate? But a sorrowful thought swept it instantly away; he was only a king in name, these grave veterans and great nobles were his masters; to them his mother was only the creature of a diseased mind; they would simply listen to his project with unbelieving ears, then send for the doctor.

The dull work went tediously on. Petitions were read, and proclamations, patents, and all manner of wordy, repetitious, and wearisome papers relating to the public business; and at last Tom sighed pathetically and murmured to himself, "In what have I offended, that the good God should take me away from the fields and the free air and the sunshine, to shut me up here and make me a king and afflict me so?" Then his poor muddled head nodded awhile, and presently dropped to his shoulder; and the business of the empire came to a standstill for want of that august factor, the ratifying power. Silence ensued around the slumbering child, and the sages of the realm ceased from their deliberations.

[1] Hume.

During the forenoon, Tom had an enjoyable hour, by permission of his keepers, Hertford and St. John, with the Lady Elizabeth and the little Lady Jane Grey; though the spirits of the princesses were rather subdued by the mighty stroke that had fallen upon the royal house; and at the end of the visit his "elder sister"—afterward the "Bloody Mary" of history—chilled him with a solemn interview which had but one merit in his eyes, its brevity. He had a few moments to himself, and then a slim lad of about twelve years of age was admitted to his presence, whose clothing, except his snowy ruff and the laces about his wrists, was of black—doublet, hose and all. He bore no badge of mourning but a knot of purple ribbon on his shoulder. He advanced hesitatingly, with head bowed and bare, and dropped upon one knee in front of Tom. Tom sat still and contemplated him soberly for a moment. Then he said:

"Rise, lad. Who art thou? What wouldst have?"

The boy rose, and stood at graceful ease, but with an aspect of concern in his face. He said:

"Of a surety thou must remember me, my lord. I am thy whipping-boy."

"My *whipping*-boy?"

"The same, your grace. I am Humphrey—Humphrey Marlow."

Tom perceived that here was some one whom his keepers ought to have posted him about. The situation was delicate. What should he do?—pretend he knew this lad, and then betray, by his every utterance, that he had never heard of him before? No, that would not do. An idea came to his relief: accidents like this might be likely to happen with some frequency, now that business urgencies would often call Hertford and St. John from his side, they being members of the council of executors; therefore perhaps it would be well to strike out a plan himself to meet the requirements of such emergencies. Yes, that would be a wise course—he would practise on this boy, and see what sort of success he might achieve. So he stroked his brow, perplexedly, a moment or two, and presently said:

"Now I seem to remember thee somewhat—but my wit is clogged and dim with suffering—"

"Alack, my poor master!" ejaculated the whipping-boy, with feeling; adding, to himself, "In truth 'tis as they said—his mind is gone—alas, poor soul! But misfortune catch me, how am I forgetting! they said one must not seem to observe that aught is wrong with him."

" 'Tis strange how my memory doth wanton with me these days," said Tom. "But mind it not—I mend apace—a little clue doth often serve to bring me back again the things and names which had escaped me. [And not they, only, forsooth, but e'en such as I ne'er heard before—as this lad shall see.] Give thy business speech."

" 'Tis matter of small weight, my liege, yet will I touch upon it, an it please your grace. Two days gone by, when your majesty faulted thrice in your Greek—in the morning lessons—dost remember it?"

"Ye-e-s—methinks I do. [It is not much of a lie—an I had meddled with the Greek at all, I had not faulted simply thrice, but forty times.] Yes, I do recall it now—go on."

—"The master, being wroth with what he termed such slovenly and doltish work, did promise that he would soundly whip me for it—and—"

"Whip *thee!*" said Tom, astonished out of his presence of mind. "Why should he whip *thee* for faults of mine?"

"Ah, your grace forgetteth again. He always scourgeth me, when thou dost fail in thy lessons."

"True, true—I had forgot. Thou teachest me in private—then if I fail, he argueth that thy office was lamely done, and—"

"Oh, my liege, what words are these? I, the humblest of thy servants, presume to teach *thee?*"

"Then where is thy blame? What riddle is this? Am I in truth gone mad, or is it thou? Explain—speak out."

"But, good your majesty, there's naught that needeth simplifying. None may visit the sacred person of the Prince of Wales with blows; wherefore when he faulteth, 'tis I that take them; and meet it is and right, for that it is mine office and my livelihood."

Tom stared at the tranquil boy, observing to himself, "Lo, it is a wonderful thing—a most strange and curious trade; I marvel they have not hired a boy to take my combings and my dressings for me—would heaven they would!—an they will do this thing, I will take my lashings in mine own person, giving God thanks for the change." Then he said aloud:

"And hast thou been beaten, poor friend, according to the promise?"

"No, good your majesty, my punishment was appointed for this day, and peradventure it may be annulled, as unbefitting the season of mourning that is come upon us; I know not, and so have made bold to come hither and remind your grace about your gracious promise to intercede in my behalf—"

"With the master? To save thee thy whipping?"

"Ah, thou dost remember!"

"My memory mendeth, thou seest. Set thy mind at ease—thy back shall go unscathed—I will see to it."

"Oh, thanks, my good lord!" cried the boy, dropping upon his knee again. "Mayhap I have ventured far enow; and yet". . . .

Seeing Master Humphrey hesitate, Tom encouraged him to go on, saying he was "in the granting mood."

"Then will I speak it out, for it lieth near my heart. Sith thou art no more Prince of Wales but king, thou canst order matters as thou wilt, with none to say thee nay; wherefore it is not in reason that thou wilt longer vex thyself with dreary studies, but wilt burn thy books and turn thy mind to things less irksome. Then am I ruined, and mine orphan sisters with me!"

"Ruined? Prithee, how?"

"My back is my bread, O my gracious liege! if it go idle, I starve. An thou cease from study, mine office is gone, thou'lt need no whipping-boy. Do not turn me away!"

Tom was touched with this pathetic distress. He said, with a right royal burst of generosity:

"Discomfort thyself no further, lad. Thine office shall be permanent in thee and thy line, forever." Then he struck the boy a light blow on the shoulder with the flat of his sword, exclaiming, "Rise, Humphrey Marlow, Hereditary Grand Whipping-Boy to the royal house of England! Banish sorrow—I will betake me to my books again, and study so ill that they must in justice treble thy wage, so mightily shall the business of thine office be augmented."

The grateful Humphrey responded fervidly:

"Thanks, oh, most noble master, this princely lavishness doth far surpass my most distempered dreams of fortune. Now shall I be happy all my days, and all the house of Marlow after me."

Tom had wit enough to perceive that here was a lad who could be useful to him. He encouraged Humphrey to talk, and he was nothing loath. He was delighted to believe that he was helping in Tom's "cure"; for always, as soon as he had finished calling back to Tom's diseased mind the various particulars of his experiences and adventures in the royal schoolroom and elsewhere about the palace, he noticed that Tom was then able to "recall" the circumstances quite clearly. At the end of an hour Tom found himself well freighted with very valuable information concerning personages and matters pertaining to the court; so he resolved to draw instruction from this source daily; and to this end he would give order to admit Humphrey to the royal closet whenever he might come, provided the majesty of England was not engaged with other people.

Humphrey had hardly been dismissed when my Lord Hertford arrived with more trouble for Tom. He said that the lords of the council, fearing that some overwrought report of the king's damaged health might have leaked out and got abroad, they deemed it wise and best that his majesty should begin to dine in public after a day or two—his wholesome complexion and vigorous step, assisted by a carefully guarded repose of manner and ease and grace of demeanor, would more surely quiet the general pulse—in case any evil rumors *had* gone about—than any other scheme that could be devised.

Then the earl proceeded, very delicately, to instruct Tom as to the observances proper to the stately occasion, under the rather thin disguise of "reminding" him concerning things already known to him; but to his vast gratification it turned out that Tom needed very little help in this line—he had been making use of Humphrey in that direction, for Humphrey had mentioned that within a few days he was to begin to dine in public; having gathered it from the swift-winged gossip of the court. Tom kept these facts to himself, however.

Seeing the royal memory so improved, the earl ventured to apply a few tests to it, in an apparently casual way, to find out how far its amendment had progressed. The results were happy, here and there, in spots—spots where Humphrey's tracks remained—and, on the whole, my lord was greatly pleased and encouraged. So encouraged was he, indeed, that he spoke up and said in a quite hopeful voice:

"Now am I persuaded that if your majesty will but tax your memory yet a little further, it will resolve the puzzle of the Great Seal—a loss which was of moment yesterday, although of none to-day, since its term of service ended with our late lord's life. May it please your grace to make the trial?"

Tom was at sea—a Great Seal was a something which he was totally unacquainted with. After a moment's hesitation he looked up innocently and asked:

"What was it like, my lord?"

The earl started, almost imperceptibly, muttering to himself, "Alack, his wits are flown again!—it was ill wisdom to lead him on to strain them"—then he deftly turned the talk to other matters, with the purpose of sweeping the unlucky Seal out of Tom's thoughts—a purpose which easily succeeded.

15

Tom as King

THE NEXT DAY the foreign ambassadors came, with their gorgeous trains; and Tom, throned in awful state, received them. The splendors of the scene delighted his eye and fired his imagination at first, but the audience was long and dreary, and so were most of the addresses—wherefore, what began as a pleasure, grew into weariness and homesickness by and by. Tom said the words which Hertford put into his mouth from time to time, and tried hard to acquit himself satisfactorily, but he was too new to such things, and too ill at ease to accomplish more than a tolerable success. He looked sufficiently like a king, but he was ill able to feel like one. He was cordially glad when the ceremony was ended.

The larger part of his day was "wasted"—as he termed it, in his own mind—in labors pertaining to his royal office. Even the two hours devoted to certain princely pastimes and recreations were rather a burden to him than otherwise, they were so fettered by restrictions and ceremonious observances. However, he had a private hour with his whipping-boy which he counted clear gain, since he got both entertainment and needful information out of it.

The third day of Tom Canty's kingship came and went much as the others had done, but there was a lifting of his cloud in one way—he felt less uncomfortable than at first; he was getting a little used to his circumstances and surroundings; his chains still galled, but not all the time; he found that the presence and homage of the great afflicted and embarrassed him less and less sharply with every hour that drifted over his head.

But for one single dread, he could have seen the fourth day approach without serious distress—the dining in public; it was to begin that day. There were greater matters in the program— for on that day he would have to preside at a council which would take his views and commands concerning the policy to be pursued toward various foreign nations scattered far and near over the great globe; on that day, too, Hertford would be formally chosen to the grand office of Lord Protector; other things of note were appointed for that fourth day also, but to Tom they were all insignificant compared with the ordeal of dining all by himself with a multitude of curious eyes fastened upon him and a multitude of mouths whispering comments upon his performance—and upon his mistakes, if he should be so unlucky as to make any.

Still, nothing could stop that fourth day, and so it came. It found poor Tom low-spirited and absent-minded, and this mood continued; he could not shake it off. The ordinary duties of the morning dragged upon his hands, and wearied him. Once more he felt the sense of captivity heavy upon him.

Late in the forenoon he was in a large audience chamber, conversing with the Earl of Hertford and duly awaiting the striking of the hour appointed for a visit of ceremony from a considerable number of great officials and courtiers.

After a little while Tom, who had wandered to a window and become interested in the life and movement of the great highway beyond the palace gates—and not idly interested, but longing with all his heart to take part in person in its stir and freedom —saw the van of a hooting and shouting mob of disorderly men, women, and children of the lowest and poorest degree approaching from up the road.

"I would I knew what 'tis about!" he exclaimed, with all a boy's curiosity in such happenings.

"Thou art the king!" solemnly responded the earl, with a reverence. "Have I your grace's leave to act?"

"Oh, blithely, yes! Oh, gladly, yes!" exclaimed Tom, excitedly, adding to himself with a lively sense of satisfaction, "In truth, being a king is not all dreariness—it hath its compensations and conveniences."

The earl called a page, and sent him to the captain of the guard with the order:

"Let the mob be halted, and inquiry made concerning the occasion of its movement. By the king's command!"

A few seconds later a long rank of the royal guards, cased in flashing steel, filed out at the gates and formed across the highway in front of the multitude. A messenger returned, to report that the crowd were following a man, a woman, and a young girl to execution for crimes committed against the peace and dignity of the realm.

Death—and a violent death—for these poor unfortunates! The thought wrung Tom's heartstrings. The spirit of compassion took control of him, to the exclusion of all other considerations; he never thought of the offended laws, or of the grief or loss which these three criminals had inflicted upon their victims, he could think of nothing but the scaffold and the grisly fate hanging over the heads of the condemned. His concern made him even forget, for the moment, that he was but the false shadow of a king, not the substance; and before he knew it he had blurted out the command:

"Bring them here!"

Then he blushed scarlet, and a sort of apology sprung to his lips; but observing that his order had wrought no sort of surprise in the earl or the waiting page, he suppressed the words he was about to utter. The page, in the most matter-of-course way, made a profound obeisance and retired backward out of the room to deliver the command. Tom experienced a glow of pride and a renewed sense of the compensating advantages of the kingly office. He said to himself, "Truly it is like what I used to feel when I read the old priest's tales, and did imagine mine own self a prince, giving law and command to all, saying, 'Do this, do that,' while none durst offer let or hindrance to my will."

Now the doors swung open; one high-sounding title after another was announced, the personages owning them followed, and the place was quickly half filled with noble folk and finery. But Tom was hardly conscious of the presence of these people, so wrought up was he and so intensely absorbed in that other and more interesting matter. He seated himself, absently, in his chair of state, and turned his eyes upon the door with manifestations of impatient expectancy; seeing which, the company forbore to trouble him, and fell to chatting a mixture of public business and court gossip one with another.

In a little while the measured tread of military men was heard approaching, and the culprits entered the presence in charge of an under-sheriff and escorted by a detail of the king's guard. The civil officer knelt before Tom, then stood aside; the three doomed persons knelt also, and remained so; the guard took position behind Tom's chair. Tom scanned the prisoners curiously. Something about the dress or appearance of the man had stirred a vague memory in him. "Methinks I have seen this man ere now . . . but the when or the where fail me"—such was Tom's thought. Just then the man glanced quickly up, and quickly dropped his face again, not being able to endure the awful port of sovereignty; but the one full glimpse of the face, which Tom got, was sufficient. He said to himself: "Now is the matter clear; this is the stranger that plucked Giles Witt out of the Thames, and saved his life that windy, bitter first day of the New Year— a brave, good deed—pity he hath been doing baser ones and got himself in this sad case. . . . I have not forgot the day, neither the hour; by reason that an hour after, upon the stroke of eleven, I did get a hiding by the hand of Gammer Canty which was of so goodly and admired severity that all that went before or followed after it were but fondlings and caresses by comparison."

Tom now ordered that the woman and the girl be removed from the presence for a little time; then addressed himself to the under-sheriff, saying:

"Good sir, what is this man's offense?"

The officer knelt, and answered:

"So please your majesty, he hath taken the life of a subject by poison."

Tom's compassion for the prisoner, and admiration of him as

the daring rescuer of a drowning boy, experienced a most damaging shock.

"The thing was proven upon him?" he asked.

"Most clearly, sire."

Tom sighed, and said:

"Take him away—he hath earned his death. 'Tis a pity, for he was a brave heart—na—na, I mean he hath the *look* of it!"

The prisoner clasped his hands together with sudden energy, and wrung them despairingly, at the same time appealing imploringly to the "king" in broken and terrified phrases:

"Oh, my lord the king, an thou canst pity the lost, have pity upon me! I am innocent—neither hath that wherewith I am charged been more than but lamely proved—yet I speak not of that; the judgment is gone forth against me and may not suffer alteration; yet in mine extremity I beg a boon, for my doom is more than I can bear. A grace, a grace, my lord the king! in thy royal compassion grant my prayer—give commandment that I be hanged!"

Tom was amazed. This was not the outcome he had looked for.

"Odds my life, a strange *boon!* Was it not the fate intended thee?"

"Oh, good my liege, not so! It is ordered that I be *boiled alive!*"

The hideous surprise of these words almost made Tom spring from his chair. As soon as he could recover his wits he cried out:

"Have thy wish, poor soul! an thou had poisoned a hundred men thou shouldst not suffer so miserable a death."

The prisoner bowed his face to the ground and burst into passionate expressions of gratitude—ending with:

"If ever thou shouldst know misfortune—which God forbid!— may thy goodness to me this day be remembered and requited!"

Tom turned to the Earl of Hertford, and said:

"My lord, is it believable that there was warrant for this man's ferocious doom?"

"It is the law, your grace—for poisoners. In Germany coiners be boiled to death in *oil*—not cast in of a sudden, but by a rope let down into the oil by degrees, and slowly; first the feet, then the legs, then—"

"Oh, prithee, no more, my lord, I cannot bear it!" cried Tom, covering his eyes with his hands to shut out the picture. "I beseech your good lordship that order be taken to change this law —oh, let no more poor creatures be visited with its tortures."

The earl's face showed profound gratification, for he was a man of merciful and generous impulses—a thing not very common with his class in that fierce age. He said:

"These your grace's noble words have sealed its doom. History will remember it to the honor of your royal house."

The under-sheriff was about to remove his prisoner; Tom gave him a sign to wait; then he said:

"Good sir, I would look into this matter further. The man has said his deed was but lamely proved. Tell me what thou knowest."

"If the king's grace please, it did appear upon the trial, that this man entered into a house in the hamlet of Islington where one lay sick—three witnesses say it was at ten of the clock in the morning and two say it was some minutes later—the sick man being alone at the time, and sleeping—and presently the man came forth again, and went his way. The sick man died within the hour, being torn with spasm and retchings."

"Did any see the poison given? Was poison found?"

"Marry, no, my liege."

"Then how doth one know there was poison given at all?"

"Please your majesty, the doctors testified that none die with such symptoms but by poison."

Weighty evidence, this—in that simple age. Tom recognized its formidable nature, and said:

"The doctor knoweth his trade—belike they were right. The matter hath an ill look for this poor man."

"Yet was not this all, your majesty; there is more and worse. Many testified that a witch, since gone from the village, none know whither, did foretell, and speak it privately in their ears, that the sick man *would die by poison*—and more, that a stranger would give it—a stranger with brown hair and clothed in a worn and common garb; and surely this prisoner doth answer woundily to the bill. Please, your majesty, to give the circumstance that solemn weight which is its due, seeing it was *foretold*."

This was an argument of tremendous force, in that superstitious day. Tom felt that the thing was settled; if evidence was worth anything, this poor fellow's guilt was proved. Still he offered the prisoner a chance, saying:

"If thou canst say aught in thy behalf, speak."

"Naught that will avail, my king. I am innocent, yet cannot I make it appear. I have no friends, else might I show that I was not in Islington that day; so also might I show that at that hour they name I was above a league away, seeing I was at Wapping Old Stairs; yea more, my king, for I could show, that while they say I was *taking* life, I was *saving* it. A drowning boy—"

"Peace! Sheriff, name the day the deed was done!"

"At ten in the morning, or some minutes later, the first day of the new year, most illustrious—"

"Let the prisoner go free—it is the king's will!"

Another blush followed this unregal outburst, and he covered his indecorum as well as he could by adding:

"It enrageth me that a man should be hanged upon such idle, hare-brained evidence!"

A low buzz of admiration swept through the assemblage. It was not admiration of the decree that had been delivered by Tom, for the propriety or expediency of pardoning a convicted poisoner was a thing which few there would have felt justified in either admitting or admiring—no, the admiration was for the intelligence and spirit which Tom had displayed. Some of the low-voiced remarks were to this effect:

"This is no mad king—he hath his wits sound."

"How sanely he put his questions—how like his former natural self was this abrupt, imperious disposal of the matter!"

"God be thanked his infirmity is spent! This is no weakling, but a king. He hath borne himself like to his own father."

The air being filled with applause, Tom's ear necessarily caught a little of it. The effect which this had upon him was to put him greatly at his ease, and also to charge his system with very gratifying sensations.

However, his juvenile curiosity soon rose superior to these pleasant thoughts and feelings; he was eager to know what sort of deadly mischief the woman and the little girl could have been about; so, by his command the two terrified and sobbing creatures were brought before him.

"What is it that these have done?" he inquired of the sheriff.

"Please your majesty, a black crime is charged upon them, and clearly proven; wherefore the judges have decreed, according to the law, that they be hanged. They sold themselves to the devil —such is their crime."

Tom shuddered. He had been taught to abhor people who did this wicked thing. Still, he was not going to deny himself the pleasure of feeding his curiosity, for all that; so he asked:

"Where was this done?—and when?"

"On a midnight, in December—in a ruined church, your majesty."

Tom shuddered again.

"Who was there present?"

"Only these two, your grace—and *that other*."

"Have these confessed?"

"Nay, not so, sire—they do deny it."

"Then, prithee, how was it known?"

"Certain witnesses did see them wending thither, good your majesty; this bred the suspicion, and dire effects have since confirmed and justified it. In particular, it is in evidence that through the wicked power so obtained, they did invoke and bring about a storm that wasted all the region round about. Above forty witnesses have proved the storm; and sooth one might have had a thousand, for all had reason to remember it, sith all had suffered by it."

"Certes this is a serious matter." Tom turned this dark piece of scoundrelism over in his mind awhile, then asked:

"Suffered the woman, also, by the storm?"

Several old heads among the assemblage nodded their recognition of the wisdom of this question. The sheriff, however, saw nothing consequential in the inquiry; he answered, with simple directness:

"Indeed, did she, your majesty, and most righteously, as all aver. Her habitation was swept away, and herself and child left shelterless."

"Methinks the power to do herself so ill a turn was dearly bought. She had been cheated, had she paid but a farthing for it; that she paid her soul, and her child's, argueth that she is mad; if she is mad she knoweth not what she doth, therefore sinneth not."

The elderly heads nodded recognition of Tom's wisdom once more, and one individual murmured, "An the king be mad himself, according to report, then it is a madness of a sort that would improve the sanity of some I wot of, if by the gentle providence of God they could but catch it."

"What age hath the child?" asked Tom.

"Nine years, please your majesty."

"By the law of England may a child enter into covenant and sell itself, my lord?" asked Tom, turning to a learned judge.

"The law doth not permit a child to make or meddle in any weighty matter, good my liege, holding that its callow wit unfitteth it to cope with the riper wit and evil schemings of them that are its elders. The *devil* may buy a child, if he so choose, and the child agree thereto, but not an Englishman—in this latter case the contract would be null and void."

"It seemeth a rude unchristian thing, and ill contrived, that English law denieth privileges to Englishmen, to waste them on the devil!" cried Tom, with honest heat.

This novel view of the matter excited many smiles, and was stored away in many heads to be repeated about the court as evidence of Tom's originality as well as progress toward mental health.

The elder culprit had ceased from sobbing, and was hanging upon Tom's words with an excited interest and a growing hope. Tom noticed this, and it strongly inclined his sympathies toward her in her perilous and unfriended situation. Presently he asked:

"How wrought they, to bring the storm?"

"*By pulling off their stockings, sire.*"

This astonished Tom, and also fired his curiosity to fever heat. He said, eagerly:

"It is wonderful! Hath it always this dread effect?"

"Always, my liege—at least if the woman desire it, and utter the needful words, either in her mind or with her tongue."

Tom turned to the woman, and said with impetuous zeal:

"Exert thy power—I would see a storm!"

There was a sudden paling of cheeks in the superstitious assemblage, and a general, though unexpressed, desire to get out of the place—all of which was lost upon Tom, who was dead to everything but the proposed cataclysm. Seeing a puzzled and astonished look in the woman's face, he added, excitedly:

"Never fear—thou shalt be blameless. More—thou shalt go free —none shall touch thee. Exert thy power."

"O, my lord the king, I have it not—I have been falsely accused."

"Thy fears stay thee. Be of good heart, thou shalt suffer no harm. Make a storm—it mattereth not how small a one—I require naught great or harmful, but indeed prefer the opposite—do this and thy life is spared—thou shalt go out free, with thy child, bearing the king's pardon, and safe from hurt or malice from any in the realm."

The woman prostrated herself, and protested, with tears, that she had no power to do the miracle, else she would gladly win her child's life alone, and be content to lose her own, if by obedience to the king's command so precious a grace might be acquired.

Tom urged—the woman still adhered to her declarations. Finally, he said:

"I think the woman hath said true. An *my* mother were in her place and gifted with the devil's functions, she had not stayed a moment to call her storms and lay the whole land in ruins, if the saving of my forfeit life were the price she got! It is argument that other mothers are made in like mold. Thou art free, good wife—thou and thy child—for I do think thee innocent. *Now* thou'st naught to fear, being pardoned—pull off thy stockings!— an thou canst make me a storm, thou shalt be rich!"

The redeemed creature was loud in her gratitude, and proceeded to obey, while Tom looked on with eager expectancy, a little marred by apprehension; the courtiers at the same time manifesting decided discomfort and uneasiness. The woman stripped her own feet and her little girl's also, and plainly did her best to reward the king's generosity with an earthquake, but it was all a failure and a disappointment. Tom sighed, and said:

"There, good soul, trouble thyself no further, thy power is departed out of thee. Go thy way in peace; and if it return to thee at any time, forget me not, but fetch me a storm."

16

The State Dinner

THE DINNER-HOUR drew near—yet, strangely enough, the thought brought but slight discomfort to Tom, and hardly any terror. The morning's experiences had wonderfully built up his confidence; the poor little ash-cat was already more wonted to his strange garret, after four days' habit, than a mature person could have become in a full month. A child's facility in accommodating itself to circumstances was never more strikingly illustrated.

Let us privileged ones hurry to the great banqueting-room and have a glance at matters there while Tom is being made ready for the imposing occasion. It is a spacious apartment, with gilded pillars and pilasters, and pictured walls and ceilings. At the door stand tall guards, as rigid as statues, dressed in rich and picturesque costumes, and bearing halberds. In a high gallery which runs all around the place is a band of musicians and a packed company of citizens of both sexes, in brilliant attire. In the center of the room, upon a raised platform, is Tom's table. Now let the ancient chronicler speak:

"A gentleman enters the room bearing a rod, and along with him another bearing a table-cloth, which, after they have both kneeled three times with the utmost veneration, he spreads upon the table, and after kneeling again they both retire; then come two others, one with the rod again, the other with a salt-cellar, a plate, and bread; when they have kneeled as the others had done, and placed what was brought upon the table, they too retire with the same ceremonies performed by the first; at last come two nobles, richly clothed, one bearing a tasting-knife, who, after prostrating themselves in the most graceful manner, approach and rub the table with bread and salt, with as much awe as if the king had been present."[1]

So end the solemn preliminaries. Now, far down the echoing corridors we hear a bugle-blast, and the indistinct cry, "Place for the king! way for the king's most excellent majesty!" These sounds are momently repeated—they grow nearer and nearer—and presently, almost in our faces, the martial note peals and the cry rings out, "Way for the king!" At this instant the shining pageant appears, and files in at the door, with a measured march. Let the chronicler speak again:

"First come Gentlemen, Barons, Earls, Knights of the Garter, all richly dressed and bareheaded; next comes the Chancellor, between two, one of which carries the royal scepter, the other the Sword of State in a red scabbard, studded with golden fleurs-de-lis, the point upwards; next comes the King himself—whom, upon his appearing, twelve trumpets and many drums salute with a great burst of welcome, whilst all in the galleries rise in their places, crying 'God save the King!' After him come nobles attached to his person, and on his right and left march his guard of honor, his fifty Gentlemen Pensioners, with gilt battle-axes."

This was all fine and pleasant. Tom's pulse beat high and a glad light was in his eye. He bore himself right gracefully, and all the more so because he was not thinking of how he was doing it, his mind being charmed and occupied with the blithe sights and sounds about him—and besides, nobody can be very ungraceful

[1] Leigh Hunt's *The Town*, p. 408, quotation from an early tourist.

in nicely fitting beautiful clothes after he has grown a little used to them—especially if he is for the moment unconscious of them. Tom remembered his instructions, and acknowledged his greeting with a slight inclination of his plumed head, and a courteous "I thank ye, my good people."

He seated himself at table without removing his cap; and did it without the least embarrassment: for to eat with one's cap on was the one solitary royal custom upon which the kings and the Cantys met upon common ground, neither party having any advantage over the other in the matter of old familiarity with it. The pageant broke up and grouped itself picturesquely, and remained bareheaded.

Now, to the sound of gay music, the Yeomen of the Guard entered—"the tallest and mightiest men in England, they being selected in this regard"—but we will let the chronicler tell about it:

"The Yeomen of the Guard entered bareheaded, clothed in scarlet, with golden roses upon their backs; and these went and came, bringing in each turn a course of dishes, served in plate. These dishes were received by a gentleman in the same order they were brought, and placed upon the table, while the taster gave to each guard a mouthful to eat of the particular dish he had brought, for fear of any poison."

Tom made a good dinner, notwithstanding he was conscious that hundreds of eyes followed each morsel to his mouth and watched him eat it with an interest which could not have been more intense if it had been a deadly explosive and was expected to blow him up and scatter him all over the place. He was careful not to hurry, and equally careful not to do anything whatever for himself, but wait till the proper official knelt down and did it for him. He got through without a mistake—flawless and precious triumph.

When the meal was over at last and he marched away in the midst of his bright pageant, with the happy noises in his ears of blaring bugles, rolling drums, and thundering acclamations, he felt that if he had seen the worst of dining in public, it was an ordeal which he would be glad to endure several times a day if by that means he could but buy himself free from some of the more formidable requirements of his royal office.

17

Foo-Foo the First

MILES HENDON hurried along toward the Southwark end of the bridge, keeping a sharp lookout for the persons he sought, and hoping and expecting to overtake them presently. He was disappointed in this, however. By asking questions, he was enabled to track them part of the way through Southwark; then all traces ceased, and he was perplexed as to how to proceed. Still, he continued his efforts as best he could during the rest of the day. Nightfall found him leg-weary, half famished, and his desire as far from accomplishment as ever; so he supped at the Tabard inn and went to bed, resolved to make an early start in the morning, and give the town an exhaustive search. As he lay thinking and planning, he presently began to reason thus: The boy would escape from the ruffian, his reputed father, if possible; would he go back to London and seek his former haunts? No, he would not do that, he would avoid recapture. What, then, would he do? Never having had a friend in the world, or a protector, until he met Miles Hendon, he would naturally try to find that friend again, provided the effort did not require him to go toward London and danger. He would strike for Hendon Hall, that is what he would do, for he knew Hendon was homeward bound, and there he might expect to find him. Yes, the case was plain to Hendon—he must lose no more time in Southwark, but move at once through Kent, toward Monk's Holm, searching the wood and inquiring as he went. Let us return to the vanished little king now.

The ruffian, whom the waiter at the inn on the Bridge saw "about to join" the youth and the king, did not exactly join them, but fell in close behind them and followed their steps. He said nothing. His left arm was in a sling, and he wore a large green patch over his left eye; he limped slightly, and used an oaken staff as a support. The youth led the king a crooked course through Southwark, and by and by struck into the highroad beyond. The king was irritated now, and said he would stop here —it was Hendon's place to come to him, not his to go to Hendon. He would not endure such insolence; he would stop where he was. The youth said:

"Thou'lt tarry here, and thy friend lying wounded in the wood yonder? So be it, then."

The king's manner changed at once. He cried out:

"Wounded? And who hath dared to do it? But that is apart; lead on, lead on! Faster, sirrah! art shod with lead? Wounded, is he? Now though the doer of it be a duke's son, he shall rue it!"

It was some distance to the wood, but the space was speedily traversed. The youth looked about him, discovered a bough sticking in the ground, with a small bit of rag tied to it, then led the way into the forest, watching for similar boughs and finding them at intervals; they were evidently guides to the point he was aiming at. By and by an open place was reached, where were the charred remains of a farmhouse, and near them a barn which was falling to ruin and decay. There was no sign of life anywhere, and utter silence prevailed. The youth entered the barn, the king following eagerly upon his heels. No one there! The king shot a surprised and suspicious glance at the youth, and asked:

"Where is he?"

A mocking laugh was his answer. The king was in a rage in a moment; he seized a billet of wood and was in the act of charging upon the youth when another mocking laugh fell upon his ear. It was from the lame ruffian, who had been following at a distance. The king turned and said angrily:

"Who art thou? What is thy business here?"

"Leave thy foolery," said the man, "and quiet thyself. My disguise is none so good that thou canst pretend thou knowest not thy father through it."

"Thou art not my father. I know thee not. I am the king. If thou hast hid my servant, find him for me, or thou shalt sup sorrow for what thou hast done."

John Canty replied, in a stern and measured voice:

"It is plain thou art mad, and I am loath to punish thee; but if thou provoke me, I must. Thy prating doth no harm here, where there are no ears that need to mind thy follies, yet is it well to practise thy tongue to wary speech, that it may do no hurt when our quarters change. I have done a murder, and may not tarry at home—neither shalt thou, seeing I need thy service. My name is changed, for wise reasons; it is Hobbs—John Hobbs; thine is Jack —charge thy memory accordingly. Now, then, speak. Where is thy mother? Where are thy sisters? They came not to the place appointed—knowest thou whither they went?"

The king answered, sullenly:

"Trouble me not with these riddles. My mother is dead; my sisters are in the palace."

The youth near by burst into a derisive laugh, and the king would have assaulted him, but Canty—or Hobbs, as he now called himself—prevented him, and said:

"Peace, Hugo, vex him not; his mind is astray, and thy ways fret him. Sit thee down, Jack, and quiet thyself; thou shalt have a morsel to eat, anon."

Hobbs and Hugo fell to talking together, in low voices, and the king removed himself as far as he could from their disagreeable company. He withdrew into the twilight of the farther end of the barn, where he found the earthen floor bedded a foot deep with straw. He lay down here, drew straw over himself in lieu of blankets, and was soon absorbed in thinking. He had many griefs, but the minor ones were swept almost into forgetfulness by the supreme one, the loss of his father. To the rest of the world the name of Henry VIII. brought a shiver, and suggested an ogre whose nostrils breathed destruction and whose hand dealt scourgings and death; but to this boy the name brought only sensations of pleasure, the figure it invoked wore a countenance that was all gentleness and affection. He called to mind a long succession of loving passages between his father and himself, and dwelt fondly upon them, his unstinted tears attesting how deep and real was the grief that possessed his heart. As the afternoon wasted away, the lad, wearied with his troubles, sunk gradually into a tranquil and healing slumber.

After a considerable time—he could not tell how long—his senses struggled to a half-consciousness, and as he lay with closed eyes vaguely wondering where he was and what had been happening, he noted a murmurous sound, the sullen beating of rain upon the roof. A snug sense of comfort stole over him, which was rudely broken, the next moment, by a chorus of piping cackles and coarse laughter. It startled him disagreeably, and he unmuffled his head to see whence this interruption proceeded. A grim and unsightly picture met his eye. A bright fire was burning in the middle of the floor, at the other end of the barn; and around it, and lit weirdly up by the red glare, lolled and sprawled the motliest company of tattered gutter-scum and ruffians, of both sexes, he had ever read or dreamed of. There were huge, stalwart men, brown with exposure, long-haired, and clothed in fantastic rags; there were middle-sized youths, of truculent countenance, and similarly clad; there were blind mendicants, with patched or bandaged eyes; crippled ones, with wooden legs and crutches; there was a villain-looking peddler with his pack; a knife-grinder, a tinker, and a barber-surgeon, with the implements of their trades; some of the females were hardly grown girls, some were at prime, some were old and wrinkled hags, and all were loud, brazen, foul-mouthed; and all soiled and slatternly; there were three sore-faced babies; there were a couple of starveling curs, with strings about their necks, whose office was to lead the blind.

The night was come, the gang had just finished feasting, an orgy was beginning, the can of liquor was passing from mouth to mouth. A general cry broke forth:

"A song! a song from the Bat and Dick Dot-and-go-One!"

One of the blind men got up, and made ready by casting aside the patches that sheltered his excellent eyes, and the pathetic placard which recited the cause of his calamity. Dot-and-go-One disencumbered himself of his timber leg and took his place, upon sound and healthy limbs, beside his fellow-rascal; then they roared out a rollicking ditty, and were reinforced by the whole crew, at the end of each stanza, in a rousing chorus. By the time the last stanza was reached, the half-drunken enthusiasm had risen to such a pitch that everybody joined in and sang it clear through from the beginning, producing a volume of villainous sound that made the rafters quake. These were the inspiring words:

> "Bien Darkmans then, Bouse Mort and Ken,
> The bien Coves bings awast,
> On Chates to trine by Rome Coves dine
> For his long lib at last.
> Bing'd out bien Morts and toure, and toure,
> Bing out of the Rome vile bine,
> And toure the Cove that cloy'd your duds,
> Upon the Chates to trine."[1]

Conversation followed; not in the thieves' dialect of the song, for that was only used in talk when unfriendly ears might be listening. In the course of it it appeared that "John Hobbs" was not altogether a new recruit, but had trained in the gang at some former time. His later history was called for, and when he said he had "accidentally" killed a man, considerable satisfaction was expressed; when he added that the man was a priest, he was roundly applauded, and had to take a drink with everybody. Old acquaintances welcomed him joyously, and new ones were proud to shake him by the hand. He was asked why he had "tarried away so many months." He answered:

"London is better than the country, and safer these late years, the laws be so bitter and so diligently enforced. An I had not had that accident, I had stayed there. I had resolved to stay, and nevermore venture countrywards—but the accident had ended that."

He inquired how many persons the gang numbered now. The "Ruffler," or chief, answered:

[1] From "The English Rogue": London, 1665.

"Five and twenty sturdy budges, bulks, files, clapperdogeons and maunders, counting the dells and doxies and other morts.[1] Most are here, the rest are wandering eastward, along the winter lay. We follow at dawn."

"I do not see the Wen among the honest folk about me. Where may he be?"

"Poor lad, his diet is brimstone now, and over hot for a delicate taste. He was killed in a brawl, somewhere about midsummer."

"I sorrow to hear that; the Wen was a capable man, and brave."

"That was he, truly. Black Bess, his dell, is of us yet, but absent on the eastward tramp; a fine lass, of nice ways and orderly conduct, none ever seeing her drunk above four days in the seven."

"She was ever strict—I remember it well—a goodly wench and worthy all commendation. Her mother was more free and less particular; a troublesome and ugly-tempered beldame, but furnished with a wit above the common."

"We lost her through it. Her gift of palmistry and other sorts of fortune-telling begot for her at last a witch's name and fame. The law roasted her to death at a slow fire. It did touch me to a sort of tenderness to see the gallant way she met her lot—cursing and reviling all the crowd that gaped and gazed around her, whilst the flames licked upward toward her face and catched her thin locks and crackled about her old gray head—cursing them, said I?—cursing them! why an thou shouldst live a thousand years thou'dst never hear so masterful a cursing. Alack, her art died with her. There be base and weakling imitations left, but no true blasphemy."

The Ruffler sighed; the listeners sighed in sympathy; a general depression fell upon the company for a moment, for even hardened outcasts like these are not wholly dead to sentiment, but are able to feel a fleeting sense of loss and affliction at wide intervals and under peculiarly favoring circumstances—as in cases like to this, for instance, when genius and culture depart and leave no heir. However, a deep drink all round soon restored the spirits of the mourners.

---

[1] Canting terms for various kinds of thieves, beggars, and vagabonds, and their female companions.

"Have any other of our friends fared hardly?" asked Hobbs.

"Some—yes. Particularly new-comers—such as small husband-men turned shiftless and hungry upon the world because their farms were taken from them to be changed to sheep-ranges. They begged, and were whipped at the cart's tail, naked from the girdle up, till the blood ran; then set in the stocks to be pelted; they begged again, were whipped again, and deprived of an ear; they begged a third time—poor devils, what else could they do?— and were branded on the cheek with a red-hot iron, then sold for slaves; they ran away, were hunted down, and hanged. 'Tis a brief tale, and quickly told. Others of us have fared less hardly. Stand forth, Yokel, Burns, and Hodge—show your adornments!"

These stood up and stripped away some of their rags, exposing their backs, crisscrossed with ropy old welts left by the lash; one turned up his hair and showed the place where a left ear had once been; another showed a brand upon his shoulder—the letter V—and a mutilated ear; the third said:

"I am Yokel, once a farmer and prosperous, with loving wife and kids—now am I somewhat different in estate and calling; and the wife and kids are gone; mayhap they are in heaven, mayhap in—in the other place—but the kindly God be thanked, they bide no more in *England!* My good old blameless mother strove to earn bread by nursing the sick; one of these died, the doctors knew not how, so my mother was burned for a witch, whilst my babes looked on and wailed. English law!—up, all, with your cups! —now all together and with a cheer!—drink to the merciful English law that delivered *her* from the English hell! Thank you, mates, one and all. I begged, from house to house—I and the wife —bearing with us the hungry kids—but it was crime to be hungry in England—so they stripped us and lashed us through three towns. Drink ye all again to the merciful English law!—for its lash drank deep of my Mary's blood and its blessed deliverance came quick. She lies there, in the potter's field, safe from all harms. And the kids—well, whilst the law lashed me from town to town, they starved. Drink lads—only a drop—a drop to the poor kids, that never did any creature harm. I begged again—begged for a crust, and got the stocks and lost an ear—see, here bides the stump; I begged again, and here is the stump of the other to keep me minded of it. And still I begged again, and was sold for a slave—here on my cheek under this stain, if I washed it off, ye might see the red S the branding-iron left there! A SLAVE! Do ye understand that word! An English SLAVE!—that is he that stands before ye. I have run from my master, and when I am found—the heavy curse of heaven fall on the law of the land that hath commanded it!—I shall hang!"

A ringing voice came through the murky air:

"Thou shalt *not!*—and this day the end of that law is come!"

All turned, and saw the fantastic figure of the little king approaching hurriedly; as it emerged into the light and was clearly revealed, a general explosion of inquiries broke out:

"Who is it? *What* is it? Who art thou, manikin?"

The boy stood unconfused in the midst of all those surprised and questioning eyes, and answered with princely dignity:

"I am Edward, king of England."

A wild burst of laughter followed, partly of derision and partly of delight in the excellence of the joke. The king was stung. He said sharply:

"Ye mannerless vagrants, is this your recognition of the royal boon I have promised?"

He said more, with angry voice and excited gesture, but it was lost in a whirlwind of laughter and mocking exclamations. "John Hobbs" made several attempts to make himself heard above the din, and at last succeeded—saying:

"Mates, he is my son, a dreamer, a fool, and stark mad—mind him not—he thinketh he *is* the king."

"I *am* the king," said Edward, turning toward him, "as thou shalt know to thy cost, in good time. Thou hast confessed a murder—thou shalt swing for it."

"*Thou'lt* betray me!—*thou?* An I get my hands upon thee—"

"Tut-tut!" said the burly Ruffler, interposing in time to save the king, and emphasizing this service by knocking Hobbs down with his fist, "hast respect for neither kings *nor* Rufflers? An thou insult my presence so again, I'll hang thee up myself." Then he said to his majesty, "Thou must make no threats against thy mates, lad;

and thou must guard thy tongue from saying evil of them else-where. *Be* king, if it please thy mad humor, but be not harmful in it. Sink the title thou hast uttered—'tis treason; we be bad men, in some few trifling ways, but none among us is so base as to be traitor to his king; we be loving and loyal hearts, in that regard. Note if I speak truth. Now—all together: 'Long live Edward, king of England!'"

"LONG LIVE EDWARD, KING OF ENGLAND!"

The response came with such a thunder-gust from the motley crew that the crazy building vibrated to the sound. The little king's face lighted with pleasure for an instant, and he slightly inclined his head and said with grave simplicity:

"I thank you, my good people."

This unexpected result threw the company into convulsions of merriment. When something like quiet was presently come again, the Ruffler said, firmly, but with an accent of good nature:

"Drop it, boy, 'tis not wise, nor well. Humor thy fancy, if thou must, but choose some other title."

A tinker shrieked out a suggestion:

"Foo-foo the First, king of the Mooncalves!"

The title "took" at once, every throat responded, and a roaring shout went up, of:

"Long live Foo-foo the First, king of the Mooncalves!" followed by hootings, cat-calls, and peals of laughter.

"Hale him forth, and crown him!"

"Robe him!"

"Scepter him!"

"Throne him!"

These and twenty other cries broke out at once; and almost before the poor little victim could draw a breath he was crowned with a tin basin, robed in a tattered blanket, throned upon a barrel, and sceptered with the tinker's soldering-iron. Then all flung themselves upon their knees about him and sent up a chorus of ironical wailings, and mocking supplications, while they swabbed their eyes with their soiled and ragged sleeves and aprons:

"Be gracious to us, O sweet king!"

"Trample not upon thy beseeching worms, O noble majesty!"

"Pity thy slaves, and comfort them with a royal kick!"

"Cheer us and warm us with thy gracious rays, O flaming sun of sovereignty!"

"Sanctify the ground with the touch of thy foot, that we may eat the dirt and be ennobled!"

"Deign to spit upon us, O sire, that our children's children may tell of thy princely condescension, and be proud and happy forever!"

But the humorous tinker made the "hit" of the evening and carried off the honors. Kneeling, he pretended to kiss the king's foot, and was indignantly spurned; whereupon he went about begging for a rag to paste over the place upon his face which had been touched by the foot, saying it must be preserved from contact with the vulgar air, and that he should make his fortune by going on the highway and exposing it to view at the rate of a hundred shillings a sight. He made himself so killingly funny that he was the envy and admiration of the whole mangy rabble.

Tears of shame and indignation stood in the little monarch's eyes; and the thought in his heart was, "Had I offered them a deep wrong they could not be more cruel—yet have I proffered naught but to do them a kindness—and it is thus they use me for it!"

18

The Prince with the Tramps

THE TROOP of vagabonds turned out at early dawn, and set forward on their march. There was a lowering sky overhead, sloppy ground under foot, and a winter chill in the air. All gaiety was gone from the company; some were sullen and silent, some were irritable and petulant, none were gentle-humored, all were thirsty.

The Ruffler put "Jack" in Hugo's charge, with some brief instructions, and commanded John Canty to keep away from him and let him alone; he also warned Hugo not to be too rough with the lad.

After a while the weather grew milder, and the clouds lifted somewhat. The troop ceased to shiver, and their spirits began to improve. They grew more and more cheerful, and finally began to chaff each other and insult passengers along the highway. This showed that they were awaking to an appreciation of life and its joys once more. The dread in which their sort was held was apparent in the fact that everybody gave them the road, and took their ribald insolences meekly, without venturing to talk back. They snatched linen from the hedges, occasionally, in full view of the owners, who made no protest, but only seemed grateful that they did not take the hedges, too.

By and by they invaded a small farmhouse and made themselves at home while the trembling farmer and his people swept the larder clean to furnish a breakfast for them. They chucked the housewife and her daughters under the chin while receiving the food from their hands, and made coarse jests about them, accompanied with insulting epithets and bursts of horse-laughter. They threw bones and vegetables at the farmer and his sons, kept them dodging all the time, and applauded uproariously when a good hit was made. They ended by buttering the head of one of the daughters who resented some of their familiarities. When they took their leave they threatened to come back and burn the house over the heads of the family if any report of their doings got to the ears of the authorities.

About noon, after a long and weary tramp, the gang came to a halt behind a hedge on the outskirts of a considerable village. An hour was allowed for rest, then the crew scattered themselves abroad to enter the village at different points to ply their various trades. "Jack" was sent with Hugo. They wandered hither and thither for some time, Hugo watching for opportunities to do a stroke of business but finding none—so he finally said:

"I see naught to steal; it is a paltry place. Wherefore we will beg."

"*We*, forsooth! Follow thy trade—it befits thee. But *I* will not beg."

"Thou'lt not beg!" exclaimed Hugo, eying the king with surprise. "Prithee, since when hast thou reformed?"

"What dost thou mean?"

"Mean? Hast thou not begged the streets of London all thy life?"

"I? Thou idiot!"

"Spare thy compliments—thy stock will last the longer. Thy father says thou hast begged all thy days. Mayhap he lied. Peradventure you will even make so bold as to *say* he lied," scoffed Hugo.

"Him *you* call my father? Yes, he lied."

"Come, play not thy merry game of madman so far, mate; use it for thy amusement, not thy hurt. An I tell him this, he will scorch thee finely for it."

"Save thyself the trouble. I will tell him."

"I like thy spirit, I do in truth; but I do not admire thy judgment. Bone-rackings and bastings be plenty enow in this life, without going out of one's way to invite them. But a truce to these matters; *I* believe your father. I doubt not he can lie; I doubt not he *doth* lie, upon occasion, for the best of us do that; but there is no occasion here. A wise man does not waste so good a commodity as lying for naught. But come; sith it is thy humor to give over begging, wherewithal shall we busy ourselves? With robbing kitchens?"

The king said, impatiently:

"Have done with this folly—you weary me!"

Hugo replied, with temper:

"Now harkee, mate; you will not beg, you will not rob; so be it. But I will tell you what you *will* do. You will play decoy whilst *I* beg. Refuse, an you think you may venture!"

The king was about to reply contemptuously, when Hugo said, interrupting:

"Peace! Here comes one with a kindly face. Now will I fall

down in a fit. When the stranger runs to me, set you up a wail, and fall upon your knees, seeming to weep; then cry out as if all the devils of misery were in your belly, and say, 'Oh, sir, it is my poor afflicted brother, and we be friendless; o' God's name cast through your merciful eyes one pitiful look upon a sick, forsaken, and most miserable wretch; bestow one little penny out of thy riches upon one smitten of God and ready to perish!'—and mind you, keep you *on* wailing, and abate not till we bilk him of his penny, else shall you rue it."

Then immediately Hugo began to moan, and groan, and roll his eyes, and reel and totter about; and when the stranger was close at hand, down he sprawled before him, with a shriek, and began to writhe and wallow in the dirt, in seeming agony.

"O dear, O dear!" cried the benevolent stranger. "Oh, poor soul, poor soul, how he doth suffer! There—let me help thee up."

"O, noble sir, forbear, and God love you for a princely gentleman—but it giveth me cruel pain to touch me when I am taken so. My brother there will tell your worship how I am racked with anguish when these fits be upon me. A penny, dear sir, a penny, to buy a little food; then leave me to my sorrows."

"A penny! thou shalt have three, thou hapless creature"—and he fumbled in his pocket with nervous haste and got them out. "There, poor lad, take them, and most welcome. Now come hither, my boy, and help me carry thy stricken brother to yon house, where—"

"I am not his brother," said the king, interrupting.

"What! not his brother?"

"Oh, hear him!" groaned Hugo, then privately ground his teeth. "He denies his own brother—and he with one foot in the grave!"

"Boy, thou art indeed hard of heart, if this is thy brother. For shame!—and he scarce able to move hand or foot. If he is not thy brother, who is he, then?"

"A beggar and a thief! He has got your money and has picked your pocket likewise. An thou wouldst do a healing miracle, lay thy staff over his shoulders and trust Providence for the rest."

But Hugo did not tarry for the miracle. In a moment he was

up and off like the wind, the gentleman following after and
raising the hue and cry lustily as he went. The king, breathing
deep gratitude to Heaven for his own release, fled in the opposite direction and did not slacken his pace until he was out of
harm's reach. He took the first road that offered, and soon put
the village behind him. He hurried along, as briskly as he could,
during several hours, keeping a nervous watch over his shoulder
for pursuit; but his fears left him at last, and a grateful sense of
security took their place. He recognized now that he was
hungry; and also very tired. So he halted at a farmhouse; but
when he was about to speak, he was cut short and driven rudely
away. His clothes were against him.

He wandered on, wounded and indignant, and was resolved
to put himself in the way of light treatment no more. But
hunger is pride's master; so as the evening drew near, he made
an attempt at another farmhouse; but here he fared worse than
before; for he was called hard names and was promised arrest
as a vagrant except he moved on promptly.

The night came on, chilly and overcast; and still the footsore
monarch labored slowly on. He was obliged to keep moving, for
every time he sat down to rest he was soon penetrated to the
bone with the cold. All his sensations and experiences, as he
moved through the solemn gloom and the empty vastness of the
night, were new and strange to him. At intervals he heard voices
approach, pass by, and fade into silence; and as he saw nothing
more of the bodies they belonged to than a sort of formless
drifting blur, there was something spectral and uncanny about
it all that made him shudder. Occasionally he caught the twinkle
of a light—always far away, apparently—almost in another world;
if he heard the tinkle of a sheep's bell, it was vague, distant,
indistinct; the muffled lowing of the herds floated to him on the
night wind in vanishing cadences, a mournful sound; now and
then came the complaining howl of a dog over viewless expanses
of field and forest; all sounds were remote; they made the little
king feel that all life and activity were far removed from him,
and that he stood solitary, companionless, in the center of a
measureless solitude.

He stumbled along, through the gruesome fascinations of this new experience, startled occasionally by the soft rustling of the dry leaves overhead, so like human whispers they seemed to sound; and by and by he came suddenly upon the freckled light of a tin lantern near at hand. He stepped back into the shadows and waited. The lantern stood by the open door of a barn. The king waited some time—there was no sound, and nobody stirring. He got so cold, standing still, and the hospitable barn looked so enticing, that at last he resolved to risk everything and enter. He started swiftly and stealthily, and just as he was crossing the threshold he heard voices behind him. He darted behind a cask, within the barn, and stooped down. Two farm laborers came in, bringing the lantern with them, and fell to work, talking meanwhile. Whilst they moved about with the light, the king made good use of his eyes and took the bearings of what seemed to be a good-sized stall at the further end of the place, purposing to grope his way to it when he should be left to himself. He also noted the position of a pile of horse-blankets, midway of the route, with the intent to levy upon them for the service of the crown of England for one night.

By and by the men finished and went away, fastening the door behind them and taking the lantern with them. The shivering king made for the blankets, with as good speed as the darkness would allow; gathered them up and then groped his way safely to the stall. Of two of the blankets he made a bed, then covered himself with the remaining two. He was a glad monarch now, though the blankets were old and thin, and not quite warm enough; and besides gave out a pungent horsy odor that was almost suffocatingly powerful.

Although the king was hungry and chilly, he was also so tired and so drowsy that these latter influences soon began to get the advantage of the former, and he presently dozed off into a state of semi-consciousness. Then, just as he was on the point of losing himself wholly, he distinctly felt something touch him! He was broad awake in a moment, and gasping for breath. The cold horror of that mysterious touch in the dark almost made his heart stand still. He lay motionless, and listened, scarcely breathing.

But nothing stirred, and there was no sound. He continued to listen, and wait, during what seemed a long time, but still nothing stirred, and there was no sound. So he began to drop into a drowse once more at last; and all at once he felt that mysterious touch again! It was a grisly thing, this light touch from this noiseless and invisible presence; it made the boy sick with ghostly fears. What should he do? That was the question; but he did not know how to answer it. Should he leave these reasonably comfortable quarters and fly from this inscrutable horror? But fly whither? He could not get out of the barn; and the idea of scurrying blindly hither and thither in the dark, within the captivity of the four walls, with this phantom gliding after him, and visiting him with that soft hideous touch upon cheek or shoulder at every turn, was intolerable. But to stay where he was, and endure this living death all night—was that better? No. What, then, was there left to do? Ah, there was but one course; he knew it well—he must put out his hand and find that thing!

It was easy to think this; but it was hard to brace himself up to try it. Three times he stretched his hand a little way out into the dark gingerly; and snatched it suddenly back, with a gasp—not because it had encountered anything, but because he had felt so sure it was just *going* to. But the fourth time he groped a little further, and his hand lightly swept against something soft and warm. This petrified him nearly with fright—his mind was in such a state that he could imagine the thing to be nothing else than a corpse, newly dead and still warm. He thought he would rather die than touch it again. But he thought this false thought because he did not know the immortal strength of human curiosity. In no long time his hand was tremblingly groping again—against his judgment, and without his consent—but groping persistently on, just the same. It encountered a bunch of long hair; he shuddered, but followed up the hair and found what seemed to be a warm rope; followed up the rope and found an innocent calf!—for the rope was not a rope at all, but the calf's tail.

The king was cordially ashamed of himself for having gotten all that fright and misery out of so paltry a matter as a slumbering calf; but he need not have felt so about it, for it was not the calf that frightened him but a dreadful non-existent something which the calf stood for; and any other boy, in those old superstitious times, would have acted and suffered just as he had done.

The king was not only delighted to find that the creature was only a calf, but delighted to have the calf's company; for he had been feeling so lonesome and friendless that the company and comradeship of even this humble animal was welcome. And he had been so buffeted, so rudely entreated by his own kind, that it was a real comfort to him to feel that he was at last in the society of a fellow-creature that had at least a soft heart and a gentle spirit, whatever loftier attributes might be lacking. So he resolved to waive rank and make friends with the calf.

While stroking its sleek, warm back—for it lay near him and within easy reach—it occurred to him that this calf might be utilized in more ways than one. Whereupon he rearranged his bed, spreading it down close to the calf; then he cuddled himself up to the calf's back, drew the covers up over himself and his friend, and in a minute or two was as warm and comfortable as he had ever been in the downy couches of the regal palace of Westminster.

Pleasant thoughts came at once; life took on a cheerfuler seeming. He was free of the bonds of servitude and crime, free of the companionship of base and brutal outlaws; he was warm, he was sheltered; in a word, he was happy. The night wind was rising; it swept by in fitful gusts that made the old barn quake and rattle, then its forces died down at intervals, and went moaning and wailing around corners and projections—but it was all music to the king, now that he was snug and comfortable; let it blow and rage, let it batter and bang, let it moan and wail, he minded it not, he only enjoyed it. He merely snuggled the closer to his friend, in a luxury of warm contentment, and drifted blissfully out of consciousness into a deep and dreamless sleep that was full of serenity and peace. The distant dogs howled, the melancholy kine complained, and the winds went on raging, whilst furious sheets of rain drove along the roof; but the majesty of England slept on undisturbed, and the calf did the same, it being a simple creature and not easily troubled by storms or embarrassed by sleeping with a king.

19

The Prince with the Peasants

WHEN the king awoke in the early morning, he found that a wet but thoughtful rat had crept into the place during the night and made a cozy bed for itself in his bosom. Being disturbed now, it scampered away. The boy smiled, and said, "Poor fool, why so fearful? I am as forlorn as thou. 'Twould be a shame in me to hurt the helpless, who am myself so helpless. Moreover, I owe you thanks for a good omen; for when a king has fallen so low that the very rats do make a bed of him, it surely meaneth that his fortunes be upon the turn, since it is plain he can no lower go."

He got up and stepped out of the stall, and just then he heard the sound of children's voices. The barn door opened and a couple of little girls came in. As soon as they saw him their talking and laughing ceased, and they stopped and stood still, gazing at him with strong curiosity; they presently began to whisper together, then they approached nearer, and stopped again to gaze and whisper. By and by they gathered courage and began to discuss him aloud. One said:

"He hath a comely face."

The other added:

"And pretty hair."

"But is ill clothed enow."

"And how starved he looketh."

They came still nearer, sidling shyly around and about him, examining him minutely from all points, as if he were some strange new kind of animal; but warily and watchfully the while, as if they half feared he might be a sort of animal that would bite, upon occasion. Finally they halted before him, holding each other's hands for protection, and took a good satisfying stare with their innocent eyes; then one of them plucked up all her courage and inquired with honest directness:

"Who art thou, boy?"

"I am the king," was the grave answer.

The children gave a little start, and their eyes spread themselves wide open and remained so during a speechless half-minute. Then curiosity broke the silence:

"The *king?* What king?"

"The king of England."

The children looked at each other—then at him—then at each other again—wonderingly, perplexedly—then one said:

"Didst hear him, Margery?—he saith he is the king. Can that be true?"

"How can it be else but true, Prissy? Would he say a lie? For look you, Prissy, an it were not true, it *would* be a lie. It surely would be. Now think on't. For all things that be not true, be lies —thou canst make naught else out of it."

It was a good, tight argument, without a leak in it anywhere; and it left Prissy's half-doubts not a leg to stand on. She considered a moment, then put the king upon his honor with the simple remark:

"If thou art truly the king, then I believe thee."

"I am truly the king."

This settled the matter. His majesty's royalty was accepted without further question or discussion, and the two little girls began at once to inquire into how he came to be where he was, and how he came to be so unroyally clad, and whither he was bound, and all about his affairs. It was a mighty relief to him to pour out his troubles where they would not be scoffed at or doubted; so he told his tale with feeling, forgetting even his hunger for the time; and it was received with the deepest and tenderest sympathy by the gentle little maids. But when he got down to his latest experiences and they learned how long he had been without food, they cut him short and hurried him away to the farmhouse to find a breakfast for him.

The king was cheerful and happy now, and said to himself, "When I am come to mine own again, I will always honor little children, remembering how that these trusted me and believed in me in my time of trouble; whilst they that were older, and thought themselves wiser, mocked at me and held me for a liar."

The children's mother received the king kindly, and was full of pity; for his forlorn condition and apparently crazed intellect touched her womanly heart. She was a widow, and rather poor; consequently she had seen trouble enough to enable her to feel for the unfortunate. She imagined that the demented boy had wandered away from his friends or keepers; so she tried to find out whence he had come, in order that she might take measures to return him; but all her references to neighboring towns and villages, and all her inquiries in the same line, went for nothing —the boy's face, and his answers, too, showed that the things she was talking of were not familiar to him. He spoke earnestly and simply about court matters; and broke down, more than once, when speaking of the late king "his father"; but whenever the conversation changed to baser topics, he lost interest and became silent.

The woman was mightily puzzled; but she did not give up. As she proceeded with her cooking, she set herself to contriving devices to surprise the boy into betraying his real secret. She talked about cattle—he showed no concern; then about sheep— the same result—so her guess that he had been a shepherd boy was an error; she talked about mills; and about weavers, tinkers, smiths, trades and tradesmen of all sorts; and about Bedlam, and jails, and charitable retreats; but no matter, she was baffled at all points. Not altogether, either; for she argued that she had narrowed the thing down to domestic service. Yes, she was sure she was on the right track now—he must have been a house-servant. So she led up to that. But the result was discouraging. The subject of sweeping appeared to weary him; fire-building failed to stir him; scrubbing and scouring awoke no enthusiasm. Then the goodwife touched, with a perishing hope, and rather as a matter of form, upon the subject of cooking. To her surprise, and her vast delight, the king's face lighted at once! Ah, she had hunted him down at last, she thought; and she was right proud, too, of the devious shrewdness and tact which had accomplished it.

Her tired tongue got a chance to rest now; for the king's, inspired by gnawing hunger and the fragrant smells that came from the sputtering pots and pans, turned itself loose and delivered itself up to such an eloquent dissertation upon certain toothsome dishes, that within three minutes the woman said to herself, "Of a truth I was right—he hath holpen in a kitchen!" Then he broadened his bill of fare, and discussed it with such appreciation and animation, that the goodwife said to herself, "Good lack! how can he know so many dishes, and so fine ones withal? For these belong only upon the tables of the rich and great. Ah, now I see! ragged outcast as he is, he must have served in the palace before his reason went astray; yes, he must have helped in the very kitchen of the king himself! I will test him."

Full of eagerness to prove her sagacity, she told the king to mind the cooking a moment—hinting that he might manufacture and add a dish or two, if he chose—then she went out of the room and gave her children a sign to follow after. The king muttered:

"Another English king had a commission like to this, in a by-gone time—it is nothing against my dignity to undertake an office which the great Alfred stooped to assume. But I will try to better serve my trust than he; for he let the cakes burn."

The intent was good, but the performance was not answerable to it; for this king, like the other one, soon fell into deep thinkings concerning his vast affairs, and the same calamity resulted—the cookery got burned. The woman returned in time to save the breakfast from entire destruction; and she promptly brought the king out of his dreams with a brisk and cordial tongue-lashing. Then, seeing how troubled he was over his violated trust, she softened at once and was all goodness and gentleness toward him.

The boy made a hearty and satisfying meal, and was greatly refreshed and gladdened by it. It was a meal which was distinguished by this curious feature, that rank was waived on both sides; yet neither recipient of the favor was aware that it had been extended. The goodwife had intended to feed this young tramp with broken victuals in a corner, like any other tramp, or like a dog; but she was so remorseful for the scolding she had given him, that she did what she could to atone for it by allowing him to sit at the family table and eat with his betters, on ostensible terms of equality with them; and the king, on his side, was so remorseful for having broken his trust, after the family had been so kind to him, that he forced himself to atone for it by humbling himself to the family level, instead of requiring the woman and her children to stand and wait upon him while he occupied their table in the solitary state due his birth and dignity. It does us all good to unbend sometimes. This good woman was made happy all the day long by the applauses she got out of herself for her magnanimous condescension to a tramp; and the king was just as self-complacent over his gracious humility toward a humble peasant woman.

When breakfast was over, the housewife told the king to wash up the dishes. This command was a staggerer for a moment, and the king came near rebelling; but then he said to himself, "Alfred the Great watched the cakes; doubtless he would have washed the dishes, too—therefore will I essay it."

He made a sufficiently poor job of it; and to his surprise, too, for the cleaning of wooden spoons and trenchers had seemed an easy thing to do. It was a tedious and troublesome piece of work, but he finished it at last. He was becoming impatient to get away on his journey now; however, he was not to lose this thrifty dame's society so easily. She furnished him some little odds and ends of employment, which he got through with after a fair fashion and with some credit. Then she set him and the little girls to paring some winter apples; but he was so awkward at this service that she retired him from it and gave him a butcher-knife to grind. Afterward she kept him carding wool until he began to think he had laid the good King Alfred about far enough in the shade for the present, in the matter of showy menial heroisms that would read picturesquely in story-books and histories, and so he was half minded to resign. And when, just after the noonday dinner, the goodwife gave him a basket of kittens to drown, he did resign. At least he was just going to resign—for he felt that he must draw the line somewhere, and it seemed to him that to draw it at kitten-drowning was about the right thing —when there was an interruption. The interruption was John Canty—with a peddler's pack on his back—and Hugo!

The king discovered these rascals approaching the front gate before they had had a chance to see him; so he said nothing about drawing the line, but took up his basket of kittens and stepped quietly out the back way, without a word. He left the creatures in an outhouse, and hurried on into a narrow lane at the rear.

20

The Prince and the Hermit

THE HIGH HEDGE hid him from the house now; and so, under the impulse of a deadly fright, he let out all his forces and sped toward a wood in the distance. He never looked back until he had almost gained the shelter of the forest; then he turned and descried two figures in the distance. That was sufficient; he did not wait to scan them critically, but hurried on, and never abated his pace till he was far within the twilight depths of the wood. Then he stopped; being persuaded that he was now tolerably safe. He listened intently, but the stillness was profound and solemn—awful, even, and depressing to the spirits. At wide intervals his straining ear did detect sounds, but they were so remote, and hollow, and mysterious, that they seemed not to be real sounds, but only the moaning and complaining ghosts of departed ones. So the sounds were yet more dreary than the silence which they interrupted.

It was his purpose, in the beginning, to stay where he was, the rest of the day; but a chill soon invaded his perspiring body, and he was at last obliged to resume movement in order to get warm. He struck straight through the forest, hoping to pierce to a road presently, but he was disappointed in this. He traveled on and on; but the farther he went, the denser the wood became, apparently. The gloom began to thicken, by and by, and the king realized that the night was coming on. It made him shudder to think of spending it in such an uncanny place; so he tried to hurry faster, but he only made the less speed, for he could not now see well enough to choose his steps judiciously; consequently he kept tripping over roots and tangling himself in vines and briers.

And how glad he was when at last he caught the glimmer of a light! He approached it warily, stopping often to look about him and listen. It came from an unglazed window-opening in a little hut. He heard a voice now, and felt a disposition to run and hide; but he changed his mind at once, for this voice was praying, evidently. He glided to the one window of the hut, raised himself on tiptoe, and stole a glance within. The room was small; its floor was the natural earth, beaten hard by use; in a corner was a bed of rushes and a ragged blanket or two; near it was a pail, a cup, a basin, and two or three pots and pans; there was a short bench and a three-legged stool; on the hearth the remains of a fagot fire were smoldering; before a shrine, which was lighted by a single candle, knelt an aged man, and on an old wooden box at his side lay an open book and a human skull. The man was of large, bony frame; his hair and whiskers were very long and snowy white; he was clothed in a robe of sheepskins which reached from his neck to his heels.

"A holy hermit!" said the king to himself; "now am I indeed fortunate."

The hermit rose from his knees; the king knocked. A deep voice responded:

"Enter!—but leave sin behind, for the ground whereon thou shalt stand is holy!"

The king entered, and paused. The hermit turned a pair of gleaming, unrestful eyes upon him, and said:

"Who art thou?"

"I am the king," came the answer, with placid simplicity.

"Welcome, king!" cried the hermit, with enthusiasm. Then, bustling about with feverish activity, and constantly saying "Welcome, welcome," he arranged his bench, seated the king on it, by the hearth, threw some fagots on the fire, and finally fell to pacing the floor, with a nervous stride.

"Welcome! Many have sought sanctuary here, but they were not worthy, and were turned away. But a king who casts his crown away, and despises the vain splendors of his office, and clothes his body in rags, to devote his life to holiness and the mortification of the flesh—he is worthy, he is welcome!—here shall he abide all his days till death come." The king hastened to interrupt and explain, but the hermit paid no attention to him—did not even hear him, apparently, but went right on with his talk, with a raised voice and a growing energy. "And thou shalt be at peace here. None shall find out thy refuge to disquiet thee with supplications to return to that empty and foolish life which God hath moved thee to abandon. Thou shalt pray here; thou shalt study the Book; thou shalt meditate upon the follies and delusions of this world, and upon the sublimities of the world to come; thou shalt feed upon crusts and herbs, and scourge thy body with whips daily, to the purifying of thy soul. Thou shalt wear a hair shirt next thy skin; thou shalt drink water only; and thou shalt be at peace; yes, wholly at peace; for whoso comes to seek thee shall go his way again baffled; he shall not find thee, he shall not molest thee."

The old man, still pacing back and forth, ceased to speak aloud, and began to mutter. The king seized this opportunity to state his case; and he did it with an eloquence inspired by uneasiness and apprehension. But the hermit went on muttering, and gave no heed. And still muttering, he approached the king and said, impressively:

"'Sh! I will tell you a secret!" He bent down to impart it, but checked himself, and assumed a listening attitude. After a moment or two he went on tiptoe to the window-opening, put his head out and peered around in the gloaming, then came tiptoeing back again, put his face close down to the king's and whispered:

"I am an archangel!"

The king started violently, and said to himself, "Would God I were with the outlaws again; for lo, now am I the prisoner of a madman!" His apprehensions were heightened, and they showed plainly in his face. In a low, excited voice, the hermit continued:

"I see you feel my atmosphere! There's awe in your face! None may be in this atmosphere and not be thus affected; for it is the very atmosphere of heaven. I go thither and return, in the twinkling of an eye. I was made an archangel on this very spot, it is five years ago, by angels sent from heaven to confer that awful dignity. Their presence filled this place with an intolerable brightness. And they knelt to me, king! yes, they knelt to me! for I was greater than they. I have walked in the courts of heaven, and held speech with the patriarchs. Touch my hand— be not afraid—touch it. There—now thou hast touched a hand which has been clasped by Abraham, and Isaac, and Jacob! For I have walked in the golden courts, I have seen the Deity face to face!" He paused, to give this speech effect; then his face suddenly changed, and he started to his feet again, saying, with angry energy, "Yes, I am an archangel; *a mere archangel!*—I that might have been pope! It is verily true. I was told it from heaven in a dream, twenty years ago; ah, yes, I was to be pope!—and I *should* have been pope, for Heaven had said it—but the king dissolved my religious house, and I, poor obscure unfriended monk, was cast homeless upon the world, robbed of my mighty destiny!" Here he began to mumble again, and beat his forehead in futile rage, with his fist; now and then articulating a venomous curse, and now and then a pathetic "Wherefore I am naught but an archangel—I that should have been pope!"

So he went on for an hour, while the poor little king sat and suffered. Then all at once the old man's frenzy departed, and he became all gentleness. His voice softened, he came down out of his clouds, and fell to prattling along so simply and so humanely, that he soon won the king's heart completely. The old devotee moved the boy nearer to the fire and made him comfortable; doctored his small bruises and abrasions with a deft and tender hand; and then set about preparing and cooking a supper— chatting pleasantly all the time, and occasionally stroking the lad's cheek or patting his head, in such a gently caressing way that in a little while all the fear and repulsion inspired by the archangel were changed to reverence and affection for the man.

This happy state of things continued while the two ate the supper; then, after a prayer before the shrine, the hermit put the boy to bed, in a small adjoining room, tucking him in as snugly and lovingly as a mother might; and so, with a parting caress, left him and sat down by the fire, and began to poke the brands about in an absent and aimless way. Presently he paused; then tapped his forehead several times with his fingers, as if trying to recall some thought which had escaped from his mind. Apparently he was unsuccessful. Now he started quickly up, and entered his guest's room, and said:

"Thou art king?"

"Yes," was the response, drowsily uttered.

"What king?"

"Of England."

"Of England. Then Henry is gone!"

"Alack, it is so. I am his son."

A black frown settled down upon the hermit's face, and he clenched his bony hands with a vindictive energy. He stood a few moments, breathing fast and swallowing repeatedly, then said in a husky voice:

"Dost know it was he that turned us out into the world houseless and homeless?"

There was no response. The old man bent down and scanned the boy's reposeful face and listened to his placid breathing. "He sleeps—sleeps soundly"; and the frown vanished away and gave place to an expression of evil satisfaction. A smile flitted across the dreaming boy's features. The hermit muttered, "So—his heart is happy"; and he turned away. He went stealthily about the place, seeking here and there for something; now and then halting to listen, now and then jerking his head around and casting a quick glance toward the bed; and always muttering, always mumbling to himself. At last he found what he seemed to want —a rusty old butcher-knife and a whetstone. Then he crept to his place by the fire, sat himself down, and began to whet the knife softly on the stone, still muttering, mumbling, ejaculating. The winds sighed around the lonely place, the mysterious voices of the night floated by out of the distances. The shining eyes of venture some mice and rats peered out at the old man from cracks and coverts, but he went on with his work, rapt, absorbed, and noted none of these things.

At long intervals he drew his thumb along the edge of his knife, and nodded his head with satisfaction. "It grows sharper," he said; "yes, it grows sharper."

He took no note of the flight of time, but worked tranquilly on, entertaining himself with his thoughts, which broke out occasionally in articulate speech:

"His father wrought us evil, he destroyed us—and is gone down into the eternal fires! Yes, down into the eternal fires! He escaped us—but it was God's will, yes it was God's will, we must not repine. But he hath not escaped the fires! no, he hath not escaped the fires, the consuming, unpitying, remorseless fires—and *they* are everlasting!"

And so he wrought; and still wrought; mumbling—chuckling a low rasping chuckle at times—and at times breaking again into words:

"It was his father that did it all. I am but an archangel—but for him, I should be pope!"

The king stirred. The hermit sprang noiselessly to the bedside, and went down upon his knees, bending over the prostrate form with his knife uplifted. The boy stirred again; his eyes came open for an instant, but there was no speculation in them, they saw nothing; the next moment his tranquil breathing showed that his sleep was sound once more.

The hermit watched and listened for a time, keeping his position and scarcely breathing; then he slowly lowered his arm, and presently crept away, saying:

"It is long past midnight—it is not best that he should cry out, lest by accident some one be passing."

He glided about his hovel, gathering a rag here, a thong there, and another one yonder; then he returned, and by careful and gentle handling he managed to tie the king's ankles together without waking him. Next he essayed to tie the wrists; he made several attempts to cross them, but the boy always drew one hand or the other away, just as the cord was ready to be applied; but at last, when the archangel was almost ready to despair, the boy crossed his hands himself, and the next moment they were bound. Now a bandage was passed under the sleeper's chin and brought up over his head and tied fast—and so softly, so gradually, and so deftly were the knots drawn together and compacted, that the boy slept peacefully through it all without stirring.

21

Hendon to the Rescue

THE OLD MAN glided away, stooping, stealthily, catlike, and brought the low bench. He seated himself upon it, half his body in the dim and flickering light, and the other half in shadow; and so, with his craving eyes bent upon the slumbering boy, he kept his patient vigil there, heedless of the drift of time, and softly whetted his knife, and mumbled and chuckled; and in aspect and attitude he resembled nothing so much as a grizzly, monstrous spider, gloating over some hapless insect that lay bound and helpless in his web.

After a long while, the old man, who was still gazing—yet not seeing, his mind having settled into a dreamy abstraction—observed on a sudden that the boy's eyes were open—wide open and staring!—staring up in frozen horror at the knife. The smile of a gratified devil crept over the old man's face, and he said, without changing his attitude or occupation:

"Son of Henry the Eighth, hast thou prayed?"

The boy struggled helplessly in his bonds; and at the same time forced a smothered sound through his closed jaws, which the hermit chose to interpret as an affirmative answer to his question.

"Then pray again. Pray the prayer for the dying!"

A shudder shook the boy's frame, and his face blenched. Then he struggled again to free himself—turning and twisting himself this way and that; tugging frantically, fiercely, desperately—but uselessly—to burst his fetters; and all the while the old ogre smiled down upon him, and nodded his head, and placidly whetted his knife, mumbling, from time to time, "The moments are precious, they are few and precious—pray the prayer for the dying!"

The boy uttered a despairing groan, and ceased from his struggles, panting. The tears came, then, and trickled, one after the other, down his face; but this piteous sight wrought no softening effect upon the savage old man.

The dawn was coming now; the hermit observed it, and spoke up sharply, with a touch of nervous apprehension in his voice:

"I may not indulge this ecstasy longer! The night is already gone. It seems but a moment—only a moment; would it had endured a year! Seed of the Church's spoiler, close thy perishing eyes, an thou fearest to look upon . . ."

The rest was lost in inarticulate mutterings. The old man sank upon his knees, his knife in his hand, and bent himself over the moaning boy—

Hark! There was a sound of voices near the cabin—the knife dropped from the hermit's hand; he cast a sheepskin over the boy and started up, trembling. The sounds increased, and presently the voices became rough and angry; then came blows, and cries for help; then a clatter of swift footsteps retreating. Immediately came a succession of thundering knocks upon the cabin door, followed by:

"Hullo-o-o! Open! And despatch, in the name of all the devils!"

Oh, this was the blessedest sound that had ever made music in the king's ears; for it was Miles Hendon's voice!

The hermit, grinding his teeth in impotent rage, moved swiftly out of the bedchamber, closing the door behind him; and straightway the king heard a talk, to this effect, proceeding from the "chapel":

"Homage and greeting, reverend sir! Where is the boy—my boy?"

"What boy, friend?"

"What boy! Lie me no lies, sir priest, play me no deceptions! —I am not in the humor for it. Near to this place I caught the scoundrels who I judged did steal him from me, and I made them confess; they said he was at large again, and they had tracked him to your door. They showed me his very footprints. Now palter no more; for look you, holy sir, an thou produce him not— Where is the boy?"

"Oh, good sir, peradventure you mean the ragged regal vagrant that tarried here the night. If such as you take interest in such as he, know, then, that I have sent him of an errand. He will be back anon."

"How soon? How soon? Come, waste not the time—cannot I overtake him? How soon will he be back?"

"Thou needst not stir; he will return quickly."

"So be it then. I will try to wait. But stop!—you sent him of an errand?—you! Verily, this is a lie—he would not go. He would pull thy old beard, an thou didst offer him such an insolence.

Thou hast lied, friend; thou hast surely lied! He would not go for thee nor for any man."

"For any *man*—no; haply not. But I am not a man."

"*What!* Now o' God's name what art thou, then?"

"It is a secret—mark thou reveal it not. I am an archangel!"

There was a tremendous ejaculation from Miles Hendon—not altogether unprofane—followed by:

"This doth well and truly account for his complaisance! Right well I knew he would budge nor hand nor foot in the menial service of any mortal; but lord, even a king must obey when an archangel gives the word o' command! Let me—'sh! What noise was that?"

All this while the king had been yonder, alternately quaking with terror and trembling with hope; and all the while, too, he had thrown all the strength he could into his anguished moanings, constantly expecting them to reach Hendon's ear, but always realizing, with bitterness, that they failed, or at least made no impression. So this last remark of his servant came as comes a reviving breath from fresh fields to the dying; and he exerted himself once more, and with all his energy, just as the hermit was saying:

"Noise? I heard only the wind."

"Mayhap it was. Yes, doubtless that was it. I have been hearing it faintly all the—there it is again! It is not the wind! What an odd sound! Come, we will hunt it out!"

Now the king's joy was nearly insupportable. His tired lungs did their utmost—and hopefully, too—but the sealed jaws and the muffling sheepskin sadly crippled the effort. Then the poor fellow's heart sank, to hear the hermit say:

"Ah, it came from without—I think from the copse yonder. Come, I will lead the way."

The king heard the two pass out talking; heard their footsteps die quickly away—then he was alone with a boding, brooding, awful silence.

It seemed an age till he heard the steps and voices approaching again—and this time he heard an added sound—the trampling of hoofs, apparently. Then he heard Hendon say:

"I will not wait longer. I *cannot* wait longer. He has lost his way in this thick wood. Which direction took he? Quick—point it out to me."

"He—but wait; I will go with thee."

"Good—good! Why, truly thou art better than thy looks. Marry, I do think there's not another archangel with so right a heart as thine. Wilt ride? Wilt take the wee donkey that's for my boy, or wilt thou fork thy holy legs over this ill-conditioned slave of a mule that I have provided for myself?—and had been cheated in, too, had he cost but the indifferent sum of a month's usury on a brass farthing let to a tinker out of work."

"No—ride thy mule, and lead thine ass; I am surer on mine own feet, and will walk."

"Then, prithee, mind the little beast for me while I take my life in my hands and make what success I may toward mounting the big one."

Then followed a confusion of kicks, cuffs, tramplings and plungings, accompanied by a thunderous intermingling of volleyed curses, and finally a bitter apostrophe to the mule, which must have broken its spirit, for hostilities seemed to cease from that moment.

With unutterable misery the fettered little king heard the voices and footsteps fade away and die out. All hope forsook him now for the moment, and a dull despair settled down upon his heart. "My only friend is deceived and got rid of," he said; "the hermit will return and—" He finished with a gasp; and at once fell to struggling so frantically with his bonds again, that he shook off the smothering sheepskin.

And now he heard the door open! The sound chilled him to the marrow—already he seemed to feel the knife at his throat. Horror made him close his eyes; horror made him open them again—and before him stood John Canty and Hugo!

He would have said "Thank God!" if his jaws had been free.

A moment or two later his limbs were at liberty, and his captors, each gripping him by an arm, were hurrying him with all speed through the forest.

22

A Victim of Treachery

ONCE MORE "King Foo-foo the First" was roving with the tramps and outlaws, a butt for their coarse jests and dull-witted railleries, and sometimes the victim of small spitefulnesses at the hands of Canty and Hugo when the Ruffler's back was turned. None but Canty and Hugo really disliked him. Some of the others liked him, and all admired his pluck and spirit. During two or three days, Hugo, in whose ward and charge the king was, did what he covertly could to make the boy uncomfortable; and at night, during the customary orgies, he amused the company by putting small indignities upon him—always as if by accident. Twice he stepped upon the king's toes—accidentally—and the king, as became his royalty, was contemptuously unconscious of it and indifferent to it; but the third time Hugo entertained himself in that way, the king felled him to the ground with a cudgel, to the prodigious delight of the tribe. Hugo, consumed with anger and shame, sprang up, seized a cudgel, and came at his small adversary in a fury. Instantly a ring was formed around the gladiators, and the betting and cheering began. But poor Hugo stood no chance whatever. His frantic and lubberly 'prentice-work found but a poor market for itself when pitted against an arm which had been trained by the first masters of Europe in single-stick, quarter-staff, and every art and trick of swordsmanship. The little king stood, alert but at graceful ease, and caught and turned aside the thick rain of blows with a facility and precision which set the motley onlookers wild with admiration; and every now and then, when his practised eye detected an opening, and a lightning-swift rap upon Hugo's head followed as a result, the storm of cheers and laughter that swept the place was something wonderful to hear. At the end of fifteen minutes, Hugo, all battered, bruised, and the target for a pitiless bombardment of ridicule, slunk from the field; and the unscathed hero of the fight was seized and borne aloft upon the shoulders of the joyous rabble to the place of honor beside the Ruffler, where with vast ceremony he was crowned King of the Game-Cocks; his meaner title being at the same time solemnly canceled and annulled, and a decree of banishment from the gang pronounced against any who should henceforth utter it.

All attempts to make the king serviceable to the troop had failed. He had stubbornly refused to act; moreover, he was always trying to escape. He had been thrust into an unwatched kitchen, the first day of his return; he not only came forth empty-handed, but tried to rouse the housemates. He was sent out with a tinker to help him at his work; he would not work; moreover, he threatened the tinker with his own soldering-iron; and finally both Hugo and the tinker found their hands full with the mere matter of keeping him from getting away. He delivered the thunders of his royalty upon the heads of all who hampered his liberties or tried to force him to service. He was sent out, in Hugo's charge, in company with a slatternly woman and a diseased baby, to beg; but the result was not encouraging—he declined to plead for the mendicants, or be a party to their cause in any way.

Thus several days went by; and the miseries of this tramping life, and the weariness and sordidness and meanness and vulgarity of it, became gradually and steadily so intolerable to the captive that he began at last to feel that his release from the hermit's knife must prove only a temporary respite from death, at best.

But at night, in his dreams, these things were forgotten, and he was on his throne, and master again. This, of course, intensified the sufferings of the awakening—so the mortifications of each succeeding morning of the few that passed between his return to bondage and the combat with Hugo, grew bitterer and bitterer, and harder and harder to bear.

The morning after that combat, Hugo got up with a heart filled with vengeful purposes against the king. He had two plans in particular. One was to inflict upon the lad what would be, to his proud spirit and "imagined" royalty, a peculiar humiliation; and if he failed to accomplish this, his other plan was to put a crime of some kind upon the king and then betray him into the implacable clutches of the law.

In pursuance of the first plan, he proposed to put a "clime" upon the king's leg, rightly judging that that would mortify him to the last and perfect degree; and as soon as the clime should operate, he meant to get Canty's help, and *force* the king to expose his leg in the highway and beg for alms. "Clime" was the cant term for a sore, artificially created. To make a clime, the operator made a paste or poultice of unslaked lime, soap, and the rust of old iron, and spread it upon a piece of leather, which was then bound tightly upon the leg. This would presently fret off the skin, and make the flesh raw and angry-looking; blood was then rubbed upon the limb, which, being fully dried, took on a dark and repulsive color. Then a bandage of soiled rags was put on in a cleverly careless way which would allow the hideous ulcer to be seen and move the compassion of the passer-by.[1]

Hugo got the help of the tinker whom the king had cowed with the soldering-iron; they took the boy out on a tinkering tramp, and as soon as they were out of sight of the camp they threw him down and the tinker held him while Hugo bound the poultice tight and fast upon his leg.

The king raged and stormed, and promised to hang the two the moment the scepter was in his hand again; but they kept a firm grip upon him and enjoyed his impotent struggling and jeered at his threats. This continued until the poultice began to bite; and in no long time its work would have been perfected, if there had been no interruption. But there was; for about this time the "slave" who had made the speech denouncing England's laws, appeared on the scene and put an end to the enterprise, and stripped off the poultice and bandage.

[1] From "The English Rogue"; London, 1665.

The king wanted to borrow his deliverer's cudgel and warm the jackets of the two rascals on the spot; but the man said no, it would bring trouble—leave the matter till night; the whole tribe being together, then, the outside world would not venture to interfere or interrupt. He marched the party back to camp and reported the affair to the Ruffler, who listened, pondered, and then decided that the king should not be again detailed to beg, since it was plain he was worthy of something higher and better —wherefore, on the spot he promoted him from the mendicant rank and appointed him to steal!

Hugo was overjoyed. He had already tried to make the king steal, and failed; but there would be no more trouble of that sort now, for, of course, the king would not dream of defying a distinct command delivered directly from headquarters. So he planned a raid for that very afternoon, purposing to get the king in the law's grip in the course of it; and to do it, too, with such ingenious strategy, that it should seem to be accidental and unintentional; for the King of the Game-Cocks was popular now, and the gang might not deal over-gently with an unpopular member who played so serious a treachery upon him as the delivering him over to the common enemy, the law.

Very well. All in good time Hugo strolled off to a neighboring village with his prey; and the two drifted slowly up and down one street after another, the one watching sharply for a sure chance to achieve his evil purpose, and the other watching as sharply for a chance to dart away and get free of his infamous captivity forever.

Both threw away some tolerably fair-looking opportunities; for both, in their secret hearts, were resolved to make absolutely sure work this time, and neither meant to allow his fevered desires to seduce him into any venture that had much uncertainty about it.

Hugo's chance came first. For at last a woman approached who carried a fat package of some sort in a basket. Hugo's eyes sparkled with sinful pleasure as he said to himself, "Breath o' my life, an I can but put *that* upon him, 'tis good-den and God keep thee, King of the Game-Cocks!" He waited and watched—outwardly patient, but inwardly consuming with excitement—till the woman had passed by, and the time was ripe; then said, in a low voice: "Tarry here till I come again," and darted stealthily after the prey.

The king's heart was filled with joy—he could make his escape now, if Hugo's quest only carried him far enough away.

But he was to have no such luck. Hugo crept behind the woman, snatched the package, and came running back, wrapping it in an old piece of blanket which he carried on his arm. The hue and cry was raised in a moment by the woman, who knew her loss by the lightening of her burden, although she had not seen the pilfering done. Hugo thrust the bundle into the king's hands without halting, saying:

"Now speed ye after me with the rest, and cry 'Stop thief!' but mind ye lead them astray!"

The next moment Hugo turned a corner and darted down a crooked alley—and in another moment or two he lounged into view again, looking innocent and indifferent, and took up a position behind a post to watch results.

The insulted king threw the bundle on the ground; and the blanket fell away from it just as the woman arrived, with an augmenting crowd at her heels; she seized the king's wrist with one hand, snatched up her bundle with the other, and began to pour out a tirade of abuse upon the boy while he struggled, without success, to free himself from her grip.

Hugo had seen enough—his enemy was captured and the law would get him now—so he slipped away, jubilant and chuckling, and wended campward, framing a judicious version of the matter to give to the Ruffler's crew as he strode along.

The king continued to struggle in the woman's grasp, and now and then cried out, in vexation:

"Unhand me, thou foolish creature; it was not I that bereaved thee of thy paltry goods."

The crowd closed around, threatening the king and calling him names; a brawny blacksmith in leather apron, and sleeves rolled to his elbows, made a reach for him, saying he would trounce him well, for a lesson; but just then a long sword flashed in the air and fell with convincing force upon the man's arm, flat-side down, the fantastic owner of it remarking, pleasantly at the same time:

"Marry, good souls, let us proceed gently, not with ill blood and uncharitable words. This is matter for the law's consideration, not private and unofficial handling. Loose thy hold from the boy, goodwife."

The blacksmith averaged the stalwart soldier with a glance, then went muttering away, rubbing his arm; the woman released the boy's wrist reluctantly; the crowd eyed the stranger unlovingly, but prudently closed their mouths. The king sprang to his deliverer's side, with flushed cheeks and sparkling eyes, exclaiming:

"Thou hast lagged sorely, but thou comest in good season now, Sir Miles; carve me this rabble to rags!"

23

The Prince a Prisoner

HENDON forced back a smile, and bent down and whispered in the king's ear:

"Softly, softly my prince, wag thy tongue warily—nay, suffer it not to wag at all. Trust in me—all shall go well in the end." Then he added, to himself: "*Sir* Miles! Bless me, I had totally forgot I was a knight! Lord how marvelous a thing it is, the grip his memory doth take upon his quaint and crazy fancies! . . . An empty and foolish title is mine, and yet it is something to have deserved it, for I think it is more honor to be held worthy to be a specter-knight in his Kingdom of Dreams and Shadows, than to be held base enough to be an earl in some of the *real* kingdoms of this world."

The crowd fell apart to admit a constable, who approached and was about to lay his hand upon the king's shoulder, when Hendon said:

"Gently, good friend, withhold your hand—he shall go peaceably; I am responsible for that. Lead on, we will follow."

The officer led, with the woman and her bundle; Miles and the king followed after, with the crowd at their heels. The king was inclined to rebel; but Hendon said to him in a low voice:

"Reflect, sire—your laws are the wholesome breath of your own royalty; shall their source resist them, yet require the branches to respect them? Apparently, one of these laws has been broken; when the king is on his throne again, can it ever grieve him to remember that when he was seemingly a private person he loyally sunk the king in the citizen and submitted to its authority?"

"Thou art right; say no more; thou shalt see that whatsoever the king of England requires a subject to suffer under the law, he will himself suffer while he holdeth the station of a subject."

When the woman was called upon to testify before the justice of the peace, she swore that the small prisoner at the bar was the person who had committed the theft; there was none able to show the contrary, so the king stood convicted. The bundle was now unrolled, and when the contents proved to be a plump little dressed pig, the judge looked troubled, while Hendon turned pale, and his body was thrilled with an electric shiver of dismay; but the king remained unmoved, protected by his ignorance. The judge meditated, during an ominous pause, then turned to the woman, with the question:

"What dost thou hold this property to be worth?"

The woman courtesied and replied:

"Three shillings and eightpence, your worship—I could not abate a penny and set forth the value honestly."

The justice glanced around uncomfortably upon the crowd, then nodded to the constable and said:

"Clear the court and close the doors."

It was done. None remained but the two officials, the accused, the accuser, and Miles Hendon. This latter was rigid and colorless, and on his forehead big drops of cold sweat gathered, broke and blended together, and trickled down his face. The judge turned to the woman again, and said, in a compassionate voice:

" 'Tis a poor ignorant lad, and mayhap was driven hard by hunger, for these be grievous times for the unfortunate; mark you, he hath not an evil face—but when hunger driveth— Good woman! dost know that when one steals a thing above the value of thirteen pence ha'penny the law saith he shall *hang* for it?"

The little king started, wide-eyed with consternation, but controlled himself and held his peace; but not so the woman. She sprang to her feet, shaking with fright, and cried out:

"Oh, good lack, what have I done! God-a-mercy, I would not hang the poor thing for the whole world! Ah, save me from this, your worship—what shall I do, what *can* I do?"

The justice maintained his judicial composure, and simply said:

"Doubtless it is allowable to revise the value, since it is not yet writ upon the record."

"Then in God's name call the pig eightpence, and heaven bless the day that freed my conscience of this awesome thing!"

Miles Hendon forgot all decorum in his delight; and surprised the king and wounded his dignity by throwing his arms around him and hugging him. The woman made her grateful adieux and started away with her pig; and when the constable opened the door for her, he followed her out into the narrow hall. The justice proceeded to write in his record-book. Hendon, always alert, thought he would like to know why the officer followed the woman out; so he slipped softly into the dusky hall and listened. He heard a conversation to this effect:

"It is a fat pig, and promises good eating; I will buy it of thee; here is the eightpence."

"Eightpence, indeed! Thou'lt do no such thing. It cost me three shillings and eightpence, good honest coin of the last reign, that old Harry that's just dead ne'er touched nor tampered with. A fig for thy eightpence!"

"Stands the wind in that quarter? Thou wast under oath, and so swore falsely when thou saidst the value was but eightpence. Come straightway back with me before his worship, and answer for the crime!—and then the lad will hang."

"There, there, dear heart, say no more, I am content. Give me the eightpence, and hold thy peace about the matter."

The woman went off crying; Hendon slipped back into the court-room, and the constable presently followed, after hiding his prize in some convenient place. The justice wrote a while longer, then read the king a wise and kindly lecture, and sentenced him to a short imprisonment in the common jail, to be followed by a public flogging. The astounded king opened his mouth and was probably going to order the good judge to be beheaded on the spot; but he caught a warning sign from Hendon, and succeeded in closing his mouth again before he lost anything out of it. Hendon took him by the hand, now made reverence to the justice, and the two departed in the wake of the constable toward the jail. The moment the street was reached, the inflamed monarch halted, snatched away his hand, and exclaimed:

"Idiot, dost imagine I will enter a common jail *alive?*"

Hendon bent down and said, somewhat sharply:

"*Will* you trust in me? Peace! and forbear to worsen our chances with dangerous speech. What God wills, will happen; thou canst not hurry it, thou canst not alter it; therefore wait, and be patient—'twill be time enow to rail or rejoice when what is to happen has happened."

24

The Escape

THE SHORT winter day was nearly ended. The streets were deserted, save for a few random stragglers, and these hurried straight along, with the intent look of people who were only anxious to accomplish their errands as quickly as possible and then snugly house themselves from the rising wind and the gathering twilight. They looked neither to the right nor to the left; they paid no attention to our party, they did not even seem to see them. Edward the Sixth wondered if the spectacle of a king on his way to jail had ever encountered such marvelous indifference before. By and by the constable arrived at a deserted market-square and proceeded to cross it. When he had reached the middle of it, Hendon laid his hand upon his arm, and said in a low voice:

"Bide a moment, good sir, there is none in hearing, and I would say a word to thee."

"My duty forbids it, sir; prithee, hinder me not, the night comes on."

"Stay, nevertheless, for the matter concerns thee nearly. Turn thy back a moment and seem not to see; *let this poor lad escape.*"

"This to me, sir! I arrest thee in—"

"Nay, be not too hasty. See thou be careful and commit no foolish error"—then he shut his voice down to a whisper, and said in the man's ear—"the pig thou hast purchased for eightpence may cost thee thy neck, man!"

The poor constable, taken by surprise, was speechless at first, then found his tongue and fell to blustering and threatening; but Hendon was tranquil, and waited with patience till his breath was spent; then said:

"I have a liking to thee, friend, and would not willingly see thee come to harm. Observe, I heard it all—every word. I will prove it to thee." Then he repeated the conversation which the officer and the woman had had together in the hall, word for word, and ended with:

"There—have I set it forth correctly? Should not I be able to set it forth correctly before the judge, if occasion required?"

The man was dumb with fear and distress for a moment; then he rallied and said with forced lightness:

"'Tis making a mighty matter indeed, out of a jest; I but plagued the woman for mine amusement."

"Kept you the woman's pig for amusement?"

The man answered sharply:

"Naught else, good sir—I tell thee 'twas but a jest."

"I do begin to believe thee," said Hendon, with a perplexing mixture of mockery and half-conviction in his tone; "but tarry thou here a moment whilst I run and ask his worship—for nathless, he being a man experienced in law, in jests, in—"

He was moving away, still talking; the constable hesitated, fidgeted, spat out an oath or two, then cried out:

"Hold, hold, good sir—prithee, wait a little—the judge! why man, he hath no more sympathy with a jest than hath a dead corpse!—come, and we will speak further. Ods body! I seem to be in evil case—and all for an innocent and thoughtless pleasantry. I am a man of family; and my wife and little ones— List to reason, good your worship; what wouldst thou of me?"

"Only that thou be blind and dumb and paralytic whilst one may count a hundred thousand—counting slowly," said Hendon, with the expression of a man who asks but a reasonable favor, and that a very little one.

"It is my destruction!" said the constable despairingly. "Ah, be reasonable, good sir; only look at this matter, on all its sides, and see how mere a jest it is—how manifestly and how plainly it is so. And even if one granted it were not a jest, it is a fault so small that e'en the grimmest penalty it could call forth would be but a rebuke and warning from the judge's lips."

Hendon replied with a solemnity which chilled the air about him:

"This jest of thine hath a name in law—wot you what it is?"

"I knew it not! Peradventure I have been unwise. I never dreamed it had a name—ah, sweet heaven, I thought it was original."

"Yes, it hath a name. In the law this crime is called *Non compos mentis lex talionis sic transit gloria Mundi.*"

"Ah, my God!"

"And the penalty is death!"

"God be merciful to me, a sinner!"

"By advantage taken of one in fault, in dire peril, and at thy mercy, thou hast seized goods worth above thirteen pence ha'-penny, paying but a trifle for the same; and this, in the eye of the law, is constructive barratry, misprision of treason, malfeasance in office, *ad hominem expurgatis in statu quo*—and the penalty is death by the halter, without ransom, commutation, or benefit of clergy."

"Bear me up, bear me up, sweet sir, my legs do fail me! Be thou merciful—spare me this doom, and I will turn my back and see naught that shall happen."

"Good! now thou'rt wise and reasonable. And thou'lt restore the pig?"

"I will, I will, indeed—nor ever touch another, though heaven send it and an archangel fetch it. Go—I am blind for thy sake—I see nothing. I will say thou didst break in and wrest the prisoner from my hands by force. It is but a crazy, ancient door—I will batter it down myself betwixt midnight and the morning."

"Do it, good soul, no harm will come of it; the judge hath a loving charity for this poor lad, and will shed no tears and break no jailer's bones for his escape."

25

Hendon Hall

As soon as Hendon and the king were out of sight of the constable, his majesty was instructed to hurry to a certain place outside the town, and wait there, whilst Hendon should go to the inn and settle his account. Half an hour later the two friends were blithely jogging eastward on Hendon's sorry steeds. The king was warm and comfortable now, for he had cast his rags and clothed himself in the second-hand suit which Hendon had bought on London Bridge.

Hendon wished to guard against over-fatiguing the boy; he

judged that hard journeys, irregular meals, and illiberal measures of sleep would be bad for his crazed mind; while rest, regularity, and moderate exercise would be pretty sure to hasten its cure; he longed to see the stricken intellect made well again and its diseased visions driven out of the tormented little head; therefore he resolved to move by easy stages toward the home whence he had so long been banished, instead of obeying the impulse of his impatience and hurrying along night and day.

When he and the king had journeyed about ten miles, they reached a considerable village, and halted there for the night, at a good inn. The former relations were resumed; Hendon stood behind the king's chair while he dined, and waited upon him; undressed him when he was ready for bed; then took the floor for his own quarters, and slept athwart the door, rolled up in a blanket.

The next day, and the next day after, they jogged lazily along talking over the adventures they had met since their separation, and mightily enjoying each other's narratives. Hendon detailed all his wide wanderings in search of the king, and described how the archangel had led him a fool's journey all over the forest, and taken him back to the hut finally, when he found he could not get rid of him. Then—he said—the old man went into the bed-chamber and came staggering back looking broken-hearted, and saying he had expected to find that the boy had returned and lain down in there to rest, but it was not so. Hendon had waited at the hut all day; hope of the king's return died out then, and he departed upon the quest again.

"And old Sanctum Sanctorum *was* truly sorry your Highness came not back," said Hendon; "I saw it in his face."

"Marry, I will never doubt *that!*" said the king—and then told his own story; after which Hendon was sorry he had not destroyed the archangel.

During the last day of the trip, Hendon's spirits were soaring. His tongue ran constantly. He talked about his old father, and his brother Arthur, and told of many things which illustrated their high and generous characters; he went into loving frenzies over his Edith, and was so glad-hearted that he was even able to say some gentle and brotherly things about Hugh. He dwelt a deal on the coming meeting at Hendon Hall; what a surprise it would be to everybody, and what an outburst of thanksgiving and delight there would be.

It was a fair region, dotted with cottages and orchards, and the road led through broad pasturelands whose receding expanses, marked with gentle elevations and depressions, suggested the swelling and subsiding undulations of the sea. In the afternoon the returning prodigal made constant deflections from his course to see if by ascending some hillock he might not pierce the distance and catch a glimpse of his home. At last he was successful, and cried out excitedly:

"There is the village, my prince, and there is the Hall close by! You may see the towers from here; and that wood there—that is my father's park. Ah, *now* thou'lt know what state and grandeur be! A house with seventy rooms—think of that!—and seven and twenty servants! A brave lodging for such as we, is it not so? Come, let us speed—my impatience will not brook further delay."

All possible hurry was made; still, it was after three o'clock before the village was reached. The travelers scampered through it, Hendon's tongue going all the time. "Here is the church—covered with the same ivy—none gone, none added." "Yonder is the inn, the old Red Lion—and yonder is the market-place." "Here is the Maypole, and here the pump—nothing is altered; nothing but the people, at any rate; ten years make a change in people; some of these I seem to know, but none know me." So his chat ran on. The end of the village was soon reached; then the travelers struck into a crooked, narrow road, walled in with tall hedges, and hurried briskly along it for a half-mile, then passed into a vast flower-garden through an imposing gateway whose huge stone pillars bore sculptured armorial devices. A noble mansion was before them.

"Welcome to Hendon Hall, my king!" exclaimed Miles. "Ah, 'tis a great day! My father and my brother and the Lady Edith will be so mad with joy that they will have eyes and tongue for none but me in the first transports of the meeting, and so thou'lt seem but coldly welcomed—but mind it not; 'twill soon seem otherwise;

for when I say thou art my ward, and tell them how costly is my love for thee, thou'lt see them take thee to their breasts for Miles Hendon's sake, and make their house and hearts thy home forever after!"

The next moment Hendon sprang to the ground before the great door, helped the king down, then took him by the hand and rushed within. A few steps brought him to a spacious apartment; he entered, seated the king with more hurry than ceremony, then ran toward a young man who sat at a writing-table in front of a generous fire of logs.

"Embrace me, Hugh," he cried, "and say thou'rt glad I am come again! and call our father, for home is not home till I shall touch his hand, and see his face, and hear his voice once more!"

But Hugh only drew back, after betraying a momentary surprise, and bent a grave stare upon the intruder—a stare which indicated somewhat of offended dignity at first, then changed, in response to some inward thought or purpose, to an expression of marveling curiosity, mixed with a real or assumed compassion. Presently he said, in a mild voice:

"Thy wits seem touched, poor stranger; doubtless thou hast suffered privations and rude buffetings at the world's hands; thy looks and dress betoken it. Whom dost thou take me to be?"

"Take thee? Prithee, for whom else than whom thou art? I take thee to be Hugh Hendon," said Miles, sharply.

The other continued, in the same soft tone:

"And whom dost thou imagine thyself to be?"

"Imagination hath naught to do with it! Dost thou pretend thou knowest me not for thy brother Miles Hendon?"

An expression of pleased surprise flitted across Hugh's face, and he exclaimed:

"What! thou art not jesting? can the dead come to life? God be praised if it be so! Our poor lost boy restored to our arms after all these cruel years! Ah, it seems too good to be true, it *is* too good to be true—I charge thee, have pity, do not trifle with me! Quick—come to the light—let me scan thee well!"

He seized Miles by the arm, dragged him to the window, and began to devour him from head to foot with his eyes, turning him this way and that, and stepping briskly around him and about him to prove him from all points of view; whilst the returned prodigal, all aglow with gladness, smiled, laughed, and kept nodding his head and saying:

"Go on, brother, go on, and fear not; thou'lt find nor limb nor feature that cannot bide the test. Scour and scan me to thy content, my dear old Hugh—I am indeed thy old Miles, thy same old Miles, thy lost brother, is't not so? Ah, 'tis a great day—I *said* 'twas a great day! Give me thy hand, give me thy cheek—lord, I am like to die of very joy!"

He was about to throw himself upon his brother; but Hugh put up his hand in dissent, then dropped his chin mournfully upon his breast, saying with emotion:

"Ah, God of his mercy give me strength to bear this grievous disappointment!"

Miles, amazed, could not speak for a moment; then he found his tongue, and cried out:

"*What* disappointment? Am I not thy brother?"

Hugh shook his head sadly, and said:

"I pray heaven it may prove so, and that other eyes may find the resemblances that are hid from mine. Alack, I fear me the letter spoke but too truly."

"What letter?"

"One that came from oversea, some six or seven years ago. It said my brother died in battle."

"It was a lie! Call thy father—he will know me."

"One may not call the dead."

"Dead?" Miles's voice was subdued, and his lips trembled. "My father dead!—oh, this is heavy news. Half my new joy is withered now. Prithee, let me see my brother Arthur—he will know me; he will know me and console me."

"He, also, is dead."

"God be merciful to me, a stricken man! Gone—both gone—the worthy taken and the worthless spared in me! Ah! I crave your mercy!—do not say the Lady Edith—"

"Is dead? No, she lives."

"Then, God be praised, my joy is whole again! Speed thee,

brother—let her come to me! An *she* say I am not myself—but she will not; no, no, *she* will know me, I were a fool to doubt it. Bring her—bring the old servants; they, too, will know me."

"All are gone but five—Peter, Halsey, David, Bernard, and Margaret."

So saying, Hugh left the room. Miles stood musing awhile, then began to walk the floor, muttering:

"The five arch villains have survived the two-and-twenty leal and honest—'tis an odd thing."

He continued walking back and forth, muttering to himself; he had forgotten the king entirely. By and by his majesty said gravely, and with a touch of genuine compassion, though the words themselves were capable of being interpreted ironically:

"Mind not thy mischance, good man; there be others in the world whose identity is denied, and whose claims are derided. Thou hast company."

"Ah, my king," cried Hendon, coloring slightly, "do not thou condemn me—wait, and thou shalt see. I am no impostor—she will say it; you shall hear it from the sweetest lips in England. I an impostor? Why I know this old hall, these pictures of my ancestors, and all these things that are about us, as a child knoweth its own nursery. Here was I born and bred, my lord; I speak the truth; I would not deceive thee; and should none else believe, I pray thee do not *thou* doubt me—I could not bear it."

"I do not doubt thee," said the king, with a childlike simplicity and faith.

"I thank thee out of my heart!" exclaimed Hendon, with a fervency which showed that he was touched. The king added, with the same gentle simplicity:

"Dost thou doubt *me?*"

A guilty confusion seized upon Hendon, and he was grateful that the door opened to admit Hugh, at that moment, and saved him the necessity of replying.

A beautiful lady, richly clothed, followed Hugh, and after her came several liveried servants. The lady walked slowly, with her head bowed and her eyes fixed upon the floor. The face was unspeakably sad. Miles Hendon sprang forward, crying out:

"Oh, my Edith, my darling—"

But Hugh waved him back, gravely, and said to the lady:

"Look upon him. Do you know him?"

At the sound of Miles's voice the woman had started slightly, and her cheeks had flushed; she was trembling now. She stood still, during an impressive pause of several moments; then slowly lifted up her head and looked into Hendon's eyes with a stony and frightened gaze; the blood sank out of her face, drop by drop, till nothing remained but the gray pallor of death; then she said, in a voice as dead as the face, "I know him not!" and turned, with a moan and a stifled sob, and tottered out of the room.

Miles Hendon sank into a chair and covered his face with his hands. After a pause, his brother said to the servants:

"You have observed him. Do you know him?"

They shook their heads; then the master said:

"The servants know you not, sir. I fear there is some mistake. You have seen that my wife knew you not."

"Thy *wife!*" In an instant Hugh was pinned to the wall, with an iron grip about his throat. "Oh, thou fox-hearted slave, I see it all! Thou'st writ the lying letter thyself, and my stolen bride and goods are its fruit. There—now get thee gone, lest I shame mine honorable soldiership with the slaying of so pitiful a manikin!"

Hugh, red-faced and almost suffocated, reeled to the nearest chair, and commanded the servants to seize and bind the murderous stranger. They hesitated, and one of them said:

"He is armed, Sir Hugh, and we are weaponless."

"Armed? What of it, and ye so many? Upon him, I say!"

But Miles warned them to be careful what they did, and added:

"Ye know me of old—I have not changed; come on, an it like you."

This reminder did not hearten the servants much; they still held back.

"Then go, ye paltry cowards, and arm yourselves and guard the doors, while I send one to fetch the watch," said Hugh. He turned, at the threshold, and said to Miles, "You'll find it to your advantage to offend not with useless endeavors at escape."

"Escape? Spare thyself discomfort, an that is all that troubles thee. For Miles Hendon is master of Hendon Hall and all its belongings. He will remain—doubt it not."

26

Disowned

THE KING sat musing a few moments, then looked up and said:

"'Tis strange—most strange. I cannot account for it."

"No, it is not strange, my liege. I know him, and this conduct is but natural. He was a rascal from his birth."

"Oh, I spake not of *him*, Sir Miles."

"Not of him? Then of what? What is it that is strange?"

"That the king is not missed."

"How? Which? I doubt I do not understand."

"Indeed! Doth it not strike you as being passing strange that the land is not filled with couriers and proclamations describing my person and making search for me? Is it no matter for commotion and distress that the head of the state is gone?—that I am vanished away and lost?"

"Most true, my king, I had forgot." Then Hendon sighed, and muttered to himself, "Poor ruined mind—still busy with its pathetic dream."

"But I have a plan that shall right us both. I will write a paper, in three tongues—Latin, Greek, and English—and thou shalt haste away with it to London in the morning. Give it to none but my uncle, the Lord Hertford; when he shall see it, he will know and say I wrote it. Then he will send for me."

"Might it not be best, my prince, that we wait here until I prove myself and make my rights secure to my domains? I should be so much the better able then to—"

The king interrupted him imperiously:

"Peace! What are thy paltry domains, thy trivial interests, contrasted with matters which concern the weal of a nation and the integrity of a throne!" Then he added, in a gentle voice, as if he were sorry for his severity, "Obey and have no fear; I will right thee, I will make thee whole—yes, more than whole. I shall remember, and requite."

So saying, he took the pen, and set himself to work. Hendon contemplated him lovingly awhile, then said to himself:

"An it were dark, I should think it *was* a king that spoke; there's no denying it, when the humor's upon him he doth thunder and lighten like your true king—now where got he that trick? See him scribble and scratch away contentedly at his meaningless pothooks, fancying them to be Latin and Greek—and except my wit shall serve me with a lucky device for diverting him from his purpose, I shall be forced to pretend to post away to-morrow on this wild errand he hath invented for me."

The next moment Sir Miles's thoughts had gone back to the recent episode. So absorbed was he in his musings, that when the king presently handed him the paper which he had been writing, he received it and pocketed it without being conscious of the act. "How marvelous strange she acted," he muttered. "I think she knew me—and I think she did *not* know me. These opinions do conflict, I perceive it plainly; I cannot reconcile them, neither can I, by argument, dismiss either of the two, or even persuade one to outweigh the other. The matter standeth simply thus: she *must* have known my face, my figure, my voice, for how could it be otherwise? yet she *said* she knew me not, and that is proof perfect, for she cannot lie. But stop—I think I begin to see. Peradventure he hath influenced her—commanded her—compelled her to lie. That is the solution! The riddle is unriddled. She seemed dead with fear—yes, she was under his compulsion. I will seek her; I will find her; now that he is away, she will speak her true mind. She will remember the old times when we were little playfellows together, and this will soften her heart, and she will no more betray me, but will confess me. There is no treacherous blood in her—no, she was always honest and true. She has loved me in those old days—this is my security; for whom one has loved, one cannot betray."

He stepped eagerly toward the door; at that moment it opened, and the Lady Edith entered. She was very pale, but she walked with a firm step, and her carriage was full of grace and gentle dignity. Her face was as sad as before.

Miles sprang forward, with a happy confidence, to meet her, but she checked him with a hardly perceptible gesture, and he stopped where he was. She seated herself, and asked him to do likewise. Thus simply did she take the sense of old-comradeship out of him, and transform him into a stranger and a guest. The surprise of it, the bewildering unexpectedness of it, made him begin to question, for a moment, if he *was* the person he was pretending to be, after all. The Lady Edith said:

"Sir, I have come to warn you. The mad cannot be persuaded out of their delusions, perchance; but doubtless they may be persuaded to avoid perils. I think this dream of yours hath the seeming of honest truth to you, and therefore is not criminal—but do not tarry here with it; for here it is dangerous." She looked steadily into Miles's face a moment, then added, impressively, "It is the more dangerous for that you *are* much like what our lost lad must have grown to be, if he had lived."

"Heavens, madam, but I *am* he!"

"I truly think you think it, sir. I question not your honesty in that—I but warn you, that is all. My husband is master in this region; his power hath hardly any limit; the people prosper or starve, as he wills. If you resembled not the man whom you profess to be, my husband might bid you pleasure yourself with your dream in peace; but trust me, I know him well, I know what he will do; he will say to all that you are but a mad impostor, and straightway all will echo him." She bent upon Miles that same steady look once more, and added: "If you *were* Miles Hendon, and he knew it and all the region knew it—consider what I am saying, weigh it well—you would stand in the same peril, your punishment would be no less sure; he would deny you and denounce you, and none would be bold enough to give you countenance."

"Most truly I believe it," said Miles, bitterly. "The power that can command one lifelong friend to betray and disown another, and be obeyed, may well look to be obeyed in quarters where bread and life are on the stake and no cobweb ties of loyalty and honor are concerned."

A faint tinge appeared for a moment in the lady's cheek, and she dropped her eyes to the floor; but her voice betrayed no emotion when she proceeded:

"I have warned you, I must still warn you, to go hence. This man will destroy you else. He is a tyrant who knows no pity. I, who am his fettered slave, know this. Poor Miles, and Arthur, and my dear guardian, Sir Richard, are free of him, and at rest—better that you were with them than that you bide here in the clutches of this miscreant. Your pretensions are a menace to his title and possessions; you have assaulted him in his own house—you are ruined if you stay. Go—do not hesitate. If you lack money, take this purse, I beg of you, and bribe the servants to let you pass. Oh, be warned, poor soul, and escape while you may."

Miles declined the purse with a gesture, and rose up and stood before her.

"Grant me one thing," he said. "Let your eyes rest upon mine, so that I may see if they be steady. There—now answer me. Am I Miles Hendon?"

"No. I know you not."

"Swear it!"

The answer was low, but distinct:

"I swear."

"Oh, this passes belief!"

"Fly! Why will you waste the precious time? Fly and save yourself."

At that moment the officers burst into the room and a violent struggle began; but Hendon was soon overpowered and dragged away. The king was taken also, and both were bound and led to prison.

27

In Prison

THE CELLS were all crowded; so the two friends were chained in a large room where persons charged with trifling offenses were commonly kept. They had company, for there were some twenty manacled or fettered prisoners here, of both sexes and of varying ages—an obscene and noisy gang. The king chafed bitterly over the stupendous indignity thus put upon his royalty, but Hendon was moody and taciturn. He was pretty thoroughly bewildered. He had come home, a jubilant prodigal, expecting to find everybody wild with joy over his return; and instead had got the cold shoulder and a jail. The promise and the fulfilment differed so widely, that the effect was stunning; he could not decide whether it was most tragic or most grotesque. He felt much as a man might who had danced blithely out to enjoy a rainbow, and got struck by lightning.

But gradually his confused and tormenting thoughts settled down into some sort of order, and then his mind centered itself upon Edith. He turned her conduct over, and examined it in all lights, but he could not make anything satisfactory out of it. Did she know him?—or didn't she know him? It was a perplexing puzzle, and occupied him a long time; but he ended, finally, with the conviction that she did know him, and had repudiated him for interested reasons. He wanted to load her name with curses now; but this name had so long been sacred to him that he found he could not bring his tongue to profane it.

Wrapped in prison blankets of a soiled and tattered condition, Hendon and the king passed a troubled night. For a bribe the jailer had furnished liquor to some of the prisoners; singing of ribald songs, fighting, shouting, and carousing, was the natural consequence. At last, awhile after midnight, a man attacked a woman and nearly killed her by beating her over the head with his manacles before the jailer could come to the rescue. The jailer restored peace by giving the man a sound clubbing about the head and shoulders—then the carousing ceased; and after that, all had an opportunity to sleep who did not mind the annoyance of the moanings and groanings of the two wounded people.

During the ensuing week, the days and nights were of a monotonous sameness, as to events; men whose faces Hendon remembered more or less distinctly came, by day, to gaze at the "impostor" and repudiate and insult him; and by night the carousing and crawling went on, with symmetrical regularity. However, there was a change of incident at last. The jailer brought in an old man, and said to him:

"The villain is in this room—cast thy old eyes about and see if thou canst say which is he."

Hendon glanced up, and experienced a pleasant sensation for the first time since he had been in the jail. He said to himself, "This is Blake Andrews, a servant all his life in my father's family —a good honest soul, with a right heart in his breast. That is, formerly. But none are true now; all are liars. This man will know me—and will deny me, too, like the rest."

The old man gazed around the room, glanced at each face in turn, and finally said:

"I see none here but paltry knaves, scum o' the streets. Which is he?"

The jailer laughed.

"Here," he said; "scan this big animal, and grant me an opinion."

The old man approached, and looked Hendon over, long and earnestly, then shook his head and said:

"Marry, *this* is no Hendon—nor ever was!"

"Right! Thy old eyes are sound yet. An I were Sir Hugh, I would take the shabby carle and—"

The jailer finished by lifting himself a-tiptoe with an imaginary halter, at the same time making a gurgling noise in his throat suggestive of suffocation. The old man said, vindictively:

"Let him bless God an he fare no worse. An *I* had the handling o' the villain, he should roast, or I am no true man!"

The jailer laughed a pleasant hyena laugh, and said:

"Give him a piece of thy mind, old man—they all do it. Thou'lt find it good diversion."

Then he sauntered toward his anteroom and disappeared. The old man dropped upon his knees and whispered:

"God be thanked, thou'rt come again, my master! I believed thou wert dead these seven years, and lo, here thou art alive! I knew thee the moment I saw thee; and main hard work it was to keep a stony countenance and seem to see none here but tuppenny knaves and rubbish o' the streets. I am old and poor, Sir Miles; but say the word and I will go forth and proclaim the truth though I be strangled for it."

"No," said Hendon, "thou shalt not. It would ruin thee, and yet help but little in my cause. But I thank thee; for thou hast given me back somewhat of my lost faith in my kind."

The old servant became very valuable to Hendon and the king; for he dropped in several times a day to "abuse" the former, and always smuggled in a few delicacies to help out the prison bill of fare; he also furnished the current news. Hendon reserved the dainties for the king; without them his majesty might not have survived, for he was not able to eat the coarse and wretched food provided by the jailer. Andrews was obliged to confine himself to brief visits, in order to avoid suspicion; but he managed to impart a fair degree of information each time—information delivered in a low voice, for Hendon's benefit, and interlarded with insulting epithets delivered in a louder voice, for the benefit of other hearers.

So, little by little, the story of the family came out. Arthur had been dead six years. This loss, with the absence of news from Hendon, impaired the father's health; he believed he was going to die, and he wished to see Hugh and Edith settled in life before he passed away; but Edith begged hard for delay, hoping for

Miles's return; then the letter came which brought the news of Miles's death; the shock prostrated Sir Richard; he believed his end was very near, and he and Hugh insisted upon the marriage; Edith begged for and obtained a month's respite; then another, and finally a third; the marriage then took place, by the death-bed of Sir Richard. It had not proved a happy one. It was whispered about the country that shortly after the nuptials the bride found among her husband's papers several rough and incomplete drafts of the fatal letter, and had accused him of precipitating the marriage—and Sir Richard's death, too—by a wicked forgery. Tales of cruelty to the Lady Edith and the servants were to be heard on all hands; and since the father's death Sir Hugh had thrown off all soft disguises and become a pitiless master toward all who in any way depended upon him and his domains for bread.

There was a bit of Andrew's gossip which the king listened to with a lively interest:

"There is rumor that the king is mad. But in charity forbear to say *I* mentioned it, for 'tis death to speak of it, they say."

His majesty glared at the old man and said:

"The king is *not* mad, good man—and thou'lt find it to thy advantage to busy thyself with matters that nearer concern thee than this seditious prattle."

"What doth the lad mean?" said Andrews, surprised at this brisk assault from such an unexpected quarter. Hendon gave him a sign, and he did not pursue his question, but went on with his budget:

"The late king is to be buried at Windsor in a day or two—the sixteenth of the month—and the new king will be crowned at Westminster the twentieth."

"Methinks they must needs find him first," muttered his majesty; then added, confidently, "but they will look to that—and so also shall I."

"In the name of—"

But the old man got no further—a warning sign from Hendon checked his remark. He resumed the thread of his gossip.

"Sir Hugh goeth to the coronation—and with grand hopes. He confidently looketh to come back a peer, for he is high in favor with the Lord Protector."

"What Lord Protector?" asked his majesty.

"His grace the Duke of Somerset."

"What Duke of Somerset?"

"Marry, there is but one—Seymour, Earl of Hertford."

The king asked, sharply:

"Since when is *he* a duke, and Lord Protector?"

"Since the last day of January."

"And, prithee, who made him so?"

"Himself and the Great Council—with help of the king."

His majesty started violently. "The *king!*" he cried. "*What* king, good sir?"

"What king, indeed! (God-a-mercy, what aileth the boy?) Sith we have but one, 'tis not difficult to answer—his most sacred majesty King Edward the Sixth—whom God preserve! Yea, and a dear and gracious little urchin is he, too; and whether he be mad or no—and they say he mendeth daily—his praises are on all men's lips; and all bless him likewise, and offer prayers that he may be spared to reign long in England; for he began humanely, with saving the old Duke of Norfolk's life, and now is he bent on destroying the cruelest of the laws that harry and oppress the people."

This news struck his majesty dumb with amazement, and plunged him into so deep and dismal a reverie that he heard no more of the old man's gossip. He wondered if the "little urchin" was the beggar-boy whom he left dressed in his own garments in the palace. It did not seem possible that this could be, for surely his manners and speech would betray him if he pretended to be the Prince of Wales—then he would be driven out, and search made for the true prince. Could it be that the court had set up some sprig of the nobility in his place? No, for his uncle would not allow that—he was all-powerful and could and would crush such a movement, of course. The boy's musings profited him nothing; the more he tried to unriddle the mystery the more perplexed he became, the more his head ached, and the worse he slept. His impatience to get to London grew hourly, and his captivity became almost unendurable.

Hendon's arts all failed with the king—he could not be comforted, but a couple of women who were chained near him, succeeded better. Under their gentle ministrations he found peace and learned a degree of patience. He was very grateful, and came to love them dearly and to delight in the sweet and soothing influence of their presence. He asked them why they were in prison, and when they said they were Baptists, he smiled, and inquired:

"Is that a crime to be shut up for in a prison? Now I grieve, for I shall lose ye—they will not keep ye long for such a little thing."

They did not answer; and something in their faces made him uneasy. He said, eagerly:

"You do not speak—be good to me, and tell me—there will be no other punishment? Prithee, tell me there is no fear of that."

They tried to change the topic, but his fears were aroused, and he pursued it:

"Will they scourge thee? No, no, they would not be so cruel! Say they would not. Come, they *will* not, will they?"

The women betrayed confusion and distress, but there was no avoiding an answer, so one of them said, in a voice choked with emotion:

"Oh, thou'lt break our hearts, thou gentle spirit! God will help us to bear our—"

"It is a confession!" the king broke in. "Then they *will* scourge thee, the stony-hearted wretches! But oh, thou must not weep, I cannot bear it. Keep up thy courage—I shall come to my own in time to save thee from this bitter thing, and I will do it!"

When the king awoke in the morning, the women were gone.

"They are saved!" he said, joyfully; then added, despondently, "but woe is me!—for they were my comforters."

Each of them had left a shred of ribbon pinned to his clothing, in token of remembrance. He said he would keep these things always; and that soon he would seek out these dear good friends of his and take them under his protection.

Just then the jailer came in with some subordinates and commanded that the prisoners be conducted to the jail-yard. The king was overjoyed—it would be a blessed thing to see the blue sky and breathe the fresh air once more. He fretted and chafed at the slowness of the officers, but his turn came at last and he was released from his staple and ordered to follow the other prisoners, with Hendon.

The court, or quadrangle, was stone-paved, and open to the sky. The prisoners entered it through a massive archway of masonry, and were placed in file, standing, with their backs against the wall. A rope was stretched in front of them, and they were also guarded by their officers. It was a chill and lowering morning, and a light snow which had fallen during the night whitened the great empty space and added to the general dismalness of its aspect. Now and then a wintry wind shivered through the place and sent the snow eddying hither and thither.

In the center of the court stood two women, chained to posts. A glance showed the king that these were his good friends. He shuddered, and said to himself, "Alack, they are not gone free, as I had thought. To think that such as these should know the lash! —in England! Ay, there's the shame of it—not in Heathenesse, but Christian England! They will be scourged; and I, whom they have comforted and kindly entreated, must look on and see the great wrong done; it is strange, so strange! that I, the very source of power in this broad realm, am helpless to protect them. But let these miscreants look well to themselves, for there is a day coming when I will require of them a heavy reckoning for this work. For every blow they strike now they shall feel a hundred then."

A great gate swung open and a crowd of citizens poured in. They flocked around the two women, and hid them from the king's view. A clergyman entered and passed through the crowd, and he also was hidden. The king now heard talking, back and forth, as if questions were being asked and answered, but he could not make out what was said. Next there was a deal of bustle and preparation, and much passing and repassing of officials through that part of the crowd that stood on the further side of the women; and while this proceeded a deep hush gradually fell upon the people.

Now, by command, the masses parted and fell aside, and the king saw a spectacle that froze the marrow in his bones. Fagots had been piled about the two women, and a kneeling man was lighting them!

The women bowed their heads, and covered their faces with their hands; the yellow flames began to climb upward among the snapping and crackling fagots, and wreaths of blue smoke to stream away on the wind; the clergyman lifted his hands and began a prayer—just then two young girls came flying through the great gate, uttering piercing screams, and threw themselves upon the women at the stake. Instantly they were torn away by the officers, and one of them was kept in a tight grip, but the other broke loose, saying she would die with her mother; and before she could be stopped she had flung her arms about her mother's neck again. She was torn away once more, and with her gown on fire. Two or three men held her, and the burning portion of her gown was snatched off and thrown flaming aside, she struggling all the while to free herself, and saying she would be alone in the world now, and begging to be allowed to die with her mother. Both the girls screamed continually, and fought for freedom; but suddenly this tumult was drowned under a volley of heart-piercing shrieks of mortal agony. The king glanced from the frantic girls to the stake, then turned away and leaned his ashen face against the wall, and looked no more. He said, "That which I have seen, in that one little moment, will never go out from my memory, but will abide there; and I shall see it all the days, and dream of it all the nights, till I die. Would God I had been blind!"

Hendon was watching the king. He said to himself, with satisfaction, "His disorder mendeth; he hath changed, and groweth gentler. If he had followed his wont, he would have stormed at these varlets, and said he was king, and commanded that the women be turned loose unscathed. Soon his delusion will pass away and be forgotten, and his poor mind will be whole again. God speed the day!"

That same day several prisoners were brought in to remain overnight, who were being conveyed, under guard, to various places in the kingdom, to undergo punishment for crimes committed. The king conversed with these—he had made it a point, from the beginning, to instruct himself for the kingly office by questioning prisoners whenever the opportunity offered—and the tale of their woes wrung his heart. One of them was a poor half-witted woman who had stolen a yard or two of cloth from a weaver—she was to be hanged for it. Another was a man who had been accused of stealing a horse; he said the proof had failed, and he had imagined that he was safe from the halter; but no— he was hardly free before he was arraigned for killing a deer in the king's park; this was proved against him, and now he was on his way to the gallows. There was a tradesman's apprentice whose case particularly distressed the king; this youth said he found a hawk one evening that had escaped from its owner, and he took it home with him, imagining himself entitled to it; but the court convicted him of stealing it, and sentenced him to death.

The king was furious over these inhumanities, and wanted Hendon to break jail and fly with him to Westminster, so that he could mount his throne and hold out his scepter in mercy over these unfortunate people and save their lives. "Poor child," sighed Hendon, "these woeful tales have brought his malady upon him again—alack, but for this evil hap, he would have been well in a little time."

Among these prisoners was an old lawyer—a man with a strong face and a dauntless mien. Three years past, he had written a pamphlet against the Lord Chancellor, accusing him of injustice, and had been punished for it by the loss of his ears in the pillory and degradation from the bar, and in addition had been fined £3,000 and sentenced to imprisonment for life. Lately he had repeated his offense; and in consequence was now under sentence to lose *what remained of his ears,* pay a fine of £5,000, be branded on both cheeks, and remain in prison for life.

"These be honorable scars," he said, and turned back his gray hair and showed the mutilated stubs of what had once been his ears.

The king's eye burned with passion. He said:

"None believe in me—neither wilt thou. But no matter—within the compass of a month thou shalt be free; and more, the laws that have dishonored thee, and shamed the English name, shall be swept from the statute-books. The world is made wrong, kings should go to school to their own laws at times, and so learn mercy."

28

The Sacrifice

MEANTIME Miles was growing sufficiently tired of confinement and inaction. But now his trial came on, to his great gratification, and he thought he could welcome any sentence provided a further imprisonment should not be a part of it. But he was mistaken about that. He was in a fine fury when he found himself described as a "sturdy vagabond" and sentenced to sit two hours in the pillory for bearing that character and for assaulting the master of Hendon Hall. His pretensions as to brothership with his prosecutor, and rightful heirship to the Hendon honors and estates, were left contemptuously unnoticed, as being not even worth examination.

He raged and threatened on his way to punishment, but it did no good; he was snatched roughly along by the officers, and got an occasional cuff, besides, for his unreverent conduct.

The king could not pierce through the rabble that swarmed behind; so he was obliged to follow in the rear, remote from his good friend and servant. The king had been nearly condemned to the stocks himself, for being in such bad company, but had been let off with a lecture and a warning, in consideration of his youth. When the crowd at last halted, he flitted feverishly from point to point around its outer rim, hunting a place to get through; and at last, after a deal of difficulty and delay, succeeded. There sat his poor henchman in the degrading stocks, the sport and butt of a dirty mob—he, the body servant of the king of England! Edward had heard the sentence pronounced, but he had not realized the half that it meant. His anger began to rise as the sense of this new indignity which had been put upon him sank home; it jumped to summer heat the next moment, when he saw an egg sail through the air and crush itself against Hendon's cheek, and heard the crowd roar its enjoyment of the episode. He sprang across the open circle and confronted the officer in charge, crying:

"For shame! This is my servant—set him free! I am the—"

"Oh, peace!" exclaimed Hendon, in a panic, "thou'lt destroy thyself. Mind him not, officer, he is mad."

"Give thyself no trouble as to the matter of minding him, good man, I have small mind to mind him; but as to teaching him somewhat, to that I am well inclined." He turned to a subordinate and said, "Give the little fool a taste or two of the lash, to mend his manners."

"Half a dozen will better serve his turn," suggested Sir Hugh, who had ridden up a moment before to take a passing glance at the proceedings.

The king was seized. He did not even struggle, so paralyzed was he with the mere thought of the monstrous outrage that was proposed to be inflicted upon his sacred person. History was already defiled with the record of the scourging of an English king with whips—it was an intolerable reflection that he must furnish a duplicate of that shameful page. He was in the toils, there was no help for him; he must either take this punishment or beg for its remission. Hard conditions; he would take the stripes—a king might do that, but a king could not beg.

But meantime, Miles Hendon was resolving the difficulty. "Let the child go," said he; "ye heartless dogs, do ye not see how young and frail he is? Let him go—I will take his lashes."

"Marry, a good thought—and thanks for it," said Sir Hugh, his face lighting with a sardonic satisfaction. "Let the little beggar go, and give this fellow a dozen in his place—an honest dozen, well laid on." The king was in the act of entering a fierce protest, but Sir Hugh silenced him with the potent remark, "Yes, speak up, do, and free thy mind—only, mark ye, that for each word you utter he shall get six strokes the more."

Hendon was removed from the stocks, and his back laid bare; and while the lash was applied the poor little king turned away his face and allowed unroyal tears to channel his cheeks unchecked. "Ah, brave good heart," he said to himself, "this loyal deed shall never perish out of my memory. I will not forget it— and neither shall *they!*" he added, with passion. While he mused, his appreciation of Hendon's magnanimous conduct grew to greater and still greater dimensions in his mind, and so also did his gratefulness for it. Presently he said to himself, "Who saves his prince from wounds and possible death—and this he did for me—performs high service; but it is little—it is nothing!—oh, less than nothing!—when 'tis weighed against the act of him who saves his prince from SHAME!"

Hendon made no outcry under the scourge, but bore the heavy blows with soldierly fortitude. This, together with his redeeming the boy by taking his stripes for him, compelled the respect of even that forlorn and degraded mob that was gathered there; and its gibes and hootings died away, and no sound remained but the sound of the falling blows. The stillness that pervaded the place when Hendon found himself once more in the stocks, was in strong contrast with the insulting clamor which had prevailed there so little a while before. The king came softly to Hendon's side, and whispered in his ear:

"Kings cannot ennoble thee, thou good, great soul, for One who is higher than kings hath done that for thee; but a king can confirm thy nobility to men." He picked up the scourge from the ground, touched Hendon's bleeding shoulders lightly with it, and whispered, "Edward of England dubs thee earl!"

Hendon was touched. The water welled to his eyes, yet at the same time the grisly humor of the situation and circumstances so undermined his gravity that it was all he could do to keep some sign of his inward mirth from showing outside. To be suddenly hoisted, naked and gory, from the common stocks to the Alpine altitude and splendor of an earldom, seemed to him the last possibility in the line of the grotesque. He said to himself, "Now am I finely tinseled, indeed! The specter-knight of the Kingdom of Dreams and Shadows is become a specter-earl!—a dizzy flight for a callow wing! An this go on, I shall presently be hung like a very May-pole with fantastic gauds and make-believe honors. But I shall value them, all valueless as they are, for the love that doth bestow them. Better these poor mock dignities of mine, that come unasked from a clean hand and a right spirit, than real ones bought by servility from grudging and interested power."

The dreaded Sir Hugh wheeled his horse about, and, as he spurred away, the living wall divided silently to let him pass, and as silently closed together again. And so remained; nobody went so far as to venture a remark in favor of the prisoner, or in compliment to him; but no matter, the absence of abuse was a sufficient homage in itself. A late comer who was not posted as to the present circumstances, and who delivered a sneer at the "impostor" and was in the act of following it with a dead cat, was promptly knocked down and kicked out, without any words, and then the deep quiet resumed sway once more.

29

To London

WHEN Hendon's term of service in the stocks was finished, he was released and ordered to quit the region and come back no more. His sword was restored to him, and also his mule and his donkey. He mounted and rode off, followed by the king, the crowd opening with quiet respectfulness to let them pass, and then dispersing when they were gone.

Hendon was soon absorbed in thought. There were questions of high import to be answered. What should he do? Whither should he go? Powerful help must be found somewhere, or he must relinquish his inheritance and remain under the imputation of being an impostor besides. Where could he hope to find this powerful help? Where, indeed! It was a knotty question. By and by a thought occurred to him which pointed to a possibility—the slenderest of slender possibilities, certainly, but still worth considering, for lack of any other that promised anything at all. He remembered what old Andrews had said about the young king's goodness and his generous championship of the wronged and unfortunate. Why not go and try to get speech of him and beg for justice? Ah, yes, but could so fantastic a pauper get admission to the august presence of a monarch? Never mind—let that matter take care of itself; it was a bridge that would not need to be crossed till he should come to it. He was an old campaigner, and used to inventing shifts and expedients; no doubt he would be able to find a way. Yes, he would strike for the capital. Maybe his father's old friend, Sir Humphrey Marlow, would help him— "good old Sir Humphrey, Head Lieutenant of the late king's kitchen, or stables, or something"—Miles could not remember just what or which. Now that he had something to turn his energies to, a distinctly defined object to accomplish, the fog of humiliation and depression which had settled down upon his spirits lifted and blew away, and he raised his head and looked about him. He was surprised to see how far he had come; the village was away behind him. The king was jogging along in his wake, with his head bowed; for he, too, was deep in plans and thinkings. A sorrowful misgiving clouded Hendon's new-born cheerfulness; would the boy be willing to go again to a city where, during all his brief life, he had never known anything but ill usage and pinching want? But the question must be asked; it could not be avoided; so Hendon reined up, and called out:

"I had forgotten to inquire whither we are bound. Thy commands, my liege?"

"To London!"

Hendon moved on again, mightily contented with the answer —but astonished at it, too.

The whole journey was made without an adventure of importance. But it ended with one. About ten o'clock on the night of the 19th of February, they stepped upon London Bridge, in the midst of a writhing, struggling jam of howling and hurrahing people, whose beer-jolly faces stood out strongly in the glare from manifold torches—and at that instant the decaying head of some former duke or other grandee tumbled down between them, striking Hendon on the elbow and then bounding off among the hurrying confusion of feet. So evanescent and unstable are men's works in this world!—the late good king is but three weeks dead and three days in his grave, and already the adornments which he took such pains to select from prominent people for his noble bridge are falling. A citizen stumbled over that head, and drove his own head into the back of somebody in front of him, who turned and knocked down the first person that came handy, and was promptly laid out himself by that person's friend. It was the right ripe time for a free fight, for the festivities of the morrow—Coronation Day—were already beginning; everybody was full of strong drink and patriotism; within five minutes the free fight was occupying a good deal of ground; within ten or twelve it covered an acre or so, and was become a riot. By this time Hendon and the king were hopelessly separated from each other and lost in the rush and turmoil of the roaring masses of humanity. And so we leave them.

30

Tom's Progress

WHILST the true king wandered about the land, poorly clad, poorly fed, cuffed and derided by tramps one while, herding with thieves and murderers in a jail another, and called idiot and impostor by all impartially, the mock King Tom Canty enjoyed a quiet different experience.

When we saw him last, royalty was just beginning to have a bright side for him. This bright side went on brightening more and more every day; in a very little while it was become almost all sunshine and delightfulness. He lost his fears; his misgivings faded out and died; his embarrassments departed, and gave place to an easy and confident bearing. He worked the whipping-boy mine to ever-increasing profit.

He ordered my Lady Elizabeth and my Lady Jane Grey into his presence when he wanted to play or talk, and dismissed them when he was done with them, with the air of one familiarly accustomed to such performances. It no longer confused him to have these lofty personages kiss his hand at parting.

He came to enjoy being conducted to bed in state at night, and dressed with intricate and solemn ceremony in the morning. It came to be a proud pleasure to march to dinner attended by a glittering procession of officers of state and gentlemen-at-arms;

insomuch, indeed, that he doubled his guard of gentlemen-at-arms, and made them a hundred. He liked to hear the bugles sounding down the long corridors, and the distant voices responding, "Way for the King!"

He even learned to enjoy sitting in throned state in council, and seeming to be something more than the Lord Protector's mouthpiece. He liked to receive great ambassadors and their gorgeous trains, and listen to the affectionate messages they brought from illustrious monarchs who called him "brother." Oh, happy Tom Canty, late of Offal Court!

He enjoyed his splendid clothes, and ordered more; he found his four hundred servants too few for his proper grandeur, and trebled them. The adulation of salaaming courtiers came to be sweet music to his ears. He remained kind and gentle, and a sturdy and determined champion of all that were oppressed, and he made tireless war upon unjust laws; yet upon occasion, being offended, he could turn upon an earl, or even a duke, and give him a look that would make him tremble. Once, when his royal "sister," the grimly holy Lady Mary, set herself to reason with him against the wisdom of his course in pardoning so many people who would otherwise be jailed, or hanged, or burned, and reminded him that their august late father's prisons had sometimes contained as high as sixty thousand convicts at one time, and that during his admirable reign he had delivered seventy-two thousand thieves and robbers over to death by the executioner,[1] the boy was filled with generous indignation, and commanded her to go to her closet, and beseech God to take away the stone that was in her breast, and give her a human heart.

Did Tom Canty never feel troubled about the poor little rightful prince who had treated him so kindly, and flown out with such hot zeal to avenge him upon the insolent sentinel at the palace gate? Yes; his first royal days and nights were pretty well sprinkled with painful thoughts about the lost prince, and with sincere longings for his return and happy restoration to his native

[1] Hume's *England*.

rights and splendors. But as time wore on, and the prince did not come, Tom's mind became more and more occupied with his new and enchanting experiences, and by little and little the vanished monarch faded almost out of his thoughts; and finally, when he did intrude upon them at intervals, he was become an unwelcome specter, for he made Tom feel guilty and ashamed.

Tom's poor mother and sisters traveled the same road out of his mind. At first he pined for them, sorrowed for them, longed to see them; but later, the thought of their coming some day in their rags and dirt, and betraying him with their kisses, and pulling him down from his lofty place, and dragging him back to penury and degradation and the slums, made him shudder. At last they ceased to trouble his thoughts almost wholly. And he was content, even glad; for, whenever their mournful and accusing faces did rise before him now, they made him feel more despicable than the worms that crawl.

At midnight of the 19th of February, Tom Canty was sinking to sleep in his rich bed in the palace, guarded by his loyal vassals, and surrounded by the pomps of royalty, a happy boy; for to-morrow was the day appointed for his solemn crowning as king of England. At that same hour, Edward, the true king, hungry and thirsty, soiled and draggled, worn with travel, and clothed in rags and shreds—his share of the results of the riot— was wedged in among a crowd of people who were watching with deep interest certain hurrying gangs of workmen who streamed in and out of Westminster Abbey, busy as ants; they were making the last preparation for the royal coronation.

31

The Recognition Procession

WHEN Tom Canty awoke the next morning, the air was heavy with a thunderous murmur; all the distances were charged with it. It was music to him; for it meant that the English world was out in its strength to give loyal welcome to the great day.

Presently Tom found himself once more the chief figure in a wonderful floating pageant on the Thames; for by ancient custom the "recognition procession" through London must start from the Tower, and he was bound thither.

When he arrived there, the sides of the venerable fortress seemed suddenly rent in a thousand places, and from every rent leaped a red tongue of flame and a white gush of smoke; a deafening explosion followed, which drowned the shoutings of the multitude, and made the ground tremble; the flame-jets, the smoke, and the explosions were repeated over and over again with marvelous celerity, so that in a few moments the old Tower disappeared in the vast fog of its own smoke, all but the very top of the tall pile called the White Tower; this, with its banners, stood out above the dense bank of vapor as a mountain peak projects above a cloud-rack.

Tom Canty, splendidly arrayed, mounted a prancing war-steed, whose rich trappings almost reached to the ground; his "uncle," the Lord Protector Somerset, similarly mounted, took place in his rear; the King's Guard formed in single ranks on either side, clad in burnished armor; after the Protector followed a seemingly interminable procession of resplendent nobles attended by their vassals; after these came the lord mayor and the aldermanic body, in crimson velvet robes, and with their gold chains across their breasts; and after these the officers and members of all the guilds of London, in rich raiment, and bearing the showy banners of the several corporations. Also in the procession, as a special guard of honor through the city, was the Ancient and Honorable Artillery Company—an organization already three hundred years old at that time, and the only military body in England possessing the privilege (which it still possesses in our day) of holding itself independent of the commands of Parliament. It was a brilliant spectacle, and was hailed with acclamations all along the line, as it took its stately way through the packed multitudes of citizens. The chronicler says, "The king, as he entered the city, was received by the people with prayers, welcomings, cries, and tender words, and all signs which argue an earnest love of subjects toward their sovereign; and the king, by holding up his glad countenance to such as stood afar off, and most tender language to those that stood nigh his Grace, showed himself no less thankful to receive the people's good will than they to offer it. To all that wished him well, he gave thanks. To such as bade 'God save his Grace,' he said in return, 'God save you all!' and added that 'he thanked them with all his heart.' Wonderfully transported were the people with the loving answers and gestures of their king."

In Fenchurch Street a "fair child, in costly apparel," stood on a stage to welcome his majesty to the city. The last verse of his greeting was in these words:

Welcome, O King! as much as hearts can think;
    Welcome again, as much as tongue can tell—
Welcome to joyous tongues, and hearts that will not shrink;
    God thee preserve, we pray, and wish thee ever well.

The people burst forth in a glad shout, repeating with one voice what the child had said. Tom Canty gazed abroad over the surging sea of eager faces, and his heart swelled with exultation; and he felt that the one thing worth living for in this world was to be a king, and a nation's idol. Presently he caught sight, at a distance, of a couple of his ragged Offal Court comrades—one of them the lord high admiral in his late mimic court, the other the first lord of the bedchamber in the same pretentious fiction; and his pride swelled higher than ever. Oh, if they could only recognize him now! What unspeakable glory it would be, if they could recognize him, and realize that the derided mock king of the slums and back alleys was become a real king, with illustrious dukes and princes for his humble menials, and the English world at his feet! But he had to deny himself, and choke down his desire, for such a recognition might cost more than it would come to; so he turned away his head, and left the two soiled lads to go on with their shoutings and glad adulations, unsuspicious of whom it was they were lavishing them upon.

Every now and then rose the cry, "A largess! a largess!" and Tom responded by scattering a handful of bright new coins abroad for the multitude to scramble for.

The chronicler says, "At the upper end of Gracechurch Street, before the sign of the Eagle, the city had erected a gorgeous arch, beneath which was a stage, which stretched from one side of the street to the other. This was a historical pageant, representing the king's immediate progenitors. There sat Elizabeth of York in the midst of an immense white rose, whose petals formed elaborate furbelows around her; by her side was Henry VII., issuing out of a vast red rose, disposed in the same manner; the hands of the royal pair were locked together, and the wedding-ring ostentatiously displayed. From the red and white roses proceeded a stem, which reached up to a second stage, occupied by Henry VIII., issuing from a red-and-white rose, with the effigy of the new king's mother, Jane Seymour, represented by his side. One branch sprang from this pair, which mounted to a third stage, where sat the effigy of Edward VI. himself, enthroned in royal majesty; and the whole pageant was framed with wreaths of roses, red and white."

This quaint and gaudy spectacle so wrought upon the rejoicing people, that their acclamations utterly smothered the small voice of the child whose business it was to explain the thing in eulogistic rhymes. But Tom Canty was not sorry; for this loyal uproar was sweeter music to him than any poetry, no matter what its quality might be. Whithersoever Tom turned his happy young face, the people recognized the exactness of his effigy's likeness to himself, the flesh-and-blood counterpart; and new whirlwinds of applause burst forth.

The great pageant moved on, and still on, under one triumphal arch after another, and past a bewildering succession of spectacular and symbolical tableaux, each of which typified and exalted some virtue, or talent, or merit, of the little king's. "Throughout the whole of Cheapside, from every penthouse and window, hung banners and streamers; and the richest carpets, stuffs, and cloth-of-gold tapestried the streets—specimens of the great wealth of the stores within; and the splendor of this thoroughfare was equaled in the other streets, and in some even surpassed."

"And all these wonders and these marvels are to welcome me— me!" murmured Tom Canty.

The mock king's cheeks were flushed with excitement, his eyes were flashing, his senses swam in a delirium of pleasure. At this point, just as he was raising his hand to fling another rich largess, he caught sight of a pale, astounded face which was strained forward out of the second rank of the crowd, its intense eyes riveted upon him. A sickening consternation struck through him; he recognized his mother! and up flew his hand, palm outward, before his eyes—that old involuntary gesture, born of a forgotten episode, and perpetuated by habit. In an instant more she had torn her way out of the press, and past the guards, and was at his side. She embraced his leg, she covered it with kisses, she cried, "O, my child, my darling!" lifting toward him a face that was transfigured with joy and love. The same instant an officer of the King's Guard snatched her away with a curse, and sent her reeling back whence she came with a vigorous impulse from his strong arm. The words "I do not know you, woman!" were falling from Tom Canty's lips when this piteous thing occurred; but it smote him to the heart to see her treated so; and as she turned for a last glimpse of him, whilst the crowd was swallowing her from his sight, she seemed so wounded, so broken-hearted, that a shame fell upon him which consumed his pride to ashes, and withered his stolen royalty. His grandeurs were stricken valueless; they seemed to fall away from him like rotten rags.

The procession moved on, and still on, through ever-augmenting splendors and ever-augmenting tempests of welcome; but to Tom Canty they were as if they had not been. He neither saw nor heard. Royalty had lost its grace and sweetness; its pomps were become a reproach. Remorse was eating his heart out. He said, "Would God I were free of my captivity!"

He had unconsciously dropped back into the phraseology of the first days of his compulsory greatness.

The shining pageant still went winding like a radiant and interminable serpent down the crooked lanes of the quaint old city, and through the huzzaing hosts; but still the king rode with bowed head and vacant eyes, seeing only his mother's face and that wounded look in it.

"Largess, largess!" The cry fell upon an unheeding ear.

"Long live Edward of England!" It seemed as if the earth shook with the explosion; but there was no response from the king. He heard it only as one hears the thunder of the surf when it is blown to the ear out of a great distance, for it was smothered under another sound which was still nearer, in his own breast, in his accusing conscience—a voice which kept repeating those shameful words, "I do not know you, woman!"

The words smote upon the king's soul as the strokes of a funeral bell smite upon the soul of a surviving friend when they remind him of secret treacheries suffered at his hands by him that is gone.

New glories were unfolded at every turning; new wonders, new marvels, sprung into view; the pent clamors of waiting batteries were released; new raptures poured from the throats of the waiting multitudes; but the king gave no sign, and the accusing voice that went moaning through his comfortless breast was all the sound he heard.

By and by the gladness in the faces of the populace changed a little, and became touched with a something like solicitude or anxiety; an abatement in the volume of applause was observable too. The Lord Protector was quick to notice these things; he was as quick to detect the cause. He spurred to the king's side, bent low in his saddle, uncovered, and said:

"My liege, it is an ill time for dreaming. The people observe thy downcast head, thy clouded mien, and they take it for an omen. Be advised; unveil the sun of royalty, and let it shine upon these boding vapors, and disperse them. Lift up thy face, and smile upon the people."

So saying, the duke scattered a handful of coins to right and left, then retired to his place. The mock king did mechanically as he had been bidden. His smile had no heart in it, but few eyes were near enough or sharp enough to detect that. The noddings of his plumed head as he saluted his subjects were full of grace and graciousness; the largess which he delivered from his hand was royally liberal; so the people's anxiety vanished, and the acclamations burst forth again in as mighty a volume as before.

Still once more, a little before the progress was ended, the duke was obliged to ride forward, and make remonstrance. He whispered:

"O dread sovereign! shake off these fatal humors; the eyes of the world are upon thee." Then he added with sharp annoyance, "Perdition catch that crazy pauper! 'twas she that hath disturbed your Highness."

The gorgeous figure turned a lusterless eye upon the duke, and said in a dead voice:

"She was my mother!"

"My God!" groaned the Protector as he reined his horse backward to his post, "the omen was pregnant with prophecy. He is gone mad again!"

32

Coronation Day

LET US GO backward a few hours, and place ourselves in Westminster Abbey, at four o'clock in the morning of this memorable
Coronation Day. We are not without company; for although it is
still night, we find the torch-lighted galleries already filling up
with people who are well content to sit still and wait seven or
eight hours till the time shall come for them to see what they may
not hope to see twice in their lives—the coronation of a king. Yes,
London and Westminster have been astir ever since the warning
guns boomed at three o'clock, and already crowds of untitled
rich folk who have bought the privilege of trying to find sitting-
room in the galleries are flocking in at the entrances reserved for
their sort.

The hours drag along, tediously enough. All stir has ceased for
some time, for every gallery has long ago been packed. We may
sit now, and look and think at our leisure. We have glimpses,
here and there and yonder, through the dim cathedral twilight,
of portions of many galleries and balconies, wedged full with
people, the other portions of these galleries and balconies being
cut off from sight by intervening pillars and architectural projections. We have in view the whole of the great north transept—
empty, and waiting for England's privileged ones. We see also
the ample area or platform, carpeted with rich stuffs, whereon
the throne stands. The throne occupies the center of the platform, and is raised above it upon an elevation of four steps.
Within the seat of the throne is inclosed a rough flat rock—the
stone of Scone—which many generations of Scottish kings sat on

to be crowned, and so it in time became holy enough to answer a like purpose for English monarchs. Both the throne and its footstool are covered with cloth-of-gold.

Stillness reigns, the torches blink dully, the time drags heavily. But at last the lagging daylight asserts itself, the torches are extinguished, and a mellow radiance suffuses the great spaces. All features of the noble building are distinct now, but soft and dreamy, for the sun is lightly veiled with clouds.

At seven o'clock the first break in the drowsy monotony occurs; for on the stroke of this hour the first peeress enters the transept, clothed like Solomon for splendor, and is conducted to her appointed place by an official clad in satins and velvets, whilst a duplicate of him gathers up the lady's long train, follows after, and, when the lady is seated, arranges the train across her lap for her. He then places her footstool according to her desire, after which he puts her coronet where it will be convenient to her hand when the time for the simultaneous coroneting of the nobles shall arrive.

By this time the peeresses are flowing in in a glittering stream, and satin-clad officials are flitting and glinting everywhere, seating them and making them comfortable. The scene is animated enough now. There is stir and life, and shifting color everywhere. After a time, quiet reigns again; for the peeresses are all come, and are all in their places—a solid acre, or such a matter, of human flowers, resplendent in variegated colors, and frosted like a Milky Way with diamonds. There are all ages here: brown, wrinkled, white-haired dowagers who are able to go back, and still back, down the stream of time, and recall the crowning of Richard III. and the troublous days of that old forgotten age; and there are handsome middle-aged dames; and lovely and gracious young matrons; and gentle and beautiful young girls, with beaming eyes and fresh complexions, who may possibly put on their jeweled coronets awkwardly when the great time comes; for the matter will be new to them, and their excitement will be a sore hindrance. Still, this may not happen, for the hair of all these ladies has been arranged with a special view to the swift and successful lodging of the crown in its place when the signal comes.

We have seen that this massed array of peeresses is sown thick with diamonds, and we also see that it is a marvelous spectacle —but now we are about to be astonished in earnest. About nine, the clouds suddenly break away and a shaft of sunshine cleaves the mellow atmosphere, and drifts slowly along the ranks of ladies; and every rank it touches flames into a dazzling splendor of many-colored fires, and we tingle to our finger-tips with the electric thrill that is shot through us by the surprise and the beauty of the spectacle! Presently a special envoy from some distant corner of the Orient, marching with the general body of foreign ambassadors, crosses this bar of sunshine, and we catch our breath, the glory that streams and flashes and palpitates about him is so overpowering; for he is crusted from head to heels with gems, and his slightest movement showers a dancing radiance all around him.

Let us change the tense for convenience. The time drifted along—one hour—two hours—two hours and a half; then the deep booming of artillery told that the king and his grand procession had arrived at last; so the waiting multitude rejoiced. All knew that a further delay must follow, for the king must be prepared and robed for the solemn ceremony; but this delay would be pleasantly occupied by the assembling of the peers of the realm in their stately robes. These were conducted ceremoniously to their seats, and their coronets placed conveniently at hand; and meanwhile the multitude in the galleries were alive with interest, for most of them were beholding for the first time, dukes, earls, and barons, whose names had been historical for five hundred years. When all were finally seated, the spectacle from the galleries and all coigns of vantage was complete; a gorgeous one to look upon and to remember.

Now the robed and mitered great heads of the church, and their attendants, filed in upon the platform and took their appointed places; these were followed by the Lord Protector and other great officials, and these again by a steel-clad detachment of the Guard.

There was a waiting pause; then, at a signal, a triumphant peal of music burst forth, and Tom Canty, clothed in a long robe of cloth-of-gold, appeared at a door, and stepped upon the platform. The entire multitude rose, and the ceremony of the Recognition ensued.

Then a noble anthem swept the Abbey with its rich waves of sound; and thus heralded and welcomed, Tom Canty was conducted to the throne. The ancient ceremonies went on with impressive solemnity, whilst the audience gazed; and as they drew nearer and nearer to completion, Tom Canty grew pale, and still paler, and a deep and steadily deepening woe and despondency settled down upon his spirits and upon his remorseful heart.

At last the final act was at hand. The Archbishop of Canterbury lifted up the crown of England from its cushion and held it out over the trembling mock king's head. In the same instant a rainbow radiance flashed along the spacious transept; for with one impulse every individual in the great concourse of nobles lifted a coronet and poised it over his or her head—and paused in that attitude.

A deep hush pervaded the Abbey. At this impressive moment, a startling apparition intruded upon the scene—an apparition observed by none in the absorbed multitude, until it suddenly appeared, moving up the great central aisle. It was a boy, bareheaded, ill shod, and clothed in coarse plebeian garments that were falling to rags. He raised his hand with a solemnity which ill comported with his soiled and sorry aspect, and delivered this note of warning:

"I forbid you to set the crown of England upon that forfeited head. *I* am the king!"

In an instant several indignant hands were laid upon the boy; but in the same instant Tom Canty, in his regal vestments, made a swift step forward and cried out in a ringing voice:

"Loose him and forbear! He *is* the king!"

A sort of panic of astonishment swept the assemblage, and they partly rose in their places and stared in a bewildered way at one another and at the chief figures in this scene, like persons who wondered whether they were awake and in their senses, or asleep and dreaming. The Lord Protector was as amazed as the rest, but quickly recovered himself and exclaimed in a voice of authority:

"Mind not his Majesty, his malady is upon him again—seize the vagabond!"

He would have been obeyed, but the mock king stamped his foot and cried out:

"On your peril! Touch him not, he is the king!"

The hands were withheld; a paralysis fell upon the house; no one moved, no one spoke; indeed, no one knew how to act or what to say, in so strange and surprising an emergency. While all minds were struggling to right themselves, the boy still moved steadily forward, with high port and confident mien; he had never halted from the beginning; and while the tangled minds still floundered helplessly, he stepped upon the platform, and the mock king ran with a glad face to meet him; and fell on his knees before him and said:

"O, my lord the king, let poor Tom Canty be first to swear fealty to thee, and say 'Put on thy crown and enter into thine own again!'"

The Lord Protector's eye fell sternly upon the new-comer's face; but straightway the sternness vanished away, and gave place to an expression of wondering surprise. This thing happened also to the other great officers. They glanced at each other, and retreated a step by a common and unconscious impulse. The thought in each mind was the same: "What a strange resemblance!"

The Lord Protector reflected a moment or two in perplexity, then he said, with grave respectfulness:

"By your favor, sir, I desire to ask certain questions which—"

"I will answer them, my lord."

The duke asked him many questions about the court, the late king, the prince, the princesses. The boy answered them correctly and without hesitating. He described the rooms of state in the palace, the late king's apartments, and those of the Prince of Wales.

It was strange; it was wonderful; yes, it was unaccountable— so all said that heard it. The tide was beginning to turn, and

Tom Canty's hopes to run high, when the Lord Protector shook his head and said:

"It is true it is most wonderful—but it is no more than our lord the king likewise can do." This remark, and this reference to himself as still the king, saddened Tom Canty, and he felt his hopes crumbling from under him. "These are not *proofs,*" added the Protector.

The tide was turning very fast now, very fast, indeed—but in the wrong direction; it was leaving poor Tom Canty stranded on the throne, and sweeping the other out to sea. The Lord Protector communed with himself—shook his head—the thought forced itself upon him, "It is perilous to the state and to us all, to entertain so fateful a riddle as this; it could divide the nation and undermine the throne." He turned and said:

"Sir Thomas, arrest this— No, hold!" His face lighted, and he confronted the ragged candidate with this question:

"Where lieth the Great Seal? Answer me this truly, and the riddle is unriddled; for only he that was Prince of Wales *can* so answer! On so trivial a thing hang a throne and a dynasty!"

It was a lucky thought, a happy thought. That it was so considered by the great officials was manifested by the silent applause that shot from eye to eye around their circle in the form of bright approving glances. Yes, none but the true prince could dissolve the stubborn mystery of the vanished Great Seal—this forlorn little impostor had been taught his lesson well, but here his teachings must fail, for his teacher himself could not answer *that* question—ah, very good, very good indeed: now we shall be rid of this troublesome and perilous business in short order! And so they nodded invisibly and smiled inwardly with satisfaction, and looked to see this foolish lad stricken with a palsy of guilty confusion. How surprised they were, then, to see nothing of the sort happen—how they marveled to hear him answer up promptly, in a confident and untroubled voice, and say:

"There is naught in this riddle that is difficult." Then, without so much as a by-your-leave to anybody, he turned and gave this command, with the easy manner of one accustomed to doing such things: "My Lord St. John, go you to my private cabinet in the palace—for none knoweth the place better than you—and, close down to the floor, in the left corner remotest from the door that opens from the antechamber, you shall find in the wall a brazen nail-head; press upon it and a little jewel-closet will fly open which not even you do know of—no, nor any soul else in all the world but me and the trusty artisan that did contrive it for me. The first thing that falleth under your eye will be the Great Seal—fetch it hither."

All the company wondered at this speech, and wondered still more to see the little mendicant pick out this peer without hesitancy or apparent fear of mistake, and call him by name with such a placidly convincing air of having known him all his life. The peer was almost surprised into obeying. He even made a movement as if to go, but quickly recovered his tranquil attitude and confessed his blunder with a blush. Tom Canty turned upon him and said, sharply:

"Why dost thou hesitate? Hast not heard the king's command? Go!"

The Lord St. John made a deep obeisance—and it was observed that it was a significantly cautious and non-committal one, it not being delivered at either of the kings, but at the neutral ground about half-way between the two—and took his leave.

Now began a movement of the gorgeous particles of that official group which was slow, scarcely perceptible, and yet steady and persistent—a movement such as is observed in a kaleidoscope that is turned slowly, whereby the components of one splendid cluster fall away and join themselves to another—a movement which, little by little, in the present case, dissolved the glittering crowd that stood about Tom Canty and clustered it together again in the neighborhood of the new-comer. Tom Canty stood almost alone. Now ensued a brief season of deep suspense and waiting—during which even the few faint-hearts still remaining near Tom Canty gradually scraped together courage enough to glide, one by one, over to the majority. So at last Tom Canty, in his royal robes and jewels, stood wholly alone and isolated from the world, a conspicuous figure, occupying an eloquent vacancy.

Now the Lord St. John was seen returning. As he advanced up the mid-aisle the interest was so intense that the low murmur of conversation in the great assemblage died out and was succeeded by a profound hush, a breathless stillness, through which his footfalls pulsed with a dull and distant sound. Every eye was fastened upon him as he moved along. He reached the platform, paused a moment, then moved toward Tom Canty with a deep obeisance, and said:

"Sire, the Seal is not there!"

A mob does not melt away from the presence of a plague-patient with more haste than the band of pallid and terrified courtiers melted away from the presence of the shabby little claimant of the Crown. In a moment he stood all alone, without friend or supporter, a target upon which was concentrated a bitter fire of scornful and angry looks. The Lord Protector called out fiercely:

"Cast the beggar into the street, and scourge him through the town—the paltry knave is worth no more consideration!"

Officers of the guard sprang forward to obey, but Tom Canty waved them off and said:

"Back! Whoso touches him perils his life!"

The Lord Protector was perplexed in the last degree. He said to the Lord St. John:

"Searched you well?—but it boots not to ask that. It doth seem passing strange. Little things, trifles, slip out of one's ken, and one does not think it matter for surprise; but how a so bulky thing as the Seal of England can vanish away and no man be able to get track of it again—a massy golden disk—"

Tom Canty, with beaming eyes, sprang forward and shouted:

"Hold, that is enough! Was it round?—and thick?—and had it letters and devices graved upon it?—Yes? Oh, *now* I know what this Great Seal is that there's been such worry and pother about! An ye had described it to me, ye could have had it three weeks ago. Right well I know where it lies; but it was not I that put it there—first."

"Who, then, my liege?" asked the Lord Protector.

"He that stands there—the rightful king of England. And he

shall tell you himself where it lies—then you will believe he knew it of his own knowledge. Bethink thee, my king—spur thy memory—it was the last, the very *last* thing thou didst that day before thou didst rush forth from the palace, clothed in my rags, to punish the soldier that insulted me."

A silence ensued, undisturbed by a movement or a whisper, and all eyes were fixed upon the new-comer, who stood, with bent head and corrugated brow, groping in his memory among a thronging multitude of valueless recollections for one single little elusive fact, which found, would seat him upon a throne—unfound, would leave him as he was, for good and all—a pauper and an outcast. Moment after moment passed—the moments built themselves into minutes—still the boy struggled silently on, and gave no sign. But at last he heaved a sigh, shook his head slowly, and said, with a trembling lip and in a despondent voice:

"I call the scene back—all of it—but the Seal hath no place in it." He paused, then looked up, and said with gentle dignity, "My lords and gentlemen, if ye will rob your rightful sovereign of his own for lack of this evidence which he is not able to furnish, I may not stay ye, being powerless. But—"

"O folly, O madness, my king!" cried Tom Canty, in a panic, "wait!—think! Do not give up!—the cause is not lost! Nor *shall* be, neither! List to what I say—follow every word—I am going to bring that morning back again, every hap just as it happened. We talked—I told you of my sisters, Nan and Bet—ah, yes, you remember that; and about mine old grandam—and the rough games of the lads of Offal Court—yes, you remember these things also; very well, follow me still, you shall recall everything. You gave me food and drink, and did with princely courtesy send away the servants, so that my low breeding might not shame me before them—ah, yes, this also you remember."

As Tom checked off his details, and the other boy nodded his head in recognition of them, the great audience and the officials stared in puzzled wonderment; the tale sounded like true history, yet how could this impossible conjunction between a prince and a beggar boy have come about? Never was a company of people so perplexed, so interested, and so stupefied, before.

"For a jest, my prince, we did exchange garments. Then we stood before a mirror; and so alike were we that both said it seemed as if there had been no change made—yes, you remember that. Then you noticed that the soldier had hurt my hand—look! here it is, I cannot yet even write with it, the fingers are so stiff. At this your Highness sprang up, vowing vengeance upon that soldier, and ran toward the door—you passed a table—that thing you call the Seal lay on that table—you snatched it up and looked eagerly about, as if for a place to hide it—your eye caught sight of—"

"There, 'tis sufficient!—and the dear God be thanked!" exclaimed the ragged claimant, in a mighty excitement. "Go, my good St. John—in an arm-piece of the Milanese armor that hangs on the wall, thou'lt find the Seal!"

"Right, my king! right!" cried Tom Canty; "now the scepter of England is thine own; and it were better for him that would dispute it that he had been born dumb! Go, my Lord St. John, give thy feet wings!"

The whole assemblage was on its feet now, and well-nigh out of its mind with uneasiness, apprehension, and consuming excitement. On the floor and on the platform a deafening buzz of frantic conversation burst forth, and for some time nobody knew anything or heard anything or was interested in anything but what his neighbor was shouting into his ear, or he was shouting into his neighbor's ear. Time—nobody knew how much of it—swept by unheeded and unnoted. At last a sudden hush fell upon the house, and in the same moment St. John appeared upon the platform and held the Great Seal aloft in his hand. Then such a shout went up!

"Long live the true king!"

For five minutes the air quaked with shouts and the crash of musical instruments, and was white with a storm of waving handkerchiefs; and through it all a ragged lad, the most conspicuous figure in England, stood, flushed and happy and proud, in the center of the spacious platform, with the great vassals of the kingdom kneeling around him.

Then all rose, and Tom Canty cried out:

"Now, O my king, take these regal garments back, and give poor Tom, thy servant, his shreds and remnants again."

The Lord Protector spoke up:

"Let the small varlet be stripped and flung into the Tower."

But the new king, the true king, said:

"I will not have it so. But for him I had not got my crown again—none shall lay a hand upon him to harm him. And as for thee, my good uncle, my Lord Protector, this conduct of thine is not grateful toward this poor lad, for I hear he hath made thee a duke"—the Protector blushed—"yet he was not a king; wherefore, what is thy fine title worth now? To-morrow you shall sue to me, *through him,* for its confirmation, else no duke, but a simple earl, shalt thou remain."

Under this rebuke, his grace the Duke of Somerset retired a little from the front for the moment. The king turned to Tom, and said, kindly:

"My poor boy, how was it that you could remember where I hid the Seal when I could not remember it myself?"

"Ah, my king, that was easy, since I used it divers days."

"Used it—yet could not explain where it was?"

"I did not know it was *that* they wanted. They did not describe it, your majesty."

"Then how used you it?"

The red blood began to steal up into Tom's cheeks, and he dropped his eyes and was silent.

"Speak up, good lad, and fear nothing," said the king. "How used you the Great Seal of England?"

Tom stammered a moment, in a pathetic confusion, then got it out:

"To crack nuts with!"

Poor child, the avalanche of laughter that greeted this, nearly swept him off his feet. But if a doubt remained in any mind that Tom Canty was not the king of England and familiar with the august appurtenances of royalty, this reply disposed of it utterly.

Meantime the sumptuous robe of state had been removed from Tom's shoulders to the king's, whose rags were effectually hidden from sight under it. Then the coronation ceremonies were resumed; the true king was anointed and the crown set upon his head, whilst cannon thundered the news to the city, and all London seemed to rock with applause.

33

Edward as King

MILES HENDON was picturesque enough before he got into the riot on London Bridge—he was more so when he got out of it. He had but little money when he got in, none at all when he got out. The pickpockets had stripped him of his last farthing.

But no matter, so he found his boy. Being a soldier, he did not go at his task in a random way, but set to work, first of all, to arrange his campaign.

What would the boy naturally do? Where would he naturally go? Well—argued Miles—he would naturally go to his former haunts, for that is the instinct of unsound minds, when homeless and forsaken, as well as of sound ones. Whereabouts were his former haunts? His rags, taken together with the low villain who seemed to know him and who even claimed to be his father, indicated that his home was in one or another of the poorest and meanest districts of London. Would the search for him be difficult, or long? No, it was likely to be easy and brief. He would not hunt for the boy, he would hunt for a crowd; in the center of a big crowd or a little one, sooner or later, he should find his poor little friend, sure; and the mangy mob would be entertaining itself with pestering and aggravating the boy, who would be proclaiming himself king, as usual. Then Miles Hendon would cripple some of those people, and carry off his little ward, and comfort and cheer him with loving words, and the two would never be separated any more.

So Miles started on his quest. Hour after hour he tramped through back alleys and squalid streets, seeking groups and crowds, and finding no end of them, but never any sign of the boy. This greatly surprised him, but did not discourage him. To his notion, there was nothing the matter with his plan of campaign; the only miscalculation about it was that the campaign was becoming a lengthy one, whereas he had expected it to be short.

When daylight arrived at last, he had made many a mile, and canvassed many a crowd, but the only result was that he was tolerably tired, rather hungry, and very sleepy. He wanted some breakfast, but there was no way to get it. To beg for it did not occur to him; as to pawning his sword, he would as soon have thought of parting with his honor; he could spare some of his clothes—yes, but one could as easily find a customer for a disease as for such clothes.

At noon he was still tramping—among the rabble which followed after the royal procession now; for he argued that this regal display would attract his little lunatic powerfully. He followed the pageant through all its devious windings about London, and all the way to Westminster and the Abbey. He drifted here and there among the multitudes that were massed in the vicinity for a weary long time, baffled and perplexed, and finally wandered off thinking, and trying to contrive some way to better his plan of campaign. By and by, when he came to himself out of his musings, he discovered that the town was far behind him and that the day was growing old. He was near the river, and in the country; it was a region of fine rural seats—not the sort of district to welcome clothes like his.

It was not at all cold; so he stretched himself on the ground in the lee of a hedge to rest and think. Drowsiness presently began to settle upon his senses; the faint and far-off boom of cannon was wafted to his ear, and he said to himself, "The new king is crowned," and straightway fell asleep. He had not slept or rested, before, for more than thirty hours. He did not wake again until near the middle of the next morning.

He got up, lame, stiff, and half famished, washed himself in the river, stayed his stomach with a pint or two of water, and trudged off toward Westminster grumbling at himself for having wasted so much time. Hunger helped him to a new plan now; he would try to get speech with old Sir Humphrey Marlow and borrow a few marks, and—but that was enough of a plan for the present; it would be time enough to enlarge it when this first stage should be accomplished.

Toward eleven o'clock he approached the palace; and although a host of showy people were about him, moving in the same direction, he was not inconspicuous—his costume took care of that. He watched these people's faces narrowly, hoping to find a charitable one whose possessor might be willing to carry his name to the old lieutenant—as to trying to get into the palace himself, that was simply out of the question.

Presently our whipping-boy passed him, then wheeled about and scanned his figure well, saying to himself, "An that is not the very vagabond his majesty is in such a worry about, then am I an ass—though belike I was that before. He answereth the description to a rag—that God should make two such, would be to cheapen miracles, by wasteful repetition. I would I could contrive an excuse to speak with him."

Miles Hendon saved him the trouble; for he turned about, then, as a man generally will when somebody mesmerizes him by gazing hard at him from behind; and observing a strong interest in the boy's eyes, he stepped toward him and said:

"You have just come out from the palace; do you belong there?"

"Yes, your worship."

"Know you Sir Humphrey Marlow?"

The boy started, and said to himself, "Lord! mine old departed father!" Then he answered, aloud, "Right well, your worship."

"Good—is he within?"

"Yes," said the boy; and added, to himself, "within his grave."

"Might I crave your favor to carry my name to him, and say I beg to say a word in his ear?"

"I will despatch the business right willingly, fair sir."

"Then say Miles Hendon, son of Sir Richard, is here without —I shall be greatly bounden to you, my good lad."

The boy looked disappointed—"the king did not name him so," he said to himself—"but it mattereth not, this is his twin brother, and can give his majesty news of t'other Sir-Odds-and-Ends, I warrant." So he said to Miles, "Step in there a moment, good sir, and wait till I bring you word."

Hendon retired to the place indicated—it was a recess sunk in the palace wall, with a stone bench in it—a shelter for sentinels in bad weather. He had hardly seated himself when some halberdiers, in charge of an officer, passed by. The officer saw him, halted his men, and commanded Hendon to come forth. He obeyed, and was promptly arrested as a suspicious character prowling within the precincts of the palace. Things began to look ugly. Poor Miles was going to explain, but the officer roughly silenced him, and ordered his men to disarm him and search him.

"God of his mercy grant that they find somewhat," said poor Miles; "I have searched enow, and failed, yet is my need greater than theirs."

Nothing was found but a document. The officer tore it open, and Hendon smiled when he recognized the "pot-hooks" made by his lost little friend that black day at Hendon Hall. The officer's face grew dark as he read the English paragraph, and Miles blenched to the opposite color as he listened.

"Another new claimant of the crown!" cried the officer. "Verily they breed like rabbits to-day. Seize the rascal, men, and see ye keep him fast while I convey this precious paper within and send it to the king."

He hurried away, leaving the prisoner in the grip of the halberdiers.

"Now is my evil luck ended at last," muttered Hendon, "for I shall dangle at a rope's end for a certainty, by reason of that bit of writing. And what will become of my poor lad!—ah, only the good God knoweth."

By and by he saw the officer coming again, in a great hurry; so he plucked his courage together, purposing to meet his trouble as became a man. The officer ordered the men to loose the prisoner and return his sword to him; then bowed respectfully, and said:

"Please you, sir, to follow me."

Hendon followed, saying to himself, "An I were not traveling to death and judgment, and so must needs economize in sin, I would throttle this knave for his mock courtesy."

The two traversed a populous court, and arrived at the grand entrance of the palace, where the officer, with another bow, delivered Hendon into the hands of a gorgeous official, who received him with profound respect and led him forward through a great hall, lined on both sides with rows of splendid flunkies (who made reverential obeisance as the two passed along, but fell into death-throes of silent laughter at our stately scarecrow the moment his back was turned), and up a broad staircase, among flocks of fine folk, and finally conducted him to a vast room, clove a passage for him through the assembled nobility of England, then made a bow, reminded him to take his hat off, and left him standing in the middle of the room, a mark for all eyes, for plenty of indignant frowns, and for a sufficiency of amused and derisive smiles.

Miles Hendon was entirely bewildered. There sat the young king, under a canopy of state, five steps away, with his head bent down and aside, speaking with a sort of human bird of paradise—a duke, maybe; Hendon observed to himself that it was hard enough to be sentenced to death in the full vigor of life, without having this peculiarly public humiliation added. He wished the king would hurry about it—some of the gaudy people near by were becoming pretty offensive. At this moment the king raised his head slightly and Hendon caught a good view of his face. The sight nearly took his breath away! He stood gazing at the fair young face like one transfixed; then presently ejaculated:

"Lo, the lord of the Kingdom of Dreams and Shadows on his throne!"

He muttered some broken sentences, still gazing and marveling; then turned his eyes around and about, scanning the gorgeous throng and the splendid saloon, murmuring, "But these are *real*—verily these are *real*—surely it is not a dream."

He stared at the king again—and thought, "*Is* it a dream? . . . or *is* he the veritable sovereign of England, and not the friendless poor Tom o' Bedlam I took him for—who shall solve me this riddle?"

A sudden idea flashed in his eye, and he strode to the wall, gathered up a chair, brought it back, planted it on the floor, and sat down in it!

A buzz of indignation broke out, a rough hand was laid upon him, and a voice exclaimed:

"Up, thou mannerless clown!—wouldst sit in the presence of the king?"

The disturbance attracted his majesty's attention, who stretched forth his hand and cried out:

"Touch him not, it is his right!"

The throng fell back, stupefied. The king went on:

"Learn ye all, ladies, lords and gentlemen, that this is my trusty and well-beloved servant, Miles Hendon, who interposed his good sword and saved his prince from bodily harm and possible death—and for this he is a knight, by the king's voice. Also learn, that for a higher service, in that he saved his sovereign stripes and shame, taking these upon himself, he is a peer of England, Earl of Kent, and shall have gold and lands meet for the dignity. More—the privilege which he hath just exercised is his by royal grant; for we have ordained that the chiefs of his line shall have and hold the right to sit in the presence of the majesty of England henceforth, age after age, so long as the crown shall endure. Molest him not."

Two persons, who, through delay, had only arrived from the country during this morning, and had now been in this room only five minutes, stood listening to these words and looking at the king, then at the scarecrow, then at the king again, in a sort of torpid bewilderment. These were Sir Hugh and the Lady Edith. But the new earl did not see them. He was still staring at the monarch, in a dazed way, and muttering:

"Oh, body o' me! *This* my pauper! This my lunatic! This is he whom *I* would show what grandeur was, in my house of seventy rooms and seven and twenty servants! This is he who had never known aught but rags for raiment, kicks for comfort, and offal for diet! This is he whom *I* adopted and would make respectable! Would God I had a bag to hide my head in!"

Then his manners suddenly came back to him, and he dropped upon his knees, with his hands between the king's, and swore allegiance and did homage for his lands and titles. Then he rose and stood respectfully aside, a mark still for all eyes—and much envy, too.

Now the king discovered Sir Hugh, and spoke out, with wrathful voice and kindling eye:

"Strip this robber of his false show and stolen estates, and put him under lock and key till I have need of him."

The late Sir Hugh was led away.

There was a stir at the other end of the room now; the assemblage fell apart, and Tom Canty, quaintly but richly clothed, marched down, between these living walls, preceded by an usher. He knelt before the king, who said:

"I have learned the story of these past few weeks, and am well pleased with thee. Thou hast governed the realm with right royal gentleness and mercy. Thou hast found thy mother and thy sisters again? Good; they shall be cared for—and thy father shall hang, if thou desire it and the law consent. Know, all ye that hear my voice, that from this day, they that abide in the shelter of Christ's Hospital and share the king's bounty, shall have their minds and hearts fed, as well as their baser parts; and this boy shall dwell there, and hold the chief place in its honorable body of governors, during life. And for that he hath been a king, it is meet that other than common observance shall be his due; wherefore, note this his dress of state, for by it he shall be known, and none shall copy it; and wheresoever he shall come, it shall remind the people that he hath been royal, in his time, and none shall deny him his due of reverence or fail to give him salutation. He hath the throne's protection, he hath the crown's support, he shall be known and called by the honorable title of the King's Ward."

The proud and happy Tom Canty rose and kissed the king's hand, and was conducted from the presence. He did not waste any time, but flew to his mother, to tell her and Nan and Bet all about it and get them to help him enjoy the great news.

CONCLUSION

Justice and Retribution

WHEN the mysteries were all cleared up, it came out, by confession of Hugh Hendon, that his wife had repudiated Miles by his command that day at Hendon Hall—a command assisted and supported by the perfectly trustworthy promise that if she did not deny that he was Miles Hendon, and stand firmly to it, he would have her life; whereupon she said take it, she did not value it—and she would not repudiate Miles; then the husband said he would spare her life, but have Miles assassinated! This was a different matter; so she gave her word and kept it.

Hugh was not prosecuted for his threats or for stealing his brother's estates and title, because the wife and brother would not testify against him—and the former would not have been allowed to do it, even if she had wanted to. Hugh deserted his wife and went over to the continent, where he presently died; and by and by the Earl of Kent married his relict. There were grand times and rejoicings at Hendon village when the couple paid their first visit to the Hall.

Tom Canty's father was never heard of again.

The king sought out the farmer who had been branded and sold as a slave, and reclaimed him from his evil life with the Ruffler's gang, and put him in the way of a comfortable livelihood.

He also took that old lawyer out of prison and remitted his

fine. He provided good homes for the daughters of the two Baptist women whom he saw burned at the stake, and roundly punished the official who laid the undeserved stripes upon Miles Hendon's back.

He saved from the gallows the boy who had captured the stray falcon, and also the woman who had stolen a remnant of cloth from a weaver; but he was too late to save the man who had been convicted of killing a deer in the royal forest.

He showed favor to the justice who had pitied him when he was supposed to have stolen a pig, and he had the gratification of seeing him grow in the public esteem and become a great and honored man.

As long as the king lived he was fond of telling the story of his adventures, all through, from the hour that the sentinel cuffed him away from the palace gate till the final midnight when he deftly mixed himself into a gang of hurrying workmen and so slipped into the Abbey and climbed up and hid himself in the Confessor's tomb, and then slept so long, next day, that he came within one of missing the Coronation altogether. He said that the frequent rehearsing of the precious lesson kept him strong in his purpose to make its teachings yield benefits to his people; and so, while his life was spared he should continue to tell the story, and thus keep its sorrowful spectacles fresh in his memory and the springs of pity replenished in his heart.

Miles Hendon and Tom Canty were favorites of the king, all through his brief reign, and his sincere mourners when he died. The good Earl of Kent had too much good sense to abuse his peculiar privilege; but he exercised it twice after the instance we have seen of it before he was called from the world; once at the accession of Queen Mary, and once at the accession of Queen Elizabeth. A descendant of his exercised it at the accession of James I. Before this one's son chose to use the privilege, near a quarter of a century had elapsed, and the "privilege of the Kents" had faded out of most people's memories; so, when the Kent of that day appeared before Charles I. and his court and sat down in the sovereign's presence to assert and perpetuate the right of his house, there was a fine stir, indeed! But the matter was soon explained and the right confirmed. The last earl of the line fell in the wars of the Commonwealth fighting for the king, and the odd privilege ended with him.

Tom Canty lived to be a very old man, a handsome, white-haired old fellow, of grave and benignant aspect. As long as he lasted he was honored; and he was also reverenced, for his striking and peculiar costume kept the people reminded that "in his time he had been royal"; so, wherever he appeared the crowd fell apart, making way for him, and whispering, one to another, "Doff thy hat, it is the King's Ward!"—and so they saluted, and got his kindly smile in return—and they valued it, too, for his was an honorable history.

Yes, King Edward VI. lived only a few years, poor boy, but he lived them worthily. More than once, when some great dignitary, some gilded vassal of the crown, made argument against his leniency, and urged that some law which he was bent upon amending was gentle enough for its purpose, and wrought no suffering or oppression which any one need mightily mind, the young king turned the mournful eloquence of his great compassionate eyes upon him and answered:

"What dost *thou* know of suffering and oppression? I and my people know, but not thou."

The reign of Edward VI. was a singularly merciful one for those harsh times. Now that we are taking leave of him let us try to keep this in our minds, to his credit.

NOTES

Note 1—Page 14
Christ's Hospital Costume

It is most reasonable to regard the dress as copied from the costume of the citizens of London of that period, when long blue coats were the common habit of apprentices and serving-men, and yellow stockings were generally worn; the coat fits closely to the body, but has loose sleeves, and beneath is worn a sleeveless yellow undercoat; around the waist is a red leathern girdle; a clerical band around the neck, and a small flat black cap, about the size of a saucer, completes the costume.—*Timbs's "Curiosities of London."*

Note 2—Page 15

It appears that Christ's Hospital was not originally founded as a *school;* its object was to rescue children from the streets, to shelter, feed, clothe them, etc.—*Timbs's "Curiosities of London."*

Note 3—Page 22
The Duke of Norfolk's Condemnation Commanded

The King was now approaching fast toward his end; and fearing lest Norfolk should escape him, he sent a message to the Commons, by which he desired them to hasten the bill, on pretense that Norfolk enjoyed the dignity of earl marshal, and it was necessary to appoint another, who might officiate at the ensuing ceremony of installing his son Prince of Wales.—*Hume,* vol. iii, p. 307.

Note 4—Page 32

It was not till the end of this reign [Henry VIII.] that any salads, carrots, turnips, or other edible roots were produced in England. The little of these vegetables that was used was formerly imported from Holland and Flanders. Queen Catherine, when she wanted a salad, was obliged to despatch a messenger thither on purpose.—*Hume's History of England,* vol. iii, p. 314.

NOTE 5—Page 36

Attainder of Norfolk

THE house of peers, without examining the prisoner, without trial or evidence, passed a bill of attainder against him and sent it down to the commons. . . . The obsequious commons obeyed his [the King's] directions; and the King, having affixed the royal assent to the bill by commissioners, issued orders for the execution of Norfolk on the morning of the twenty-ninth of January [the next day].— *Hume's England,* vol. iii, p. 306.

NOTE 6—Page 46

The Loving-Cup

THE loving-cup, and the peculiar ceremonies observed in drinking from it, are older than English history. It is thought that both are Danish importations. As far back as knowledge goes, the loving-cup has always been drunk at English banquets. Tradition explains the ceremonies in this way: in the rude ancient times it was deemed a wise precaution to have both hands of both drinkers employed, lest while the pledger pledged his love and fidelity to the pledgee the pledgee take that opportunity to slip a dirk into him!

NOTE 7—Page 51

The Duke of Norfolk's Narrow Escape

HAD Henry VIII. survived a few hours longer, his order for the duke's execution would have been carried into effect. "But news being carried to the Tower that the King himself had expired that night, the lieutenant deferred obeying the warrant; and it was not thought advisable by the council to begin a new reign by the death of the greatest nobleman in the Kingdom, who had been condemned by a sentence so unjust and tyrannical."—*Hume's England,* vol. iii, p. 307.

NOTE 8—Page 75

The Whipping-Boy

JAMES I. and Charles II. had whipping-boys when they were little fellows, to take their punishment for them when they fell short in their lessons; so I have ventured to furnish my small prince with one, for my own purposes.

NOTES TO CHAPTER 15—Pages 78–88

Character of Hertford

THE young king discovered an extreme attachment to his uncle, who was, in the main, a man of moderation and probity.—*Hume's England,* vol. iii, p. 324.

But if he [the Protector] gave offense by assuming too much state, he deserves great praise on account of the laws passed this session, by which the rigor of former statutes was much mitigated, and some security given to the freedom of the constitution. All laws were repealed which extended the crime of treason beyond the statute of the twenty-fifth of Edward III.; all laws enacted during the late reign extending the crime of felony; all the former laws against Lollardy or heresy, together with the statute of the Six Articles. None were to be accused for words, but within a month after they were spoken. By these repeals several of the most rigorous laws that ever had passed in England were annulled; and some dawn, both of civil and religious liberty, began to appear to the people. A repeal also passed of that law, the destruction of all laws, by which the king's proclamation was made of equal force with a statute.—*Ibid.,* vol. iii, p. 339.

Boiling to Death

IN the reign of Henry VIII., poisoners were, by act of parliament, condemned to be *boiled to death.* This act was repealed in the following reign.

In Germany, even in the 17th century, this horrible punishment was inflicted on coiners and counterfeiters. Taylor, the Water Poet, describes an execution he witnessed in Hamburg, in 1616. The judgment pronounced against a coiner of false money was that he should "be *boiled to death in oil:* not thrown into the vessel at once, but with a pulley or rope to be hanged under the armpits, and then let down into the oil *by degrees;* first the feet, and next the legs, and so to boil his flesh from his bones alive."—*Dr. J. Hammond Trumbull's "Blue Laws, True and False,"* p. 13.

The Famous Stocking Case

A WOMAN and her daughter, *nine years old,* were hanged in Huntingdon for selling their souls to the devil, and raising a storm by pulling off their stockings!—*Ibid.,* p. 20.

NOTE 10—Page 98
Enslaving

So young a king, and so ignorant a peasant were likely to make mistakes—and this is an instance in point. This peasant was suffering from this law *by anticipation;* the king was venting his indignation against a law which was not yet in existence: for this hideous statute was to have birth in this little king's own reign. However, we know, from the humanity of his character, that it could never have been suggested by him.

NOTES TO CHAPTER 23—Pages 129–32
Death for Trifling Larcenies

WHEN Connecticut and New Haven were framing their first codes, larceny above the value of twelve pence was a capital crime in England, as it had been since the time of Henry I.—*Dr. J. Hammond Trumbull's "Blue Laws, True and False,"* p. 17.

The curious old book called *The English Rogue* makes the limit thirteen pence ha'penny; death being the portion of any who steal a thing "above the value of thirteen pence ha'penny."

NOTES TO CHAPTER 27—Pages 146–55

FROM many descriptions of larceny, the law expressly took away the benefit of clergy; to steal a horse, or a *hawk,* or woolen cloth from the weaver, was a hanging matter. So it was to kill a deer from the king's forest, or to export sheep from the Kingdom.—*Dr. J. Hammond Trumbull's "Blue Laws, True and False,"* p. 13.

William Prynne, a learned barrister, was sentenced—[long after Edward the Sixth's time]—to lose both his ears in the pillory; to degradation from the bar; a fine of £3,000, and imprisonment for life. Three years afterward, he gave new offense to Laud, by publishing a pamphlet against the hierarchy. He was again prosecuted, and was sentenced to lose *what remained of his ears;* to pay a fine of £5,000; to be *branded on both his cheeks* with the letters of S. L. (for Seditious Libeler), and to remain in prison for life. The severity of this sentence was equaled by the savage rigor of its execution.—*Ibid.,* p. 12.

NOTES TO CHAPTER 33—Pages 181–88

CHRIST'S HOSPITAL or BLUE COAT SCHOOL, "the Noblest Institution in the World."

The ground on which the Priory of the Grey Friars stood was conferred by Henry the Eighth on the Corporation of London [who caused the institution there of a home for poor boys and girls]. Subsequently, Edward the Sixth caused the old Priory to be properly repaired, and founded within it that noble establishment called the Blue Coat School, or Christ's Hospital, for the *education* and maintenance of orphans and the children of indigent persons. . . . Edward would not let him [Bishop Ridley] depart till the letter was written [to the Lord Mayor], and then charged him to deliver it himself, and signify his special request and commandment that no time might be lost in proposing what was convenient, and apprising him of the proceedings. The work was zealously undertaken, Ridley himself engaging in it; and the result was, the founding of Christ's Hospital for the Education of Poor Children. [The king endowed several other charities at the same time.] "Lord God," said he, "I yield thee most hearty thanks that thou hast given me life thus long, to finish this work to the glory of thy name!" That innocent and most exemplary life was drawing rapidly to its close, and in a few days he rendered up his spirit to his Creator, praying God to defend the realm from Papistry. —*J. Heneage Jesse's "London, its Celebrated Characters and Places."*

In the Great Hall hangs a large picture of King Edward VI. seated on his throne, in a scarlet and ermined robe, holding the scepter in his left hand, presenting with the other the Charter to the kneeling Lord Mayor. By his side stands the Chancellor, holding the seals, and next to him are other officers of state. Bishop Ridley kneels before him with uplifted hands, as if supplicating a blessing on the event; while the Aldermen, etc., with the Lord Mayor, kneel on both sides, occupying the middle ground of the picture; and lastly, in front, are a double row of boys on one side, and girls on the other, from the master and matron down to the boy and girl who have stepped forward from their respective rows, and kneel with raised hands before the king.—*Timbs's "Curiosities of London,"* p. 98.

Christ's Hospital, by ancient custom, possesses the privilege of addressing the Sovereign on the occasion of his or her coming into the City to partake of the hospitality of the Corporation of London.—*Ibid.*

The Dining-Hall, with its lobby and organ-gallery, occupies the entire story, which is 187 feet long, 51 feet wide, and 47 feet high; it is lit by nine large windows, filled with stained glass on the south side; that is, next to Westminster Hall, the noblest room in the metropolis. Here the boys, now about 800 in number, dine; and here are held the "Suppings in Public," to which visitors are admitted by tickets, issued by the Treasurer and by the Governors of Christ's Hospital. The tables are laid with cheese in wooden bowls; beer in wooden piggins, poured from leathern jacks; and bread brought in large baskets. The official company enter; the Lord Mayor, or President, takes his seat in a state chair, made of oak from St. Catherine's Church by the Tower; a hymn is sung, accompanied by the organ; a "Grecian," or head boy, reads the prayers from the pulpit, silence being enforced by three drops of a wooden hammer. After prayer the supper commences, and the visitors walk between the tables. At its close, the "trade-boys" take up the baskets, bowls, jacks, piggins, and candlesticks, and pass in procession, the bowing to the Governors being curiously formal. This spectacle was witnessed by Queen Victoria and Prince Albert in 1845.

Among the more eminent Blue Coat Boys are Joshua Barnes, editor of Anacreon and Euripides; Jeremiah Markland, the eminent critic, particularly in Greek literature; Camden, the antiquary; Bishop Stillingfleet; Samuel Richardson, the novelist; Thomas Mitchell, the translator of Aristophanes; Thomas Barnes, many years editor of the London *Times;* Coleridge, Charles Lamb, and Leigh Hunt.

No boy is admitted before he is seven years old, or after he is nine; and no boy can remain in the school after he is fifteen, King's boys and "Grecians" alone excepted. There are about 500 Governors, at the head of whom are the Sovereign and the Prince of Wales. The qualification for a Governor is payment of £ 500.—*Ibid.*

GENERAL NOTE

ONE *hears much about the "hideous Blue-Laws of Connecticut," and is accustomed to shudder piously when they are mentioned. There are people in America—and even in England!—who imagine that they were a very monument of malignity, pitilessness, and inhumanity; whereas, in reality they were about the first* SWEEPING DEPARTURE FROM JUDICIAL ATROCITY *which the "civilized" world had seen. This humane and kindly Blue-Law code, of two hundred and forty years ago, stands all by itself, with ages of bloody law on the further side of it, and a century and three-quarters of bloody English law on* THIS *side of it.*

There has never been a time—under the Blue-Laws or any other—when above FOURTEEN *crimes were punishable by death in Conneticut. But in England, within the memory of men who are still hale in body and mind,* TWO HUNDRED AND TWENTY-THREE *crimes were punishable by death![1] These facts are worth knowing—and worth thinking about, too.*

[1] See Dr. J. Hammond Trumbull's *Blue Laws, True and False*, p. 11.

THOSE
EXTRAORDINARY TWINS

CONTENTS

THOSE EXTRAORDINARY TWINS

A MAN who is born with the novel-writing gift has a troublesome time of it when he tries to build a novel. I know this from experience. He has no clear idea of his story; in fact he has no story. He merely has some people in his mind, and an incident or two, also a locality. He knows these people, he knows the selected locality, and he trusts that he can plunge those people into those incidents with interesting results. So he goes to work. To write a novel? No—that is a thought which comes later; in the beginning he is only proposing to tell a little tale; a very little tale; a six-page tale. But as it is a tale which he is not acquainted with, and can only find out what it is by listening as it goes along telling itself, it is more than apt to go on and on and on till it spreads itself into a book. I know about this, because it has happened to me so many times.

And I have noticed another thing: that as the short tale grows into the long tale, the original intention (or motif) is apt to get abolished and find itself superseded by a quite different one. It was so in the case of a magazine sketch which I once started to write—a funny and fantastic sketch about a prince and a pauper; it presently assumed a grave cast of its own accord, and in that new shape spread itself out into a book. Much the same thing happened with "Pudd'nhead Wilson." I had a sufficiently hard time with that tale, because it changed itself from a farce to a tragedy while I was going along with it—a most embarrassing circumstance. But what was a great deal worse was, that it was not one story, but two stories tangled together; and they obstructed and interrupted each other at every turn and created no end of confusion and annoyance. I could not offer the book for publication, for I was afraid it would unseat the reader's reason. I did not know what was the matter with it, for I had not noticed, as yet, that it was two stories in one. It took me months to make that discovery. I carried the manuscript back and forth across the Atlantic two or three times, and read it and studied over it on shipboard; and at last I saw where the difficulty lay. I had no further trouble. I pulled one of the stories out by the roots, and left the other one—a kind of literary Cæsarean operation.

Would the reader care to know something about the story which I pulled out? He has been told many a time how the born-and-trained novelist works. Won't he let me round and complete his knowledge by telling him how the jack-leg does it?

Originally the story was called "Those Extraordinary Twins." I meant to make it very short. I had seen a picture of a youthful Italian "freak"—or "freaks"—which was—or which were—on exhibition in our cities—a combination consisting of two heads and four arms joined to a single body and a single pair of legs—and I thought I would write an extravagantly fantastic little story with this freak of nature for hero—or heroes—a silly young miss for heroine, and two old ladies and two boys for the minor parts. I lavishly elaborated these people and their doings, of course. But the tale kept spreading along, and spreading along, and other people got to intruding themselves and taking up more and more room with their talk and their affairs. Among them came a stranger named Pudd'nhead Wilson, and a woman named Roxana; and presently the doings of these two pushed up into prominence a young fellow named Tom Driscoll, whose proper place was away in the obscure background. Before the book was half finished those three were taking things almost entirely into their own hands and working the whole tale as a private venture of their own—a tale which they had nothing at all to do with, by rights.

When the book was finished and I came to look around to see what had become of the team I had originally started out with —Aunt Patsy Cooper, Aunt Betsy Hale, the two boys, and Rowena the light-weight heroine—they were nowhere to be seen; they had disappeared from the story some time or other. I hunted about and found them—found them stranded, idle, forgotten, and permanently useless. It was very awkward. It was awkward all around; but more particularly in the case of Rowena, because there was a love-match on, between her and one of the twins that constituted the freak, and I had worked it up to a blistering heat and thrown in a quite dramatic love-quarrel, wherein Rowena scathingly denounced her betrothed for getting drunk, and scoffed at his explanation of how it had happened, and wouldn't listen to it, and had driven him from her in the usual "forever" way; and now here she sat crying and broken-hearted; for she had found that he had spoken only the truth; that it was not he, but the other half of the freak, that had drunk the liquor that made him drunk; that her half was a prohibitionist and had never drunk a drop in his life, and, although tight as a brick three days in the week, was wholly innocent of blame; and indeed, when sober, was constantly doing all he could to reform his brother, the other half, who never got any satisfaction out of drinking, anyway, because liquor never affected him. Yes, here she was, stranded with that deep injustice of hers torturing her poor torn heart.

I didn't know what to do with her. I was as sorry for her as anybody could be, but the campaign was over, the book was finished, she was sidetracked, and there was no possible way of crowding her in, anywhere. I could not leave her there, of course; it would not do. After spreading her out so, and making such a to-do over her affairs, it would be absolutely necessary to account to the reader for her. I thought and thought and studied and studied; but I arrived at nothing. I finally saw plainly that there was really no way but one—I must simply give her the grand bounce. It grieved me to do it, for after associating with her so much I had come to kind of like her after a fashion, notwithstanding she was such an ass and said such stupid, irritating things and was so nauseatingly sentimental. Still it had to be done. So, at the top of Chapter XVII, I put a "Calendar" remark concerning July Fourth, and began the chapter with this statistic:

"Rowena went out in the back yard after supper to see the fireworks and fell down the well and got drowned."

It seemed abrupt, but I thought maybe the reader wouldn't notice it, because I changed the subject right away to something else. Anyway it loosened up Rowena from where she was stuck and got her out of the way, and that was the main thing. It seemed a prompt good way of weeding out people that had got stalled, and a plenty good enough way for those others; so I hunted up the two boys and said "they went out back one night to stone the cat and fell down the well and got drowned." Next I searched around and found old Aunt Patsy Cooper and Aunt Betsy Hale where they were aground, and said "they went out back one night to visit the sick and fell down the well and got drowned." I was going to drown some of the others, but I gave up the idea, partly because I believed that if I kept that up it would arouse attention, and perhaps sympathy with those people, and partly because it was not a large well and would not hold any more anyway.

Still the story was unsatisfactory. Here was a set of new characters who were become inordinately prominent and who persisted in remaining so to the end; and back yonder was an older set who made a large noise and a great to-do for a little while and then suddenly played out utterly and fell down the well. There was a radical defect somewhere, and I must search it out and cure it.

The defect turned out to be the one already spoken of—two stories in one, a farce and a tragedy. So I pulled out the farce and left the tragedy. This left the original team in, but only as mere names, not as characters. Their prominence was wholly gone; they were not even worth drowning; so I removed that detail. Also I took those twins apart and made two separate men of them. They had no occasion to have foreign names now, but it was too much trouble to remove them all through, so I left them christened as they were and made no explanation.

1

The Twins as They Really Were

THE CONGLOMERATE TWINS were brought on the stage in Chapter
I of the original extravaganza. Aunt Patsy Cooper has received
their letter applying for board and lodging, and Rowena, her
daughter, insane with joy, is begging for a hearing of it:

"Well, set down then, and be quiet a minute and don't fly
around so; it fairly makes me tired to see you. It starts off so:
'HONORED MADAM—'"

"I like that, ma, don't you? It shows they're high-bred."

"Yes, I noticed that when I first read it. 'My brother and I have
seen your advertisement, by chance, in a copy of your local
journal—'"

"It's so beautiful and smooth, ma—don't you think so?"

"Yes, seems so to me—'and beg leave to take the room you offer.
We are twenty-four years of age, and twins—'"

"Twins! How sweet! I do hope they are handsome, and I just
know they are! Don't you hope they are, ma?"

"Land, I ain't particular. 'We are Italians by birth—'"

"It's so romantic! Just think—there's never been one in this
town, and everybody will want to see them, and they're all *ours!*
Think of that!"

"—'but have lived long in the various countries of Europe, and
several years in the United States.'"

"Oh, just think what wonders they've seen, ma! Won't it be
good to hear them talk?"

"I reckon so; yes, I reckon so. 'Our names are Luigi and
Angelo Capello—'"

"Beautiful, perfectly beautiful! Not like Jones and Robinson and those horrible names."

" 'You desire but one guest, but dear madam, if you will allow us to pay for two we will not discommode you. We will sleep together in the same bed. We have always been used to this, and prefer it.' And then he goes on to say they will be down Thursday."

"And this is Tuesday—I don't know how I'm ever going to wait, ma! The time does drag along so, and I'm so dying to see them! Which of them do you reckon is the tallest, ma?"

"How do you s'pose I can tell, child? Mostly they are the same size—twins are."

"Well then, which do you reckon is the best looking?"

"Goodness knows—I don't."

"I think Angelo is; it's the prettiest name, anyway. Don't you think it's a sweet name, ma?"

"Yes, it's well enough. I'd like both of them better if I knew the way to pronounce them—the Eyetalian way, I mean. The Missouri way and the Eyetalian way is different, I judge."

"Maybe—yes. It's Luigi that writes the letter. What do you reckon is the reason Angelo didn't write it?"

"Why, how can I tell? What's the difference who writes it, so long as it's done?"

"Oh, I hope it wasn't because he is sick! You don't think he is sick, do you, ma?"

"Sick your granny; what's to make him sick?"

"Oh, there's never any telling. These foreigners with that kind of names are so delicate, and of course that kind of names are not suited to our climate—you wouldn't expect it."

[And so-on and so-on, no end. The time drags along; Thursday comes: the boat arrives in a pouring storm toward midnight.]

At last there was a knock at the door and the anxious family jumped to open it. Two negro men entered, each carrying a trunk, and proceeded upstairs toward the guest-room. Then followed a stupefying apparition—a double-headed human creature with four arms, one body, and a single pair of legs! It—or they, as you please—bowed with elaborate foreign formality, but the Coopers could not respond immediately; they were paralyzed. At this moment there came from the rear of the group a fervent ejaculation—"My lan'!"—followed by a crash of crockery, and the slave-wench Nancy stood petrified and staring, with a tray of wrecked tea-things at her feet. The incident broke the spell, and brought the family to consciousness. The beautiful heads of the new-comer bowed again, and one of them said with easy grace and dignity:

"I crave the honor, madam and miss, to introduce to you my brother, Count Luigi Capello," (the other head bowed) "and myself—Count Angelo; and at the same time offer sincere apologies for the lateness of our coming, which was unavoidable," and both heads bowed again.

The poor old lady was in a whirl of amazement and confusion, but she managed to stammer out:

"I'm sure I'm glad to make your acquaintance, sir—I mean, gentlemen. As for the delay, it is nothing, don't mention it. This is my daughter Rowena, sir—gentlemen. Please step into the parlor and sit down and have a bite and sup; you are dreadful wet and must be uncomfortable—both of you, I mean."

But to the old lady's relief they courteously excused themselves, saying it would be wrong to keep the family out of their beds longer; then each head bowed in turn and uttered a friendly good night, and the singular figure moved away in the wake of Rowena's small brothers, who bore candles, and disappeared up the stairs.

The widow tottered into the parlor and sank into a chair with a gasp, and Rowena followed, tongue-tied and dazed. The two sat silent in the throbbing summer heat unconscious of the million-voiced music of the mosquitoes, unconscious of the roaring gale, the lashing and thrashing of the rain along the windows and the roof, the white glare of the lightning, the tumultuous booming and bellowing of the thunder; conscious of nothing but that prodigy, that uncanny apparition that had come and gone so suddenly—that weird strange thing that was so soft-spoken and so gentle of manner and yet had shaken them up like an earthquake with the shock of its gruesome aspect. At last a cold little shudder quivered along down the widow's meager frame and she said in a weak voice:

"Ugh, it was awful—just the mere look of that phillipene!"

Rowena did not answer. Her faculties were still caked, she had not yet found her voice. Presently the widow said, a little resentfully:

"Always been *used* to sleeping together—in fact, *prefer* it. And I was thinking it was to accommodate me. I thought it was very good of them, whereas a person situated as that young man is—"

"Ma, you oughtn't to begin by getting up a prejudice against him. I'm sure he is good-hearted and means well. Both of his faces show it."

"I'm not so certain about that. The one on the left—I mean the one on *it's* left—hasn't near as good a face, in my opinion, as its brother."

"That's Luigi."

"Yes, Luigi; anyway it's the dark-skinned one; the one that was west of his brother when they stood in the door. Up to all kinds of mischief and disobedience when he was a boy, I'll be bound. I lay his mother had trouble to lay her hand on him when she wanted him. But the one on the right is as good as gold, I can see that."

"That's Angelo."

"Yes, Angelo, I reckon, though I can't tell t'other from which by their names, yet awhile. But it's the right-hand one—the blond one. He has such kind blue eyes, and curly copper hair and fresh complexion—"

"And such a noble face!—oh, it *is* a noble face, ma, just royal, you may say! And beautiful—deary me, how beautiful! But both are that; the dark one's as beautiful as a picture. There's no such wonderful faces and handsome heads in this town—none that even begin. And such hands—especially Angelo's—so shapely and—"

"Stuff, how could you tell which they belonged to?—they had gloves on."

"Why, didn't I see them take off their hats?"

"That don't signify. They might have taken off each other's hats. Nobody could tell. There was just a wormy squirming of arms in the air—seemed to be a couple of dozen of them, all writhing at once, and it just made me dizzy to see them go."

"Why, ma, I hadn't any difficulty. There's two arms on each shoulder—"

"There, now. One arm on each shoulder belongs to each of the creatures, don't it? For a person to have two arms on one shoulder wouldn't do him any good, would it? Of course not. Each has an arm on each shoulder. Now then, you tell me which of them belongs to which, if you can. *They* don't know, themselves—they just work whichever arm comes handy. Of course they do; especially if they are in a hurry and can't stop to think which belongs to which."

The mother seemed to have the rights of the argument, so the daughter abandoned the struggle. Presently the widow rose with a yawn and said:

"Poor thing, I hope it won't catch cold; it was powerful wet, just drenched, you may say. I hope it has left its boots outside, so they can be dried." Then she gave a little start, and looked perplexed. "Now I remember I heard one of them ask Joe to call him at half after seven—I think it was the one on the left—no, it was the one to the east of the other one—but I didn't hear the other one say anything. I wonder if he wants to be called too. Do you reckon it's too late to ask?"

"Why, ma, it's not necessary. Calling one is calling both. If one gets up, the other's *got* to."

"Sho, of course; I never thought of that. Well, come along, maybe we can get some sleep, but I don't know, I'm so shook up with what we've been through."

The stranger had made an impression on the boys, too. They had a word of talk as they were getting to bed. Henry, the gentle, the humane, said:

"I feel ever so sorry for it, don't you, Joe?"

But Joe was a boy of this world, active, enterprising, and had a theatrical side to him:

"Sorry? Why, how you talk! It can't stir a step without attracting attention. It's just grand!"

Henry said, reproachfully:

"Instead of pitying it, Joe, you talk as if—"

"Talk as if *what?* I know one thing mighty certain: if you can fix me so I can eat for two and only have to stub toes for one, I ain't going to fool away no such chance just for sentiment."

The twins were wet and tired, and they proceeded to undress without any preliminary remarks. The abundance of sleeve made the partnership coat hard to get off, for it was like skinning a tarantula; but it came at last, after much tugging and perspiring. The mutual vest followed. Then the brothers stood up before the glass, and each took off his own cravat and collar. The collars were of the standing kind, and came high up under the ears, like the sides of a wheelbarrow, as required by the fashion of the day. The cravats were as broad as a bank-bill, with fringed ends which stood far out to right and left like the wings of a dragon-fly, and this also was strictly in accordance with the fashion of the time. Each cravat, as to color, was in perfect taste, so far as its owner's complexion was concerned—a delicate pink, in the case of the blond brother, a violent scarlet in the case of the brunette —but as a combination they broke all the laws of taste known to civilization. Nothing more fiendish and irreconcilable than those shrieking and blaspheming colors could have been contrived. The wet boots gave no end of trouble—to Luigi. When they were off at last, Angelo said, with bitterness:

"I wish you wouldn't wear such tight boots, they hurt my feet."

Luigi answered with indifference:

"My friend, when I am in command of our body, I choose my apparel according to my own convenience, as I have remarked more than several times already. When you are in command, I beg you will do as you please."

Angelo was hurt, and the tears came into his eyes. There was gentle reproach in his voice, but not anger, when he replied:

"Luigi, I often consult your wishes, but you never consult mine. When I am in command I treat you as a guest; I try to make you feel at home; when you are in command you treat me as an intruder, you make me feel unwelcome. It embarrasses me cruelly in company, for I can see that people notice it and comment on it."

"Oh, damn the people," responded the brother languidly, and with the air of one who is tired of the subject.

A slight shudder shook the frame of Angelo, but he said nothing and the conversation ceased. Each buttoned his own share of the nightshirt in silence; then Luigi, with Paine's *Age of Reason* in his hand, sat down in one chair and put his feet in another and lit his pipe, while Angelo took his *Whole Duty of Man,* and both began to read. Angelo presently began to cough; his coughing increased and became mixed with gaspings for breath, and he was finally obliged to make an appeal to his brother's humanity:

"Luigi, if you would only smoke a little milder tobacco, I am sure I could learn not to mind it in time, but this is so strong, and the pipe is so rank that—"

"Angelo, I wouldn't be such a baby! I have learned to smoke in a week, and the trouble is already over with me; if you would try, you could learn too, and then you would stop spoiling my comfort with your everlasting complaints."

"Ah, brother, that is a strong word—everlasting—and isn't quite fair. I only complain when I suffocate; you know I don't complain when we are in the open air."

"Well, anyway, you could learn to smoke yourself."

"But my *principles,* Luigi, you forget my principles. You would not have me do a thing which I regard as a sin?"

"Oh, bosh!"

The conversation ceased again, for Angelo was sick and discouraged and strangling; but after some time he closed his book and asked Luigi to sing "From Greenland's Icy Mountains" with him, but he would not, and when he tried to sing by himself Luigi did his best to drown his plaintive tenor with a rude and rollicking song delivered in a thundering bass.

After the singing there was silence, and neither brother was happy. Before blowing the light out Luigi swallowed half a tumbler of whisky, and Angelo, whose sensitive organization could not endure intoxicants of any kind, took a pill to keep it from giving him the headache.

2

Ma Cooper Gets All Mixed Up

THE FAMILY sat in the breakfast-room waiting for the twins to come down. The widow was quiet, the daughter was alive with happy excitement. She said:

"Ah, they're a boon, ma, just a boon! don't you think so?"

"Laws, I hope so, I don't know."

"Why, ma, yes you do. They're so fine and handsome, and high-bred and polite, so every way superior to our gawks here in this village; why, they'll make life different from what it was —so humdrum and commonplace, you know—oh, you may be sure they're full of accomplishments, and knowledge of the world, and all that, that will be an immense advantage to society here. Don't you think so, ma?"

"Mercy on me, how should I know, and I've hardly set eyes on them yet." After a pause she added, "They made considerable noise after they went up."

"Noise? Why, ma, they were singing! And it was beautiful, too."

"Oh, it was well enough, but too mixed-up, seemed to me."

"Now, ma, honor bright, did you ever hear 'Greenland's Icy Mountains' sung sweeter—now did you?"

"If it had been sung by itself, it would have been uncommon sweet, I don't deny it; but what they wanted to mix it up with 'Old Bob Ridley' for, I can't make out. Why, they don't go together, at all. They are not of the same nature. 'Bob Ridley' is a common rackety slam-bang secular song, one of the rippingest and rantingest and noisiest there is. I am no judge of music, and I don't claim it, but in my opinion nobody can make those two songs go together right."

"Why, ma, I thought—"

"It don't make any difference what you thought, it can't be done. They tried it, and to my mind it was a failure. I never heard such a crazy uproar; seemed to me, sometimes, the roof would come off; and as for the cats—well, I've lived a many a year, and seen cats aggravated in more ways than one, but I've never seen cats take on the way they took on last night."

"Well, I don't think that that goes for anything, ma, because it is the nature of cats that any sound that is unusual—"

"Unusual! You may well call it so. Now if they are going to sing duets every night, I do hope they will both sing the same tune at the same time, for in my opinion a duet that is made up of two different tunes is a mistake; especially when the tunes ain't any kin to one another, that way."

"But, ma, I think it must be a foreign custom; and it must be right too; and the best way, because they have had every opportunity to know what is right, and it don't stand to reason that with their education they would do anything but what the highest musical authorities have sanctioned. You can't help but admit that, ma."

The argument was formidably strong; the old lady could not find any way around it; so, after thinking it over awhile she gave in with a sigh of discontent, and admitted that the daughter's position was probably correct. Being vanquished, she had no mind to continue the topic at that disadvantage, and was about to seek a change when a change came of itself. A footstep was heard on the stairs, and she said:

"There—he's coming!"

"*They*, ma—you ought to say *they*—it's nearer right."

The new lodger, rather shoutingly dressed but looking superbly handsome, stepped with courtly carriage into the trim little breakfast-room and put out all his cordial arms at once, like one of those pocket-knives with a multiplicity of blades, and shook hands with the whole family simultaneously. He was so easy and pleasant and hearty that all embarrassment presently thawed away and disappeared, and a cheery feeling of friendliness and comradeship took its place. He—or preferably they—were asked to occupy the seat of honor at the foot of the table. They consented with thanks, and carved the beefsteak with one set of their hands while they distributed it at the same time with the other set.

"Will you have coffee, gentlemen, or tea?"

"Coffee for Luigi, if you please, madam, tea for me."

"Cream and sugar?"

"For me, yes, madam; Luigi takes his coffee black. Our natures differ a good deal from each other, and our tastes also."

The first time the negro girl Nancy appeared in the door and saw the two heads turned in opposite directions and both talking at once, then saw the commingling arms feed potatoes into one mouth and coffee into the other at the same time, she had to pause and pull herself out of a faintness that came over her; but after that she held her grip and was able to wait on the table with fair courage.

Conversation fell naturally into the customary grooves. It was a little jerky, at first, because none of the family could get smoothly through a sentence without a wabble in it here and a break there, caused by some new surprise in the way of attitude or gesture on the part of the twins. The weather suffered the most. The weather was all finished up and disposed of, as a subject, before the simple Missourians had gotten sufficiently wonted to the spectacle of one body feeding two heads to feel composed and reconciled in the presence of so bizarre a miracle. And even after everybody's mind became tranquilized there was still one slight distraction left: the hand that picked up a biscuit carried it to the wrong head, as often as any other way, and the wrong mouth devoured it. This was a puzzling thing, and marred the talk a little. It bothered the widow to such a degree that she presently dropped out of the conversation without knowing it, and fell to watching and guessing and talking to herself:

"Now that hand is going to take that coffee to—no, it's gone to the other mouth; I can't understand it; and now, here is the dark-complected hand with a potato on its fork, I'll see what goes with it—there, the light-complected head's got it, as sure as I live!" Finally Rowena said:

"Ma, what is the matter with you? Are you dreaming about something?"

The old lady came to herself and blushed; then she explained with the first random thing that came into her mind: "I saw Mr. Angelo take up Mr. Luigi's coffee, and I thought maybe he— sha'n't I give *you* a cup, Mr. Angelo?"

"Oh no, madam, I am very much obliged, but I never drink coffee, much as I would like to. You did see me take up Luigi's cup, it is true, but if you noticed, I didn't carry it to my mouth, but to his."

"Y-es, I thought you did. Did you mean to?"

"How?"

The widow was a little embarrassed again. She said:

"I don't know but what I'm foolish, and you mustn't mind; but you see, he got the coffee I was expecting to see you drink, and you got a potato that I thought he was going to get. So I thought it might be a mistake all around, and everybody getting what wasn't intended for him."

Both twins laughed and Luigi said:

"Dear madam, there wasn't any mistake. We are always help-ing each other that way. It is a great economy for us both; it saves time and labor. We have a system of signs which nobody can notice or understand but ourselves. If I am using both my hands and want some coffee, I make the sign and Angelo fur-nishes it to me; and you saw that when he needed a potato I delivered it."

"How convenient!"

"Yes, and often of the extremest value. Take the Mississippi boats, for instance. They are always overcrowded. There is table-room for only half of the passengers, therefore they have to set a second table for the second half. The stewards rush both parties, they give them no time to eat a satisfying meal, both divisions leave the table hungry. It isn't so with us. Angelo books himself for the one table, I book myself for the other. Neither of us eats anything at the other's table, but just simply works— works. Thus, you see there are four hands to feed Angelo, and the same four to feed me. Each of us eats two meals."

The old lady was dazed with admiration, and kept saying, "It is *per*fectly wonderful, perfectly wonderful!" and the boy Joe licked his chops enviously, but said nothing—at least aloud.

"Yes," continued Luigi, "our construction may have its disadvantages—in fact, *has*—but it also has its compensations of one sort and another. Take travel, for instance. Travel is enormously expensive, in all countries; we have been obliged to do a vast deal of it—come, Angelo, don't put any more sugar in your tea, I'm just over one indigestion and don't want another right away —been obliged to do a deal of it, as I was saying. Well, we always travel as one person, since we occupy but one seat; so we save half the fare."

"How romantic!" interjected Rowena, with effusion.

"Yes, my dear young lady, and how practical too, and economical. In Europe, beds in the hotels are not charged with the board, but separately—another saving, for we stood to our rights and paid for the one bed only. The landlords often insisted that as both of us occupied the bed we ought—"

"No, they didn't," said Angelo. "They did it only twice, and in both cases it was a double bed—a rare thing in Europe—and the double bed gave them some excuse. Be fair to the landlords; twice doesn't constitute 'often.'"

"Well, that depends—that depends. I knew a man who fell down a well twice. He said he didn't mind the first time, but he thought the second time was once too often. Have I misused that word, Mrs. Cooper?"

"To tell the truth, I was afraid you had, but it seems to look, now, like you hadn't." She stopped, and was evidently struggling with the difficult problem a moment, then she added in the tone of one who is convinced without being converted, "It seems so, but I can't somehow tell why."

Rowena thought Luigi's retort was wonderfully quick and

bright, and she remarked to herself with satisfaction that there wasn't any young native of Dawson's Landing that could have risen to the occasion like that. Luigi detected the applause in her face, and expressed his pleasure and his thanks with his eyes; and so eloquently withal, that the girl was proud and pleased, and hung out the delicate sign of it on her cheeks.

Luigi went on, with animation:

"Both of us get a bath for one ticket, theater seat for one ticket, pew-rent is on the same basis, but at peep-shows we pay double."

"We have much to be thankful for," said Angelo, impressively, with a reverent light in his eye and a reminiscent tone in his voice, "we have been greatly blessed. As a rule, what one of us has lacked, the other, by the bounty of Providence, has been able to supply. My brother is hardy, I am not; he is very masculine, assertive, aggressive; I am much less so. I am subject to illness, he is never ill. I cannot abide medicines, and cannot take them, but he has no prejudice against them, and—"

"Why, goodness gracious," interrupted the widow, "When you are sick, does he take the medicine for you?"

"Always, madam."

"Why, I never heard such a thing in my life! I think it's beautiful of you."

"Oh, madam, it's nothing, don't mention it, it's really nothing at all."

"But I say it's beautiful, and I stick to it!" cried the widow, with a speaking moisture in her eye. "A well brother to take the medicine for his poor sick brother—I wish I had such a son," and she glanced reproachfully at her boys. "I declare I'll never rest till I've shook you by the hand," and she scrambled out of her chair in a fever of generous enthusiasm, and made for the twins, blind with her tears, and began to shake. The boy Joe corrected her:

"You're shaking the wrong one, ma."

This flurried her, but she made a swift change and went on shaking.

"Got the wrong one again, ma," said the boy.

"Oh, shut up, can't you!" said the widow, embarrassed and irritated. "Give me *all* your hands, I want to shake them all; for I know you are both just as good as you can be."

It was a victorious thought, a master-stroke of diplomacy, though that never occurred to her and she cared nothing for diplomacy. She shook the four hands in turn cordially, and went back to her place in a state of high and fine exultation that made her look young and handsome.

"Indeed I owe everything to Luigi," said Angelo, affectionately. "But for him I could not have survived our boyhood days, when we were friendless and poor—ah, so poor! We lived from hand to mouth—lived on the coarse fare of unwilling charity, and for weeks and weeks together not a morsel of food passed my lips, for its character revolted me and I could not eat it. But for Luigi I should have died. He ate for us both."

"How noble!" sighed Rowena.

"Do you hear that?" said the widow, severely, to her boys. "Let it be an example to you—I mean you, Joe."

Joe gave his head a barely perceptible disparaging toss and said: "Et for both. It ain't anything—I'd 'a' done it."

"Hush, if you haven't got any better manners than that. You don't see the point at all. It wasn't good food."

"I don't care—it was food, and I'd 'a' et it if it was rotten."

"Shame! Such language! Can't you understand? They were starving—actually starving—and he ate for both, and—"

"Shucks! you gimme a chance and I'll—"

"There, now—close your head! and don't you open it again till you're asked."

[Angelo goes on and tells how his parents the Count and Countess had to fly from Florence for political reasons, and died poor in Berlin bereft of their great property by confiscation; and how he and Luigi had to travel with a freak-show during two years and suffer semi-starvation.]

"That hateful black-bread; but I seldom ate anything during that time; that was poor Luigi's affair—"

"I'll never *Mister* him again!" cried the widow, with strong emotion, "he's Luigi to me, from this out!"

"Thank you a thousand times, madam, a thousand times! though in truth I don't deserve it."

"Ah, Luigi is always the fortunate one when honors are showering," said Angelo, plaintively; "now what have I done, Mrs. Cooper, that you leave me out? Come, you must strain a point in my favor."

"Call you Angelo? Why, certainly I will; what are you thinking of! In the case of twins, why—"

"But, ma, you're breaking up the story—do let him go on."

"You keep still, Rowena Cooper, and he can go on all the better, I reckon. One interruption don't hurt, it's two that makes the trouble."

"But you've added one, now, and that is three."

"Rowena! I will not allow you to talk back at me when you have got nothing rational to say."

3

Angelo Is Blue

[After breakfast the whole village crowded in, and there was a grand reception in honor of the twins; and at the close of it the gifted "freak" captured everybody's admiration by sitting down at the piano and knocking out a classic four-handed piece in great style. Then the Judge took it—or them —driving in his buggy and showed off his village.]

ALL ALONG the streets the people crowded the windows and stared at the amazing twins. Troops of small boys flocked after the buggy, excited and yelling. At first the dogs showed no interest. They thought they merely saw three men in a buggy—a matter of no consequence; but when they found out the facts of the case, they altered their opinion pretty radically, and joined the boys, expressing their minds as they came. Other dogs got interested; indeed, all the dogs. It was a spirited sight to see them come leaping fences, tearing around corners, swarming out of every by-street and alley. The noise they made was something beyond belief—or praise. They did not seem to be moved by malice but only by prejudice, the common human prejudice against lack of conformity. If the twins turned their heads, they broke and fled in every direction, but stopped at a safe distance and faced about; and then formed and came on again as soon as the strangers showed them their back. Negroes and farmers' wives took to the woods when the buggy came upon them suddenly, and altogether the drive was pleasant and animated, and a refreshment all around.

[It was a long and lively drive. Angelo was a Methodist, Luigi was a Free-thinker. The Judge was very proud of his Free-thinkers' Society, which was flourishing along in a most prosperous way and already had two members—himself and the obscure and neglected Pudd'nhead Wilson. It was to meet that evening, and he invited Luigi to join; a thing which Luigi was glad to do, partly because it would please himself, and partly because it would gravel Angelo.]

They had now arrived at the widow's gate, and the excursion was ended. The twins politely expressed their obligations for the pleasant outing which had been afforded them; to which the Judge bowed his thanks, and then said he would now go and arrange for the Free-thinkers' meeting, and would call for Count Luigi in the evening.

"For you also, dear sir," he added hastily, turning to Angelo and bowing. "In addressing myself particularly to your brother, I was not meaning to leave you out. It was an unintentional rudeness, I assure you, and due wholly to accident—accident and preoccupation. I beg you to forgive me."

His quick eye had seen the sensitive blood mount into Angelo's face, betraying the wound that had been inflicted. The sting of the slight had gone deep, but the apology was so prompt, and so evidently sincere, that the hurt was almost immediately healed, and a forgiving smile testified to the kindly Judge that all was well again.

Concealed behind Angelo's modest and unassuming exterior, and unsuspected by any but his intimates, was a lofty pride, a pride of almost abnormal proportions, indeed, and this rendered him ever the prey of slights; and although they were almost always imaginary ones, they hurt none the less on that account. By ill fortune Judge Driscoll had happened to touch his sorest point, *i.e.*, his conviction that his brother's presence was welcomer everywhere than his own; that he was often invited, out of mere courtesy, where only his brother was wanted, and that in a majority of cases he would not be included in an invitation if he could be left out without offense. A sensitive nature like this is necessarily subject to moods; moods which traverse the whole gamut of feeling; moods which know all the climes of emotion, from the sunny heights of joy to the black abysses of despair. At times, in his seasons of deepest depressions, Angelo almost wished that he and his brother might become segregated from each other and be separate individuals, like other men. But of course as soon as his mind cleared and these diseased imaginings passed away, he shuddered at the repulsive thought, and earnestly prayed that it might visit him no more. To be separate, and as other men are! How awkward it would seem; how unendurable. What would he do with his hands, his arms? How would his legs feel? How odd, and strange, and grotesque every action, attitude, movement, gesture would be. To sleep by himself, eat by himself, walk by himself—how lonely, how unspeakably lonely! No, no, any fate but that. In every way and from every point, the idea was revolting.

This was of course natural; to have felt otherwise would have been unnatural. He had known no life but a combined one; he had been familiar with it from his birth; he was not able to conceive of any other as being agreeable, or even bearable. To him, in the privacy of his secret thoughts, all other men were monsters, deformities: and during three-fourths of his life their aspect had filled him with what promised to be an unconquerable aversion. But at eighteen his eye began to take note of female beauty; and little by little, undefined longings grew up in his heart, under whose softening influences the old stubborn aversion gradually diminished, and finally disappeared. Men were still monstrosities to him, still deformities, and in his sober moments he had no desire to be like them, but their strange and unsocial and uncanny construction was no longer offensive to him.

This had been a hard day for him, physically and mentally. He had been called in the morning before he had quite slept off the effects of the liquor which Luigi had drunk; and so, for the first half-hour had had the seedy feeling, and languor, the brooding depression, the cobwebby mouth and druggy taste that come of dissipation and are so ill a preparation for bodily or intellectual activities; the long violent strain of the reception had followed; and this had been followed, in turn, by the dreary sight-seeing, the Judge's wearying explanations and laudations of the sights, and the stupefying clamor of the dogs. As a congruous conclusion, a fitting end, his feelings had been hurt, a slight had been put upon him. He would have been glad to forego dinner and betake himself to rest and sleep, but he held his peace and said no word, for he knew his brother, Luigi, was fresh, unweary, full of life, spirit, energy; he would have scoffed at the idea of wasting valuable time on a bed or a sofa, and would have refused permission.

4

Supernatural Chronometry

ROWENA was dining out, Joe and Harry were belated at play, there were but three chairs and four persons that noon at the home dinner table—the twins, the widow, and her chum, Aunt Betsy Hale. The widow soon perceived that Angelo's spirits were as low as Luigi's were high, and also that he had a jaded look. Her motherly solicitude was aroused, and she tried to get him interested in the talk and win him to a happier frame of mind, but the cloud of sadness remained on his countenance. Luigi lent his help, too. He used a form and a phrase which he was always accustomed to employ in these circumstances. He gave his brother an affectionate slap on the shoulder and said, encouragingly:

"Cheer up, the worst is yet to come!"

But this did no good. It never did. If anything, it made the matter worse, as a rule, because it irritated Angelo. This made it a favorite with Luigi. By and by the widow said:

"Angelo, you are tired, you've overdone yourself; you go right to bed after dinner, and get a good nap and a rest, then you'll be all right."

"Indeed, I would give anything if I could do that, madam."

"And what's to hender, I'd like to know? Land, the room's yours to do what you please with! The idea that you can't do what you like with your own!"

"But, you see, there's one prime essential—an essential of the very first importance—which isn't my own."

"What is that?"

"My body."

The old ladies looked puzzled, and Aunt Betsy Hale said:

"Why bless your heart, how is that?"

"It's my brother's."

"Your brother's! I don't quite understand. I supposed it belonged to both of you."

"So it does. But not to both at the same time."

"That is mighty curious; I don't see how it can be. I shouldn't think it could be managed that way."

"Oh, it's a good enough arrangement, and goes very well; in fact, it wouldn't do to have it otherwise. I find that the teetotalers and the anti-teetotalers hire the use of the same hall for their meetings. Both parties don't use it at the same time, do they?"

"You bet they don't!" said both old ladies in a breath.

"And, moreover," said Aunt Betsy, "the Free-thinkers and the Baptist Bible class use the same room over the Market house, but you can take my word for it they don't mush up together and use it at the same time."

"Very well," said Angelo, "you understand it now. And it stands to reason that the arrangement couldn't be improved. I'll prove it to you. If our legs tried to obey two wills, how could we ever get anywhere? I would start one way, Luigi would start another, at the same moment—the result would be a standstill, wouldn't it?"

"As sure as you are born! Now ain't that wonderful! A body would never have thought of it."

"We should always be arguing and fussing and disputing over the merest trifles. We should lose worlds of time, for we couldn't go down-stairs or up, couldn't go to bed, couldn't rise, couldn't wash, couldn't dress, couldn't stand up, couldn't sit down, couldn't even cross our legs, without calling a meeting first and explaining the case and passing resolutions, and getting consent. It wouldn't ever do—now would it?"

"Do? Why, it would wear a person out in a week! Did you ever hear anything like it, Patsy Cooper?"

"Oh, you'll find there's more than one thing about them that ain't commonplace," said the widow, with the complacent air of a person with a property right in a novelty that is under admiring scrutiny.

"Well, now, how ever do you manage it? I don't mind saying I'm suffering to know."

"He who made us," said Angelo reverently, "and with us this difficulty, also provided a way out of it. By a mysterious law of our being, each of us has utter and indisputable command of our body a week at a time, turn and turn about."

"Well, I never! Now ain't that beautiful!"

"Yes, it is beautiful and infinitely wise and just. The week ends every Saturday at midnight to the minute, to the second, to the last shade of a fraction of a second, infallibly, unerringly, and in that instant the one brother's power over the body vanishes and the other brother takes possession, asleep or awake."

"How marvelous are His ways, and past finding out!"

Luigi said: "So exactly to the instant does the change come, that during our stay in many of the great cities of the world, the public clocks were regulated by it; and as hundreds of thousands of private clocks and watches were set and corrected in accordance with the public clocks, we really furnished the standard time for the entire city."

"Don't tell me that He don't do miracles any more! Blowing down the walls of Jericho with rams' horns wa'n't as difficult, in my opinion."

"And that is not all," said Angelo. "A thing that is even more marvelous, perhaps, is the fact that the change takes note of longitude and fits itself to the meridian we are on. Luigi is in command this week. Now, if on Saturday night at a moment before midnight we could fly in an instant to a point fifteen degrees west of here, he would hold possession of the power another hour, for the change observes *local* time and no other."

Betsy Hale was deeply impressed, and said with solemnity:

"Patsy Cooper, for *de*tail it lays over the Passage of the Red Sea."

"Now, I shouldn't go as far as that," said Aunt Patsy, "but if you've a mind to say Sodom and Gomorrah, I am with you, Betsy Hale."

"I am agreeable, then, though I do think I was right, and I believe Parson Maltby would say the same. Well, now, there's another thing. Suppose one of you wants to borrow the legs a minute from the one that's got them, could he let him?"

"Yes, but we hardly ever do that. There were disagreeable results, several times, and so we very seldom ask or grant the privilege, nowadays, and we never even think of such a thing unless the case is extremely urgent. Besides, a week's possession at a time seems so little that we can't bear to spare a minute of it. People who have the use of their legs all the time never think of what a blessing it is, of course. It never occurs to them; it's just their natural ordinary condition, and so it does not excite them at all. But when I wake up, on Sunday morning, and it's my week and I feel the power all through me, oh, such a wave of exultation and thanksgiving goes surging over me, and I want to shout 'I can walk! I can walk!' Madam, do you ever, at your uprising, want to shout 'I can walk! I can walk!'?"

"No, you poor unfortunate cretur', but I'll never get out of my bed again without *doing* it! Laws, to think I've had this unspeakable blessing all my long life and never had the grace to thank the good Lord that gave it to me!"

Tears stood in the eyes of both the old ladies and the widow said, softly:

"Betsy Hale, we have learned something, you and me."

The conversation now drifted wide, but by and by floated back once more to that admired detail, the rigid and beautiful impartiality with which the possession of power had been distributed between the twins. Aunt Betsy saw in it a far finer justice than human law exhibits in related cases. She said:

"In my opinion it ain't right now, and never has been right, the way a twin born a quarter of a minute sooner than the other one gets all the land and grandeurs and nobilities in the old countries and his brother has to go bare and be a nobody. Which of you was born first?"

Angelo's head was resting against Luigi's; weariness had overcome him, and for the past five minutes he had been peacefully sleeping. The old ladies had dropped their voices to a lulling drone, to help him to steal the rest his brother wouldn't take him up-stairs to get. Luigi listened a moment to Angelo's regular breathing, then said in a voice barely audible:

"We were both born at the same time, but I am six months older than he is."

"For the land's sake!"

" 'Sh! don't wake him up; he wouldn't like my telling this. It has always been kept secret till now."

"But how in the world can it be? If you were both born at the same time, how can one of you be older than the other?"

"It is very simple, and I assure you it is true. I was born with a full crop of hair, he was as bald as an egg for six months. I could walk six months before he could make a step. I finished teething six months ahead of him. I began to take solids six months before he left the breast. I began to talk six months before he could say a word. Last, and absolutely unassailable proof, *the sutures in my skull closed six months ahead of his.* Always just that six months' difference to a day. Was that accident? Nobody is going to claim that, I'm sure. It was ordained—it was law—it had its meaning, and we know what that meaning was. Now what does this overwhelming body of evidence establish? It establishes just one thing, and that thing it establishes beyond any peradventure whatever. Friends, we would not have it known for the world, and I must beg you to keep it strictly to yourselves, but the truth is, *we are no more twins than you are.*"

The two old ladies were stunned, paralyzed—petrified, one may almost say—and could only sit and gaze vacantly at each other for some moments; then Aunt Betsy Hale said impressively:

"There's no getting around proof like that. I do believe it's the most amazing thing I ever heard of." She sat silent a moment or two and breathing hard with excitement, then she looked up and surveyed the strangers steadfastly a little while, and added: "Well, it does beat me, but I would have took you for twins anywhere."

"So would I, so would I," said Aunt Patsy with the emphasis of a certainty that is not impaired by any shade of doubt.

"*Any*body would—anybody in the world, I don't care who he is," said Aunt Betsy with decision.

"You won't tell," said Luigi, appealingly.

"Oh, dear, no!" answered both ladies promptly, "you can trust us, don't you be afraid."

"That is good of you, and kind. Never let on; treat us always as if we were twins."

"You can depend on us," said Aunt Betsy, "but it won't be easy, because now that I know you ain't you don't *seem* so."

Luigi muttered to himself with satisfaction: "That swindle has gone through without change of cars."

It was not very kind of him to load the poor things up with a secret like that, which would be always flying to their tongues' ends every time they heard any one speak of the strangers as twins, and would become harder and harder to hang on to with every recurrence of the temptation to tell it, while the torture of retaining it would increase with every new strain that was applied; but he never thought of that, and probably would not have worried much about it if he had.

A visitor was announced—some one to see the twins. They withdrew to the parlor, and the two old ladies began to discuss with interest the strange things which they had been listening to. When they had finished the matter to their satisfaction, and Aunt Betsy rose to go, she stopped to ask a question:

"How does things come on between Roweny and Tom Driscoll?"

"Well, about the same. He writes tolerable often, and she answers tolerable seldom."

"Where is he?"

"In St. Louis, I believe, though he's such a gadabout that a body can't be very certain of him, I reckon."

"Don't Roweny know?"

"Oh, yes, like enough. I haven't asked her lately."

"Do you know how him and the Judge are getting along now?"

"First rate, I believe. Mrs. Pratt says so; and being right in the house, and sister to the one and aunt to t'other, of course she ought to know. She says the Judge is real fond of him when he's away; but frets when he's around and is vexed with his ways, and not sorry to have him go again. He has been gone three weeks this time—a pleasant thing for both of them, I reckon."

"Tom's ruther harum-scarum, but there ain't anything bad in him, I guess."

"Oh, no, he's just young, that's all. Still, twenty-three is old, in one way. A young man ought to be earning his living by that time. If Tom were doing that, or was even trying to do it, the Judge would be a heap better satisfied with him. Tom's always going to begin, but somehow he can't seem to find just the opening he likes."

"Well, now, it's partly the Judge's own fault. Promising the boy his property wasn't the way to set him to earning a fortune of his own. But what do you think—is Roweny beginning to lean any toward him, or ain't she?"

Aunt Patsy had a secret in her bosom; she wanted to keep it there, but nature was too strong for her. She drew Aunt Betsy aside, and said in her most confidential and mysterious manner:

"Don't you breathe a syllable to a soul—I'm going to tell you something. In my opinion Tom Driscoll's chances were considerable better yesterday than they are to-day."

"Patsy Cooper, what *do* you mean?"

"It's so, as sure as you're born. I wish you could 'a' been at breakfast and seen for yourself."

"You don't mean it!"

"Well, if I'm any judge, there's a leaning—there's a leaning, sure."

"My land! Which one of 'em is it?"

"I can't say for certain, but I think it's the youngest one—Anjy."

Then there were handshakings, and congratulations, and hopes, and so on, and the old ladies parted, perfectly happy—the one in knowing something which the rest of the town didn't, and the other in having been the sole person able to furnish that knowledge.

The visitor who had called to see the twins was the Rev. Mr. Hotchkiss, pastor of the Baptist church. At the reception Angelo had told him he had lately experienced a change in his religious views, and was now desirous of becoming a Baptist, and would immediately join Mr. Hotchkiss's church. There was no time to say more, and the brief talk ended at that point. The minister was much gratified, and had dropped in for a moment now, to invite the twins to attend his Bible class at eight that evening. Angelo accepted, and was expecting Luigi to decline, but he did not, because he knew that the Bible class and the Free-thinkers met in the same room, and he wanted to treat his brother to the embarrassment of being caught in free-thinking company.

5

Guilt and Innocence Finely Blent

[A long and vigorous quarrel follows, between the twins. And there is plenty to quarrel about, for Angelo was always seeking truth, and this obliged him to change and improve his religion with frequency, which wearied Luigi, and annoyed him too; for he had to be present at each new enlistment—which placed him in the false position of seeming to indorse and approve his brother's fickleness; moreover, he had to go to Angelo's prohibition meetings, and he hated them. On the other hand, when it was *his* week to command the legs he gave Angelo just cause of complaint, for he took him to circuses and horse-races and fandangoes, exposing him to all sorts of censure and criticism; and he drank, too; and whatever he drank went to Angelo's head instead of his own and made him act disgracefully. When the evening was come, the two attended the Free-thinkers' meeting, where Angelo was sad and silent; then came the Bible class and looked upon him coldly, finding him in such company. Then they went to Wilson's house and Chapter XI of *Pudd'n-*

head Wilson follows, which tells of the girl seen in Tom
Driscoll's room; and closes with the kicking of Tom by Luigi
at the anti-temperance mass-meeting of the Sons of Liberty;
with the addition of some account of Roxy's adventures as a
chambermaid on a Mississippi boat. Her exchange of the
children had been flippantly and farcically described in an
earlier chapter.]

NEXT MORNING all the town was a-buzz with great news; Pudd'n-
head Wilson had a law case! The public astonishment was so
great and the public curiosity so intense, that when the justice of
the peace opened his court, the place was packed with people,
and even the windows were full. Everybody was flushed and
perspiring; the summer heat was almost unendurable.

Tom Driscoll had brought a charge of assault and battery
against the twins. Robert Allen was retained by Driscoll, David
Wilson by the defense. Tom, his native cheerfulness unannihi-
lated by his back-breaking and bone-bruising passage across the
massed heads of the Sons of Liberty the previous night, laughed
his little customary laugh, and said to Wilson:

"I've kept my promise, you see; I'm throwing my business your
way. Sooner than I was expecting, too."

"It's very good of you—particularly if you mean to keep it up."

"Well, I can't tell about that yet. But we'll see. If I find you
deserve it I'll take you under my protection and make your fame
and fortune for you."

"I'll try to deserve it, Tom."

A jury was sworn in; then Mr. Allen said:

"We will detain your honor but a moment with this case. It is
not one where any doubt of the fact of the assault can enter in.
These gentlemen—the accused—kicked my client at the Market
Hall last night; they kicked him with violence; with extraordinary
violence; with even unprecedented violence, I may say; insomuch
that he was lifted entirely off his feet and discharged into the
midst of the audience. We can prove this by four hundred witnesses—we shall call but three. Mr. Harkness will take the stand."

Mr. Harkness, being sworn, testified that he was chairman upon the occasion mentioned; that he was close at hand and saw the defendants in this action kick the plaintiff into the air and saw him descend among the audience.

"Take the witness," said Allen.

"Mr. Harkness," said Wilson, "you say you saw these gentlemen, my clients, kick the plaintiff. Are you sure—and please remember that you are on oath—are you perfectly sure that you saw *both* of them kick him, or only one? Now be careful."

A bewildered look began to spread itself over the witness's face. He hesitated, stammered, but got out nothing. His eyes wandered to the twins and fixed themselves there with a vacant gaze.

"Please answer, Mr. Harkness, you are keeping the court waiting. It is a very simple question."

Counsel for the prosecution broke in with impatience:

"Your honor, the question is an irrelevant triviality. Necessarily, they both kicked him, for they have but the one pair of legs, and both are responsible for them."

Wilson said, sarcastically:

"Will your honor permit this new witness to be sworn? He seems to possess knowledge which can be of the utmost value just at this moment—knowledge which would at once dispose of what every one must see is a very difficult question in this case. Brother Allen, will you take the stand?"

"Go on with your case!" said Allen, petulantly. The audience laughed, and got a warning from the court.

"Now, Mr. Harkness," said Wilson, insinuatingly, "we shall have to insist upon an answer to that question."

"I—er—well, of course, I do not absolutely *know*, but in my opinion—"

"Never mind your opinion, sir—answer the question."

"I—why, I *can't* answer it."

"That will do, Mr. Harkness. Stand down."

The audience tittered, and the discomfited witness retired in a state of great embarrassment.

Mr. Wakeman took the stand and swore that he saw the twins kick the plaintiff off the platform. The defense took the witness.

"Mr. Wakeman, you have sworn that you saw these gentlemen kick the plaintiff. Do I understand you to swear that you saw them *both* do it?"

"Yes, sir,"—with decision.

"How do you know that both did it?"

"Because I *saw* them do it."

The audience laughed, and got another warning from the court.

"But by what means do you know that both, and not one, did it?"

"Well, in the first place, the insult was given to both of them equally, for they were called a pair of scissors. Of course they would both want to resent it, and so—"

"Wait! You are theorizing now. Stick to facts—counsel will attend to the arguments. Go on."

"Well, they both went over there—*that* I saw."

"Very good. Go on."

"And they both kicked him—I swear to it."

"Mr. Wakeman, was Count Luigi, here, willing to join the Sons of Liberty last night?"

"Yes, sir, he was. He did join, too, and drank a glass or two of whisky, like a man."

"Was his brother willing to join?"

"No, sir, he wasn't. He is a teetotaler, and was elected through a mistake."

"Was he given a glass of whisky?"

"Yes, sir, but of course that was another mistake, and not intentional. He wouldn't drink it. He set it down." A slight pause, then he added, casually and quite simply: "The plaintiff reached for it and hogged it."

There was a fine outburst of laughter, but as the justice was caught out himself, his reprimand was not very vigorous.

Mr. Allen jumped up and exclaimed: "I protest against these foolish irrelevancies. What have they to do with the case?"

Wilson said: "Calm yourself, brother, it was only an experiment. Now, Mr. Wakeman, if one of these gentlemen chooses to join an association and the other doesn't; and if one of them enjoys whisky and the other doesn't, but sets it aside and leaves it unprotected" (titter from the audience), "it seems to show that they have independent minds, and tastes, and preferences, and that one of them is able to approve of a thing at the very moment that the other is heartily disapproving of it. Doesn't it seem so to you?"

"Certainly it does. It's perfectly plain."

"Now, then, it might be—I only say it might be—that one of these brothers wanted to kick the plaintiff last night, and that the other didn't want that humiliating punishment inflicted upon him in that public way and before all those people. Isn't that possible?"

"Of course it is. It's more than possible. I don't believe the blond one would kick anybody. It was the other one that—"

"Silence!" shouted the plaintiff's counsel, and went on with an angry sentence which was lost in the wave of laughter that swept the house.

"That will do, Mr. Wakeman," said Wilson, "you may stand down."

The third witness was called. He had seen the twins kick the plaintiff. Mr. Wilson took the witness.

"Mr. Rogers, you say you saw these accused gentlemen kick the plaintiff?"

"Yes, sir."

"Both of them?"

"Yes, sir."

"Which of them kicked him first?"

"Why—they—they both kicked him at the same time."

"Are you perfectly sure of that?"

"Yes, sir."

"What makes you sure of it?"

"Why, I stood right behind them, and *saw* them do it."

"How many kicks were delivered?"

"Only one."

"If two men kick, the result should be two kicks, shouldn't it?"

"Why—why—yes, as a rule."

"Then what do you think went with the other kick?"

"I—well—the fact is, I wasn't thinking of two being necessary, this time."

"What do you think now?"

"Well, I—I'm sure I don't quite know what to think, but I reckon that one of them did half of the kick and the other one did the other half."

Somebody in the crowd sung out: "It's the first sane thing that any of them has said."

The audience applauded. The judge said: "Silence! or I will clear the court."

Mr. Allen looked pleased, but Wilson did not seem disturbed. He said:

"Mr. Rogers, you have favored us with what you think and what you reckon, but as thinking and reckoning are not evidence, I will now give you a chance to come out with something positive, one way or the other, and shall require you to produce it. I will ask the accused to stand up and repeat the phenomenal kick of last night." The twins stood up. "Now, Mr. Rogers, please stand behind them."

A Voice: "No, stand in front!" (Laughter. Silenced by the court.) Another Voice: "No, give Tommy another highst!" (Laughter. Sharply rebuked by the court.)

"Now, then, Mr. Rogers, two kicks shall be delivered, one after the other, and I give you my word that at least one of the two shall be delivered by one of the twins alone, without the slightest assistance from his brother. Watch sharply, for you have got to render a decision without any if's and and's in it." Rogers bent himself behind the twins with his palms just above his knees, in the modern attitude of the catcher at a baseball match, and riveted his eyes on the pair of legs in front of him. "Are you ready, Mr. Rogers?"

"Ready, sir."

"Kick!"

The kick was launched.

"Have you got that one classified, Mr. Rogers?"

"Let me study a minute, sir."

"Take as much time as you please. Let me know when you are ready."

For as much as a minute Rogers pondered, with all eyes and a breathless interest fastened upon him. Then he gave the word: "Ready, sir."

"Kick!"

The kick that followed was an exact duplicate of the first one.

"Now, then, Mr. Rogers, one of those kicks was an individual kick, not a mutual one. You will now state positively which was the mutual one."

The witness said, with a crestfallen look:

"I've got to give it up. There ain't any man in the world that could tell t'other from which, sir."

"Do you still assert that last night's kick was a mutual kick!"

"Indeed, I don't, sir."

"That will do, Mr. Rogers. If my brother Allen desires to address the court, your honor, very well; but as far as I am concerned I am ready to let the case be at once delivered into the hands of this intelligent jury without comment."

Mr. Justice Robinson had been in office only two months, and in that short time had not had many cases to try, of course. He had no knowledge of laws and courts except what he had picked up since he came into office. He was a sore trouble to the lawyers, for his rulings were pretty eccentric sometimes, and he stood by them with Roman simplicity and fortitude; but the people were well satisfied with him, for they saw that his intentions were always right, that he was entirely impartial, and that he usually made up in good sense what he lacked in technique, so to speak. He now perceived that there was likely to be a miscarriage of justice here, and he rose to the occasion.

"Wait a moment, gentlemen," he said, "it is plain that an assault has been committed—it is plain to anybody; but the way things are going, the guilty will certainly escape conviction. I cannot allow this. Now—"

"But, your honor!" said Wilson, interrupting him, earnestly but respectfully, "you are deciding the case yourself, whereas the jury—"

"Never mind the jury, Mr. Wilson; the jury will have a chance when there is a reasonable doubt for them to take hold of—which there isn't, so far. There is no doubt whatever that an assault has been committed. The attempt to show that both of the accused committed it has failed. Are they both to escape justice on that account? Not in this court, if I can prevent it. It appears to have been a mistake to bring the charge against them as a corporation; each should have been charged in his capacity as an individual, and—"

"But, your honor!" said Wilson, "in fairness to my clients I must insist that inasmuch as the prosecution did not separate the—"

"No wrong will be done your clients, sir—they will be protected; also the public and the offended laws. Mr. Allen, you will amend your pleadings, and put one of the accused on trial at a time."

Wilson broke in: "But, your honor! this is wholly unprecedented! To imperil an accused person by arbitrarily altering and widening the charge against him in order to compass his conviction when the charge as originally brought promises to fail to convict, is a thing unheard of before."

"Unheard of *where?*"

"In the courts of this or any other state."

The Judge said with dignity: "I am not acquainted with the customs of other courts, and am not concerned to know what they are. I am responsible for this court, and I cannot conscientiously allow my judgment to be warped and my judicial liberty hampered by trying to conform to the caprices of other courts, be they—"

"But, your honor, the oldest and highest courts in Europe—"

"This court is not run on the European plan, Mr. Wilson; it is not run on any plan but its own. It has a plan of its own; and that plan is, to find justice for both State and accused, no matter what happens to be practice and custom in Europe or anywhere else." (Great applause.) "Silence! It has not been the custom of this court to imitate other courts; it has not been the custom of this court to take shelter behind the decisions of other courts, and we will not begin now. We will do the best we can by the light that God has given us, and while this court continues to have His approval, it will remain indifferent to what other organizations may think of it." (Applause.) "Gentlemen, I *must* have order!—quiet yourselves! Mr. Allen, you will now proceed against the prisoners one at a time. Go on with the case."

Allen was not at his ease. However, after whispering a moment with his client and with one or two other people, he rose and said:

"Your honor, I find it to be reported and believed that the accused are able to act independently in many ways, but that this independence does not extend to their legs, authority over their legs being vested exclusively in the one brother during a specific term of days, and then passing to the other brother for a like term, and so on, by regular alternation. I could call witnesses who would prove that the accused had revealed to them the existence of this extraordinary fact, and had also made known which of them was in possession of the legs yesterday—and this would, of course, indicate where the guilt of the assault belongs— but as this would be mere hearsay evidence, these revelations not having been made under oath—"

"Never mind about that, Mr. Allen. It may not all be hearsay. We shall see. It may at least help to put us on the right track. Call the witnesses."

"Then I will call Mr. John Buckstone, who is now present, and I beg that Mrs. Patsy Cooper may be sent for. Take the stand, Mr. Buckstone."

Buckstone took the oath, and then testified that on the previous evening the Count Angelo Capello had protested against going to the hall, and had called all present to witness that he was going by compulsion and would not go if he could help himself. Also, that the Count Luigi had replied sharply that he would *go,* just the same, and that he, Count Luigi, would see to that himself. Also, that upon Count Angelo's complaining about being kept on his legs so long, Count Luigi retorted with apparent surprise, "*Your* legs!—I like your impudence!"

"*Now* we are getting at the kernel of the thing," observed the Judge, with grave and earnest satisfaction. "It looks as if the Count Luigi was in possession of the battery at the time of the assault."

Nothing further was elicited from Mr. Buckstone on direct examination. Mr. Wilson took the witness.

"Mr. Buckstone, about what time was it that that conversation took place?"

"Toward nine yesterday evening, sir."

"Did you then proceed directly to the hall?"

"Yes, sir."

"How long did it take you to go there?"

"Well, we walked; and as it was from the extreme edge of the town, and there was no hurry, I judge it took us about twenty minutes, maybe a trifle more."

"About what hour was the kick delivered?"

"About thirteen minutes and a half to ten."

"Admirable! You are a pattern witness, Mr. Buckstone. How did you happen to look at your watch at that particular moment?"

"I always do it when I see an assault. It's likely I shall be called as a witness, and it's a good point to have."

"It would be well if others were as thoughtful. Was anything said, between the conversation at my house and the assault, upon the detail which we are now examining into?"

"No, sir."

"If power over the mutual legs was in the possession of one brother at nine, and passed into the possession of the other one during the next thirty or forty minutes, do you think you could have detected the change?"

"By no means!"

"That is all, Mr. Buckstone."

Mrs. Patsy Cooper was called. The crowd made way for her, and she came smiling and bowing through the narrow human lane, with Betsy Hale, as escort and support, smiling and bowing in her wake, the audience breaking into welcoming cheers as the old favorites filed along. The Judge did not check this kindly demonstration of homage and affection, but let it run its course unrebuked.

The old ladies stopped and shook hands with the twins with effusion, then gave the Judge a friendly nod, and bustled into the seats provided for them. They immediately began to deliver a volley of eager questions at the friends around them: "What is this thing for?" "What is that thing for?" "Who is that young man that's writing at the desk? Why, I declare, it's Jack Bunce! I thought he was sick." "Which is the jury? Why, is *that* the jury? Billy Price and Job Turner, and Jack Lounsbury, and—well, I never!" "Now who would ever 'a' thought—"

But they were gently called to order at this point, and asked not to talk in court. Their tongues fell silent, but the radiant interest in their faces remained, and their gratitude for the blessing of a new sensation and a novel experience still beamed undimmed from their eyes. Aunt Patsy stood up and took the oath, and Mr. Allen explained the point in issue, and asked her to go on now, in her own way, and throw as much light upon it as she could. She toyed with her reticule a moment or two, as if considering where to begin, then she said:

"Well, the way of it is this. They are Luigi's legs a week at a time, and then they are Angelo's, and he can do whatever he wants to with them."

"You are making a mistake, Aunt Patsy Cooper," said the Judge. "You shouldn't state that as a *fact*, because you don't know it to *be* a fact."

"What's the reason I don't?" said Aunt Patsy, bridling a little.

"What is the reason that you do know it?"

"The best in the world—because they told me."

"That isn't a reason."

"Well, for the land's sake! Betsy Hale, do you hear that?"

"*Hear* it? I should think so," said Aunt Betsy, rising and facing the court. "Why, Judge, I was there and heard it myself. Luigi says to Angelo—no, it was Angelo said it to—"

"Come, come, Mrs. Hale, pray sit down, and—"

"Certainly, it's all right, I'm going to sit down presently, but not until I've—"

"But you *must* sit down!"

"*Must!* Well, upon my word if things ain't getting to a pretty pass when—"

The house broke into laughter, but was promptly brought to

order, and meantime Mr. Allen persuaded the old lady to take her seat. Aunt Patsy continued:

"Yes, they told me that, and I know it's true. They're Luigi's legs this week, but—"

"Ah, *they* told you that did they?" said the Justice, with interest.

"Well, no, I don't know that *they* told me, but that's neither here nor there. I know, without that, that at dinner yesterday, Angelo was as tired as a dog, and yet Luigi wouldn't lend him the legs to go up-stairs and take a nap with."

"Did he ask for them?"

"Let me see—it seems to me somehow, that—that—Aunt Betsy, do you remember whether he—"

"Never mind about what Aunt Betsy remembers—she is not a witness; we only want to know what you remember yourself," said the Judge.

"Well, it does seem to me that you are most cantankerously particular about a little thing, Sim Robinson. Why, when I can't remember a thing myself, I always—"

"Ah, *please* go on!"

"Now how *can* she when you keep fussing at her all the time?" said Aunt Betsy. "Why, with a person pecking at *me* that way, I should get that fuzzled and fuddled that—"

She was on her feet again, but Allen coaxed her into her seat once more, while the court squelched the mirth of the house. Then the Judge said:

"Madam, do you know—do you absolutely *know*, independently of anything these gentlemen have told you—that the power over their legs passes from the one to the other regularly every week?"

"Regularly? Bless your heart, regularly ain't any name for the exactness of it! All the big cities in Europe used to set the clocks by it." (Laughter, *suppressed by the court.*)

"How do you *know*? That is the question. Please answer it plainly and squarely."

"Don't you talk to me like that, Sim Robinson—I won't have it. How do I know, indeed! How do *you* know what you know?

Because somebody told you. You didn't invent it out of your own head, did you? Why, these twins are the truthfulest people in the world; and I don't think it becomes you to sit up there and throw slurs at them when they haven't been doing anything to you. And they are orphans besides—both of them. All—"

But Aunt Betsy was up again now, and both old ladies were talking at once and with all their might; but as the house was weltering in a storm of laughter, and the Judge was hammering his desk with an iron paper-weight, one could only see them talk, not hear them. At last, when quiet was restored, the court said:

"Let the ladies retire."

"But, your honor, I have the right, in the interest of my clients, to cross-exam—"

"You'll not need to exercise it, Mr. Wilson—the evidence is thrown out."

"Thrown out!" said Aunt Patsy, ruffled; "and what's it thrown out for, I'd like to know."

"And so would I, Patsy Cooper. It seems to me that if we can save these poor persecuted strangers, it is our bounden duty to stand up here and talk for them till—"

"There, there, there, *do* sit down!"

It cost some trouble and a good deal of coaxing, but they were got into their seats at last. The trial was soon ended now. The twins themselves became witnesses in their own defense. They established the fact, upon oath, that the leg-power passed from one to the other every Saturday night at twelve o'clock sharp. But on cross-examination their counsel would not allow them to tell whose week of power the current week was. The Judge insisted upon their answering, and proposed to compel them, but even the prosecution took fright and came to the rescue then, and helped stay the sturdy jurist's revolutionary hand. So the case had to go to the jury with that important point hanging in the air. They were out an hour and brought in this verdict:

"We the jury do find: 1, that an assault was committed, as charged; 2, that it was committed by one of the persons accused, he having been seen to do it by several credible witnesses; 3, but that his identity is so merged in his brother's that we have not been able to tell which was him. We cannot convict both, for only one is guilty. We cannot acquit both, for only one is innocent. Our verdict is that justice has been defeated by the dispensation of God, and ask to be discharged from further duty."

This was read aloud in court and brought out a burst of hearty applause. The old ladies made a spring at the twins, to shake and congratulate, but were gently disengaged by Mr. Wilson and softly crowded back into their places.

The Judge rose in his little tribune, laid aside his silver-bowed spectacles, roached his gray hair up with his fingers, and said, with dignity and solemnity, and even with a certain pathos:

"In all my experience on the bench, I have not seen justice bow her head in shame in this court until this day. You little realize what far-reaching harm has just been wrought here under the fickle forms of law. Imitation is the bane of courts—I thank God that this one is free from the contamination of that vice— and in no long time you will see the fatal work of this hour seized upon by profligate so-called guardians of justice in all the wide circumstance of this planet and perpetuated in their pernicious decisions. I wash my hands of this iniquity. I would have compelled these culprits to expose their guilt, but support failed me where I had most right to expect aid and encouragement. And I was confronted by a law made in the interest of crime, which protects the criminal from testifying against himself. Yet I had precedents of my own whereby I had set aside that law on two different occasions and thus succeeded in convicting criminals to whose crimes there were no witnesses but themselves. What have you accomplished this day? Do you realize it? You have set adrift, unadmonished, in this community, two men endowed with an awful and mysterious gift, a hidden and grisly power for evil—a power by which each in his turn may commit crime after crime of the most heinous character, and no man be able to tell which is the guilty or which the innocent party in any case of them all. Look to your homes—look to your property—look to your lives—for you have need!

"Prisoners at the bar, stand up. Through suppression of evidence, a jury of your—our—countrymen have been obliged to deliver a verdict concerning your case which stinks to heaven with the rankness of its injustice. By its terms you, the guilty one, go free with the innocent. Depart in peace, and come no more! The costs devolve upon the outraged plaintiff—another iniquity. The court stands dissolved."

Almost everybody crowded forward to overwhelm the twins and their counsel with congratulations; but presently the two old aunties dug the duplicates out and bore them away in triumph through the hurrahing crowd, while lots of new friends carried Pudd'nhead Wilson off tavernward to feast him and "wet down" his great and victorious entry into the legal arena. To Wilson, so long familiar with neglect and depreciation, this strange new incense of popularity and admiration was as a fragrance blown from the fields of paradise. A happy man was Wilson.

6

The Amazing Duel

A deputation came in the evening and conferred upon Wilson the welcome honor of a nomination for mayor; for the village has just been converted into a city by charter. Tom skulks out of challenging the twins. Judge Driscoll thereupon challenges Angelo (accused by Tom of doing the kicking); he declines, but Luigi accepts in his place against Angelo's timid protest.

IT WAS LATE Saturday night—nearing eleven.

The Judge and his second found the rest of the war party at the further end of the vacant ground, near the haunted house.

Pudd'nhead Wilson advanced to meet them, and said anxiously:

"I must say a word in behalf of my principal's proxy, Count Luigi, to whom you have kindly granted the privilege of fighting my principal's battle for him. It is growing late, and Count Luigi is in great trouble lest midnight shall strike before the finish."

"It is another testimony," said Howard, approvingly. "That young man is fine all through. He wishes to save his brother the sorrow of fighting on the Sabbath, and he is right; it is the right and manly feeling and does him credit. We will make all possible haste."

Wilson said: "There is also another reason—a consideration, in fact, which deeply concerns Count Luigi himself. These twins have command of their mutual legs turn about. Count Luigi is in command now; but at midnight, possession will pass to my principal, Count Angelo, and—well, you can foresee what will happen. He will march straight off the field, and carry Luigi with him."

"Why! sure enough!" cried the Judge, "we have heard something about that extraordinary law of their being, already—nothing very definite, it is true, as regards dates and durations of power, but I see it is definite enough as regards to-night. Of course we must give Luigi every chance. Omit all the ceremonial possible, gentlemen, and place us in position."

The seconds at once tossed up a coin; Howard won the choice. He placed the Judge sixty feet from the haunted house and facing it; Wilson placed the twins within fifteen feet of the house and facing the Judge—necessarily. The pistol-case was opened and the long slim tubes taken out; when the moonlight glinted from them a shiver went through Angelo. The doctor was a fool, but a thoroughly well-meaning one, with a kind heart and a sincere disposition to oblige, but along with it an absence of tact which often hurt its effectiveness. He brought his box of lint and bandages, and asked Angelo to feel and see how soft and comfortable they were. Angelo's head fell over against Luigi's in a faint, and precious time was lost in bringing him to; which provoked Luigi into expressing his mind to the doctor with a good deal of vigor and frankness. After Angelo came to he was still so weak that Luigi was obliged to drink a stiff horn of brandy to brace him up.

The seconds now stepped at once to their posts, halfway between the combatants, one of them on each side of the line of fire. Wilson was to count, very deliberately, "One—two—three—fire!—stop!" and the duelists could bang away at any time they chose during that recitation, but not after the last word. Angelo grew very nervous when he saw Wilson's hand rising slowly into the air as a sign to make ready, and he leaned his head against Luigi's and said:

"Oh, please take me away from here, I can't stay, I know I can't!"

"What in the world are you doing? Straighten up! What's the matter with you?—*you're* in no danger—nobody's going to shoot at you. Straighten up, I tell you!"

Angelo obeyed, just in time to hear:

"One—!"

"Bang!" Just one report, and a little tuft of white hair floated slowly to the Judge's feet in the moonlight. The Judge did not swerve; he still stood erect and motionless, like a statue, with his pistol-arm hanging straight down at his side. He was reserving his fire.

"Two—!"

"Three—!"

"Fire—!"

Up came the pistol-arm instantly—Angelo dodged with the report. He said "Ouch!" and fainted again.

The doctor examined and bandaged the wound. It was of no consequence, he said—bullet through fleshy part of arm—no bones broken—the gentleman was still able to fight—let the duel proceed.

Next time Angelo jumped just as Luigi fired, which disordered his aim and caused him to cut a chip out of Howard's ear. The Judge took his time again, and when he fired Angelo jumped and got a knuckle skinned. The doctor inspected and dressed the wounds. Angelo now spoke out and said he was content with the satisfaction he had got, and if the Judge—but Luigi shut him roughly up, and asked him not to make an ass of himself; adding:

"And I want you to stop dodging. You take a great deal too prominent a part in this thing for a person who has got nothing to do with it. You should remember that you are here only by courtesy, and are without official recognition; officially you are not here at all; officially you do not even exist. To all intents and purposes you are absent from this place, and you ought for your own modesty's sake to reflect that it cannot become a person who is not present here to be taking this sort of public and indecent prominence in a matter in which he is not in the slightest degree concerned. Now, don't dodge again; the bullets are not for you, they are for me; if I want them dodged I will attend to it myself. I never saw a person act so."

Angelo saw the reasonableness of what his brother had said, and he did try to reform, but it was of no use; both pistols went off at the same instant, and he jumped once more; he got a sharp scrape along his cheek from the Judge's bullet, and so deflected Luigi's aim that his ball went wide and chipped a flake of skin from Pudd'nhead Wilson's chin. The doctor attended to the wounded.

By the terms, the duel was over. But Luigi was entirely out of patience, and begged for one more exchange of shots, insisting that he had had no fair chance, on account of his brother's indelicate behavior. Howard was opposed to granting so unusual a privilege, but the Judge took Luigi's part, and added that indeed he himself might fairly be considered entitled to another trial, because although the proxy on the other side was in no way to blame for his (the Judge's) humiliatingly resultless work, the gentleman with whom he was fighting this duel was to blame for it, since if he had played no advantages and had held his head still, his proxy would have been disposed of early. He added:

"Count Luigi's request for another exchange is another proof that he is a brave and chivalrous gentleman, and I beg that the courtesy he asks may be accorded him."

"I thank you most sincerely for this generosity, Judge Driscoll," said Luigi, with a polite bow, and moving to his place. Then he added—to Angelo, "Now hold your grip, hold your *grip*, I tell you, and I'll land him sure!"

The men stood erect, their pistol-arms at their sides, the two seconds stood at their official posts, the doctor stood five paces in Wilson's rear with his instruments and bandages in his hands. The deep stillness, the peaceful moonlight, the motionless figures, made an impressive picture and the impending fatal possibilities augmented this impressiveness to solemnity. Wilson's hand began to rise—slowly—slowly—higher—still higher—in another moment:

"*Boom!*"—the first stroke of midnight swung up out of the distance; Angelo was off like a deer!

"Oh, you unspeakable traitor!" wailed his brother, as they went soaring over the fence.

The others stood astonished and gazing; and so stood, watching that strange spectacle until distance dissolved it and swept it from their view. Then they rubbed their eyes like people waking out of a dream.

"Well, I've never seen anything like that before!" said the Judge. "Wilson, I am going to confess now, that I wasn't quite able to believe in that leg business, and had a suspicion that it was a put-up convenience between those twins; and when Count Angelo fainted I thought I saw the whole scheme—thought it was pretext No. 1, and would be followed by others till twelve o'clock should arrive, and Luigi would get off with all the credit of seeming to want to fight and yet not have to fight, after all. But I was mistaken. His pluck proved it. He's a brave fellow and did want to fight."

"There isn't any doubt about that," said Howard, and added, in a grieved tone, "but what an unworthy sort of Christian that Angelo is—I hope and believe there are not many like him. It is not right to engage in a duel on the Sabbath—I could not approve of that myself; but to finish one that has been begun—that is a duty, let the day be what it may."

They strolled along, still wondering, still talking.

"It is a curious circumstance," remarked the surgeon, halting Wilson a moment to paste some more court-plaster on his chin, which had gone to leaking blood again, "that in this duel neither of the parties who handled the pistols lost blood, while nearly all the persons present in the mere capacity of guests got hit. I have not heard of such a thing before. Don't you think it unusual?"

"Yes," said the Judge, "it has struck me as peculiar. Peculiar and unfortunate. I was annoyed at it, all the time. In the case of Angelo it made no great difference, because he was in a measure concerned, though not officially; but it troubled me to see the seconds compromised, and yet I knew no way to mend the matter."

"There was no way to mend it," said Howard, whose ear was being readjusted now by the doctor; "the code fixes our place, and it would not have been lawful to change it. If we could have stood at your side, or behind you, or in front of you, it—but it would not have been legitimate and the other parties would have had a just right to complain of our trying to protect ourselves from danger; infractions of the code are certainly not permissible in any case whatever."

Wilson offered no remarks. It seemed to him that there was very little place here for so much solemnity, but he judged that if a duel where nobody was in danger or got crippled but the seconds and the outsiders had nothing ridiculous about it for these gentlemen, his pointing out that feature would probably not help them to see it.

He invited them in to take a nightcap, and Howard and the Judge accepted, but the doctor said he would have to go and see how Angelo's principal wound was getting on.

[It was now Sunday, and in the afternoon Angelo was to be received into the Baptist communion by immersion—a doubtful prospect, the doctor feared.]

7

Luigi Defies Galen

WHEN the doctor arrived at Aunt Patsy Cooper's house, he found the lights going and everybody up and dressed and in a great state of solicitude and excitement. The twins were stretched on a sofa in the sitting-room, Aunt Patsy was fussing at Angelo's arm, Nancy was flying around under her commands, the two young boys were trying to keep out of the way and always getting in it, in order to see and wonder, Rowena stood apart, helpless with apprehension and emotion, and Luigi was growling in unappeasable fury over Angelo's shameful flight.

As has been reported before, the doctor was a fool—a kind-hearted and well-meaning one, but with no tact; and as he was by long odds the most learned physician in the town, and was quite well aware of it, and could talk his learning with ease and precision, and liked to show off when he had an audience, he was sometimes tempted into revealing more of a case than was good for the patient.

He examined Angelo's wound, and was really minded to say nothing for once; but Aunt Patsy was so anxious and so pressing that he allowed his caution to be overcome, and proceeded to empty himself as follows, with scientific relish:

"Without going too much into detail, madam—for you would probably not understand it, anyway—I concede that great care is going to be necessary here; otherwise exudation of the esophagus is nearly sure to ensue, and this will be followed by ossification and extradition of the maxillaris superioris, which must decompose the granular surfaces of the great infusorial ganglionic system, thus obstructing the action of the posterior varioloid arteries, and precipitating compound strangulated sorosis of the valvular tissues, and ending unavoidably in the dispersion and combustion of the marsupial fluxes and the consequent embrocation of the bicuspid populo redax referendum rotulorum."

A miserable silence followed. Aunt Patsy's heart sank, the pallor of despair invaded her face, she was not able to speak; poor Rowena wrung her hands in privacy and silence, and said to herself in the bitterness of her young grief, "There is no hope— it is plain there is no hope"; the good-hearted negro wench, Nancy, paled to chocolate, then to orange, then to amber, and thought to herself with yearning sympathy and sorrow, "Po' thing, he ain' gwyne to las' throo de half o' dat"; small Henry choked up, and turned his head away to hide his rising tears, and his brother Joe said to himself, with a sense of loss, "The baptizing's busted, that's sure." Luigi was the only person who had any heart to speak. He said, a little bit sharply, to the doctor:

"Well, well, there's nothing to be gained by wasting precious time; give him a barrel of pills—I'll take them for him."

"You?" asked the doctor.

"Yes. Did you suppose he was going to take them himself?"

"Why, of course."

"Well, it's a mistake. He never took a dose of medicine in his life. He can't."

"Well, upon my word, it's the most extraordinary thing I ever heard of!"

"Oh," said Aunt Patsy, as pleased as a mother whose child is being admired and wondered at, "you'll find that there's more about them that's wonderful than their just being made in the image of God like the rest of His creatures, now you can depend on that, *I* tell you," and she wagged her complacent head like one who could reveal marvelous things if she chose.

The boy Joe began:

"Why, ma, they *ain't* made in the im—"

"You shut up, and wait till you're asked, Joe. I'll let you know when I want help. Are you looking for something, doctor?"

The doctor asked for a few sheets of paper and a pen, and

said he would write a prescription; which he did. It was one of Galen's; in fact, it was Galen's favorite, and had been slaying people for sixteen thousand years. Galen used it for everything, applied it to everything, said it would remove everything, from warts all the way through to lungs—and it generally did. Galen was still the only medical authority recognized in Missouri; his practice was the only practice known to the Missouri doctors, and his prescriptions were the only ammunition they carried when they went out for game. By and by Dr. Claypool laid down his pen and read the result of his labors aloud, carefully and deliberately, for this battery must be constructed on the premises by the family, and mistakes could occur; for he wrote a doctor's hand—the hand which from the beginning of time has been so disastrous to the apothecary and so profitable to the undertaker:

"Take of afarabocca, henbane, corpobalsamum, each two drams and a half: of cloves, opium, myrrh, cyperus, each two drams; of opobalsamum, Indian leaf, cinnamon, zedoary, ginger, coftus, coral, cassia, euphorbium, gum tragacanth, frankincense, styrax calamita, celtic, nard, spignel, hartwort, mustard, saxifrage, dill, anise, each one dram; of xylaloes, rheum ponticum, alipta, moschata, castor, spikenard, galangals, opoponax, anacardium, mastich, brimstone, peony, eringo, pulp of dates, red and white hermodactyls, roses, thyme, acorns, pennyroyal, gentian, the bark of the root of mandrake, germander, valerian, bishop's-weed, bayberries, long and white pepper, xylobalsamum, carnabadium, macedonian, parsley seeds, lovage, the seeds of rue, and sinon, of each a dram and a half; of pure gold, pure silver, pearls not perforated, the blatta byzantina, the bone of the stag's heart, of each the quantity of fourteen grains of wheat; of sapphire, emerald and jasper stones, each one dram; of hazel-nuts, two drams; of pellitory of Spain, shavings of ivory, calamus odoratus, each the quantity of twenty-nine grains of wheat; of honey or sugar a sufficient quantity. Boil down and skim off."

"There," he said, "that will fix the patient; give his brother a dipperful every three-quarters of an hour—"

—"while he survives," muttered Luigi—

—"and see that the room is kept wholesomely hot, and the doors and windows closed tight. Keep Count Angelo nicely covered up with six or seven blankets, and when he is thirsty—which will be frequently—moisten a rag in the vapor of the tea-kettle and let his brother suck it. When he is hungry—which will also be frequently—he must not be humored oftener than every seven or eight hours; then toast part of a cracker until it begins to brown, and give it to his brother."

"That is all very well, as far as Angelo is concerned," said Luigi, "but what am I to eat?"

"I do not see that there is anything the matter with you," the doctor answered, "you may, of course, eat what you please."

"And also drink what I please, I suppose?"

"Oh, certainly—at present. When the violent and continuous perspiring has reduced your strength, I shall have to reduce your diet, of course, and also bleed you, but there is no occasion for that yet awhile." He turned to Aunt Patsy and said: "He must be put to bed, and sat up with, and tended with the greatest care, and not allowed to stir for several days and nights."

"For one, I'm sacredly thankful for that," said Luigi, "it postpones the funeral—I'm not to be drowned to-day, anyhow."

Angelo said quietly to the doctor:

"I will cheerfully submit to all your requirements, sir, up to two o'clock this afternoon, and will resume them after three, but cannot be confined to the house during that intermediate hour."

"Why, may I ask?"

"Because I have entered the Baptist communion, and by appointment am to be baptized in the river at that hour."

"Oh, insanity!—it cannot be allowed!"

Angelo answered with placid firmness:

"Nothing shall prevent it, if I am alive."

"Why, consider, my dear sir, in your condition it might prove fatal."

A tender and ecstatic smile beamed from Angelo's eyes, and he broke forth in a tone of joyous fervency:

"Ah, how blessed it would be to die for such a cause—it would be martyrdom!"

"But your brother—consider your brother; you would be risking his life, too."

"He risked mine an hour ago," responded Angelo, gloomily; "did he consider me?" A thought swept through his mind that made him shudder. "If I had not run, I might have been killed in a duel on the Sabbath day, and my soul would have been lost —lost."

"Oh, don't fret, it wasn't in any danger," said Luigi, irritably; "they wouldn't waste it for a little thing like that; there's a glass case all ready for it in the heavenly museum, and a pin to stick it up with."

Aunt Patsy was shocked, and said:

"Looy, Looy!—don't talk so, dear!"

Rowena's soft heart was pierced by Luigi's unfeeling words, and she murmured to herself, "Oh, if I but had the dear privilege of protecting and defending him with my weak voice!—but alas! this sweet boon is denied me by the cruel conventions of social intercourse."

"Get their bed ready," said Aunt Patsy to Nancy, "and shut up the windows and doors, and light their candles, and see that you drive all the mosquitoes out of their bar, and make up a good fire in their stove, and carry up some bags of hot ashes to lay to his feet—"

—"and a shovel of fire for his head, and a mustard plaster for his neck, and some gum shoes for his ears," Luigi interrupted, with temper; and added, to himself, "Damnation, I'm going to be roasted alive, I just know it!"

"Why, Looy! Do be quiet; I never saw such a fractious thing. A body would think you didn't care for your brother."

"I don't—to *that* extent, Aunt Patsy. I was glad the drowning was postponed a minute ago, but I'm not now. No, that is all gone by; I want to be drowned."

"You'll bring a judgment on yourself just as sure as you live, if you go on like that. Why, I never heard the beat of it. Now, there

—there! you've said enough. Not another word out of you—I won't have it!"

"But, Aunt Patsy—"

"Luigi! Didn't you hear what I told you?"

"But, Aunt Patsy, I—why, I'm not going to set my heart and lungs afloat in that pail of sewage which this criminal here has been prescri—"

"Yes, you are, too. You are going to be good, and do everything I tell you, like a dear," and she tapped his cheek affectionately with her finger. "Rowena, take the prescription and go in the kitchen and hunt up the things and lay them out for me. I'll sit up with my patient the rest of the night, doctor; I can't trust Nancy, she couldn't make Luigi take the medicine. Of course, you'll drop in again during the day. Have you got any more directions?"

"No, I believe not, Aunt Patsy. If I don't get in earlier, I'll be along by early candle-light, anyway. Meantime, don't allow him to get out of his bed."

Angelo said, with calm determination:

"I shall be baptized at two o'clock. Nothing but death shall prevent me."

The doctor said nothing aloud, but to himself he said:

"Why, this chap's got a manly side, after all! Physically he's a coward, but morally he's a lion. I'll go and tell the others about this; it will raise him a good deal in their estimation—and the public will follow their lead, of course."

Privately, Aunt Patsy applauded too, and was proud of Angelo's courage in the moral field as she was of Luigi's in the field of honor.

The boy Henry was troubled, but the boy Joe said, inaudibly, and gratefully, "We're all hunky, after all; and no postponement on account of the weather."

8

Baptism of the Better Half

BY NINE O'CLOCK the town was humming with the news of the midnight duel, and there were but two opinions about it: one, that Luigi's pluck in the field was most praiseworthy and Angelo's flight most scandalous; the other, that Angelo's courage in flying the field for conscience' sake was as fine and creditable as was Luigi's in holding the field in the face of the bullets. The one opinion was held by half of the town, the other one was maintained by the other half. The division was clean and exact, and it made two parties, an Angelo party and a Luigi party. The twins had suddenly become popular idols along with Pudd'nhead Wilson, and haloed with a glory as intense as his. The children talked the duel all the way to Sunday-school, their elders talked it all the way to church, the choir discussed it behind their red curtain, it usurped the place of pious thought in the "nigger gallery."

By noon the doctor had added the news, and spread it, that Count Angelo, in spite of his wound and all warnings and supplications, was resolute in his determination to be baptized at the hour appointed. This swept the town like wildfire, and mightily reinforced the enthusiasm of the Angelo faction, who said, "If any doubted that it was moral courage that took him from the field, what have they to say now!"

Still the excitement grew. All the morning it was traveling countryward, toward all points of the compass; so, whereas before only the farmers and their wives were intending to come and witness the remarkable baptism, a general holiday was now proclaimed and the children and negroes admitted to the privileges of the occasion. All the farms for ten miles around were vacated, all the converging roads emptied long processions of wagons, horses, and yeomanry into the town. The pack and cram of people vastly exceeded any that had ever been seen in that sleepy region before. The only thing that had ever even approached it, was the time long gone by, but never forgotten, nor even referred to without wonder and pride, when two circuses and a Fourth of July fell together. But the glory of that occasion was extinguished now for good. It was but a freshet to this deluge.

The great invasion massed itself on the river-bank and waited hungrily for the immense event. Waited, and wondered if it would really happen, or if the twin who was not a "professor" would stand out and prevent it.

But they were not to be disappointed. Angelo was as good as his word. He came attended by an escort of honor composed of several hundred of the best citizens, all of the Angelo party; and when the immersion was finished they escorted him back home: and would even have carried him on their shoulders, but that people might think they were carrying Luigi.

Far into the night the citizens continued to discuss and wonder over the strangely mated pair of incidents that had distinguished and exalted the past twenty-four hours above any other twenty-four in the history of their town for picturesqueness and splendid interest; and long before the lights were out and burghers asleep it had been decided on all hands that in capturing these twins Dawson's Landing had drawn a prize in the great lottery of municipal fortune.

At midnight Angelo was sleeping peacefully. His immersion had not harmed him, it had merely made him wholesomely drowsy, and he had been dead asleep many hours now. It had made Luigi drowsy, too, but he had got only brief naps, on account of his having to take the medicine every three-quarters of an hour—and Aunt Betsy Hale was there to see that he did it. When he complained and resisted, she was quietly firm with him, and said in a low voice:

"No—no, that won't do; you mustn't talk, and you mustn't retch and gag that way, either—you'll wake up your poor brother."

"Well, what of it, Aunt Betsy, he—"

"'Sh-h! Don't make a noise, dear. You mustn't forget that your poor brother is sick and—"

"Sick, is he? Well, I wish I—"

"'Sh-h-h! Will you be quiet, Luigi! Here, now, take the rest of it—don't keep me holding the dipper all night. I declare if you haven't left a good fourth of it in the bottom! Come—that's a good boy."

"Aunt Betsy, don't make me! I feel like I've swallowed a cemetery; I do, indeed. Do let me rest a little—just a little; I can't take any more of the devilish stuff now."

"Luigi! Using such language here, and him just baptized! Do you want the roof to fall on you?"

"I wish to goodness it would!"

"Why, you dreadful thing! I've a good notion to—let that blanket alone; do you want your brother to catch his death?"

"Aunt Betsy, I've *got* to have it off, I'm being roasted alive; nobody could stand it—you couldn't yourself."

"Now, then, you're sneezing again—I just expected it."

"Because I've caught a cold in my head. I always do, when I go in the water with my clothes on. And it takes me weeks to get over it, too. I think it was a shame to serve me so."

"Luigi, you are unreasonable; you know very well they couldn't baptize him dry. I should think you would be willing to undergo a little inconvenience for your brother's sake."

"Inconvenience! Now how you talk, Aunt Betsy. I came as near as anything to getting drowned—you saw that yourself; and do you call this inconvenience?—the room shut up as tight as a drum, and so hot the mosquitoes are trying to get out; and a cold in the head, and dying for sleep and no chance to get any on account of this infamous medicine that that assassin prescri—"

"There, you're sneezing again. I'm going down and mix some more of this truck for you, dear."

9

The Drinkless Drunk

DURING Monday, Tuesday, and Wednesday the twins grew steadily worse; but then the doctor was summoned South to attend his mother's funeral, and they got well in forty-eight hours. They appeared on the street on Friday, and were welcomed with enthusiasm by the new-born parties, the Luigi and Angelo factions. The Luigi faction carried its strength into the Democratic party, the Angelo faction entered into a combination with the Whigs. The Democrats nominated Luigi for alderman under the new city government, and the Whigs put up Angelo against him. The Democrats nominated Pudd'nhead Wilson for mayor, and he was left alone in this glory, for the Whigs had no man who was willing to enter the lists against such a formidable opponent. No politician had scored such a compliment as this before in the history of the Mississippi Valley.

The political campaign in Dawson's Landing opened in a pretty warm fashion, and waxed hotter every week. Luigi's whole heart was in it, and even Angelo developed a surprising amount of interest—which was natural, because he was not merely representing Whigism, a matter of no consequence to him, but he was representing something immensely finer and greater—to wit, Reform. In him was centered the hopes of the whole reform element of the town; he was the chosen and admired champion of every clique that had a pet reform of any sort or kind at heart. He was president of the great Teetotalers' Union, its chiefest prophet and mouthpiece.

But as the canvass went on, troubles began to spring up all

around—troubles for the twins, and through them for all the parties and segments and factions of parties. Whenever Luigi had possession of the legs, he carried Angelo to balls, rum shops, Sons of Liberty parades, horse-races, campaign riots, and everywhere else that could damage him with his party and the church; and when it was Angelo's week he carried Luigi diligently to all manner of moral and religious gatherings, doing his best to regain the ground he had lost before. As a result of these double performances, there was a storm blowing all the time, an ever-rising storm, too—a storm of frantic criticism of the twins, and rage over their extravagant, incomprehensible conduct.

Luigi had the final chance. The legs were his for the closing week of the canvass. He led his brother a fearful dance.

But he saved his best card for the very eve of the election. There was to be a grand turnout of the Teetotalers' Union that day, and Angelo was to march at the head of the procession and deliver a great oration afterward. Luigi drank a couple of glasses of whisky—which steadied his nerves and clarified his mind, but made Angelo drunk. Everybody who saw the march, saw that the Champion of the Teetotalers was half seas over, and noted also that his brother, who made no hypocritical pretensions to extra temperance virtues, was dignified and sober. This eloquent fact could not be unfruitful at the end of a hot political canvass. At the mass-meeting Angelo tried to make his great temperance oration, but was so discommoded by hiccoughs and thickness of tongue that he had to give it up; then drowsiness overtook him and his head drooped against Luigi's and he went to sleep. Luigi apologized for him, and was going on to improve his opportunity with an appeal for a moderation of what he called "the prevailing teetotal madness," but persons in the audience began to howl and throw things at him, and then the meeting rose in wrath and chased him home.

This episode was a crusher for Angelo in another way. It destroyed his chances with Rowena. Those chances had been growing, right along, for two months. Rowena had partly confessed that she loved him, but wanted time to consider. Now the tender dream was ended, and she told him so the moment he was sober enough to understand. She said she would never marry a man who drank.

"But I don't drink," he pleaded.

"That is nothing to the point," she said, coldly, "you get drunk, and that is worse."

[There was a long and sufficiently idiotic discussion here, which ended as reported in a previous note.]

10

So They Hanged Luigi

DAWSON'S LANDING had a week of repose, after the election, and it needed it, for the frantic and variegated nightmare which had tormented it all through the preceding week had left it limp, haggard, and exhausted at the end. It got the week of repose because Angelo had the legs, and was in too subdued a condition to want to go out and mingle with an irritated community that had come to distrust and detest him because there was such a lack of harmony between his morals, which were confessedly excellent, and his methods of illustrating them, which were distinctly damnable.

The new city officers were sworn in on the following Monday —at least all but Luigi. There was a complication in his case. His election was conceded, but he could not sit in the board of aldermen without his brother, and his brother could not sit there because he was not a member. There seemed to be no way out of the difficulty but to carry the matter into the courts, so this was resolved upon. The case was set for the Monday fortnight. In due course the time arrived. In the meantime the city government had been at a standstill, because without Luigi there was a tie in the board of aldermen, whereas with him the liquor interest—the richest in the political field—would have one majority. But the court decided that Angelo could not sit in the board with him, either in public or executive sessions, and at the same time forbade the board to deny admission to Luigi, a fairly and legally chosen alderman. The case was carried up and up from court to court, yet still the same old original decision was confirmed every time. As a result, the city government not only stood still, with its hands tied, but everything it was created to protect and care for went a steady gait toward rack and ruin. There was no way to levy a tax, so the minor officials had to resign or starve; therefore they resigned. There being no city money, the enormous legal expenses on both sides had to be defrayed by private subscription. But at last the people came to their senses, and said:

"Pudd'nhead was right at the start—we ought to have hired the official half of that human phillipene to resign; but it's too late now; some of us haven't got anything left to hire him with."

"Yes, we have," said another citizen, "we've got this"—and he produced a halter.

Many shouted: "That's the ticket." But others said: "No—Count Angelo is innocent; we mustn't hang him."

"Who said anything about hanging him? We are only going to hang the other one."

"Then that is all right—there is no objection to that."

So they hanged Luigi. And so ends the history of "Those Extraordinary Twins."

FINAL REMARKS

As YOU SEE, it was an extravagant sort of a tale, and had no purpose but to exhibit that monstrous "freak" in all sorts of   H 42 grotesque lights. But when Roxy wandered into the tale she had to be furnished with something to do; so she changed the children in the cradle; this necessitated the invention of a reason for it; this, in turn, resulted in making the children prominent personages—nothing could prevent it, of course. Their career began to take a tragic aspect, and some one had to be brought in to help work the machinery; so Pudd'nhead Wilson was introduced and taken on trial. By this time the whole show was being run by the new people and in their interest, and the original show was become side-tracked and forgotten; the twin-monster, and the heroine, and the lads, and the old ladies had dwindled to inconsequentialities and were merely in the way. Their story was one story, the new people's story was another story, and there was no connection between them, no interdependence, no kinship. It is not practicable or rational to try to tell two stories at the same time; so I dug out the farce and left the tragedy.

The reader already knew how the expert works; he knows now how the other kind do it.

MARK TWAIN.